A SUPPLEMENT TO THE ENGLISH UNIVERSAL HISTORY,

Lately publiſhed in *LONDON*:

CONTAINING

HISTORICAL and CHRONOLOGICAL DISSERTATIONS on the Reigns of the Kings of *Iſrael* and *Judah*; with curious TABLES, tending to clear up the Difficulties of that Part of the Sacred Writings; and Obſervations on the *Egyptian* HISTORY, being a free and candid Enquiry into the ancient Accounts of that celebrated People.

ALSO

REMARKS and ANNOTATIONS on the UNIVERSAL HISTORY, deſigned as an Improvement and Illuſtration of that WORK.

To which is added,

An EXAMINATION of the ſeveral Opinions of thoſe who pretend that *Abraham*'s Poſterity reigned in *Egypt*.

The Whole carefully tranſlated from the Original *German* of the Eminent

S. J.
Dr. *BAUMGARTEN*,

Profeſſor and Director of the Theological Seminary at the Univerſity of *Hall*, in *Saxony*.

VOLUME *the* FIRST.

LONDON:

Printed for EDWARD DILLY, at the *Roſe* and *Crown*, in the *Poultry*.

MDCCLX. 54

TO THE

ENGLISH READER.

THE *Universal History* of all nations being so voluminous a work, compiled with so much care, and many parts of it with uncommon accuracy, a supplement to it may at first sight appear a superfluous attempt. But considering how copious the subject is, and how infinite the materials, even in the ancient part, this objection can only be made by those, who content themselves with a general knowledge of this most useful branch of learning. Others who investigate truth with more aſſiduity, will be pleaſed to ſee any important point of hiſtory or chronology farther illuſtrated, than it could poſſibly be, in the regular method obſerved by the authors of that valuable work. It was received in *Germany* with the higheſt approbation, and opened an ample field for the laborious writers of that country.

Among the reſt, the reverend and learned Dr. *Baumgarten*, who has diſtinguiſhed himſelf there by a ſuperior genius, equally comprehenſive and indefatigable, undertook from mere motives of public ſpirit, to ſuperviſe the tranſlation, and to enrich it with notes of his own. Thoſe to whom the character of that gentleman is known, will have great curioſity to peruſe thoſe notes, and will find nothing in them unequal to the great learning and merit of their Author.

They

They appear indeed to some disadvantage. In the original they are placed, as notes usually are, at the bottom of the pages, to which they refer. And it would have been some discouragement to this translation of them, had there been any other more pleasing method of communicating them to the public. But as they are too great an addition to the work to be incorporated in any future *English* edition, since that would be an injury which the proprietors of it would never do to the purchasers and encouragers of the former editions, it has been thought expedient to offer them in this manner to the public. Some of them are almost as well connected, as if they were a continued discourse, and many of them may prove entertaining, even without a reference to the passages, which they illustrate.

In some cases he differs from the compilers in opinion; but never without assigning, what he at least thought a sufficient reason. In many other places he improves upon their observations; but with the candour and modesty of a writer, who means the instruction of the public, rather than the ostentation of himself. His extensive reading enabled him to cite many authors, which had not been consulted by them; and as some of those, which he cites, are very much unknown amongst us, and some of his *German* authorities have never been translated into *English*, it was thought needless to retain those in the translation.

These remarks, tho' not the first part of this volume, yet deserved the first mention in this prefatory account, as they are written by Doctor *Baumgarten* himself. The rest of this collection consists of a supplemental preface likewise written by him, a dissertation on the chronology of the kings of *Israel* and *Judah*, a piece intitled, remarks on the *Egyptian* chronology, and an Appendix.

The supplement to the preface discusses, in the fullest, and in a very new and entertaining manner, a point which the authors of the *Universal History* had omitted, as either too trite or too obvious, the nature and usefulness of history in general. In enlarging upon his definition of history, he examines with great judgment and good sense, the internal and external grounds of an historian's credibility, and by this examination, and the conclusions drawn from it, he establishes the faith of history upon a new and solid foundation. Then he proceeds to shew the usefulness of history, in six instances, upon which he enlarges in the most instructive manner, and whilst he is giving the strongest evidences of his parts and learning, he does honor to his subject by taking occasion from it to profess his piety. Next he answers two questions of moment to those, who cannot devote all their time to this study, which is most useful and necessary, the knowlege of ancient, or of modern history? and in what order the study should be prosecuted? After this he undertakes to answer the objections to that study, and explodes all that ever were formed, under seven heads, and leaves his reader with a full conviction, that all other knowlege is very imperfect without this, and that the neglect of this alone, hath produced the darkness of barbarous ages, as the connexion between this and all other sciences is more intimate, than that of any two sciences whatever, exclusive of this. In short, the whole is a noble lecture, preparatory to this important study; for it exhibits the advantages of it almost as

clearly

clearly to the attentive reader, as experience would.

The Chronological Dissertation on the reigns of the kings of *Israel* and *Judah* is written by another hand. It is a great undertaking to reconcile the scriptural accounts of the reigns of those kings in an unexceptionable manner. Many learned men have been deterred from the attempt by the prodigious difficulties of it, and have agreed to solve them by imputing the surprizing inconsistency of the accounts to the negligence or mistakes of transcribers; but this author has taken pains to shew that the reigns tally exactly according to the sacred historians, and that it is not at all necessary to reconcile them, by having recourse to the supposed errors of transcribers. He then proceeds to attempt a clearer connexion of the *Jewish* history from the revolt of the ten tribes to *Darius Hystaspis*, with prophane history.

history. How far he has succeeded in both these essays, must be submitted to the judgment of the learned. He has the merit at least of raising attention to a subject, which some other ingenious enquirers may be invited to consider with the care and diligence it deserves, at a time when the writers against revealed religion, select single difficulties out of the sacred books, and draw conclusions from them against the inspiration of the whole. The synchronistical tables he proposes as illustrations of what he has advanced in the dissertation.

The next piece is intitled, remarks on the *Egyptian* history in the first part of the *Universal History*. The author is Mr. *Semler*, a worthy and learned divine in *Germany*. His method in treating the subject is clear and regular. He appears perfectly well acquainted with the sources, and indisputably deserves the attention of those

those who have made this part of history their study, or have a disposition to engage in it. The point which he most labors, is to shew, that *Manetho*'s dynasties are successive, and not collateral. Of this he adduces four very strong proofs, and answers the objections very learnedly and clearly. In the latter part he states the right use of the several helps we have towards the *Egyptian* history and chronology, in six observations, which may be of considerable use to persons, who are willing to consult the original writers, rather than content themselves with accounts taken from them, perhaps, in a hasty, superficial or injudicious manner.

The Appendix is written by Dr. *Baumgarten* himself, and placed after his remarks, because these end with the *Egyptian* history. It examines and refutes four opinions concerning the government of the posterity of

Abraham

Abraham in *Egypt*. The first is that of our profligate countryman *Morgan*, who pretends that the *Israelites* were those shepherds, who appear from *Manetho* to have invaded *Egypt*, and usurped the government of it. He appeals to the scripture, from whence *Morgan* pretends to have drawn his opinion, for the full confutation of it. The second is M. *Boivin*, an ingenious *French* writer; who, from an affectation of singularity, advances a system less impious, but, in point of history, almost as exceptionable as *Morgan*'s. He supposes the *Israelites* to have spent four hundred and thirty years in *Egypt*, that during the first seventy-one years they led the life of shepherds, that after this they were sovereigns of the country for the space of two hundred and fifty-nine years, and those being expired, they were reduced for the remaining ninety-nine years, to slavery, oppression and captivity. This system is here exploded by shewing, that the

Israelites

Israelites did not spend half that time in *Egypt*, and by observing, that *Moses* could not have passed over in silence so important a part of their history, amidst all the minute particulars he mentions of the conduct and adventures of that people. Then he shews how insufficient the scriptural authorities are, which M. *Boivin* alleges.

The third opinion is that of a worthy divine in *Germany*, who supposes *Manetho*'s shepherds to have been *Israelites*, but that their kings were *Egyptians*, and that they were succeeded by *Nitocris*, a woman of *Jewish* extraction, who became a tyrant over *Egypt*, and with the assistance of the *Hebrews*, who were left behind in that country, subdued the *Egyptians* and even compelled them to receive circumcision. This opinion is refuted with great learning and candor, in three several arguments, each of which destroy the principles,

principles, and prove a misapplication of the authorities in which it is founded.

He proceeds next to the mistakes of those, who do not indeed ascribe this government to the *Israelites*, but to other descendants of *Abraham*. M. *Fourmont* gives it to the race of *Esau*, and pleads besides the similitude of the oriental names, which he makes use of to prove his point, the history of the *Amalekites* in scripture. But both arguments are shewn to be fallacious, the first from the great uncertainty which attends the illustration of mythology from history, and the other from the inconsistency of it with other passages of scripture. *Theophanes Cantabrigiensis*, an ingenious writer against *Morgan*, supposes the *Ishmaelites* to have been the shepherd kings in *Manetho*. This opinion he supports by comparing *Manetho*'s account with the condition of those *Ishmaelites*; by

alleging

alleging some passages from the books of *Genesis* and *Exodus*, and by the supposed difference of the practice of circumcision among the *Ishmaelites* from that which was prescribed to the descendants of *Isaac*. But to this our learned author objects, first, a manifest anachronism; next, difficulties arising from the aversion of the *Egyptians* to the *Hebrews*, from the state of *Egypt* at that period, from the idolatry prevailing among the *Egyptians*, and from the express distinction of the *Ishmaelites* from the *Egyptians* in scripture, after which he concludes with a short answer to the arguments, which that gentleman urges in support of his opinion.

This is a summary account of the following work, which as it has the appearance of being miscellaneous, the *English* Editor thought himself obliged to prefix. If the public should receive any use or entertainment from the design, or esteem it any improvement of the

the great work to which it is offered as a supplement, he will proceed with pleasure to communicate more of these tracts and remarks, which are now in his hands.

SUP-

SUPPLEMENT TO THE PREFACE OF THE UNIVERSAL HISTORY, &c.

THE ingenious Authors of the *Universal History*, &c. in their Preface to the first Volume, have omitted giving the Reader an Idea of the NATURE and USEFULNESS of HISTORY; supposing it improbable that any one can be ignorant or doubtful thereof. They tell us, that this Subject has been sufficiently treated by others, and that on this account they have declined troubling the Reader with a minute Detail of it. But as their Supposition is ill-grounded, and the contrary can indisputably be proved; and as the Allegation just mentioned not only contradicts that Supposition, but is as insufficient for the Conclusion they have drawn, as their Supposition would be even if it were incontestably true, I shall think myself incouraged rather than diverted from premising so necessary a part of an Introduction to an universal History.

For not to mention that many, who have an Inclination to HISTORY, and delight in that Study, without perhaps knowing the Reason why, may be pleased and instructed upon discovering whence their Taste proceeds, and how well it is grounded; it cannot be denied that the Admirers of History are so far from being as numerous as might be expected from times so much enlighten'd as the present, that there are some who publicly slight it. The various prevailing Amusements, even with Books either entirely unprofitable, or at least of much less Advantage and more pernicious Tendency, have so depraved the natural Taste of many, that they prefer fictitious Tales and Romances to a true Narration of real Events. Prejudices and Customs continually changing are as prevalent among the Learned as the rest of Mankind, and are most observable in the different Value which their Employments from time to time assume. Hence in great measure it is, that the excessive Veneration many entertain for other Sciences of a distinct and higher Nature, chiefly for Philosophy, hath almost led them to an utter Contempt of HISTORY, as a study fit for idle Persons, or such as are unfit for deep Reflection. The fashionable Propensity to raising Doubts, which many have taken for a sure sign of an improved Understanding and superior Genius, has in the vast Compass of History not only found a large Field and favourable Opportunities for new Discoveries, but likewise abundance of specious Pretences to depreciate all human Knowledge as entirely uncertain. Hence many have been deterred from making a thorough Enquiry, or to avoid the Suspicion of Credulity; and the more advantageously to defend other Sciences, they have been induced to abandon History to these Attacks, as a Subject not admitting of solid Proofs. To aggravate this Mischief some other Writers, affecting Novelty and Singularity, have endeavoured either to demolish the greatest Part of History hitherto received,

ceived, and the best ancient Records, with a view to erect a new historical Edifice (1), or, merely to distinguish themselves, have publicly controverted the whole Body of ancient *History* (2); which has been

(1) This has been attempted by *John Hardouin*, a *French* Jesuit, who denies the Authenticity of all ancient Writings, except those of *Homer*, *Herodotus*, *Plautus*, the *elder Pliny*, with some parts of *Virgil* and *Horace*, and the *Vulgate*, pretending that all the rest, and consequently the Accounts that are drawn from them, are supposititious and spurious Productions of the latest Ages of Darkness. He forms however a System of ancient History and Chronology of his own, and defends it with the warmest Confidence. An Attempt of this kind might deserve Pity, as the Produce of a disorder'd Brain, for this only can account for his charging all the primitive *Christian* Writers, and the Fathers, with an *atheistical* Conspiracy against divine Revelation. But he appears to have had his Adherents; one of them, *Joseph Berruyer* of the same Order, carried the Conceit the farthest, and would have been more extravagant, had not the Publication of his Continuation of the History of the Bible been prevented and suppressed by the Care of Cardinal *Fleury*: Mr. *Vander Hardt*'s Conceits are much such another Abuse of ancient History, chiefly of sacred Writ.

(2) Mr. *le Mascrier*, an Author of Merit, has very lately made the same Attempt where it might the least be expected, *viz.* in his Introduction to the first Part of the *Egyptian History*, which entirely consists of the ancient History of that Nation. It was published in the Year 1745, under the Title, *Idée du Gouvernement ancien & moderne de l'* Egypte. The first Part contains a preliminary Discourse of an hundred Pages, in which the general Taste for ancient History is very artfully attacked. As I propose in the Sequel of these Sheets to confute the specious Arguments he makes use of, I shall mention but two Things here, by which a Judgment may be formed of the whole Attempt. In the first place, his Intention was evidently to lessen the public Esteem for the Abbot *Guyon*'s Writings, and likewise for those of the celebrated *Rollin*, who is represented as the Author of this prevailing Taste for ancient History; which could not well have been done without attacking ancient History in general. This is not the first Instance of an Attack upon whole Sciences and Branches of Learning, from mere Envy and Malevolence to certain Writers eminent in those Sciences, and who have deserved well of the Republic of Letters in general. Secondly, the Proofs Mr. *le Mascrier* gives us, plainly shew, that he is very little versed in History, notwithstanding he has employed

been attempted by Arguments that confine all useful History to News-Papers, or at most to modern Accounts of Lives and Travels. For the History of any Kingdom or Nation, even of those that are now most powerful, flourishing, and civilized, will, if duly examined, naturally lead us into ancient History. Add to this, the well-meant Zeal of some, against either all modern Treatises on ancient History, or Translations of ancient Historians into more known Languages; from an Apprehension that the use of the proper Sources, and the reading of those genuine Patterns of good Histories are thereby lessened, and may chance to be more neglected; besides the Disadvantage resulting from thence to History, which would by all possible

ployed his Time chiefly in Works of that Nature. This *Egyptian History* would do no great Honour to its Author, should it undergo a strict Examination; tho' in the first Part he has the Credit of Novelty in an old History of that Nation, composed by him from *Manethon*'s *Dynasties*, or rather the Conjectures of *Paul Pezron* on them, setting aside the Accounts of *Herodotus* and *Diodorus*, as Sources less to be depended upon. The Additions and Emendations which he, and Abbe *Banier*, have made to the *Paris* Edition of the *Ceremonies & Coutumes religieuses de tous les Peuples du monde*, discover yet more his want of Penetration and Abilities in historical Matters; for not only *Bossuet*'s *Variations*, but even *Sanderus*'s, *Maimburg*'s, and *Varillas*'s Writings are the chief Sources, from which these Emendations have been drawn; nay, whole Pieces have been borrowed from them, and inserted as Additions to be depended upon. The Accounts of Mr. *de Maillet*, which the same Abbot *le Mascrier* has publish'd under the Title of *Description de l'Egypte*, would perhaps in many Parts have been more exact, and in general deserve much more Credit, had they not passed thro' his Hands; in which Case indeed they might have lost many of the Ornaments he has embellished them with. At least it were to be wished, that a Work, in which many Things are quoted from *Oriental* Writers, had fallen into the Hands of an Editor, whose Ignorance in Languages and History had not been so great as to make *Rabbies* of *Arabian* Authors. All the Contempt therefore which he expresses for ancient History is of no weight, whilst it is evident that his own Ignorance occasioned and prompted it.

Means

Means be facilitated, if we did not increase the number of those, who, on account of true or imaginary Difficulties, endeavour to depreciate it.

Now, though we have strong grounds to hope, that neither the natural Taste, nor the use of Reason, will ever be totally suppressed in Men; consequently that History will retain its Place among the employments of time, and it is doubtless the first both in Rank and Antiquity: Yet the Labours of such, as have endeavoured to commend the usefulness of HISTORY to others, and to rescue it from the Prejudices and Attacks of the Times, are neither useless nor superfluous; nor can we justly censure those, who by pointing out its Nature, Design, and Limits, have studied to promote its true end, and to direct a proper Choice and Judgment of the Means that conduce to it; whether such Endeavours have been used professedly in particular Writings, or incidentally. Of the former kind many were published in the 15th and 16th Centuries, on occasion of the general reformation of Learning, which hath been thereby considerably advanced, and some have appeared in later times (3). These useful Productions however, are not alone sufficient for the end proposed, which is often more successfully obtained by short

(3) *Stollii Introductio ad Hist. Litera.* Tom. 1. cap. 6. §. 5. and *Joh. Fran. Buddei Isagoge historico Theolog.* lib. 1. c. 4. §. 15. furnish large Catalogues of such Writers. Among those lately published we find the following of most use; the Abbot *Lenglet du Fresnoy*'s *Methode pour etudier l' Histoire*, which very deservedly has been translated into *English*, *German*, and *Italian*; and his *Histoire justifiée contre les* Romans. We have also from this able Pen an Epitome of an universal History in six Volumes, entitled, *Principes de l'Histoire pour l' Education de la Jeunesse.* Louis Thomassin's *Methode d' etudier & d'enseigner chretiennement & solidement les Historiens profanes*, and *Rollin*, *de la manere d'enseigner & d' etudier les belles lettres par rapport à l' Esprit & au Coeur*, where the 3d and 4th Parts of the 5th Book treat of History.

and cursory Remarks: For such Writings are seldom read by those who have no Taste for History, or by Persons prepossess'd against it, or by those who thinking the Pleasure and Advantage too evident to inquire into solid Proofs of it, are soon disgusted at a Difficulty which might have been obviated; and thus are apt to convert a blind Partiality into a direct Contempt.

Before I proceed to demonstrate and defend the Utility of HISTORY, it will be necessary briefly to define it, in order to add Perspicuity and Force to the Arguments I shall oppose to the Objections I have met with. It may likewise serve to facilitate the Judgment to be formed of historical Works, and promote the proper use of them.

HISTORY, according to the common and strict sense of the Word, is, A TRUE AND WELL-GROUNDED ACCOUNT OF PAST EVENTS, of which the essential Characteristics are two.

The ONE consists in its Object and Contents, which comprehend only *past Events*. For, tho' in many kinds of them, *viz.* in the History of Nature, or of Literature, we meet with accounts of Qualities and Opinions, of Works of Nature and Art; yet those and the like, have no other relation to HISTORY than as they are *Events*, and are deduced from Observations on past Changes. Thus, not only all Events merely possible, but likewise future ones, are excluded, how certainly soever foreseen, either from divine Prophecies, or from the Laws of Motion in the material World. And from the Diversity in the Object and Contents arises the most common Division of History, into as many Branches as there are kinds of Events; which, tho' very distinct, are connected in point of Time, Place, People, or Similitude. Now as there is an infinite number of Events, but all of them

them not of equal Importance, 'tis plain, that Hiſtory ought only to relate remarkable Events; which, on account of their Singularity or their Connection with other Matters, deſerve to be reported, and conſequently to be attended to and remember'd. This different Importance of the Events is not only a ſure mark of the Judgment and Diſcretion of the Writer, but occaſions likewiſe a proportionable Eſtimate of them in the mind of the Reader, ſince neither uncommon Diligence, nor ſtrict Impartiality, nor an elegant Style, in reporting Trifles and Events of no Importance, can deſerve the Name of a good Hiſtory; and many things may appear important to Perſons of a certain Profeſſion or place of Abode, which will hardly ſtrike the Attention of other Readers. Hence, before we form a Judgment of ancient and foreign Hiſtorians, we ought to conſider the Opinion and Cuſtoms of the Times and Places in which they were written; therefore an account of Events that were in thoſe Days thought worthy of Notice, tho' they do not appear ſo to us, ſuch as the frequent pretended Miracles and natural Prodigies reported by *Livy*, ought to be as favourably received as accounts of Travels, which might be conſider'd as trifling by every one on the Spot (4). The

(4) Many Hiſtorians, conſcious that their Readers expect memorable Events, have endeavoured by magnifying, to render them more ſo. But this ſeldom ſucceeds, and whenever it is diſcerned, which is generally the caſe, proves prejudicial to the other Properties of Hiſtory, which are at leaſt as important, chiefly to its Credibility. The more ignorant a Reader is of Hiſtory, the more apt he is to judge of the Remarkableneſs of Events merely by their Singularity or Rarity; but when his Underſtanding becomes enlarged, and he begins to form a judgment of the importance of Events from connecting and comparing them, many things will become remarkable to him, which in point of Singularity, or Rarity, appeared of little or no Moment. As all Events in the World are connected, and conſe-

The SECOND Characteristic and essential Part of HISTORY, consists in the manner of reporting such Events. If it is to be a WELL-GROUNDED ACCOUNT, *the Events must be sufficiently related*, be placed *in a natural Connection and Order*, and *there must be certain Signs and determinate Grounds of* Credibility: For without these Requisites, it is impossible to compile a clear and true Report of Events that have happen'd, or at least it can never be called a well-grounded one.

By the FIRST of these Requisites, Histories may be distinguished from mere Lists or Catalogues of Names. 'Tis therefore necessary, not only to mention all those Events that circumscribe, or are relative to the Account to be given, but likewise all the Circumstances that may contribute to a clear and lively Representation. Whoever is defective in this, cannot succeed in the other Parts; and Digressions, intermixed Reflections, or Flourishes of Rhetoric; will be so far from supplying this Defect, that they will render it more conspicuous and less supportable. I would not however be understood by a circumstantial Narration to mean Verbosity and a needless Accumulation of common and familiar Circumstances, but a judicious Choice of the peculiar distinguishing Parts and remarkable Circumstances of each Event. The Excellency of ancient Historians, and what constitutes them, the best Models for Imitation, is the uncommon Brevity with which they have related many Circumstances, of manifest Use towards comprehending the whole Event.

The SECOND Requisite is, that the Account must be connected in a manner suitable to the

consequently one Story illustrates another, a gradual Improvement in the knowledge of History will naturally secure Attention, even tho' it should cease to be kept up by an Admiration of Things of a marvellous and uncommon kind.

Event

Event related. Herein historical Works are distinguished from the Illustration of other Truths and Sciences by Examples and historical Facts. Though the Order of a Narration seems to be arbitrary, yet it ought to be natural, that is, it must always be suitable to the Matters related. But as all Events succeed, or collaterally attend each other, and according to this two-fold Relation, have an undeniable Influence over each other; this double Connection ought to be attended to with all possible Care. Hereby the Representation of single Events becomes not only clearer, but more useful for discerning and deducing general Truths, Directions and Observations, because the Motives, Causes, Views and Consequences, or the whole Spring or Principle of Action is thereby manifested. And hence it is that Chronology and Geography are so necessary in History (5).

The THIRD Requisite is indeed the most important, and those before-mention'd have likewise a Tendency to it; but it is at the same time not only in general most exposed to Doubt; at least the only possible Proofs of it have been most disputed, but it is likewise in particular Cases the most suspicious, and thus requires the greatest Circumspection and most careful Scrutiny.

(5) By observing the first Requisite, that is, by a proper Choice of Events and Circumstances that have a manifest Influence on others; and, according to the Second, by connecting them, as they illustrate each other, a History becomes practical, even tho' the Author should leave Reflections and Observations to the Reader's own Discovery, whilst he only lays before him such Grounds and Inducements to reflect, as cannot escape an ordinary Attention and may operate even imperceptibly. The Division of the Narration must be determined by the Extent of Events, and of their Connection. Hence Annals and Journals are in many Histories neither necessary, possible, nor of much use, and as for Almanacks of Events, they are almost a Burlesque upon Chronology.

In

In order to avoid the two Extremes of a blind Credulity, and the prevailing Humour of disbelieving and doubting, we must consider and attend to the Nature of that Certainty which is possible in historical Matters, and the proper grounds for determining it. This will facilitate the Answer and Confutation of the most weighty Objections that are made to historical Accounts in general.

The grounds on which the Credibility of an History is to be founded, are of two kinds. They must be taken, partly from the Events related, partly from the Evidence and Deposition of such as relate them; whence arises an internal and external Credibility.

To the INTERIOR GROUNDS of Credibility belong the POSSIBILITY as well as PROBABILITY of the Event reported. The former neither requires a perfect knowlege of the Rise, Causes, Means or the Manner whereby, and how a thing came to pass, nor a *Faculty* of imitating and executing any Part of the same at pleasure. For, we want both, in innumerable Instances, of the possibility of which we have not the least Doubt. It is only required, that the Fact do not contradict itself, nor other undeniable Truths. The interior *Probability* consists in this, that the Circumstances in which an Event is reported to have happened, be conformable or suitable thereto, or that there be some Foundation for it in the connection of the Circumstances, and that in parallel Cases the same hath frequently happened. Hence 'tis easily to be conceived, that many an Event may appear improbable, nay incredible to some, thro' mere Ignorance, or by separating it from its Circumstances and placing them in a Connection totally different (6). This

(6) This is the case with the frequent Charges of Incredibility brought against those numerous Armies we read of in ancient

This interior Credibility, tho' not alone sufficient to prove the Truth of an Account, is nevertheless indispensably necessary to it, and must be settled before its exterior Credibility is enquired into. This is as necessary in supernatural Events or Miracles, as in natural ones: for they must not only be free from all Contradiction, but likewise be neither repugnant to, nor interfere with any undeniable Truth concerning the Attributes and probable Will of God; on the contrary, they must be conformable to them. As the indispensable Necessity of God's Omnipotence, and his immediate working in an Event, otherwise impossible, derogates nothing from the Truth of it, so every claim and pretence to a Miracle is not sufficient to make it probable, and obviate all Inquiry into its interior Credibility (7).

The

cient History, raised sometimes by moderate Provinces in a few Weeks or Days, which took the Field without Provisions, as if they had sprung from the Earth, and lived upon Air; whereas we know, from the Experience of our Days, the Time, Expence, and Pains required to raise an Army, consisting only of the 10th, 20th, or 50th Part of those ancient Armies, and what distant Preparations are necessary for their Subsistence, only during one Campaign. 'Tis evident, that Armies in Pay, or regular Soldiers, are here confounded with the whole Number of fighting Men, and sometimes all the Inhabitants, male and female, of a Country, that anciently were summoned to serve in War; and that the modern Art of War in the *West* is not distinguished from that of the Ancients, and some modern *Eastern* Nations, who still use it. This has given Occasion to HENRY STEPHANUS's Attempt to confirm incredible Accounts related in ancient History, by still more incredible but undoubted Events of later Times, in a valuable Piece, intitled, *Apologie pour Herodote, ou traité de la Conformité des merveilles anciennes avec les modernes*; in which the incredible Legends of Popery are so much exposed, that the ignorant Monks of those Days certainly must have regretted the Attacks of ancient Historians.

(7) Prince DEMETRIUS CANTIMIR having asked the learned SAADI EFFENDI, how he could believe the famous Tradition, that MAHOMET had put the half Moon which fell from Heaven into his Coat Sleeve? was answered, that the

Fact

The EXTERNAL GROUNDS of Credibility, or Principles to ground our Belief upon, are the NATURE and NUMBER of Evidences on which the account of an Event is founded.

The nature of the Evidence comprehends the Genuineneſs of the Teſtimony, and the Ability and Integrity of the Witneſſes; or that the Evidence alledged is aſcribed to its true Authors, and that they were ſo circumſtanced and inclined as to relate the Truth, and add to it nothing falſe, nor omit any Truth of Conſequence to the Event reported.

The FIRST of theſe Articles is inſeparable from the other two, and affects not only hiſtorical Books and Tracts, but public Records and Monuments of paſt Events, Statues, Images, and Inſcriptions upon Coins, Columns, and Edifices. The fraudulent Practice of former Times in forging Evidences of this kind would, without a previous Enquiry, very much miſlead us, and might give Occaſion to an Hiſtory apparently corroborated with reſpectable Teſtimonies, tho' both the Story and its Evidences are equally Inventions (8). But ſuch Examination requires great

Fact being related in the KORAN, he renounced his Reaſon, becauſe God could do whatever he pleaſed. This was rather declining a Diſpute on the Merits of the Queſtion, than a Solution of the Difficulty. At leaſt the Anſwer would be weak, and cannot appear ſatisfactory to an impartial Perſon; though there are many who ignorantly pretend, that our Divines are reduced to ſuch Evaſions for vindicating the Miracles reported in holy Writ, See CANTIMIR's *Hiſtoire de l'Empire Othoman*, Tom. I. p. 89.

(8) The Omiſſion of ſuch a Judgment and Diſtinction between genuine and ſpurious Writings, has introduced innumerable Fables, and Confuſions into Hiſtory. Eccleſiaſtical Hiſtory has ſuffered moſt in this reſpect, as abundantly appears from the counterfeit GOSPELS and ACTS of the APOSTLES, the pretended Writings of CLEMENS of ROME, ABDIAS of BABYLON,

great Knowledge in the History not only of human Societies, but of the Opinions, Sciences, Languages, and Customs of different Times.

The CAPACITY of an Historian consists in a fit Relation between him and the Events he reports, as well as the Knowledge necessary to report them; in all which regard must be had to the distance of Time and Place from the Events themselves; the means of arriving at the Knowledge of them, and Judgment in the use of those means.

As to the FIRST Circumstance, immediate Eye-Witnesses of the Events, or such as were living

BABYLON, HIPPOLYTUS, DOROTHEUS, &c. and from that infinite Number of suppositititious Histories of Martyrs and Saints, forged Bulls, or solemn Instruments of Popes, Bishops and Councils. Other Histories have had their Share of these Impositions. The Writings of BEROSUS, MANETHON, MEGASTHENES, ARCHILOCHUS, XENOPHON, R. FAB. PICTOR, M. PORCUS, CATO, C. SEMPRONIUS, PHILO and MYRSILUS, with which ANNIUS of VITERBO, has, in the 15th Century, enriched History, have intermixed a Number of invented Facts with the History of the ancient Nations. The Life of the Emperor CHARLES, written by JOSEPH BEN GORION, and TURPINUS, is of the same Stamp. Hence those Writings whose Authority is doubtful, such as the Fragments of SANCHONIATHON, are not to be admitted in Evidence of Facts, till it is first demonstrated that they were neither entirely forged, nor interpolated. The same may be said of Coins, which HARDOUIN affects to prefer to all written Records; for, besides the Ignorance of the Artificer, the Fraud is more easily committed, and better paid, than the Forgery of Writing. A like Caution is absolutely necessary with respect to that Number of written Records which modern Times have produced; for else the ablest Writers may be imposed upon, as was the Case of the ingenious Mr. NORDBERG, in a Letter of the *Grand Signor* to the KING of SWEDEN, inserted in the *French* Translation of the Life of CHARLES XII, at the End of the second Book of the first Volume, Page 139. This Letter which is notoriously forged, would never have been mentioned by this careful Writer as genuine, had he been but half as much versed in the TURKISH History as he is in the SWEDISH; however this Mistake doth not affect any essential Part of his History.

and

and present, are much more to be credited than those who could have only a more remote Information of them. But as such authentic Testimony could not possibly be deliver'd in many Histories that are of any Extent, and therefore is not alone sufficient to give a full Insight into Things, unless they be Matters merely affecting the Historian, in which case his Account will be suspected of Partiality; so the Evidence of such must deserve more Credit who lived at the Time and Place of Action, where they might either receive their Intelligence from immediate Eye-Witnesses, at least before the Report has pass'd thro' too many Hands and degenerated into mere Hearsay; or where they might among various Depositions and Reports, chuse those which might most be depended upon and gather a full and circumstantial Account. A Writer therefore cannot be called an immediate Historian, on account of his having been a Cotemporary of the Event he related, unless the circumstance of Place concurs: For modern Transactions at distant Places are by far more uncertain than after the Expiration of some Time. On this account we shall in time to come, have Accounts of SCHACH NADIR, or KULI CHAN, more circumstantial and more faithful than any we have at present (9).

(9) The above-mentioned Mr. NORDBERG (Note 8), has in this Respect a great Advantage over Mr. DE VOLTAIRE, on Account of his having not only been an Eye-Witness of many Events himself, but having consulted a great Number of other Eye-Witnesses, of the principal of whom he gives us a List; not to mention other means of Assistance he has had, which Circumstances together intitle his Work to a preference to that of Mr. DE VOLTAIRE. POLYBIUS would not have been so authentic a Writer, if his long Residence at ROME and in ITALY, and his Acquaintance with SCIPIO, had not given him a more accurate Knowledge of what he relates, than he would have had, by residing in GREECE.

The

The SECOND Circumſtance in the Capacity of an Hiſtorian, or *the Means of arriving at the Knowledge of Facts*, is a point of great Conſequence in forming a Judgment of thoſe firſt and immediate Hiſtorians that relate recent Events; but it is yet more indiſpenſable, in judging of later Accounts of Tranſactions long ſince paſt. Hiſtories compiled merely from weekly or monthly News-Papers, are for this reaſon very little to be depended upon. Perſons who are unacquainted even with the known and extant Sources of an Event, ſhould not attempt a Narration of it, as it certainly cannot be amplified and enrich'd without the uſe of new and unknown Sources, or ſuch as have not before been exhibited to the Public (10).

The THIRD Circumſtance, the Parts and Judgment of the Hiſtorian, is not only abſolutely neceſſary to perfect his Work in other reſpects, but contributes greatly to the Authenticity and Credibility of his Narration. To beſtow proper Attention upon the Events to which himſelf is witneſs, to collect neceſſary Informations concerning them, to chuſe and judge of their Nature and Certainty, to diſcover the proper Connection of real Facts and their eſſential Circum-

(10) LEWIS MAIMBURG's and VEIT LEWIS DE SECKENDORF's Hiſtories of LUTHERANISM, are notable Inſtances of this Difference in the Capacity of Hiſtorians. The former could not make uſe of any *German* Book, and had but indifferent Sources in LATIN to draw from; whereas the latter, beſides thoſe neceſſary Books, had an Opportunity of conſulting the Records and Letters preſerved in the SAXON Archives. The ſame Difference appears between NIC. SANDERS's and B. BURNET's Hiſtories of the Reformation in ENGLAND; likewiſe between GREG. LETI, and SAM. DE PUFFENDORF's Hiſtories and Lives of great Men. Hence a Judgment may be formed of the different Value to be put on Abbot AUG. CALMET's Hiſtory of LORRAIN, and his *Univerſal Hiſtory*.

ſtances,

ſtances, and to make uſe of thoſe other Sources of former Tranſactions, is a Taſk of great Labour, demands indefatigable Application, as well as Sagacity and Penetration, and, in many Caſes, no ſmall Share of Learning and Knowledge. Whenever the Hiſtorian betrays an inaccurate way of thinking, a weakneſs of Judgment, Credulity, and an Inclination to Conjectures ill-founded, or to mere Imagination, his Story will, in many parts, become ſuſpicious, notwithſtanding all the other Marks of his Sincerity; ſimple and ignorant People eaſily miſrepreſent a Tranſaction to themſelves, and are apt to receive the Miſrepreſentations of others. Ignorance in Languages, Unſkilfulneſs in Records, and proper Sources, want of Reading, and of ſufficient Inſight into particular kinds of human Tranſactions, Arts and Sciences; ſometimes diſable the Hiſtorian from diſcovering and uſing the proper Helps, or from a right uſe of thoſe which he doth employ (11).

However,

(11) The Strength and Weakneſs of an Author's intellectual Faculties, together with the Bounds of his Knowledge and Penetration, are eaſily diſcoverable, not only in accounts of Travels but in other Hiſtories, and the Credibility of his Narration is conſiderable greater if he confines himſelf to the Deſcription of ſuch Things as he underſtands, and is able to judge of. Many modern French Authors on particular parts of ancient Hiſtory, manifeſtly ſhew, that not content merely with tranſlating old Hiſtorians and defective Pieces of Antiquity, they were not even qualified to make uſe of the proper Sources. We obſerve even in Plutarch's incomparable Lives of the Romans and Grecians, that his Account of Roman Occurrances, loſes much of its Credit, by his confeſſed and viſible Ignorance, or imperfect Knowledge of the Latin Tongue, tho' he had many Greek Authors on the Subject, and did not entirely neglect the Latin ones. This likewiſe accounts for the different Fate of ancient Hiſtories and thoſe of the middle Ages: The former were written by Generals and Magiſtrates of the firſt Rank, Experience, and Learning; whereas the laſt were left chiefly to the moſt unexperienced Monks. And hence we need not wonder

However, a bare insipid account of Facts, which required no other Attention than that of the Senses, may add to the Credibility of an Author, as it shews him incapable of much Invention with the appearance of Probability; whereas, on the contrary, other Writers become suspicious from their remarkable Addrefs in filling up the Gaps and Defects of their Intelligence, by Inventions of their own; giving a Glofs to the Events they relate, or courting the Reader's Approbation and Judgment by artful Embellishments. There are many Writers who, besides the more evident interior Credibility of their Story, shew that it was utterly impossible for them, either insensibly to deviate from Truth, or to be tempted to it by a probability of Succefs in the representation of a Falshood. For it happens fortunately for History, that the telling of artful and probable Lies in historical Accounts, chiefly when they are of any Extent, is so far from being an easy Task, that very few have a Capacity for it (12).

It is indeed in many Cases more difficult to examine the SINCERITY and Intention of an Historian, than his Capacity in relating the Truth;

wonder that the *Histoire de la Milice* Françoise of the ingenious and able Jesuit GABR. DANIEL, in spite of all his painful Enquiries, has been but indifferently received by all those that are skilled in the Art of War.

(12) The Eloquence and elegant Style of *F. Daniel* in Preference to *Mezeray*, cannot mislead a judicious Reader to prefer the former in Point of Credibility when they differ in their Facts, but will rather have a contrary Effect. The same may be said of SFORT, PALLAVICINI's, and Father PAUL's Histories of the Council of *Trent*, when the former attempts to confute the latter. And JACOB BEN BOSSVET's Abilities, which appear in his HISTOIRE DES VARIATIONS DES EGLISES PROTESTANTES, cannot fail of exciting Caution and Suspicion in the Readers.

and frequently the Enquiry must end in Conjecture; but the difficulty ought not to discourage the Attempt, for it is in many Cases successful. Much Caution however is requisite; and a misuse of some ambiguous Marks ought, by an exact Restriction of them, to be most carefully avoided. The surest Grounds for making Conjectures and ascertaining such Marks are the following:

As no one in general ought to be suspected without Reason, so it would be extremely unjust to charge those Historians whose Probity and Virtue are publicly known, with want of Sincerity, or to suspect them of it, without the least apparent Foundation. It must be admitted however, that neither the Language of Virtue, nor the other Marks of a conscientious Mind, are sufficient for removing Suspicions of Partiality that are supported by other Grounds; especially when an Historian discovers such Prejudices as oblige him to Partiality, or such Zeal and Passion as naturally and undesignedly produce it (13).

If an Historian has given indisputable Proofs of his Integrity, even in dangerous and critical Cases,

(13) Whoever is acquainted with the same Bossuet's Proceeding against Fenelon, and in the Affairs of the Quietists, as well as the rest of his Conduct, will not expect much Sincerity from him. The Lives and Characters of Ge. Buchanan and Paul Jovius, likewise of Machiavel and Hobbes, give but little Encouragement to look for much Sincerity in their Books; whereas the Lives of Seckendorf, Hiob Ludolph, John Sleidan, F. Paul, Thuanus, and several others, will ground a Presumption in their Favour. From the above Limitation it appears, why the Sincerity even of pious and virtuous Persons in their historical Accounts may sometimes be suspected: Witness the many fabulous Histories of Saints and Heretics, which did not always proceed from a bad Mind in the Authors, nor were always supposed by them to be true. *Epiphanius, Gregory the First*, and *Bernard de Clairvaux* are Instances of the same kind.

Cases, a strong Presumption arises of his having observed the same Conduct in other Cases, and the contrary ought not to be supposed without evident Proofs. On the other hand, if he be convicted of Falshoods or Untruths, which could neither proceed from want of Intelligence, nor be written without Design, his Sincerity upon the whole is justly liable to Suspicion (14).

As no one tells a Lie without the prospect of Advantage, nor with a Design of making such Falshood discernable, there is no Reason to suspect a want of Sincerity, when it can be gathered that the Historian probably could neither gain by departing from the Truth, nor apprehend Prejudice from strictly adhering to it, or rather when the contrary of both appears; especially when he relates such Events, at such Times and Places, that his Untruth must infallibly have been discover'd, contradicted, and punished, and when of necessity he must have foreseen this (15).

When

(14) When an Historian modestly confesses his want of Intelligence or Uncertainty with respect to some Events, this is a convincing proof both of his Ability and Sincerity, and gives the Reader a better Opinion of his Credibility, than confident Assertions of uncertain Facts. The following are likewise sure Signs of Insincerity; when he wilfully omits Facts that occurred in the Books or Records he consulted, when he mutilates and falsifies Quotations, when he misrepresents and forces the Sense of them, and when he affirms and relates either without Foundation, or upon such Grounds as himself in other Cases hath deemed insufficient and wrong. So that mistaken Conjectures upon the motives and design of the Events he reports, or the false Judgments he passes on them, are not to be ranked in this Class; for this proceeds in many Cases from a want of Ability rather than Sincerity, and the Events themselves may notwithstanding have been reported with the greatest Faithfulness and Accuracy.

(15) Under this Article all those Things must be weighed which after a Controversy has arisen, can be alledged to the Advantage of the Party, whose Cause the Historian has espoused, or the Disadvantage of the adverse Party, likewise in many

When Historians who relate Events, that have a Connection with civil, religious, or litterary Disputes, have the Character of being sincere, even from the Advocates of the other side, or when they are opposed in such a manner as betrays the Insignificancy and Weakness of the Adversary's Charge, it contributes not a little to establish the Opinion of their Integrity (16).

Thus much for the QUALITY of the Evidence: I proceed now to their NUMBER. In trying the Credibility of an Event by that, we should weigh; 1. How many Historians and known Sources are really extant of a particular Event; 2. The actual Diversity of their Testimonies; 3. Their Agreement and Contradiction; and if they cannot be reconciled, 4. The exterior and interior Credibility of the contradicting Narrations.

Cases the particular and odd Opinions an Author has broached and adopted. Hence it is evident that, 1. That no Historian of a Controversy can be above Suspicion, that has been much entangled in it; and therefore EUSEBIUS and THEODOREI were prudent in passing by the ARIAN and NESTORIAN Controversies in Silence; 2. That tho' the Historian's Remoteness, in point of Time and Place, from the Fact, renders his Capacity for a full and true Account suspicious, yet a remote Publication of his History in either Respects at his own Desire, must rather increase than lessen the Presumption of his Sincerity, which is the Case of CAMBDEN, THUANUS, and partly of BURNET. 3. That Histories published by anonimous Historians, or by fictitious Names, are not always to be suspected in point of Sincerity, tho' it is of Advantage to History if the real Names of the Authors become afterwards known; as was the Case with PET. SUAV. POLANUS.

(16) It is not necessary that an Historian's Veracity be always acknowledged in express Terms; it may likewise be inferred from a tacit Approbation and actual use of his Accounts. The NEAPOLITAN History of Mr. PET. GIANNONE will always be ranked among the most incomparable Histories, and the ingenious Author's Sincerity will be easily admitted by the Reader, though his Book had the Fate of being burnt at *Rome*, and the Author himself was at length imprisoned for writing it.

The

The FIRST Point is for this Reason to be observed, because the whole Argument for a Negative, drawn from the Silence of other Historians, depends upon it. For such Silence can never render the Truth of an Event suspicious, tho' reported by a single Historian distant both in Time and Place, untill it be first proved that more Writings are extant, whose Authors not only could have known such Event, but might, and ought to have inserted it in their Accounts; or, that it is impossible to conceive how they could have been ignorant of that Event, or designedly passed it over in silence, or undesignedly have forgot it, if it really happened. In those Cases such Silence is undoubtedly of great moment, especially if it can be proved, that the Event in Question either must have been better and more distinctly known to those Historians who make no mention thereof, than to him who reports it; or if by the use they made of the latter, his Writings appear not to have been unknown to them; and if the Fact was so connected with their Work, that they could not have passed it over in silence without a manifest Imperfection in their History, consequently must have omitted it merely from a consciousness of its Falsity. In Cases where only one or two Historians report an Event, this Enquiry cannot be made, without affecting their Credit by the want of foreign Testimony, tho' we be satisfied with the other marks they have of Credibility (17).

As

(17) The whole Controversy carried on by JOHN DAILLE, JOHN PEARSON, MATTH. LA ROCQUE, JOHN LAUNOY, and JOHN BAPT. THIERS, concerning the use to be made of the Silence of Historians, is decided by these Restrictions; which are the more absolutely necessary, as it is evident, that a wrong use might else be made of this Argument, by rejecting many genuine Writings of Antiquity and of the most important

 Events,

As to the SECOND Article, those new or later historical Books, of which it can be proved that they were copied out of ancient ones, must be excluded from the number of proper Evidences. For, tho' such subsequent Vouchers are likewise of use in many Cases for confirming the Authenticity and explaining the Sense of their Originals, they ought nevertheless not to be ranked among the principal Evidences. For, all these later Authors make out but one Evidence with the primary Source from which they drew. With respect to these capital Evidences, it is of use duly to consider the Times and Places in which they were written, and even the manifest diversity of their Contents; nay, their seeming Contradictions, in Incidents or Circumstances, may remove the Suspicion of their having transcribed from each other, or that their Harmony was concerted, or that it arises from their having made use of one and the same more ancient Writing.

Under the THIRD Head, all possible Endeavours must be used to compare and conciliate different Accounts, whereby a great number of imaginary Contradictions will fall to the Ground, at least the real ones may frequently be reduced to Circumstances merely incidental and of no Importance; in which Case the principal Event is the more corroborated.

Events, nay of sacred Writ itself. By keeping close to the Restrictions, the Foundation we have laid for forming a Judgment will appear unquestionably true and of great use, chiefly in ecclesiastical History; nor can any thing here advanced be weakened by *Eman. de Schelstraten*'s Evasion with his DISCIPLINA ARCANI, or Rules for secreting the most important Doctrines, Rites and Events. See likewise PET. BAYLE's Dict. Hist. & crit. *Tom.* 2. *p.* 105. 777. *Tom.* 3. *p.* 568. and HONOR. DE SAINTE MARIE *Reflexions sur les regles de la critique.* Tom. I. diss. 3. art. 2. p. 255----266.

The

The FOURTH and last Consideration is necessary for avoiding three occasions of Precipitancy. For, it would be highly inexcusable upon reading contradictory representations of Events, abruptly to reject the whole merely on that Account, as one of them may notwithstanding be fully entitled to Credit. It would be equally absurd, at the first sight of such Contradictions, to side with the majority without any further Enquiry; for the Report of a few, sometimes of a single Writer, may be more worthy of Credit than the opposite Accounts of many, who either are chargeable with improbability in their Reports, or with want of Abilities or Sincerity, or all of these together. Nor would our Judgment be less rash, if we should condemn as uncertain all the Events that have been differently represented or contradicted; or if we except against them rather than others, where no such Contradiction occurs; for, it is very evident from the Grounds before stated for determining the Credibility of Historians, that the same may happen to a relation of the most undoubted Facts.

To these means of establishing the authenticity of Events by several Evidences, two other kinds of Proofs must still be added, which considerably increase their Credibility.

1. One of them consists in a manifest connection of many preceeding with some subsequent Events, the latter having such a relation to the former, that without them they can hardly be supposed to have happened. Hence, besides that ocular Evidence, which is in many Cases possible, all other Witnesses remotely tend to confirm the first Authority, and the interior Credibility of ancient History is thereby greatly advanced. 2. The other kind of additional Proof, is the sight of several Monuments and remains of Antiquity,

 such

ſuch as Coins, Inſcriptions, Statues and Edifices, provided their genuineneſs can be regularly proved. For, tho' the difficulties of Hiſtory are accidentally increaſed, when ſuch Monuments contain things of which the Hiſtorians extant either make no mention at all, or even appear to relate the contrary: Yet, as it is incumbent on us to treat them as we ſhould a new diſcovery of ancient and unknown Hiſtorians, it muſt be admitted on the other hand, that great part of ancient Hiſtory has been conſiderably confirmed by them, chiefly by many inimitable Monuments and Ruins of old Edifices, of which it would be abſurd to pretend that they were forged at an immenſe expenſe, merely with a view to ſupport ſome invention of ancient Hiſtory (18).

From what has been hitherto ſaid, the five following Conſequences naturally ariſe.

First, that there is a real and demonſtrable certainty of Events, which ought not to be doubted or conteſted, becauſe it is of a different kind and founded in proofs different from MATHEMATICAL Certainty and demonſtration of general Truths. The Rules of Logic would not only be conſiderably defective, but greatly miſapplied, if we did not extend them to this kind of certainty, or ſhould apply them to controvert it, as appears from many Books on the art of Reaſoning. It is certain at leaſt, that the prevailing Scepticiſm in hiſtorical Matters, or the prejudice againſt a poſſibility of any Certainty in them, is moſt commonly, if not

(18) The Extracts from the Accounts of modern Travellers in Egypt, inſerted in the firſt Volume of the *Univerſal Hiſtory*, and in the Notes added thereto, do certainly much improve the Credibility of Herodotus and Diodorus; whoſe Accounts of the Egyptian Edifices and works of Art and Nature, would appear moſt incredible without thoſe modern Witneſſes of theſe *Ruins*, which put the whole beyond Suſpicion.

always, founded in an ignorance of the real nature of that Certainty and its Criterion, or in a consciousness of the indispensable necessity of unwearied Diligence, of farther Helps, and deeper Reflection in examining and proving, than the conveniency of many will allow. It is besides a very rash and false Conclusion, tho' frequently made, to judge an Undertaking in which we have miscarried, or which appears impossible to us, and in certain respects may be really so, to be absolutely impossible to all Mankind; and this Conclusion is the more suspicious, if a confession of Ignorance is attended with a fear of Disgrace (19).

In the second Place it follows, That the Demonstrability of a Fact, the Credibility of an Historian who reports it, and the Evidences of his whole Work, ought never to be confounded and mistaken for one and the same thing. The last is not absolutely necessary even to the second, and much less to the first. An Historian may be well worthy of credit though he be not infallible, and has actually committed Errors in some of his Reports. It is therefore an insufficient Charge against his Credibility to point out here and there a Mistake, especially if every one of those should appear to have been drawn from his Authorities, and so his Ability and Sincerity in most of his other Accounts should remain indisputable. But the

(19) Though we take *Certainty*, in the most rigorous Sense, to consist in the Necessity of a Truth, whose contrary is impossible; 'tis easily to be conceived, that, since accidental Things have a sufficient Ground for their actual Existence, and that if they do exist it is impossible that at the same Time they should not exist, there must be a Certainty, and consequent exterior necessity of Existence in them, tho' they derive not from thence an interior Necessity. This will at least be admitted by those, who admit as demonstrably true, the divine Foresight of all Contingencies; from the knowledge of God himself, by the light of Nature, without confounding this exterior Necessity with the interior.

Credibility

Credibility of an Historian is in the next place not always sufficient, nor indispensable to evidence a Fact; for as Historians, though credible, are not therefore infallible, the bare mention of an Event by any credible Historian, doth not constitute the whole proof of its Certainty. And as an Event may be certain, though expresly reported only by Historians of less Credibility, it follows that mere Credibility is not always an indispensable Proof. However a Fact is considerably more demonstrable if supported by the Credibility of the Historian; and it is greatly confirmed, if the whole Work, or at least the Substance of it, appear to be worthy of Credit (20).

THIRDLY,

(20) The anonymous History of the Popes, published in five Volumes by the Title of *Histoire des Papes depuis S. Pierre jusque à Benoit* XIII. happens in most of the Facts to be true; though the Book itself is by no means worthy of Credit; and the Author, FRANC. BRUYS, had neither the Abilities nor Sincerity requisite for such a Work, but has given evident Proofs of the contrary. Instances hereof may be met with in the 42d Part, page 130. and the following, of JOHN PET. NICERON'S *Memoires pour servir à l'Histoire des hommes illustres, dans la republique des Lettres.* We have an excellent pattern of a judicious determination of the Credibility of an Historian, as well as of the truth of the chief Contents of his Work, in Mr. PET. FRANC. LE COURAYER'S Annotations and Illustrations of PAUL SARPI'S History of the Council of *Trent*, and his subsequent Vindication of them. From what has been said, it will appear moreover, 1. That the divine Inspiration of the historical Books of Holy Writ being once proved, not only their Credibility is undoubted, but likewise the absolute certainty of the Facts there related, because their Infallibility is a consequence of that Inspiration: 2. That the Credibility of these Books and their Contents, not only may be proved by other Arguments, without previously proving such divine Inspiration, but that these Arguments likewise corroborate that Inspiration in an incontestable manner; especially as this Inspiration did not consist in an immediate revelation of Events or Facts that had happened; for the Men of God might without a Miracle, and really did procure sufficient information of them, though the Inspiration they had influenced their Narration as well as their

Doctrine:

Thirdly, The demonstrability of Events has different Degrees and Limits, and doth not reach to all Events that ever have happened, but only so far as the Records preserv'd will permit. Many of the principal Events recorded in History, may be reduced to Certainty, and many more to a preponderating Probability (21). Many Events, and many more of their Circumstances, are uncertain or doubtful, nay improbable; others are without foundation, nay evidently false. However it is as necessary towards a perfect knowledge of History to be sagacious in discerning the Falsity or Uncertainty of these, as the Truth or Probability of those.

Doctrine: 3. That their Accounts must be of use even to such as contest their divine Original, unless they will absurdly deny the whole History merely because they deny the manner of its having been recorded, which is more than we do with respect to the *Koran*, to which in point of History we allow as much credit as the interior Credibility and Mahomed's Abilities and Sincerity, as well as the agreement of other Authors, can possibly admit.

(21) When this is called a moral Certainty, it is not only because the obligation arising from divine as well as human Laws, likewise from all Covenants, and even from the Constitution of human Societies, is founded in Events that admit no other Proof, and concerns Actions which cannot be tried by Laws without such Evidence; but because this preponderating probability sufficiently authorizes and obliges every one to act according to it, and makes a contrary course of Action penal. As in Sciences, properly so called, it is not absolutely necessary in order to be convinced of a Truth, that we should know distinctly, not only the Arguments that prove it, but the Answers to all Objections, because these may be concluded wrong if the Arguments are right; so it is not necessary for establishing the Credibility of an Event, to comprehend the entire Impossibility, or only entire Improbability of the contrary, but a clear balance of probability is sufficient. The expression of an *historical Evidence*, sometimes used occasionally upon confirming general Truths by examples taken from History, which it must be confess'd are in most Cases no more than Illustrations, is perhaps in great measure the reason why many have entertained a groundless disesteem for all the Proofs which History requires and is capable of.

It

It is doubtless a vast Undertaking, but clearly shews the narrow bounds of human Knowledge; and the farther we advance in the knowledge of History, the more we are convinced of the narrowness of our Faculties by the prodigious extent of the Work.

In the fourth Place, That the Credibility of many Facts may happen to rise and fall, not only in the opinion of single Persons, but likewise with respect to their general and public Demonstrability; tho' it be impossible to determine the proportion of such Rise and Fall, or its different Degrees, by one and the same duration of Time. Many Events or Facts are not publickly credited, or known to be true, till after the death of such as either were the Actors or Parties concerned in them, and generally a long time after the Events themselves; and it frequently happens, that Records and Vouchers of Transactions long since past are discovered, which till then were either unknown, or could not be confidently published by those who knew them, because they wanted such Witnesses and Proofs. Circumstantial Accounts, even in the most notorious Events, must have some time to ripen in order to become authentic. Thus many Accounts, that were once thought credible, may in great measure, or totally, lose their Authority; whereas on the other hand, an Account which before was uncertain, nay considered as improbable and false, may be vindicated and proved by late discoveries of historical Writings and Records (22).

(22) Thus, by *John Leunclaw*'s, *Paul Ricault*'s, and *Demetrius Cantimir*'s Accounts of the *Turkish* Empire, innumerable Facts and Events, reported not only by the *Byzantine* Historians, but likewise by *Phil. Lonicer* in his collection concerning this Empire, all which formerly were not in the least suspected, have lost their Credit, and are now openly rejected.

Fifthly,

FIFTHLY, The Credit of Hiſtory can never decay by age, or diminiſh in proceſs of time, as ſome have pretended, and on that ground maintained, that not only all ancient hiſtorical Accounts are leſs authentic than modern ones, but that even the CHRISTIAN Doctrine, which is founded in Facts, muſt periſh in time, which they even take upon them to determine by calculation, at leaſt that it muſt loſe all its demonſtrability, unleſs the former accounts of theſe Events ſhould be confirmed by new Miracles.

This being premiſed, we ſhall now be able to demonſtrate with more facility and perſpicuity, both the USEFULNESS OF HISTORY in general, and that of its different Branches, and likewiſe to vindicate it againſt thoſe Objections that appear moſt ſpecious or of any weight, without having recourſe to a fulſom Panegyric in its behalf, or to the Teſtimonies and Deciſions made in its favour by Writers of Credit.

The uſefulneſs of Hiſtory in general, may be reduced to ſix Diviſions.

In the firſt place, there is an inviting agreeableneſs, a pleaſure, and an Entertainment in Hiſtory. This not only conſiderably increaſes its utility in other reſpects, but is itſelf a principal part of it, as well on account of the many Advantages to be obtained by it, as chiefly on accouut of the Obligation we are under to procure Satisfaction to ourſelves and others, which cannot be excluded from the duties of Man.

This pleaſure and enjoyment of Hiſtory is ſo univerſal, that it cannot very well be imputed to any received prejudice, nor in many caſes be ſuppreſſed by long diſuſe; nay it frequently manifeſts itſelf in thoſe who publickly treat hiſtorical Accounts

counts with Contempt (23). No sooner do the faculties of the Mind and the use of Reason exert themselves in Children, than they become sensible of this Pleasure, which is therefore of the highest Use for their Instruction, and affords the surest helps for instilling into them all other useful Knowledge. It follows that this Enjoyment must be natural, and conformable to the wise designs of the Author of human Nature. This will appear still more evident, by considering minutely the Constitution of human Nature on which the Enjoyment is founded. Narrations of Events take their rise from Sensations and a personal Knowledge of them; and therefore are not only the more easily represented to others, but are likewise infallibly impressed upon the Memory, so that the recollection nearly approaches to a revival and repetition of them. By this means the representation is suddenly changed, and all the Faculties of the human Soul, are insensibly and freely engaged, and by the perpetual change of the Objects, continued in Action, and at the same time sharpened; which, besides considerably increasing the stock of Ideas, and a Knowledge of their relations and connections, and moving the Passions or interior Springs of the human Mind, is attended with Delight (24). There

(23) *Franc. de la Mothe le Vayer*, the famous promoter of Scepticism, in spite of his vehement attacks on History and the Credit of it, has not only filled his Writings with historical Accounts and betrayed a great Reading in Travels, but employed his time in the same manner to the last Hour of his Life. It is reported of him, that just before his Death, when he recovered from a fainting Fit, upon seeing unexpectedly Mr. *Bernier*, who was returned from *India*, he pressed him to give him an account of the *Great Mogul*.

(24) It is a very common Prejudice, though not the better founded on that account, that History is a mere work of Memory, and neither requires nor engages, improves or shortens any other Faculties of the Soul. The contrary of this may be shewn,

There is moreover a Satisfaction in every view of Order and Perfection, of Variety, Resemblance and Harmony, of which Instances cannot be wanting in connected Events: Hence it appears, that History is of use in three respects, for the Instruction of others, for the relaxation of the Mind, and for a lasting, innocent and beneficial Amusement.

Idleness and want of Employment are a great Burden to many, who would sometimes chearfully pay as much to get rid of their superfluous Time, as others would give to gain it, if such a Purchase were practicable. But besides, the want of Employment is very frequently a dangerous

shewn. It is true, History has this Advantage which much contributes to its agreeableness, that it neither requires any laborious Stretch of the intellectual Faculties, nor surpasses any Understanding, nor discourages by betraying any one's Incapacity to comprehend it; yet there is not a Power of the Imagination or Understanding but what ought to be employed in History. As no Language can take place without the Representation of general Things and the use of intellectual Powers, and as all Conceptions arise from single Cases and the observation of their likeness and difference; so History employs the Understanding and Judgment as well as the Memory and Imagination: whilst it puts us upon the Observation of similar Cases it gives a clear Insight into the Connection of things; and both the Passions, and the Will, consequently both the rational and the sensitive part of our Nature are exercised. And this sensibility of Commotions, Changes and Vicissitudes within us, this Perception of so many various and connected Representations and Ideas in so easy an Explication of them, and this unexpected Observation of frequent Thoughts and Desires within us, is perfectly agreeable to our natural Inclination of Change, and must create Delight, Even the pleasure which fictitious Narrations give, shew the superior agreeableness of History; the former are but a mere Imitation of the latter, and can delight only in proportion as they come up to the Original. Art indeed can never equal Nature; and notwithstanding all the Delight which Fictions are capable of giving, a Dissatisfaction will arise from knowing them to be void of Truth and their use for Imitation unsafe; at least no other use can be made of them than by recollecting real Events or Facts of a similar kind.

Occasion

Occafion and ftrong Incentive to vicious and mifchievous Acts. It is therefore doing no fmall Service to thefe Men and others, to provide for them a fufficient Paftime. This muft in order to anfwer the Purpofe be neither tedious nor laborious, but light and agreeable; of a large Extent and containing great Variety; and it becomes yet more valuable, if attended with other folid and unexpected Advantages. Now there is nothing more effectual for this purpofe, than Hiftory; it will fill up the longeft Life of the idleft Man, the Pleafures of it will engage him to relifh it; it will infenfibly correct his Manners and improve his Underftanding; and it may excite him to other ufeful Employments, and confequently teach him not only to fpend his Time, but to make a proper ufe of it.

Men of Bufinefs and Labour find their Account in the agreeablenefs of Hiftory, by the Recreation it affords. It is true, their Mind is not wholly inactive in this Amufement, which would be an infupportable Burden to fome; but it is unbent and relieved by a lighter and more entertaining Employment; the Faculties of the Mind fatigued and almoft exhaufted, find actual Repofe, are recollected, recruited and reftored to Vigour. It is fometimes neceffary to anfwer this Purpofe by a mere Change of the moft intenfe Labour and the moft diftracting Employments, in order to reftore Alacrity to the Mind worn out by one kind of painful Study; But this end is much fooner and more readily obtained, when the Change is confiderably eafier, and attended with Pleafure. not only from the prefent Amufement, but from the Profpect of many other Advantages befides the faving of Time.

Hiftory, in the laft place, is of ufe for the Inftruction of others, not only of Children, for whom it is particularly fuited, by being eafy and pleafant, but likewife of moft Perfons of mature Underftanding, ſtanding. It raiſes and keeps up their Attention, explains and illuſtrates, clears the way for Judgment and Reflexion, much ſooner than could be done without this Help. God himſelf has uſed this Method of Teaching in his more immediate Revelation, greateſt part of which conſiſts of hiſtorical Events or Facts (25).

In the second Place, Hiſtory is the means of our acquaintance with a much greater and more remote part of the human Race than would be poſſible without it. And this is attended not only with Pleaſure, but with conſiderable Advantage, and is, at the ſame time, matter of Duty which cannot be neglected without the Omiſſion of many other Duties.

Man is of a ſociable nature, formed for a ſocial Life, and obliged to it. Now Societies cannot ſubſiſt, much leſs can all the ends of their Inſtitution be anſwered, without a Retroſpect to paſt Events; even the ſingle ſociety of a Family needs it; much more thoſe great Communities, religious or civil, as their ſeveral Prerogatives and Duties depend upon Events. The great privilege of Language which we enjoy above Brutes, tends to qua-

(25) As all human Knowledge and Science aroſe originally from Senſations and ſubſequent Reflections, conſequently took their Riſe originally from Facts; it is doubtleſs, that the primary Inſtruction Men received, was by means of Hiſtory, and conſiſted in propagated Traditions of former Events, in Experience and in Diſcoveries; This was found ſo fitting and uſeful a Method, that Fictions and Fables took their Riſe from thence, and were made to ſupply the Want or the Ignorance of ſuch real Events as might ſerve to propoſe an intereſting Truth. Hence, the earlieſt Compoſitions of Oratory now extant conſiſt of Relations of remarkable Events; which, the better to propagate and tranſmit them, as few Nations had written Records, were formed into Metre, from meaſuring the Sound of Words and Syllables, in order to be the more eaſily learned, better retained, and by being publickly ſung, more generally divulged.

lify and dispose us for social Life, which would be very much confined if we were incapable of any other knowlege but what is obtained by the immediate perception of the external Senses. Now as no one can either be a useful Member of human Society, or even enjoy all its Advantages, who is indifferent to the public Good, and therefore careless of the Concerns, the Prosperity, or Distresses of his Fellow-members; so it is doubtless no Merit to affect an unwillingness to know more of what passes in the World, than immediately concern ourselves, for this is making Self the only Object of our Thoughts. The more we consider the close Connection between all human Societies, which all together make up but one general Society, the more interesting the Events and Actions of our Fellow-members will appear to us, even those that happen in the remotest parts of the Universe. And as this Connection not only unites all Cotemporaries, but likewise extends to different Periods, whence general obligations to our Ancestors and Posterity arise; it follows, that the Attention must likewise be extended to Events of former times, if we chuse to be the better for our Predecessors, to discharge our Duty to them, and to render their Actions, and the effects they have produced, more useful to Posterity. For it would be an unaccountable Conduct to live in the World as if the human Race had begun and was to perish with us. It is therefore a duty of Humanity, it promotes and proceeds from universal Benevolence and a social Disposition, to think the Fate and Transactions of other Men worthy of our attention and enquiry, and to participate in them as much as possible.

Our natural inclination to Curiosity was designed as a Preservative against a dangerous Indifference to this band of Society; and we cannot apply

apply our Curiosity better, nor with greater advantage, nor more satisfaction, than to History, and reading historical Works. Long Voyages, attended with trouble, fatigue, expence and danger, undertaken with a view to see and know the World, to get acquaintance abroad, or acquire a knowlege of human Societies and their constitutions, and to become conversant with the Globe we inhabit, cannot answer these purposes without the help of History; they can never lead us so far as History doth, and are of most use when we extend our knowledge of History. The value of this Study will be inhanced if we consider that it represents to us whatever is uncommon or curious in the most distant places, and remotest times, and introduces us to the most useful kind of Acquaintance, with the greatest Men of our own as well as all former times: for this Acquaintance, so far from consisting in observations upon their countenances, dress, and carriage, is oftentimes rather hindered than advanced by the frequent view and attention to mere Objects of Sense (26).

In

(26) A fit distance between the place from which an Object is seen, and the Object itself, is absolutely necessary to give a pleasing and useful View of it, chiefly if it be wide in Circumference, for else the Perception is not only too much confined, but likewise too much crowded, and by the Confusion it causes render'd unfit for observation. In a great noise, where the Senses are stunned, no one is able with exactness to observe what happens nearest to him. In some intricate Transactions careful Attentiveness to ourselves, and the part we have in them, prevents our making full and accurate Observations, and rightly distinguishing between Circumstances that are memorable, and those that are not. It follows, that a Spectator, whose Mind is at peace, and at leisure, and who is at a due distance, and quite dispassionate, is the fittest Person for viewing and justly representing to himself, as well as forming a proper Judgment of an Event. History therefore not only affords more Delight and Admiration, but likewise much more facilitates a right and useful Application of human Actions, than a personal View of

them.

In the third Place, it is obſervable and undeniable, that Hiſtory lays a foundation not only for general Prudence, but for that particular kind which the circumſtances and ſituation of each Man require.

To become acquainted with the characters of Men, the marks, ſource, and effects of their Paſſions and Prejudices, the power and changes of their Cuſtoms, even of their ſhape, poſture, geſture, and changeable faſhions, whether theſe be uſual, natural, and free, or unpoliſhed, unuſual, irregular and monſtrous, conſtrained, unnatural and odd; to know all theſe is an eſſential and neceſſary ſtep to Prudence, and all this Knowlege is conſiderably improved by Hiſtory. The greater and the more extenſive our neceſſary Connections with other men are, the more we ſtand in need of this branch of Knowledge in order to conduct ourſelves with judgment, penetration, and advantage. and in this reſpect Hiſtory is of incomparable uſe..

Above all things, Experience which is ſo eſſential to prudence is prodigiouſly improved by Hiſtory. It teaches us to make other Men's experience our own, to profit by it, and to learn Wiſdom from their Misfortunes. It is by experience that we are enabled to make a judicious Choice of proper means for executing our Reſolutions, and accompliſhing our ends, to chuſe, among many more poſſible means, ſuch as are moſt ſecure, moſt innocent, eaſy, promiſing and advantageous, and to diſpoſe and apply them properly. Without experi-

them. It makes us more converſant in the Univerſe, and the Change of the Scene being frequent on this Theatre, it produces much more Acquaintance with Perſons of Importance, and better qualifies us both to judge of them, and to improve by their Example, than the moſt accurate Survey of Countries, the moſt general Converſation with Men, or any perſonal Share of ours in the Scene of Action.

experience, many poſſible concluſions and connections, cauſes and effects, deſigns and means, are apt to offer themſelves to an ingenious Head, which upon trial miſcarry and diſappoint him, nor can he depend upon Succeſs till he has been duly inſtructed by experience. Now as this Inſtruction cannot without danger be derived from mere perſonal Trials, for theſe would precipitate and perhaps ruin him beyond all recovery, or at leaſt they would be bought at too great a price; and as the Improvement would advance but ſlowly, nor reach very far, or extend to many poſſible caſes, it is obvious that attention to other Men's Conduct is one of the ſureſt Guides to Prudence, conſequently one of thoſe indiſpenſable Duties which every one owes to human Society, and chiefly to himſelf. Yet it is equally obvious, that, without the aid of Hiſtory, this attention cannot extend ſo far, nor anſwer thoſe Purpoſes ſo ſucceſsfully as with it. As paſt Events are no Dream, but are ſo connected with one another, that ſubſequent Facts are founded on preceding ones, and may conſequently be diſcerned and derived from them, it follows that a faithful Account of former Tranſactions, muſt greatly enable us to penetrate and foreſee the Conſequences of preſent Contingencies and Meaſures, and thus contribute not a little to render us cautious and provident, to prevent a blind Temerity, to furniſh immediate Expedients, and to make us ready at probable Conjectures, either in diſcovering advantages, dangers, ſnares, the ſecret and concealed deſigns of others, or in predetermining what may happen hereafter. The better we are acquainted with the Perſons and Societies with whom we have concerns, and with ſimilar caſes of Undertakings and Circumſtances that nearly reſemble our own, the eaſier it will be for us to conduct ourſelves to advantage, and the leſs reaſon we have to apprehend a surprize at unexpected Accidents, or the loss of a necessary Presence of Mind (27).

In the fourth Place; History is of eminent use in promoting Virtue. This end is effected partly by a copious and pleasing Instruction in a right and virtuous Conduct in general, partly by Opportunities that present themselves and lead us insensibly to the practice of several Virtues in particular.

As for the general Instruction; it cannot be denied, that the innumerable Examples of Virtue and Vice, of right and wrong Conduct, and the Consequences of both with which History abounds, are better suited to inculcate with Ease and Success the Properties, Marks and characteristical Differences between them, than the best System of Morals.

(27) The greatest Generals, Magistrates, and Oracles of ancient times, were very sensible of this Use of History, and frequently availed themselves of it; though many of them had neither much Inclination, Time, nor Capacity for reading, but contented themselves with oral Narrations. This use, however, is not solely confined to the Administration of public Offices, but extends to Arts, Sciences, Trade, and to the most important Transactions of social Life. But it requires not only a strong Memory for treasuring up a large Fund of prudent Expedients, and uncommon Inventions, and a happy Faculty of recollecting them, but rather a Quickness to be acquired by frequent Reflections on historical Matters, in comprehending in our Minds a sufficient Compass of Circumstances and Events that relate to each other, in discovering the true Springs, Motives, and Means made use of to bring about great Revolutious and unexpected Events, in forming a right Judgment of the Weight and Importance of concurring Circumstances from the Influence they had upon the ensuing Event, in determining our Conduct by drawing Conclusions from the known state of Things past and present, to a future Event and to its different Degrees of Probability; and thus whilst we are expecting similar Cases, in sharpening and applying both our Reason and Judgment. Many learned Men might have avoided innumerable Errors, much fruitless Pains, needless Embarrassments, and vexatious Controversies, had they been better acquainted with History in general, or only that of their own Science.

Morals. The usual Prejudices against the practicability and importance of Virtue, are at the same time obviated, and frequent Directions are given for facilitating the Practice of it, as well as avoiding the seeming Inconsistency of different Duties.

Besides, History contains strong Motives and powerful Incentives to an earnest Pursuit of Virtue, and to the utmost Caution in avoiding Vice. Not to mention the discovery of their very different Consequences; the bare image of a brave, resolute and undeviating Virtue so captivates our Affection and Esteem, that we cannot but admire and delight in it. It leaves warm Impressions of Pleasure and Approbation upon our Minds. Even the Profligate is obliged to approve and revere it with a secret Wish to be so constituted, or at least to have the appearance of it. A Person who is not quite insensible and indifferent to himself, must, upon contemplating the publick Merits of other Men, their Zeal for the common Good, their strict observance of Justice and Equity, their moderation in Prosperity and fortitude in Adversity, their magnanimous unwearied Beneficence, their inviolable Friendship, &c. feel within himself a strong, perhaps an involuntary disposition to imitate them. He will be forced in spite of all the Disguises his Character may assume, to take frequent shame to himself when he observes how different it is in the comparison. On the other hand, the sight of Perfidy and Dissoluteness, of inhuman Cruelty, mercenary Injustice, Levity and Inconstancy, Gluttony and Intemperance, brutal Lasciviousness and base Villany, must raise his Indignation and Abhorrence; even though his own Character should very much resemble that of which he abhors the Representation.

This good Effect of History extends even to those, who are subject to no Controul, superior to

Laws, and to the Cenſures of their own Times, which they are not apt either to hear or regard; but they foreſee and apprehend that their Actions will inevitably be recorded in the Annals of future Ages; that great Exploits and ſucceſsful Enterprizes cannot ſecure them the reputation of Virtue, or any degree of it; and that a ſevere Judgment will be paſs'd upon them by Poſterity.

Whole Nations have manifeſtly enjoyed this benefit of Hiſtory. For there never was a civilized People who did not honourably commemorate ſome virtuous Pattern ſet up for Imitation, and treat it with the moſt ſolemn Veneration. The more their Hiſtory comprehends diſtant and foreign Events, the leſs we find them arbitrary in their Laws, and ordinary Deciſions on the juſtice or injuſtice of Actions, or in changing real Obligations and Virtues for mere Cuſtoms and Uſages introduced for conveniency.

Beſides all this, Hiſtory almoſt unavoidably leads us to various Reflexions, which either tend to the practice of ſome particular Virtue, or remarkably promote that of all the reſt in general.

It exhibits ſuch lively Repreſentations of the periſhableneſs of all Things, the tranſient Vanity and nothingneſs of Men themſelves, and the perpetual Viciſſitudes to which all created Beings are ſubject, that we cannot poſſibly paſs them over without ſome recollection of our own Fate, and a ſuitable impreſſion on our Minds. The leaſt acquaintance with Hiſtory, convinces us how narrowly the power of the moſt potent Men is bounded, both with reſpect to time and place. Our extravagant eſtimate of preſent Things, and our own undertakings, which proceeds chiefly from ignorance of former and more remote Events, receives a great diminution from Hiſtory; exorbitant and ill-grounded Admiration is reſtrained, and we learn to admire and estimate every thing before us according to its real value. History therefore is an instructive school of Humility and Discretion; it presents us with the most emphatical warnings against Pride, and a dangerous forgetfulness of our Condition. It powerfully incites us upon the least reflection, to look with indifference upon human Things, and on the splendor of Wealth and Grandeur; to moderate whatever Joy, Sorrow, Fear, Hope, and Confidence they may cause in us; to confine ourselves to our own Bounds, not plunging into needless Embarrassments; to become careful in the use of opportunity and time, and to devote ourselves to Virtue, which alone is durable, and the only Property exempted from Vicissitude (28).

Tranquillity of Mind, and contentment with our Condition, which are very essential to human Happiness, and highly conducive to the practice of other Virtues, are greatly promoted by observing, that good and bad, profit and loss, pleasure and pain, are indiscriminately mixed in human Life, or that they are equally balanced, with respect to human Happiness, at different times

(28) As Accounts of human Transactions exhibit at the same time the History of the human Understanding and Heart, every one that is conscious of his own Humanity, must find himself deeply humbled, upon discovering the amazing and frequent Infirmities, Extravagancies, and Errors of his Fellow-Creatures; not only of those who were Monsters and a Disgrace to human Nature, but of the most specious, considerable, and amiable Characters. He cannot reflect upon these without lessening his Opinion of, and Confidence in the Perfection of great Parts and a capacious Understanding, and a Heart that pretends to be above the Necessity of Amendment. He will find it expedient to proceed with the utmost Caution and Diffidence of himself, without misapplying his Observations so far as to bring all his Fellow-Creatures under the Denomination of Fools or Knaves; though it cannot be denied that the Number of both has at all times and places been very great, and but too many now may be ranked in both Classes; which again increases the Necessity of Caution and Circumspection.

and

and places; that therefore the danger is the greater of misapplying these external distinctions of Fortune, and receiving hurt from the enjoyment of them, and that a sufficient counterpoize of Affliction, of Distresses and Troubles, is necessary for the Mind of Man; all which is taught and illustrated in History. As Discontent and Disquiet in general chiefly proceed from an inconsiderate Wish, if not for another World, yet at least for some other times and places of our Globe, which many through Ignorance represent to themselves as golden and perfect; so a knowledge of the true nature and condition of foreign Places and remote Times, and the different ways of living, and regulations of human Societies, must shut up this source of Disquiet, and help to convince us that the true happiness of Man depends not upon such external Accidents, nor is the attainment of it facilitated by such things as are commonly reputed to be the means thereto (29).

To conclude this head, History discovers to us many Obligations which we owe to other Men, even such as have been long since deceased, and without this help we should want both the opportunity, and the motives to the discharge of those

(29) A defective Knowledge of History may sometimes create and nourish this Discontent to such a Degree, that Men may think themselves in Heaven, if they could but be changed into old *Romans* or *Lacedemonians*, or perhaps into modern *Chinese*. Many learned Men have fallen into this Folly, as *Isaac Vossius* did, but the Fault was rather to be imputed to their Ignorance of History, than to History itself. History moreover prevents many possible Instances of Surprise and Despair in dejected Minds. There are some who torment themselves with the Apprehension of imaginary Dangers, or with magnifying real ones by supposing them insuperable; and disquiet their Minds with an idle dread of the total Ruin of Societies, and Destruction of public Good. The Knowledge of former Events is a sure Preservative from these distracting Fears, as well as from careless Security.

Obli-

Obligations. Besides the Patterns and Examples they left us there for our Instruction, Encouragement, and Warning, we learn from History that there is not a conveniency of Life, nor an improvement or benefit of Arts and Sciences, nor a happy constitution of any Society we now enjoy, but what we owe to our Ancestors, who have deserved so well of us, that we are under the strongest Obligation to Gratitude, which we may discharge by honouring their Memory, making a good use of their Discoveries, and carefully forwarding and improving them (30).

In the fifth Place, the greatest Advantage arising from History, doubtless consists in that it promotes the Knowlege and Service of God, by which Men are brought to true Virtue and Happiness, in the Enjoyment of the supreme Good. The following Things fall here under our Consideration.

Historical Accounts considerably improve the Knowlege, and point out the right and salutary use of God's wise, kind, and never-erring Providence. We are not only hereby assured that he

(30) This Consideration of the Obligation we lie under to our Ancestors, reminds us of our Duty to Posterity, that it is incumbent on us to take care that they may not by our means be deprived of the Advantages procured by our common Ancestors, and their Condition be thereby rendered worse. Public Spirit and the Love of one's native Country, has always been supported and animated by the Considerations of other Men's Merit and Fatigues, of their Labour and Danger, and in some Cases of their actual Sacrifices of their Lives. There is no danger of falling by this means into a blind Veneration for ancient Customs and contracting Prejudices in favour of Antiquity; for, tho' this Obligation to our Ancestors doth not allow us to be so fond of Novelty as to abolish ancient Customs without due deliberation, yet it has no Tendency to prevent our Improvements of what may contribute to public Utility; nay it rather encourages and demands it from us, if we are willing to appear the genuine Posterity of Ancestors who have deserved well of us.

actually interferes in human Affairs, and carefully inspects, guides, and directs them; but we likewise become better acquainted with the Nature and Measures of this divine Administration of the World, and the Principles on which the great Author of it acts; and consequently we learn to submit to it more cheerfully and to use it more profitably. A Man is much more liable to Perplexities and Doubts about this divine Providence and Government who knows nothing of human Actions and Events, nor considers any but his own Affairs, fancying himself the only Object of the divine care. If his Ignorance tempts him so far as to make his own Appetites and Passions the Rule of divine Providence; no wonder that every thing in the World appears to him irregular and confused. The Knowlege of God by the light of Nature is too much confined, if historical Events are excluded from the auxiliary means, the Sources and the Grounds for determining that Knowledge; for they exhibit many striking Instances of the divine Perfections, and frequently reveal as it were the Counsel of God, the Decrees of his Providence, and the Directions of his Will. Whoever observes and attentively considers these, will find many Occasions, Instructions, Motives and Encouragements, to praise and adore his Creator with Awe and Reverence, to acknowledge his Goodness with the warmest Gratitude, to resign himself freely to his Will, both in active and passive Obedience, in perfect Confidence, in Patience and Contentment, and to make God the chief Object of his Thoughts and Actions (31).

History

(31) By considering human Events, we may at the same time discover and meditate the Works and Ways of God, which are remarkably conspicuous in the Transactions of Men, even in their Follies and Errors. Such Observations have a natural

History likewise points out to us the Characteristics, Sources and Causes of Superstition and Enthusiasm, of Atheism and religious Libertinism. It discovers to us the Insufficiency and Falsity of the grounds upon which both are built, their dangerous Effects and Consequences, with respect to Individuals as well as whole Societies; and therefore abundantly warns us against either of the Extremes, and renders it impossible to fall into either without setting aside the clear Convictions of History.

Besides, History convinces us of the Necessity and of the inestimable Blessing of a more particular Revelation from God, it shews the Marks by which it may be known, the Arguments by which it is demonstrable, and the Certainty and indisputable Truth of its having been made in holy Writ; for the greatest and most important part of it consists in Events, that have a Connection with other Histories; and the grounds for proving the divine Authority of its Contents by Miracles and the Accomplishment of Prophecies, require a Knowlege of the Credibility of Accounts, and what are the proper Rules for determining it, as well as the Credibility of other Events; whereby it is at the same time made evident, that the divine Records might possibly be preserved without Falsifications, or rather, that there is a moral Impossibility of their having been falsified (32).

In

natural Tendency to a dutiful Imitation of God as well as Tranquillity of Mind, and enable us more easily to justify God to ourselves and to others.

(32) Some Objections pretended to be brought from History against the *Christian Religion*, will, upon a moderate Insight into History, lose all their Plausibility, which is founded merely on Ignorance in that Science. Such are the Pretences that the Scriptures were written in later Times, that they were introduced by artful, covetous, and ambitious Priests or Magistrates, that other kinds of religious Worship are preferable, chiefly

In the sixth Place; every other Science receives such Benefit and Advantage from History, that no Branch of Learning can conveniently dispense with the Use of it. Learning in general, is considerably indebted to History for this, that it insensibly leads those who have neither Abilities, Inclination, Time, nor Opportunity for Literature, to some Acquaintance with it, either by giving them a Taste for it, or at least a Conviction of its absolute Necessity in human Society, which must of Course create an Esteem for it; or by qualifying them, and exciting an Inclination, to understand and improve from the Writings, Labours and Conversation of learned Men; all which cannot be accomplished without History (33).

Moreover, all Men of Letters, to whatever Branch of Learning they may belong, must indispensably have a Knowlege of the History of their own Art or Science, and may reap considerable Advantage from knowing the Examples of their Predecessors. This might even have its Use in other human Discoveries and Occupations, even mechanic Trades and Agriculture not excepted (34).

chiefly with respect to the Public, &c. Other Objections become by the use of History very trifling, even to those who cannot solve every single Difficulty, especially in Chronology; for use will teach them, not to make the Credibility of Events that are most authentic and undeniable, depend upon their readiness to answer every Difficulty that may be started.

(33) As it is of use to Learning, that by the means of History, it is more adapted to every one's Capacity and Attention; so on the other hand, no small Advantage occurs to the Unlearned from this Science, as it furnishes them in a cursory way with a tolerable Knowlege of the most important Discoveries and Observations of the Learned. By which the Benefit and Pleasure of rational Conversation must be greatly promoted.

(34) The more learned Men know from History, the Helps and the Bounds of their Science; the easier will they avoid round-about ways for instructing themselves, for improving and for extending it; and an entire Knowlege of History will secure them against innumerable Temptations to *Pedantry*.

As

As for the particular ſeparate Advantages of each branch or part of Literature; even a thorough fundamental Knowlege of Languages cannot be obtained without Hiſtory. For Languages have their own Hiſtories, which well underſtood, contribute much to the underſtanding and uſe of them, as they are ſubject to great Changes from different Times and Places. There is no Language, whoſe Expreſſions, Idiom and Proverbs, are not relative to Cuſtoms and Events, and require an Acquaintance with them in order preciſely to determine their Significations: Oratory and Poetry can hardly exiſt without the knowlege and uſe of Hiſtory. The great Models of both, which Antiquity hath tranſmitted to us, cannot, without Hiſtory, be underſtood, nor rightly be made uſe of, nor duly imitated; nay both receive moſt of their Materials, Subjects as well as Thoughts, from Hiſtory; for it is from thence they draw pertinent, agreeable, charming and affecting Repreſentations, Expreſſions and Ornaments. Philoſophy and Mathematics have recourſe to Hiſtory, and to Nature, through the medium of Hiſtory, for moſt of their Objects; and in many parts of theſe Sciences, chiefly in Phyſic or natural Philoſophy, and *mix'd* or *practical* Mathematics, the whole force of the Demonſtration is founded in Experiments, which would make but an indifferent figure, if the Aſſiſtance of other Men's Experiments by the means of Hiſtory were excluded. Divines, without the help of this Science, could neither ſucceed in the Interpretation of holy Writ, nor even prove its divine Authority againſt many Objections. They could not thoroughly underſtand, nor defend the religious Doctrines, whoſe Limitation, technical Terms, and Confeſſions, are founded on former Controverſies, nor could they pay a due and well-grounded Regard to eccleſiaſtical Conſtitutions,

religious

religious Rites, and human Ordinances (35). Lawyers, without making uſe of Hiſtory, cannot fundamentally explain or defend the civil Laws of their Country, nor ſupport a Litigation, or aſſert the Rights of Communities, or of particular Bodies, founded on Covenants, Treaties, ſolemn Immunities, and preſcriptive Cuſtoms, of which even the Law of Nations conſiſts; and much leſs would they be qualified to give their Counſel in public Exigencies. The medical Art being properly Phyſic, or natural Philoſophy limited to Man and his Health, what hath been mentioned above concerning that Science is applicable to this.

From what has been ſaid, two Queſtions, which have given Occaſion to many Diſputes, may eaſily be reſolved, or rather entirely decided: The firſt is, what kind of Hiſtory or Account of Nations is preferable in point of Utility and Neceſſity, the ancient, in particular that of the *Iſraelites*, *Grecians*, *Romans*, and neighbouring Nations, or the modern, chiefly that of one's own Nation and Country? The ſecond, in what Order it ought to be learnt, and whether univerſal Hiſtory is abſolutely neceſſary for the Purpoſe?

To reſolve the FIRST Queſtion, we muſt clear it from Ambiguity. If we mean Utility and Neceſſity relative to certain Individuals, and their way of Living and particular relation to certain human Societies, it cannot be denied, that there are many Men, chiefly among the Learned, to whom ſome other Parts of Hiſtory are more uſeful and neceſſary, than the Hiſtory of Nations in general. Other Litterati, and indeed all Men, chiefly ſuch as

(35) In the Introduction to the firſt Part of my Abſtract of Church-Hiſtory, §. 2. I explained more at large the Advantage and abſolute Neceſſity of Church-Hiſtory; where, §. 1. likewiſe contains the Plan of this ſame more comprehenſive Account of the Nature of Hiſtory in general.

are in any public Office, may likewise frequently find the History of their own Country, and its Constitution, of more immediate use and necessity, than that of ancient Nations. But if we set aside these particular Relations and Restrictions, and suppose the Question to be meant of general or universal Utility and Necessity; it will not be difficult to prove incontestably, that ancient History is intitled to a Preference. For the use of it in all civilized Nations, not only in various Matters of Literature and Policy, but even in the particular History of every Nation now in being, chiefly those of the *West*; and the Number of remarkable Events and excellent Historians, are Circumstances which do not concur equally in favour of the History of any modern Nation or Country whatever (36).

However the Labours of those modern Historians are certainly laudable, useful, and necessary, who

(36) Occasions may happen where a Person stands in greater need of the History of his own Family, and can make more use of it, though no sovereign Princes belong to it, than of the History of any Nation whatever. Persons who are charged with the care of public Affairs, have greater Occasion for the History of their Country and of their Neighbours, than for the *Roman* History. But this Necessity or Use however, is confined to an infinitely less Number, than the Use of ancient History is; without which neither holy Writ, nor the best ancient Authors can be understood or used, and which the Histories of later Nations cannot dispense with; for, though ancient History may very well be learnt without the Assistance of modern, the latter cannot without the former. It proceeds therefore not from a Partiality or contemptuous Neglect of our native Country and its former Inhabitants, that our Youth is first of all instructed in the History of the ancient *Oriental* Nations, and of the *Grecians* and *Romans*, and led to the reading of those Historians, in order to get a true Taste and a sound Judgment of History in general. Our most remote Ancestors, whilst they wanted every Requisite for the formation of an illustrious Character, were not so defective in great Actions, remarkable Events, and meritorious Men, as in Historians to transmit good Accounts of them

who are employed in drawing up Accounts not yet committed to Writing, or in clearing up, supplying and digesting obscure, confused, and defective Passages and Fragments, chiefly from Sources that were unknown or not in use, and thus break up the uncultivated Lands of History, and actually extends its Boundaries. For their Productions become original Histories, which all Times are in need of; and they pave the way for more Discoveries to facilitate that important Study, and to render it more advantageous to the World in general.

The SECOND Question requires the same Limitation. Persons who read History merely for the sake of Amusement and Pastime, or having in view some particular Branch of Learning, attend only to certain Branches of History, are not confined to that Order and Connection, which is absolutely requisite for obtaining a proper Knowlege of History; though it is doubtless, that we shall always be more successful in our Study of any Part by taking in a larger Compass of the whole, and making the History of Nations or Commonwealths, with a due Attention to the Difference and Connection of Times and Places, the Foundation of our Inquiries. Hence it follows evidently, that any Degree of historical Knowlege, requires Instructions from universal History, and that to study any Branch of that Science with Success, presupposes and requires an Epitome, or connected Compendium of univerfal History; or, to speak more properly, it is only extending the Knowlege of particular Parts of it, which are connected with the whole. Unless this be our Plan, we shall only

them down to their Posterity; which is the Reason why we are obliged to draw our Knowledge of them from foreign, distant, and rather suspicious Sources.

fill

fill the Memory with some Events, which may be done without applying to History or pretending to the Knowlege of it.

From what hath been hitherto said, it will be no difficult nor tedious matter to refute and explode the trifling Arguments made use of to depreciate the Study of History.

The first is a Pretence, that History cannot properly be called a Branch of Learning; nay, that historical is the lowest and most despicable of human Knowlege, and hinders the Progress of real Sciences, not only in particular Persons, but likewise among Bodies of Men. This Pretence hath discouraged many in the present Age from stooping to History, lest they should demean and misapply their penetrating Genius, which they esteem worthy of a better Occupation. But the whole is founded in confused Prejudices, and contradicts Experience.

For, in the first Place, it is manifest, that the historical Knowlege of essential Parts of Sciences, is here confounded with the Knowlege of, and thorough Insight into historical Matters, which demands as penetrating a Genius, as the Representation of abstracted Truths. Every Inquiry into the real Grounds and different Degrees of Probability and Certainty of historical Events and Facts, a Discovery of the Connection of different Events, and their mutual Influence over each other, and a right Judgment and Application of the same, require as much Reflection and Exercise, and sharpen the reflecting Powers as much, as any other Science. The Comparisons *Plutarch* has subjoined to his Lives, shew plainly, how far *philosophical* and *mathematical* Knowlege are related to History; which yet comprehends much more than appears from thence.

In the next Place, Learning is very imperfect and too narrowly limited, if it extends only to certain Sciences, or signifies a Knowlege, which is supposed to have engaged a whole Life, and perhaps to have rendered us ignorant of every thing else that is useful. If Learning consists in a ready, fundamental, extensive and connected Knowlege of useful Truths, then History cannot be excluded from it. It is not indeed the sole Property of Scholars, but may be looked upon as the Cement of the learned and unlearned World, who are certainly of reciprocal use to each other.

Besides, to pretend that Memory is the only Faculty used in History, that a comprehensive Memory much exercised, is inconsistent with great Parts and Judgment; or that a Taste for History and for the Sciences interfere with, and destroy each other, is mere Prejudice, exploded by considering the Nature of Man and daily Experience. Not to mention many Instances in ancient History, the contrary is abundantly proved in the Characters of *Bacon*, *Sarpi*, *Grotius*, *Gassendus*, *Puffendorf*, *Leibnitz*, and *Newton*, who will be admitted as eminent for their Taste and Capacity in both. Indeed it were to be wished, that there had, at all Times, been fewer Historians destitute of all Knowlege in Sciences and other Parts of Literature, and that those who professed the Sciences had been less ignorant in History.

But besides the Advantages above-mentioned, which other Branches of Literature derive from History, the Experience of former Ages hath abundantly shewn, that whenever a Taste for History prevailed, it was not detrimental, but rather greatly beneficial, to the Sciences, and Literature in general; and that, on the contrary,

their

their Progress was considerably hindered, and Learning brought to Decay, by a prevailing Neglect, Contempt, and Ignorance of History. The barbarous Darkness of the middle Ages since the Birth of CHRIST, consisted not so much in a want of ingenious Learning and Knowlege of Sciences (for these were carried to the highest Subtleties) as in setting aside Languages and History, which were looked upon as frivolous Studies. But upon their Restoration and Revival, the Face of Literature in general was soon changed for the better. This is confirmed by the fate of Learning among the *Arabs* and *Chinese*, where it must have spread farther, and flourished longer, and have been carried much higher, had not the want of History, chiefly foreign, prevented it.

The SECOND Objection made against History, is a Complaint of its extreme Uncertainty, and the utter Impossibility of demonstrating any Facts and Events. This is commonly supported by Instances of Contradictions in historical Writings, and the different Opinions of Chronologers. Sometimes by contesting in general the Grounds of human Belief, in things which we cannot know, or are incapable of proving by Arguments drawn from general Notions and incontestible Principles.

The last Argument certainly goes too far, as it not only overthrows the Credibility of History, but the Basis of most Parts of Literature and Sciences, and even that of a divine Revelation and the right Interpretation of it. It is but one Step from *Scepticism*; at least it bids Defiance to almost all the Rules we have and can rely upon for determining those human Actions, upon which the Lives and Welfare of Men depend. The pretended Contradiction of Historians is likewise carried too far. If contrary Doctrines and different Opinions upon single Articles related by them, should necessarily produce Uncertainty and affect their Credit, then the greatest Part of Learning and Sciences, if not all Certainty of human Knowlege, would fall to the Ground. Whoever is capable of maturely considering and applying the Grounds above stated, for determining the Veracity and Evidence of historical Events, will not unreasonably demand other kinds of Proof than the Nature of the Thing admits; for this would be much the same as desiring to distinguish a Doctrine by the Senses of feeling or smelling. He will find innumerable Events, as well as their Chronology, supported by sufficient Authority; and he will place the rest to the Account of those Limits, which circumscribe all human Knowlege; without making these a Pretence for rejecting that which is certain and demonstrable, along with what is uncertain and incapable of Proof (37).

The

(37) Mr. *le Masrier*, whom we have mentioned above, in his Attacks on ancient History, has carried this Objection very far, and filled many Pages with exaggerated Representations of Things. We cannot forbear making the following Observations on them. 1. Objects are so much magnified there, and Matters so ill stated, that it is impossible not to suspect the Author, either of gross Ignorance, or designed Imposture. For Instance, he says in the above-mentioned *Discours Preliminaire*, Pag. 11. Sesoster *is represented to have led whole Armies out of* Egypt *to* Japan, *in as short a Time, and with less Trouble, than is perhaps required for the Dispatch of an Express from* Paris *to* Rome. Here he may with Propriety be asked, where he has read this? He says, Pag. 14. *The common Opinion limits historical Certainty still to* 500 *Years after the* Trojan *War, and admits no Event as authentic that is dated before the first Olympiad.* Here he manifestly confounds the Certainty of a fixed Chronology in History, with the historical Authenticity or Evidence of the Events themselves. And Pag. 9. we read, *Is there any one*

The THIRD Objection is a Pretence that History fills the Head with a Multitude of useless and unpro-

one remarkable and important Event in ancient History, concerning which the Historians do not differ, and often contradict one another? If this Assertion were true, it would not answer the Purpose of proving what it is intended for; however, such as maintain it, must either be extremely ignorant in ancient History, or impudent to the highest Degree. The Question he makes, Pag. 10. is of the same Stamp; *What else do the famous Republics of* Sparta *and* Athens *present to us, but mere deformed, and oftentimes mutilated Lists, of those who ruled them in the earliest Times?* And that of Page 13. is still more extraordinary: *What can we depend on, when we see the ablest Men, even in our Days, doubt whether the History of* Alexander the Great *is not a Romance and a Fable?* He might with more Propriety have said, *Begin in our Days to doubt*; for former Times have not furnished such able Men as have since arisen in *France*, who could change the whole History of *Alexander* into a *Fable*; a Piece of Address which demanded all the Abilities of *F. Hardouin*. 2. The Arguments made use of by him for shewing the Uncertainty of ancient History, evidently prove too much; for upon the same Grounds we might contest the Credibility of all Events in general, particularly those of holy Writ; and those Arguments are derived from Principles which are not only void of Proof, but evidently false. In Pag. 13. he concludes, because some Reigns are passed over in silence, or barely mentioned by Historians, that this is a Proof of the Uncertainty of their Narration: *When Historians*, says he, *take only a cursory Notice of the Life of a Prince, what Judgment else can I form to myself, but that either nothing remarkable happened in that Reign, or that they were not informed of his Actions?* Mr. *le Mascrier* will always be apt to infer the latter, though the former will in many Cases appear more probable to others. But granting him his own Inference, it is inconceivable how he can draw his farther Conclusion, that, since the Silence observed by Historians with respect to the Reigns of some Princes, proves, that they were not informed of them; therefore, that their Accounts in other Respects, are uncertain and not authentic. An Historian certainly may have well-grounded Intelligence of some Events, and want the same with respect to others; and surely he deserves more Credit by far, if, where his Intelligence is defective, he runs over whole Reigns with only mentioning the Names of the Princes, than if he invents unprofitable Ideas, chiefly of distant Events, which cannot, without Singularity, be imitated at other Times

Facts or Events, in order to fill up his Gaps and to conceal the unavoidable Imperfection of his Story.-----Mr. *le Mascrier*, in the same place, instances the same Contradiction between *Herodotus* and *Xenophon*, concerning the Death of *Cyrus*, as a Proof of this Uncertainty, and asks again, *Can it be thought an easy Matter to decide between these two Historians?* I might ask in Return, Is every Thing that is not very easy, for that Reason impossible? or, Are all other Truths so easily proved? or, Are there not remaining Events enough of *Cyrus*'s Life, though it should be impossible to decide this Contradiction? or farther, Is it not an additional Argument of the Certainty of those Things, in which both Historians agree? and what would be the Fate of all historical Accounts? Modern as well as ancient would be rejected, and the former much sooner than the latter, if the mere Contradiction of Historians in some Points, should be deemed sufficient to discredit their whole Narrations. He concludes these Arguments, Page 17, and the following, with the Character of most of the ancient Historians, whom he represents as Strangers to the People whose History they wrote, and tells us they were *Grecians, that is, credulous Men and Lyars. This is,* continues he, *the peculiar Characteristic of that Nation, proceeding from their Levity and Inclination to the fabulous and marvellous, which has distinguished it from other Nations, and at all Times will distinguish it.* To begin with the last Charge, it is evident that he confounds the modern with the ancient *Grecians*, and most unjustly makes it a fundamental Rule for judging of a whole Nation in all Ages, to observe the Customs of certain Times and Individuals, who perhaps might amount to a Majority, and from these to determine the Merit of all Writers of that Nation. That this is a most indefensible Proceeding, appears from the particular Observation the Author has added upon his own Countrymen, to which he was led by a natural Connection of Ideas from drawing the Character of the *Grecians*. This remarkable Passage is conceived in the following Words: *I beg leave on this Occasion to do Justice to my Country. The* French *are naturally vain and conceited, and perhaps have more Self-love than we meet with in all other Nations taken together. Yet, notwithstanding these bad Qualities, no Nation has ever produced more credible Historians:* De Thou *and* Mezeray *will, in this Respect, be standing Patterns worthy of Imitation.* I must observe, that the only two Histo-

Times and Places, nor serve in other Respects for a Rule of Action.

But as the same want of Utility may be objected to all other auxiliary Means, for forming the Manners and Understanding of Mankind, and as there is no room to apprehend, that any one will fall

Historians, which the Author had to produce, must, according to the very Rules laid down by him, forfeit that Credit he attributes to them: For he could not be ignorant how much the former is contradicted by the many Writers of the *Holy League* in *France*, and the latter by *Daniel*. And as to the vain Comparison he makes of his Countrymen with other Nations, he may be indulged in this, as probably he may not have read many foreign Historians. But, if the *French*, notwithstanding their Vanity, Conceit and Self-love, which our Author from his Conscience acknowleges, may yet have Historians worthy of Credit, and if a Pair of Examples are sufficient to prove this, it follows we owe the same Justice to the *Grecians*, among whom *Thucydides*, *Xenophon*, *Polybius*, and *Plutarch* are Characters which will always deserve Imitation with respect to Integrity and Credibility. Besides this, our Author must have been entirely unacquainted with the Taste and Manner of writing of the *Eastern* People, whereby even some of the *Grecians* were corrupted; and with the common Fate of the first Accounts of each Nation, and *Livy*'s own Confession of it, as well as with the Fate of a great Number of *Roman* Historians treating of their own domestic Affairs, and which have no relation to modern History. Lastly, the Authority of an Historian does not depend upon the Place of his Birth: For a Stranger may frequently happen to have superior Capacity and more Sincerity than many who write the History of their own Country; and we cannot refuse declaring for him, provided we are convinced that he had sufficient Intelligence, drew from good Sources, and knew how to make a proper Use of other Materials. If *de Maillet* could give an authentic Account of the present State of *Egypt*, though he was no *Egyptian*; if the Authority of *Thevenot*, *Lucas*, *Bernier*, *Tournefort*, *Spon*, *Chardin*, and *du Halde*, is not called in Question, though they were *Frenchmen*, and though the last wrote his Account of *China* even at *Paris*; why should *Herodotus*, *Diodorus*, *Polybius*, *Dionysius*, be deemed not authentic, merely because they wrote foreign Histories?

into

into an Abuse of History by a wrong and absurd Imitation, unless he be so far defective in Understanding and common Sense, as not to know how to conduct himself according to the Experience of his own Time and Country, or how to apply the Instruction he has received from common Rules and Examples: So it may be presumed, that his own Experience, and that of others, which he is to learn from History, will most easily teach him what is fit to be imitated, and what Rules he is to observe in his Conduct; even intellectual Weakness and Want of Judgment, may meet with Relief from History: For among the many Events, Transactions, Manners and Customs, that bear an undeniable Resemblance and Conformity to each other, we likewise meet with a wide and undoubted Dissimilitude and Difference in others, even such as appeared most similar, which evidently proceeded from Imitation: So that no one can be misled by History, even that of the remotest Events, to any other Imitation, than what is suited to the Circumstances he is in; at least, if he is misled, it is not to be imputed to History (38).

The

(38) Those Arguments of most weight, which Mr. *le Masceier* has made use of for supporting this Objection, are, 1. That ancient Times have been no more fertile in producing great Men than the modern, and furnish no Examples of Virtue and Prudence, but what may be observed nearer home, where they are by far more conspicuous. 2. That the public Transactions of former Ages are but indifferent Patterns for Imitation, as the Art of War, the Constitution of Governments, and the reciprocal Transactions of States, with each other, are entirely changed. 3. That Antiquity represents to us an infinite Number of Customs and Usages, of which no Traces can be found in our Times.----Though these Arguments seem only to prove the inutility of ancient History; yet they might, with equal Reason, serve to persuade us to forbear the Use of all

The FOURTH Objection consists in an Apprehension that History intangles us in almost unavoidable

all History, modern as well as ancient, because our own Experience, and the Knowlege we acquire of the great World by Travels, by much Conversation and Exercise in public Affairs, is preferable to all historical Writings; and because the personal Observation of virtuous Characters, which we meet with at all Times and Places, is far more instructive than History could render them; especially as many of the Customs and Circumstances, which occur in History, depart from those of our own Times. But without dwelling on Consequences that might be drawn from our Author's Arguments, the Reader will take notice here, that by recommending ancient History and its Use, the Use of the modern is not depreciated nor rejected. The Knowlege of the great *Condé* and *Turenne*, is no Obstruction to an Acquaintance with *Epaminondas*. And it were to be wished, we had so many moderns like *Aristides* and *Phocion*, as not to need the Exhibition of those ancient Examples; though their Number of them could hardly be great enough to render the Examples of Antiquity entirely superfluous. Besides, there are some exterior Circumstances required to constitute true Greatness, as well as rightly to distinguish it; and it is a Point hitherto undetermined, whether such Circumstances do not occur more frequently in ancient than in modern Times; as it is doubtless, that the Circumstances of former Ages were better adapted for forming great Orators than those of the present. The greatest Generals and Judges of the Art of War have esteemed the reading of *Cæsar* and *Polybius* to be of extreme Utility. If a Reader is to profit by Instructions from History, it is absolutely necessary for him to learn to discern Virtue and Prudence under very different Shapes and Appearances, in various Circumstances, and concealed in many Customs and Usages, in order to distinguish that which is essential from accidental Circumstances, and to make these subservient to the profitable Use of those. Ancient and foreign History may answer this Purpose as well, if not better than Accounts of our own Times and Countries. One more Slip of this Author deserves Notice. On Occasion of this Objection, he warmly urges, that the Men of two or three thousand Years ago, were no more different from those that are now living, than the Trees of those Days bore different Fruits from the present. Yet, it appears very odd, that notwithstanding this, he pretends, page 4. 7. and the following, upon

voidable and endless Embarassments, and in most painful and tedious Inquiries; chiefly with respect to Chronology. But this Objection is easily removed. Every Branch of Learning is more or less extensive, more easy or difficult, more intricate or clear, in proportion as Men aim at a superficial or a fundamental Knowlege, or as they vary in their natural Capacities, and the Opportunity, Instruction, and Helps they have for attaining such Knowlege. And the same is undoubtedly the case in History; every one is to examine his own Taste and Inclination how far he intends to engage in the Study, and how difficult or easy he proposes to make it to himself. History it is true is of so great an Extent, that it may employ the longest Life, and the most attentive Diligence of the most laborious Man; and it is to many so alluring and interesting a Study, that the most painful Enquiries they are oftentimes obliged to make, do not discourage them. But on this very Account it doth not appear by far so tedious and perplexing to them as others are apt to think it. Yet it would be a discouraging Circumstance, in Arts and Sciences, if the several Branches of Learning were of no Service to each other, and if each of them only could be useful to such who devote their Lives to the Profession of it, and chose themselves to undertake all the Enquiries to be made, even those that had already been carried on by others. As it

upon disputing the Pleasures of ancient History, that the Reason why modern History is preferable in point of Entertainment, is, because every body considers the People of ancient Times as Men that were of another Cast. This strange Reasoning may as fitly be applied to modern History of distant Countries, because oftentimes, not only the common People, but the Learned represent to themselves *Turks*, *Persians*, *Chinese*, &c. as Men made of different Materials.

would

would be injurious to reject *mathematical* Arts and Sciences, and to pronounce them useless, or unprofitable to such as profess a different kind of Learning, for no other Reason but because Enquiries and Calculations occur, which require much Time, great Application, and unwearied Pains; especially if every Man would prove and resolve all Propositions and Problems already resolved, without availing himself of the Labours of other Men; so it would be doing Injustice to History to suffer this Apprehension to deter us from it, especially as this Study abounds with more Assistance procured for us by the Labour of others than any other kind of Literature can produce; and as a moderate Progress in it, opens to us the evident and manifold Utility of it, and renders us sensible of the Pleasures by which it invites us to farther Attention (39).

It is objected in the FIFTH place, that, as History is inexhaustible, and affords infinite Delight

(39) Mr. *le Mascrier*, in complaining of the insurmountable Difficulties in Chronology, has employed all his Rhetoric to display its Obsurity, Darkness, and Confusion. His chief Argument is, that there is a double Chronology in Holy Scripture, the *Hebrew* and that of the *Septuagint*, and that very learned Men have declared themselves for each. He seems to have been ignorant, that as learned Men as those were who asserted the *Grecian* Chronology, have declared for a third, the *Samaritan*. He concludes with proposing, that it might perhaps be necessary, first of all to enquire how the ancient Nations computed their Years, and when they began the Use of solar Years. As he has given us such Specimens of his Penetration in Chronology, we need not wonder at his dismal Representation of it; it were however to be wished, that he had left the *Egyptian* Chronology as he found it. The best Use to be made of the Consideration of this Intricacy in History, the many Difficulties we meet with, and the undeniable Defects in many of its Parts, is a modest Acknowlegement of the Narrowness of our own Faculties, and of the Limits of human Understanding in general.

and Satisfaction, it may easily create an insatiable Curiosity and a Disgust to necessary and serious Employments, it may even make us negligent of our most important Concerns, and occasion an irreparable Loss of Time.

This Objection not only implies an actual Confutation of the preceding one, but is of no Weight; and doubtless proves too much; for the accidental Abuse is no Argument against the Use of a Thing, which has sufficient to recommend it in other respects. The Nature of History itself is such a Bar against this Abuse of it, that it cannot happen so frequently as might be apprehended. We cannot long be passionately and insatiably fond of History, unless our Enjoyment arises either from the Improvement of our Knowlege, and the Acquisition of a vast Variety of connected Ideas, or from perceiving our Passions and Dispositions to be agreeably affected. In both Cases the Evil is prevented in every Breast, unless it be that of a Man so addicted to Idleness, that this Insatiability of History is become the less and more tolerable Evil to be apprehended. For History insensibly leads such Men to Employments and Inquiries, which remove their Prejudice and Disgust to Labour, and perhaps habituate them to Industry. And it contains so many Motives and Allurements to useful Undertakings, that these must either have their proper Effect, or the Reader must become so very insensible, that his Inclination to the affecting Representations of historical Events will soon cease.

The SIXTH Objection made use of to create a Contempt of History, affects only the Learned, and chiefly Writers. It is their Concern to hear the Complaint, that nothing new can be discovered in History, especially in that of former Ages, nor any thing written but what has been written already; and that every one is qualified to compile Histories of modern Events.

This Complaint might redound to the Advantage of History, if it should deter Men from Inventions in historical Matters, from whence so much Embarrasment and Uncertainty have arisen. It might also have its Use in preventing others from compiling Histories or venturing at Illustrations of ancient Events, without having made authentic Discoveries, and learned to distinguish the Rabble of Historians from Authors worthy of Imitation. Both Ends may be answered by a regular and proper Study of History, and that so easily, that scarce any kind of learned Employment affords more Opportunities for deserving well of the Reader than this. The Subject of it must of Necessity increase with the Age of the World, and the Misrepresentations of ignorant, injudicious and partial Writers, demand and give a Scope for numberless Inquiries into their Veracity or Falshood, Confutations of the one, and Refutations of the other, and many Corrections of different kinds.

The SEVENTH Objection, with which I shall conclude this Essay, derives the pretended Dangers of History from hence, that many draw more Instruction from it in Vices, Vanity, and Cunning, are more invited to Extravagancies, Wickedness, insatiable Ambition, foolish Conceits, and irregular Desires; are more furnished with Doubts of God's Providence and Government, and with Arguments to contest a divine Revelation, than with Instructions and Motives to Virtue, Prudence and Piety. But vicious Misapplications, to which the most innocent, useful, and sacred Things are equally subject, can never be laid to the Blame of of Hiſtory ſo miſapplied, nor can this be a Reaſon for condemning it as dangerous in its Nature, ſince ſo far from miſleading to ſuch Abuſe, it rather warns every one ſufficiently againſt it. When Faults and Vices are ſpeciouſly coloured, when the artful Refinements of falſe Policy and deteſtable Villany are honoured with Encomiums, or when the Writer or Reader delights in Obſcenities, it is not Hiſtory in general that is diſgraced, but that particular Writer and Reader of it. This Abuſe however is beſt and moſt effectually prevented by a careful Endeavour to facilitate and promote the right Uſe of it.

A
CHRONOLOGICAL DISSERTATION
ON THE
REIGNS
OF THE
KINGS *of* ISRAEL *and* JUDAH;

To which are ſubjoined,

CHRONOLOGICAL TABLES,

BY

FERDINAND WILLIAM BEERS.

to the ſame purpoſe; for it changed the ſeries of the feaſts celebrated by the Egyptians: The Jews had their own preſcribed to them, in a manner and order altogether peculiar; and by the conſtant return of theſe anniverſaries, the memory and ſimilitude of the Egyptian feſtivals was totally removed. It was altogether impoſſible to change, or to fix a proper time for celebrating the Egyptian feaſts, becauſe the year and months of both the nations were ſo vaſtly different.

The Hebrew nation having ſettled in the country, which had been promiſed them, and now being governed by their judges, underwent ſeveral changes and revolutions, both in reſpect to civil polity and religion. They worſhipped the one true God, and they became idolaters by turns: however, it does not appear that an univerſal idolatry ever was introduced among them; each man choſe his own idol as he pleaſed, and worſhip'd it when he thought proper.

But things began to change afterwards, and they were quite altered when David became king of Iſrael. Succeſs and victory attending him, he freed his country from oppreſſion, and many other nations became ſubject to the Hebrews. He ruled with equal power and authority; and being very zealous in religion, a moſt ſevere puniſhment would in his time have been ſure to attend the leaſt appearance of idolatry. Hence true religion prevailed among the Jews, and was exerciſed to its full extent for the ſpace of forty years, during which he governed them.

Solomon's power and authority were as great as David's: the chief difference between him and his father was this, David was diſtinguiſhed by his military merit, Solomon by his wiſdom and learning. Religion at firſt employ'd his warmeſt attention; he built the temple, the moſt ſtately edifice

edifice in the universe; he introduced the feasts as ordered in the law of Moses, universally among the people; and, the better to secure their celebration, he thought it proper to abolish the lunar year, as proving very inconvenient in many respects: instead of this he introduced a solar year of 365 days and six hours. As the reason for the former computation ceased, it was time to abolish it. He persuaded himself that the Jews, having a magnificent temple of their own, as well as their regular feasts and ceremonies, it would be impossible for them to become idolaters: Or perhaps he thought the power of a king of Israel sufficient to prevent all error and disorder in this respect. However he shared the fate of many other princes, who rely too much on their own wisdom: He himself fell into a sin, which formerly he had looked upon as impossible ever to be committed: Thus shamefully offending his subjects, and occasioning the division of the kingdom; for ten tribes of it, by a free election, appointed Jeroboam king of Israel.

Jeroboam being afraid the zeal of these tribes might abate in time, and they might become desirous of joining the other tribes, endeavoured strenuously to prevent any such accident. According to the laws of God, the whole nation was to meet together three times every year, in order to celebrate the passover, the feast of weeks, and of tabernacles, in the temple at Jerusalem, the place of Rehoboam's residence. This was most likely to promote what he feared; he therefore contrived the worshipping of the two calves at Dan and Bethel. In what manner he persuaded the Israelites to sacrifice to them, we do not find related in the scripture; however, probably he represented Solomon's building the temple as an attempt, for which he could not have alleged any other than his own authority, as a new undertaking without any precedent: this he probably told them they should be cautious not to partake of, as the whole form of the ancient true religion had been corrupted by it. He probably pretended to set every thing right again; thus it is said in scripture, *Jeroboam ordained a feast which he had devised of his own heart*, 1 Kings xii. 33. We do not in this say, he intended to abolish true religion and to introduce idolatry; not so much as the feasts themselves were changed, but only the time for celebrating them. He again introduced the lunar year and settled the feasts accordingly, by which he obtained all that he had been aiming at. The feasts of his subjects after this not coinciding with those of Rehoboam's, the Israelites could not expect to meet with their brethren at Jerusalem, who followed altogether another computation, according to which the feasts were celebrated at a different time, seemingly new, and erroneous in the opinion of the Israelites.

The difference continued as long as the kingdom of Israel, and is taken notice of in the History of Hezekiah, in whose time the kingdom of Israel was drawing near to its period.

Hezekiah intending to open the temple and to celebrate the passover, invited his neighbours the Israelites: A few of them went to Jerusalem, the rest slighted his invitation; not because true religion and the feasts of the law had been quite abolished among them, but because they esteemed it a ridiculous proposition to invite them to celebrate the passover at a wrong time, which, according to their calender, happen'd to be on a very different day. The established religion by no means consisted in a total abolition of the true worship of the Deity; they changed the glory of the incorruptible God into images that were ob-

jects

jects of the senses: This occasioned a more gross idolatry among part of them, who adored Images not at all intended as a representation of the Deity.

This hypothesis, concerning the change of the time appointed for celebrating the feasts of the Hebrews, is warranted by the following passage of the scripture; 1 Kings xii. 26, &c. *And Jeroboam said in his heart, now shall the kingdom return to the house of* DAVID: *if this people go up to do sacrifice in the house of the LORD at Jerusalem, then shall the heart of this people turn again unto their lord, even unto Rehoboam king of Judah, and they shall kill me, and go again to Rehoboam king of Judah. Whereupon the king took counsel, and made two calves of gold, and said unto them, It is too much for you to go up to Jerusalem: behold thy gods, O Israel, which brought thee up out of the land of Egypt. And he set the one in Beth-el; and the other put he in Dan. And this thing became a sin: for the people went to worship before the one, even unto Dan. And he made an house of high places, and made priests of the lowest of the people, which were not of the sons of Levi. And Jeroboam ordained a feast in the eighth month, on the fifteenth day of the month, like unto the feast that is in Judah, and he offered upon the altar, (so did he in Beth-el) sacrificing unto the calves that he had made: and he placed in Beth-el the priests of the high places which he had made. So he offered upon the altar which he had made in Beth-el, the fifteenth day of the eighth month, even in the month which he had devised of his own heart: and ordained a feast unto the children of Israel, and he offered upon the altar, and burnt incense.*

This single expression, *Even in the month which he had devised of his own heart*, appears express and plain enough to give us the clue for removing every scruple and difficulty. The stile of the scriptures is very concise, but it is the nature of ſuch a ſtile to have no words ſuperfluous or inſignificant. *A month which he had deviſed of his own heart*, muſt needs be a month calculated as he thought it proper; and the form of the year depending on the calculation of the months, Jeroboam's changing theſe, ſuppoſes an alteration of the other, and his having ordained the feaſts, as expreſly mentioned, accordingly. For want of attending to this, it has been ſo difficult a taſk to compare the years of the kings of Judah and Iſrael. The endeavours for making them agree have hitherto proved ineffectual, becauſe the agreement was imperfect; an obſervation, which is by no means intended to derogate from the merits of thoſe who undertook the buſineſs. But how could it be otherwiſe? a perfect compariſon being quite impoſſible, their attempts ſerved to ſupport the authority of the ſcriptures as well as could be done. I appeal to all who are converſant in this part of chronology, and who know the difficulties attending this article. I am ſure they cannot help owning that this method of reconciling them, was either forced and unnatural, or too precarious and arbitrary. Nay, even the beſt, by miſtake, introduces a chronology accompanied with the greateſt difficulties, when compared with the unqueſtioned records of profane hiſtory; and ſometimes quite inconſiſtent with them. As all chronology undoubtedly depends, and is grounded upon the calculation of the Hebrews, it is impoſſible to connect the whole after any material miſtakes committed in this. The weakneſs of the whole will appear more glaring, if the miſtake relates to an epocha abundantly determined by the records of profane hiſtorians, as this part of the Jewiſh Hiſtory certainly does.

As the hiſtorical and chronological parts of ſcripture have been handed down to us, chiefly in order to convince us in the ſtrongeſt manner of the

the truth of what has been promised or prophesied from time to time among the Jews, I could not imagine how they should be attended with insurmountable Difficulties in this particular; or that it was necessary to solve those by only supposing errors and mistakes in the MSS.

On the contrary, being persuaded scripture always is its own best interpreter both in matters of religion and history, I was equally sure, that not an intrinsic impossibility of the subject itself, but the prejudice of a certain hypothesis, and the neglecting some necessary assistances must have prevented, even men of the greatest learning and genius, with whom I do not presume to compare myself, from hitting upon the true point in explaining these difficulties; just as it often happens in the doctrinal parts of religion. While I was consulting the passage I refer to, I began to suspect, a difference in the years probably might have occasioned all these difficulties; and I thought at first, the solar year had been introduced by Jeroboam, who, whilst in Egypt, very likely became acquainted with the calculation that was used there, but I became soon convinced of the contrary: then applying the same opinion to Rehoboam and his Successors, I quite unexpectedly discovered a mistake of 36 years in the common hypothesis. This induced me to repeat my accounts four times. I varied the calculation either by augmenting or diminishing the months and days of a complete year; but always found the particulars, as determined by scripture chronology, the most exact of all. These being the result of infinite wisdom, must indeed render mistakes impossible; all that is necessary is that we know how to set about the calculation. When I had erred, the scriptures always set me right again; nor could I ever make up more than two hundred nineteen years for the whole duration of the kingdom of Israel, which generally

generally is computed to be two hundred and fifty-four years. Thus we need not wonder at meeting with unsurmountable difficulties in the common systems of chronology. Those who will give themselves the trouble to compare the years of the two kingdoms according to my hypothesis, by supposing solar years for Judah, and lunar years for Israel, will be convinced of the truth of it with the greatest ease and certainty imaginable; for those very passages which are supposed the cause and origin of the difficulties mentioned before, are in this computation, the very texts which prevent any mistake, and set us right immediately. This at the same time will supply the thinking mind with the greatest evidence and arguments for the divine origin of scripture, and make every man of candour and consideration conclude it to be impossible, even for the most skillful chronologer, to connect two calculations as is done in the present case, barely by mentioning the years, without taking into consideration the days and months of them.

Thus all the Objections with which scripture so often has been charged by its enemies, are removed in respect to this part of chronology. These sacred writings never can be proved erroneous in the least particular; nay, we may assert that not a single word of them is without the utmost propriety and design. All will be convinced of this by a strict enquiry, and thus they will easily remove the suspicion of errors committed in MSS. And it will appear that the chronological parts of scripture, as well as other passages, have been a peculiar object of the care of Providence.

Some think it impossible to explain 2 Chron. xxii. 2. without supposing an error in the MS. In this place Ahaziah is said to have been forty-two years old when he began to reign, and he is said to have been but twenty-two in another passage

passage of scripture, 2 Kings. *Forty and two years old was* Ahaziah *when he began to reign, and he reigned one year in* Jerusalem. His mother's name also was Athaliah, the daughter of Omri. What can be plainer? Athaliah was not Ahaziah's mother but his grandmother, the mother of Joram, and the wife of Jehoshaphat, who taking care of Ahaziah's education after the death of his mother, was deservedly called so. In the same manner as I am my father's son by birth, I am the son of my grandfather from the year of my father's birth, when substituted in his place: Supposing this, there does not remain the least difficulty, the forty-two years refer to Jehoshaphat's marrying the daughter of Omri; for, in this very year Joram was born, and the same period points out the beginning of all the misfortunes that happened to the kingdom of Judah which was almost ruined by Athaliah; consequently this passage does not allow of a litteral explication as if Athaliah had been called a daughter of Omri, who was her grandfather, she being Ahab's daughter. It is not difficult to prove this: Joram being enticed by his wife, the daughter of Ahab, slew all his brethren with the sword: This he did, that the kingdom might devolve to Ahab's posterity; wherefore the Lord stirred up against Jehoram the spirit of the Philistines, and of the Arabians that were near the Ethiopians, and they came up into Judah and brake into it, and carried away all the substance that was found in the king's house, and his sons also and his wives; so that there was never a son left him save Jehohaz the youngest of his sons. Hence it is plain Ahaziah's mother, the daughter of Ahab was carried away a great while before Ahaziah began to reign; and it was his grandmother, a wicked and ambitious woman, who is here called his mother, and who was his counsellor to do wickedly. See 2 Chron. xxii. 3.

Thus

Thus the supposition of some is quite groundless who make exception against the chronology of the kingdom of Judah as it is determined in scripture, and against sacred chronology in general, because the overplus of days and months are not taken notice of, which in process of time must become very material; it is owing to this omission that they think it impossible to ascertain chronology as determined there. There is no occasion for subtilizing in this more than in other particulars with which revelation acquaints us, every thing being here, as well as elsewhere, regulated in the exactest and wisest manner possible. Days and months are not mentioned where it was unnecessary, the computation being infallible without them. In case the successor has been appointed king, before his father's decease, then he partakes of the last year of his father's reign. It is no matter how many months of this year belong to the father, the day wherewith he begins his last year being also the first of his son's reign, he having been regent already before that time. In case he had not been appointed king in his father's life-time, then the particulars are determined in such a manner, as make it impossible to commit any material mistake in fixing the beginning of his reign, without immediately being aware of the error; a mark of divine wisdom, which must stand clear of any objections of human subtilty; I may appeal to every one, who has made the proof of it.

According to the chronological table annexed to these observations, the reign of Rehoboam and Jeroboam begins with January the 1st. by which I do not intend to insinuate as if I really was of the opinion this was the very day they took the crown; but I have fixed upon this day in particular, only for a period to begin my computation with, and to prove

prove its intrinsic possibility, it being necessary to point out the months and days of the kings of Israel. Whatever may have been the real day, it does not interfere in the least with my chronology; and the end of the kingdom of Israel notwithstanding coincides with the 190th year after the beginning of Jeroboam's reign. According to my hypothesis, Jeroboam's reign then begins January the 1st. March the 1st, 219, is the second year of the siege of Samaria, full nine months remaining from that day to November 22d of the same year; and the ninth year of Hosea's reign not being elapsed before November the 22d of the same.

The opinion that there was a difference of the years in the kingdoms of Judah and Israel, is warranted by an express passage of scripture, 1 Kings xii. quoted before; but how it came about that the lunar years were abolished and solar years introduced in their stead, I cannot explain by any particular testimony. Most probably it happened as related before. The thing itself cannot be disputed, it is proved by many other circumstances mentioned in scripture, the explication of which depends on the difference of solar and lunar years, and the use of them; of which the following may be an instance and stand as an argument.

That a solar year was in use among the Jews, after the two kingdoms had been divided, may be seen by the sun-dial of Ahaz; Hezekiah being sick unto death, the prophet asked him, *Shall the shadow go forward ten degrees, or go back ten degrees?* which makes a difference of twenty degrees. The longest day in Palestine being but fourteen hours, a difference of twenty degrees was impossible according to them; consequently we cannot suppose this to have been a com-

common sun-dial. To say, it has been divided into twenty-eight parts, or so many half hours, would occasion a double difficulty. The first Question would be this: Why did the shadow move but ten degrees, there being no impossibility of moving thirteen at least either way? The second: What possibility was there of its moving ten degrees, either to go back or forward? An expression quite inconsistent with the wisdom of God, as it could not be brought about in any way. Consequently then it must have been a mathematical instrument, and deservedly may be called so, tho' plain and simple in itself, and well known in our days. It was composed according to the meridian, and was to shew the declination of the sun and the hours of the day, the line representing this meridian had at least twenty-three marks, or two and twenty divisions: Thus a difference of twenty was possible; the shadow moving to the last mark on the other side, to shew its moving exactly as far as foretold by the prophet, and at the same time as far as possible. This also shews the reason why neither more nor less degrees were determin'd by him. Again, it appears in the same manner that it could have moved backwards; at Noon the shadow falls upon the line exactly, and it moves the whole year to and fro through all its divisions; but here it was to move in one moment as far as it did in several months naturally at other times: This was a sign plain enough on all accounts. When the king was sick to death, the sun-dial was fastened either at a wall of his bed-chamber, or on a building opposite to him: Take which supposition you will, a solar year must have been in use at that time, for it is impossible, nor would it be of any use, to compose a dial agreeing with the lunar year. The prophet particularises a sun-dial of Ahaz, whence it is probable,

there

there were more of them at Jerusalem; and consequently a solar year must have been in common use there; if not, all, nay one of them, would have been impossible to be made, unintelligible and useless. Whereas, on the contrary, we find the king and the prophet both well acquainted with the use of it; and if we suppose those that were present, or the whole nation unacquainted with the same, how could they come to know the miracle and the greatness of it? A miracle whenever wrought must be known as such; if not, it cannot be of any use. Moses introduced a lunar year, of three hundred fifty-four days, among the Jews in general. This is known by the cycle of the jubilee, and I only just mention it, because it is nothing material to my present purpose. The contrivance of it was as follows: The months, says Moses, are to be reckoned according to the new moon: Every seventh year was a sabbatical, and every fiftieth a jubilee year. The question is, what was the meaning, what the intention of it? how to remove the difficulties arising here? especially as a sabbatical and a jubilee year, following each other immediately, the land was to lye uncultivated for two years together. I do not remember ever to have seen a solution of this; no author, known to me, has effected it, nor is it possible to give one at all, supposing an *annus mixtus* or mixt year, according to the common hypothesis. But every thing here also becomes plain, if reduced to a lunar year of 354 days. Let us suppose March the twenty-first, as the beginning of the first year in this cycle, then the beginning of the fortieth year will be September the 27th; the jubilee was proclaimed the tenth day of the seventh month of the forty-ninth year; consequently the jubilee begun April the 1st, consisting of 354 days, and the fifty-first year, or the following cycle, as plainly

plainly as all the other cycles, began March the 31st as the former. Such a cycle exactly made up forty-eight solar years of 365 days, which is easily proved; for forty-eight lunar years, each consisting of 354 days, make 16,992 days in all; six months and ten days of the forty-ninth year 186 days; the year of the jubilee itself 354; the total sum of the whole is then 17,532 days, which divided by 365 makes forty-eight years and twelve days. These twelve days are required for as many leap years in the space of forty-eight; and of consequence, forty-eight solar years exactly are required to make up the cycle of the jubilee. Hence it appears for what reason Moses chose this number of years, and neither more nor less of them; why the tenth day of the seventh month was made the beginning of the jubilee; what was the origin of intercalation among the Jews, who did not introduce their Veadar till many years after; how a sabbatical and jubilee-year could follow each other, without making the land a desart, or occasioning dearth and famine; and lastly, how by means of this cycle the chronology of the Hebrews proved as exact and regular as any of the other nations; altho' the method they followed was quite different from theirs: In short, this proves the best solution of all the difficulties which have perplex'd mens minds on this occasion.

What has been here laid down will, I doubt not, give full satisfaction to all that are proper judges, to all who are duly acquainted with the subject, by convincing them of the truth of this hypothesis, tending to remove what difficulties have occured in this part of sacred chronology. In some respect however I might have done without it, no one being obliged to prove an hypothesis or a calculation any farther, than by its answering the end he proposed; for this reason I shall

shall not think it necessary to enlarge farther upon this subject, or to allege any more particulars. For the rest, I think neither scripture nor profane history proposes the least circumstance or difficulty that is not answerable according to this hypothesis. Now the harmony and correspondence of accounts being the proofs of their mutual truth, I am obliged to bring in the same argument in behalf of what I have been advancing here. It is for this reason I have annexed some chronological tables brought down to the time of Xerxes, king of Persia.

But above all things, it is incumbent on me to mention what my proposed connexion of sacred and profane history is built upon. My principle is twofold, determining partly the olympiads, and partly the years according to the Julian period.

The years of the latter depend on fixing the year of the total eclipse of the sun, which happened at the time of the celebrated battle between the Lydians and Medes near the river Halys. This eclipse hath been the standard of chronologers, only they did not agree concerning the year in which it happened, probably, because each of them fixed upon that eclipse which he found agreed the best with his own hypothesis. Mr. Beyer, professor at Petersburg, intending to reduce every particular concerning the expedition of the Scythians into Asia, and their general history into order and to certainty, desired his friend and collegue, Mr. P. Meyer to find out the true year of this eclipse. Mr. Meyer gave himself the trouble to run thro' a period of above fifty years, in which he was sure this eclipse must have happened. Having calculated and determined all the eclipses of this interval, he made it plain, that none of all the chronologers, neither father Petavius, nor Calvisius, nor Usher nor Sca-

Scaliger, had hit upon the true one, which he asserted happened May the 17th, 4111 of the Julian period, and thus first reduced this affair to great certainty.

As to the Olympiads, I made use of the *Chronicon Marmoreum*; which reckons ninety-one years to the birth of Alexander the great; whose death happening in the month Thargelion, at the end of the first year of the 114th Olympiad, in the eighth month of the thirty-second year of his age, determines sufficiently the year in which he was born.

Again: It mentions the year of the battle of Marathon, which happened in the third year of the seventy-second Olympiad, the sixth of the month Boedromion: it ascertains the beginning of the reign of Xerxes; and the time when Crœsus sent ambassadors to the oracle at Delphi; agreeable to this and other particular epochas it is no difficult matter to reduce the time of these several events to the Julian period, without inserting here the method how it must be effected.

But one thing must here be observed; it never was designed that these marbles should determine the beginning of the reign of foreign kings, as has been attempted by some, who by this means thought themselves able to fill several blanks in history. The chronicon determines the time of no other events, but such as bear a relation to the history of Greece, and then they mention no more than the reign of this or that king; but this mention does not properly assign the beginning of that reign. We need but turn to some of the particulars in order to convince us of the truth of this observation: for instance, 1. It is said:

Since Crœsus reigned in Asia, and sent ambassadors to the oracle, 292 years.

This fixes the year of his embassy, which brought the richest present ever sent to Greece, as mentioned at at large by Herodotus, and this happened not long before the misfortunes that befell him. The next epocha determined the year of Sardes's being taken by Crœsus, but the number is become illegible. Some proposed a conjecture from the fourteen years of his reign, and made it 278, but this calculation proves false, for Sardes was taken two years after the before-mentioned embassy. The taking of this town was determined in this place, because immediately after Cyrus began to conquer the Grecians in Asia, as related by Herodotus.

In the same manner the year is mentioned of Halyattes's sending his presents to Delphi, as related by Herodotus; but the year 341, there assigned is not the first of his reign: the present was sent in the twentieth year of his reign, after the war with the Milesians, the temple having been burnt, and two new buildings being erected instead of one.

The same chronicles fix the year when Xerxes was made king of Persia, but this was not the beginning of his reign after his father's death; but it is the time when he was appointed king by his father; who himself intended to command the army in the Grecian expedition, as is expresly mentioned in Herodotus.

The chronicle itself is perfectly accurate, and appears only to mistake when it is misinterpreted. This must create a prodigious confusion in chronology; we read, for instance, the names, of the Archontes of Athens who ruled at the time of certain events there related. Hence the commentators endeavour to exhibit the series of them as very useful in other parts of history. But here they met with almost insuperable difficulties, and how could it be otherwise, as they did not rightly understand the design of the chronicle itself, nor properly explain the contents of it.

These are the assistances which with some other I have made use of, in order to reconcile prophane and sacred history. If some mistake or other has been committed, by placing an event somewhat later or earlier than it really happened, I am persuaded it is not material, nor affects the series of the whole, for I never made use of one event in order to determine another, unless I was perfectly clear in the chronology of the first. Each of them has been laid down separately, according to the years fixed by the most authentic historians; so as not to make the connection of chronology at all depend on facts of this nature. For instance, suppose the taking of Tyre by Nebuchadnezzar to have happened a year later than is assigned, this doth not at all affect the rest, as neither the beginning of his reign, nor any other fact is to be determined by that event. It is placed in the year which the series of the kings of Tyre seemed to require, and nothing depends on this series in my chronology. Neither any inaccuracy in this series, nor the difference of years when the town was taken, interferes at all with the connection as inferred from my hypothesis.

Before I proceed farther, however, it may not be improper to take notice of some objections that may be started. We read in the prophecy of Ezekiel, that he was to lie upon his left side, and to bear the iniquity of the house of Israel 390 days: then to lie again on his right side and to bear the iniquity of the house of Judah 40 days, which added makes 430 days. According to several interpreters this was meant to denote the time of God's forbearance with the Jews, and they determine the time of the temple's standing accordingly. Now as my hypothesis shortens the usual chronology of the kings of Israel by 30 years, these 430 years will not coincide with it, and so it may chance to be rejected as contradicting scripture. It is not indeed my province to explain the

writings

writings of the prophets; yet I may be allowed to offer my opinion concerning this passage, so far as it is alleged in support of a chronology. In the first place, the question is not of committing, but of bearing the iniquity; wherefore I do not see any reason why we should look for these four hundred thirty years in past, rather than in subsequent times: especially as this happened in the 6th year of the prophet's being in captivity.

Secondly, as God spared the Jews much longer than 430 years, I do not see why the time of his patience is to be confined between the building and the destruction of the temple, which supposes the building of it, as it were the beginning of all their iniquities. On the contrary it is well known, that God intended to have destroyed this nation in the desart, and they very seldom obeyed his commands. I am therefore inclined to think, that the interpretation of this passage arises from the common opinion of the temple's standing 430 years, which not being the case, I hope another interpretation may be hit upon, and sufficiently proved.

I am confident, however, that my hypothesis concerning the years of the kings of Judah, and their connection with prophane history, will shew the completion of all the prophecies in the most easy and natural method; as may be seen in these tables and will farther appear in others I intend to publish as a sequel to them. I beg leave at the same time to observe, that not one of all the particular chronologies hitherto published, has been able to clear this point; a most convincing argument this of their imperfection. A chronological system, if it were perfect, must agree with the prophecies; it becomes suspicious when its correspondence with the prophecies is the effect of artificial comments.

At present I shall mention only one prophecy, the explication of which has been difficult, according

 to

to the common system of chronology, Jerem. xxvii. 6, 7. *Now have I given all these lands into the hand of Nebuchadnezzar the king of Babylon my servant,---And all nations shall serve him, and his son, and his sons son, until the time of his land come.* This was the very king who destroyed Jerusalem. That Evilmerodach and Belshazzar were his sons is as expresly mention'd in scripture; Darius took the kingdom from the latter; now the question is, what becomes of his sons son?

This difficulty arises from the common systems of chronology, which prolong the kingdom of Judah beyond its real period, without alleging any authority for so doing, and therefore suppose Nabopolassar the second, to have taken Jerusalem; his father Nabopolassar the first is pass'd over in silence, tho' it is plain he revolted from the king of Assyria and Babylon, and possess'd himself of Babel. A prince who becomes the founder of a new kingdom by dint of arms, must necessarily make a figure in history; whereas nothing is ascrib'd to this hero, but all to his son, who is said to have conquered and destroy'd Nineveh and Jerusalem, to have vanquished a great many other nations, to have besieged Tyre for the space of 13 years, and yet to have had time enough remaining for a madness of seven years; after which he reigns in peace and quietness till the time of his death. Here are many and great difficulties, but my hypothesis fairly removes them all. Nabopolassar mention'd by the prophet was the first of this name, the same who destroy'd Jerusalem; his son succeeded him, Nabopolassar the great, then Evilmerodach, lastly Belshazzar or Nabonnadan, and in his reign was the time of Babylon.

I must mention also another difficulty here concerning Darius Medus, a king, whose chronology hath been attended with inconceivable difficulties, merely

merely because the principles upon which it was examined were false, for in itself there is no diffi-culty at all. To give all the different opinions, the arguments in behalf of them, and the confu-tation of opposite systems, wou'd be a tedious work, there being not one of them which is not loaded with almost unsurmountable difficulties. The truth of the case is this; in order to save the authority of scripture according to their hypothe-sis, they thought themselves obliged to insert a pretended Darius Medus into the catalogue of the kings of Babylon, and to make Cyrus his succes-sor; tho' this Darius is a king quite unknown in profane history, nor are they themselves able to give any particulars of his reign and actions.

My table shews the true connexion of the whole, for omitting the overplus of years in the history of the Kings of Judah, as mention'd before, it is an easy matter fairly and sufficiently to connect scrip-ture and profane history; and then it becomes evi-dent, that Darius Medus must be Darius the son of Hystaspes, who took Babylon, demolish'd the gates, lower'd the walls of it, crucified several thousands of the principal inhabitants, as may be seen at large in Herodotus, and thus fulfill'd what had been prophecy'd, concerning the punishment of the king of Babylon after the accomplishment of 70 years, Jerem. xxv. 12. From that time Babylon became a Desolation, that is to say, its glory was taken away; it was never a royal resi-dence, nor an independent state afterwards; but by degrees it became an heap of stones, till even the place where it had stood was forgot, and cannot now be pointed out, farther than by mere conjec-tures.

As to the objection that this seems to contradict scripture, where Darius expresly is call'd the son of Ahasuerus, and a Median by extraction, it is of no great weight, for Darius Hystaspis was of the same royal Median family. This is plain from what Xerxes mentions in Herodotus concerning his genealogy. The account stands thus,

Achaemenes.
Cambyses.
Cyrus.
Teispeus.
Arariamnes.
Hystaspes.
Darius.
Xerxes.

Darius being thus of the posterity of Cyrus, was descended from Cyrus's mother, Mandane, and so from Astyages, king of Media, and was truly of the Median family, tho' his Father was a Persian. As for his being call'd Ahasuerus, it is not more extraordinary than Daniel's being call'd Belshazzar, all the nobles had their particular names at court, which denoted either the king's favour, or their dignity, or they arose from mere custom; in this case the reason is very plain. Ahasuerus means the same with Xerxes, a Hero or a General; which agrees very well with Hystaspes, in the reign of Cyrus. He was alive when his son was chosen king of Persia, who made him governor of that province, and probably he was of great authority at court, enjoying titles and designations suitable to his dignity.

According to scripture, Darius Medus divided his kingdom into 120 Provinces. Esther i. 1. Herodotus gives us the names of the most considerable: Babylonia is but one of these partitions; and he mentions this division as unknown before. Scripture mentions seven Princes as counsellors of Darius, and the laws of the Medes and Persians as unchangeable: all this agrees perfectly with Darius; the Medes are always nam'd the first. Cyrus, Cambyses and Darius, were call'd Kings of of Media, as appears in Herodotus, the kingdom and their title to it being derived from that family; but this denomination was disused afterwards, the Medes being too much elated upon this their prerogative. Whoever compares scripture with the profane historians of authority, will find every thing in this part agreeing perfectly with Darius Hystaspis, and no one else, not to mention that he is call'd a Persian, as well as Cyrus, Dan. vi. 28. If an objection should be drawn from what is said to the prophet, Dan. xi. 1. in the third year of Cyrus: *Also I, in the first year of Darius the Mede, even I stood to confirm and to strengthen him*; I must be excused giving in my answer concerning a prophecy, which the prophet himself is directed to shut up and seal even to the end, Dan. xii. 4. that is, it is not to be understood by any one. On the other side, I might allege a passage from an historical Book of scripture: 2 Chron. xxxvi. 20. *Them that had escaped from the sword, carried he away to Babylon: where they were servants to him and his sons, until the reign of the kingdom of Persia:---to fulfil threescore and ten years.* Darius Medus taking the kingdom from Nebuchadnezzar's grandson, and conquering Chaldea, is very properly call'd a king of Persia. The words of Daniel are as follows, *In the first year of Darius the son of Ahasuerus, of the seed of the Medes, which was made king over the realm of the Chaldeans; In the first year of his reign, I Daniel understood by books the number of the years,---that he would accomplish seventy years in the desolations of Jerusalem.* Dan. ix. 1, 2. Thus it is evident from several of the clearest passages in scripture, that Darius the Mede and Hystaspes were one and the same person; he is call'd a Persian, the son of Ahasuerus, but of the family of the Medes; the same who slew the son of Nebuchadnezzar, and conquer'd the Chaldeans; who was king of 120 provinces, and the first

first that formed this division; who had seven princes at his court, persons not mention'd before the time of Darius Hystaspes; in whose reign Babylon being taken, and Belshazzar the last king of Chaldea being slain, the 70 years of the desolation of Jerusalem were accomplish'd. All this plainly shews, both must have been one and the same person, if it be possible to ascertain any truth in history.

The two last facts, viz. the 70 years of the Desolation of Jerusalem, and the taking of Babylon, I shall endeavour to illustrate from profane history; and in this manner to account for my chronological tables, which might otherwise appear wrong in this particular. I must confess that I had some doubt at first, for I placed the facts according to the authority of records, without any respect to the prophecies; but in this manner I became fully convinced of the truth of my calculation, and the perfect harmony of profane history and scripture. Darius laid siege to Babylon in the year 4187, of the Julian period, probably in the spring, and the siege lasted almost 22 months, this is declar'd in Herodotus. He surprised the town, and Belshazzar was slain in the first attack, in the 62d year of his age, but the demolishing of the walls and gates did not happen till the third year after the siege was begun, and this must be the first year of Darius. The year 4189 is the 70th from the Desolation of Jerusalem, which happen'd 4120, consequently this most exactly agrees with the prophecy of Jeremiah concerning the desolation of Babylon, the end of the year 4189 being also the end of the 70 years of the captivity, which being elapsed, the temple was to be rebuilt; and it really was begun 4190, in the second year of Darius, and finish'd in the 6th of his reign: See Ezra iv. 24. vi. 18. where Darius always is call'd king of Persia,

ſia, tho' the years of his reign are reckon'd from the end of the kingdom of Babylon.

Another objection that may be ſtated is this, Nebuchadnezzar took all the veſſels of the temple and carried them to Babylon. Theſe Cyrus gave to Sheſhbazzar, *who brought them up from Babylon unto Jeruſalem*, Ezra i. 11. Now if Darius Medus and Hyſtaſpis are one and the ſame perſon, he did not reign and take Babylon, till after Cyrus; how then can it be ſaid, the king of Babylon at that time drank out of the veſſels which his father Nebuchadnezzar had taken out of the temple, as expreſsly mention'd, Dan. v. 2, 3. Cyrus having reſtored thoſe veſſels to the Jews a great while before?

Now this is the fulfilling of Jeremiah's prophecy, ch. xxvii. and it is accompliſh'd in its ſtrict and moſt literal ſenſe. Nebuchadnezzar plunder'd the temple two or three times, firſt when he carried away captive Jeconiah, the ſon of Jehoiakim, v. 20. the veſſels he then took were put in his temple at Babylon. The falſe prophets, 2 Chron. xxxvi. 7. had ſaid, the veſſels of the lord's houſe ſhall now ſhortly be brought again from Babylon, v. 16. Jeremiah aſſured them, that the veſſels which were left in the houſe of the lord, and in the houſe of the king of Judah, ſhou'd be carried to Babylon, and there ſhou'd they be, until the day that I viſit them, that is, the Babylonians, then will I bring them up, and reſtore them to this place. v. 22. Theſe veſſels that had been left, were brought to Babylon at the total deſtruction of Jeruſalem, 2 Chron. xxxvi. 18. which was the fulfilling of the firſt part of the prophecy.

Afterwards Cyrus returned the veſſels to Sheſhbazzar, which Nebuchadnezzar had put in the houſe of his Gods, as is expreſly mentioned Ezra, i. 7. The reſt were left in the palace at Babylon, for he

he neither slew Nabonnadius, *i. e.* Belshazzar, nor did he take all his sovereignty from him: he only became tributary to him, and consequently he left the plate for his use. Thus we see he might use them that very night when he was slain: they being left at Babylon until the day that God visited the city, took the kingdom from it, caused its walls and gates to be demolished, and its nobles to be slain, after which, these vessels also were carried to Jerusalem, as mentioned Ezra, vi. 5. *Let the golden and silver vessels of the house of God which Nebuchadnezzar took forth out of the temple which is at Jerusalem, and brought unto Babylon, be restored, and brought again unto the temple.* This order was given in the second year of his reign, that is, after Babylon had been visited; and thus the prophecy of Jeremiah was fulfilled in the most exact and particular manner.

On the contrary, those who pretend to substitute their fictitious Darius the Mede, instead of Cyrus, contradict not only this passage, but several others, where Cyrus is mentioned expresly to have returned the first vessels which were put into the temple of Belus, as observed Ezra i. 7, 8, 12. and again Ezra vii, 13 --- 16. and suppose Darius to have returned the rest a great while after. Cyrus destroyed no part of Babylon: every thing was left there as before, according to the express testimony of Herodotus.

The king continued king, and with this difference only, that he became tributary to Cyrus. How can this be called a visitation of Babylon, a desolation and destruction of that city? In short: the thing is too plain to admit the least dispute; whatever may seem perplexing or contradictory is merely owing to a false hypothesis established by the modern chrono ogers.

The best argument of truth, in points of chronology is, the correspondence of the facts and the full

full satisfaction given in every point which it is intended to establish. This, I think, is fully done in my hypothesis; and appears in several instances already mentioned. Whoever will give himself the trouble to consult the tables themselves, will be convinced of the order of the facts as placed there, according to scripture and profane history, clearly and without confusion: and this is the most convincing proof of the truth of them. In the second section of this essay I shall endeavour to explain the connection of the facts which happened in that period, as much as the necessary conciseness of a work of this nature will allow. This second section being intended for those of my readers who do not care to perplex themselves with chronological tables and arguments; I thought it proper to anticipate them here and to place them by themselves, in order to give such readers an uninterrupted history.

I cannot leave this subject, without taking notice of one objection more; which some misapply to the scriptural method of history; especially as it gives me an opportunity to prove the truth of my hypothesis in another instance, and to shew the exact fulfilling of a prophecy which has hitherto perplexed the interpreters. It may be asked, why did not scripture take the least notice of Cambyses and the Magus? why of Cyrus only, and of no more than three years of his reign? Borrichius, in answer to this, appeals to the custom of sacred history, to pass over misfortunes, and those times in which they happened, and takes this to be the reason why nothing is said concerning the following years of the reign of Cyrus, of Cambyses, and Magus, when the Jews were forbid to go on with the temple. Whether or not this solution is taken from the Talmud I cannot determine: at least it deserves a place in that work. Let us set

set things in another light: all that scripture-history aims at, is to shew the fulfilling of prophecies, which all of them meet in one common centre as it were, which is the coming of the Messiah. The destruction of Jerusalem, and the burning of the temple by the kings of Babylon had been prophecied a long while before by Isaiah, as related in the history of Hezekiah. And this is the reason why mention is made of Merodach, then king of Babylon, but of none of his successors (Asnaphar excepted who conquered Manasseh) till Nabopolassar, or Nebuchadnezzar, by whom that prophecy was accomplished. The kingdom was promised to him, his son, and his son's son: and their names are expresly mentioned in scripture for this very reason. Again, it was prophecied, Babylon was to be visited in its turn, its glory was to be taken away for ever, and Jerusalem and the temple were to be restored. These circumstances made it necessary to name who were to bring about those great events, *viz.* Cyrus and Darius. Neither Cambyses nor the Magus destroyed Babylon, nor did they contribute in the least to the completion of prophecies: hence, as they were out of the question here, neither their names are mentioned, nor those of any other king of Babylon, after Merodach.

This is so very plain, that the years of Cyrus in scripture are computed from the destruction of Babylon, whenever the accomplishment of the prophecies is mentioned. His returning the vessels of the temple, or at least his orders given for the same, must have happened the next year after: for this was the natural consequence of Cyrus's giving the Jews leave to return into their country, after he was become the founder of the Persian monarchy. They knew their captivity was to last 70 years. All of them were not carried away at once, but some so early as the year 4105, in the first invasion of the Babylonians;

nians: others in 4109 with Jehojachin, others again after the burning of the temple 4120: they therefore thought their captivity was to end in the same manner. Cyrus, after his return from the conquest of Asia, having taken the title of the great king, in the year 4169, they begged leave of him to go into their country. He granted their request the first year 4170, the beginning of the 70th of their captivity, computed from Nebuchadnezzar conquering Jehojachim in 4102. Or if any objection be made to this calculation, they may be said to have obtained leave in the year 4174, the first of Cyrus, after he conquered Babylon, and 70 years after the invasion of the Babylonians in 4105. See Jerem. lii, 28. 2 Kings xxiv, 2. But this was not the meaning of the prophets, who reckoned from the burning of the temple: and accordingly we see that notwithstanding they had Cyrus's leave, and even his orders, they could not effect what they desired before the time was expired; *viz.* in 4190, when the temple really began to be built, and was finished a few years after. No wonder they became impatient, and longed for the end of their captivity: but on the other side, God was as exact in fulfilling the prophecies. It was not before the second year of Darius that Haggai and Zachariah prophesied in the name of the Lord, and gave them notice that their time was at hand. Then Zorobabel and Joshua began to think of building the temple, and the prophets encouraged them, as mentioned Ezra iv. 5, the 70 years now being fully expired, and they in their first year of liberty.

The reason why but 3 years of Cyrus's reign are mentioned in scripture, is because in the fourth year after the taking of Babylon he left his dominions, and set out on the expedition against the Scythians. Thus it is plain that my hypothesis fully removes all difficulties.

The

The same will hold in respect to what I have said, concerning his assuming the title of a great king: for this is the very epocha, according to Ptolomy, of the beginning of the kingdom of Persia: and that author says, Cyrus reigned nine years as such. Scripture, we see, according to its custom, fixes the taking of Babylon as the epocha most proper for the purpose intended by the prophecies. But Ptolomy having a different view, begins five years earlier from the conquest of Asia, and probably of Egypt, as mentioned by Herodotus, when Cyrus being returned victorious to the Medes, now really became monarch of Asia. This I prove in the following manner: According to his computation, Cyrus reign'd nine years, which together with eight years of Alexander's reign, being included in the duration of the Persian monarchy, make it amount to 215. The *chronicon marmoreum* which was composed in the first year of the 129th Olympiad, i. e. in the year 4443 of the Julian period, reckons 91 years back to the birth of Alexander, taking the full number of 32 years for his life; consequently Cyrus assumed the title of the Great King in the 4169th year of the Julian period: this was five years before the taking of Babylon, which happened in the year 4173, as it plainly will appear by the following calculation: in 4169 Cyrus assumes the title, allow 207 for the duration of the Persian monarchy, and 8 for Alexander's reign, the amount is, 4384. Take off 32 for Alexander's age; then 4352 will be the year of his birth; 91 the time from thence to the chronicon, and 4443 will prove the time when it was composed.

This shews how much those are mistaken, who begin these 9 years of Cyrus's reign as mention'd in

* See Dr. Baumgarten's dissertation on the chronicle of Paros, part 1. of the supplement, and additions to the universal history, p. 190.

in Ptolemy from the taking of Babylon, or, which is worse, from Belshazzar (Nabonnadius) the last king of Babylon? Whereas my hypothesis proves true in this as in every other respect. The battle of Marathon was fought in the 3d year of the 72d Olympiad, according to Plutarch, and the 31st of Darius, as mention'd by Herodotus: consequently the beginning of Darius's reign is the 1st year of the 65th Olympiad. Cambyses reigned 8 years according to Ptolemy, and therefore he must have begun to reign in the first year of the 63d Olympiad; and the 9 years being added, which the same author attributes to Cyrus, the first year of his reign is the 4th of the 60th Olympiad. The chronicle was made in the 1st year of the 129th Olympiad, which gives 68 Olympiads and two years for the interval from thence to the first of Cyrus, or 274 years, which deducted from 4443 --- 4169 is the first of Cyrus's reign.

Herodotus also takes notice of his having assumed his title before the taking of Babylon: for he mentions Cyrus's undertaking the expedition against Babylon, in quality of the great king, which means his being revered at that time as monarch of Asia. Besides, he and his successors were called monarchs of Media, not of Babylon; Babylon being but one of the 20 large provinces of his kingdom, two of which were conquered by Darius, *viz.* Egypt and India. Cyrus was master of 17 before the conquest of Babylon, and much advanced in years. This shews there is not the least reason to suppose that he deferred the assuming of that title from one expedition to another; for he really made war to the very time of his death, and made conquests in all his wars, excepting in the last campaign.

SECT. II.

The history of the Jews, *from the revolt of the ten tribes to* Darius Hystaspis, *connected with prophane history.*

JEROBOAM being chosen king of the ten tribes, established a form of worship, altogether different from that used at Jerusalem, in order to perpetuate the separation of the two kingdoms. He succeeded in his design. One kingdom considering the other as unbelievers or heretics, their mutual hatred was inflamed to such a degree, that hostility and wars between them lasted as long as the Israelites were governed by kings of Jeroboam's posterity.

This being extinct, Omri obtained the crown. He was captain of the host, and a man of great parts; he prevailed against his rival, and reigned with so great reputation, that Asa, king of Judah, thought proper to ask his daughter Athaliah in marriage for his son Jehoshaphat. A match which indeed had this good effect, that it secured a peace with Israel, during the reign of Omri's family; but on the other side, the consequences of it proved very pernicious: for now the kings of Israel had a great influence at the court of Jerusalem, which almost occasioned the utter ruin and destruction of that family. 1 Kings xv, 18. *Asa's heart was perfect with the Lord all his days; yet the high places were not removed*; probably, because it was not in his power, and because he would not preclude his daughter-in-law from the exercise of the religion in which she had been educated.

This harmony between the two courts increased in the reign of his son and successor Jehoshaphat, who married his son Joram to Ahab's daughter, made

made him a visit in person, and accompanied him in his expedition against Syria. Ahab probably had some good qualities, and might have made a tolerable figure on the throne, if he had not been ruled by the wicked Jezebel, who governed both him and the kingdom with a most absolute and arbitrary sway. The marriage with this princess proved fatal to him. She was a daughter of Ethbaal, king of Sidon, descended from a powerful family, but devoted to the worship of Baal. These matches with idolaters were expressly forbidden by God himself in the law of Moses, and were always unfortunate. She did all in her power to introduce her religion into the establishment, and actually gained her point at last, no more than 7000 being left in Israel, who had not either in hypocrisy or in sincerity bowed the knee to Baal. The prophets of the Lord were either killed or banished, except some few, who hid themselves here and there in caves, privately teaching and encouraging those who still worshipped the only true and living God, the God of Israel. The prophets of Baal filled the whole country, 400 of them, called the prophets of the groves, ate at Jezebel's table; for she dispensed the king's revenues in as arbitrary a manner, as she exercised his power. She and her favourites acted in every respect without controul. Her conduct in politics was such, as perfectly suited her religious character. She endeavoured to unite the kingdoms of Judah and Israel, intending to secure both to her own posterity; with this view she concluded the match between her daughter and Joram, the son and successor of Jehoshaphat. Jehoshaphat himself, a prince of an honest unsuspecting heart, being persuaded to join with Ahab in the expedition against Syria, put on his robes when they entered into the battle; whereas the king of Israel disguised himself. This was doubtless an insidious contrivance of the cunning and wicked Jezebel. However, he happily escaped, for God protected his innocence: on the contrary, Ahab received a mortal wound, which defeated her designs against Jehoshaphat. However Jezebel in spite of all these disappointments, far from being disheartned, was rather more successfully wicked than ever; for her son was totally under her influence.

In the mean time Jehoshaphat died, and Joram his son gave himself up to the counsels both of his mother Athaliah, and of his wife the daughter of Jezebel, probably also call'd Athaliah. He slew all his brethren with the sword, for the three queens had conspired to extirpate the royal family of Judah; he led after this an infamous and wicked life. To shew how great a proficiency he had made in the politics of Jezebel, he rose up by night and smote the captains of the Edomites, in order the more effectually to enslave that nation, altho' it was then tributary to him: but this expedition proved a very unsuccessful one; they revolted, and were never after reduced to obedience. Besides this, the Philistines and Arabians came up unexpectedly into Judah, and carried away all the substance that was found in the king's house, and his sons also, and his wives, (and among them young Jezebel or Athaliah;) they left Athaliah the mother, not willing to encumber themselves with a person of her age. Providence saved one only prince, Ahaziah the youngest of all, for the Lord wou'd not altogether destroy the house of David. After all this, the Lord smote Joram in his bowels with an incurable disease; they burst out by reason of his sickness, and he died of sore diseases.

His son however did not regard all these warnings, but still followed the wicked devices of his grandmother and of Jezebel, and in obedience to

them

them he went to war with Jehoram against the Syrians. Then divine justice exerted itself in its most terrible judgments. Jehu arose, anointed by the Lord, to cut off the house of Ahab. He particularly order'd Jezebel to be thrown out of a window: the dogs of the street devoured her; they found no more of her, than the skull and the feet, and the palms of her hands.

Athaliah was now the only person left of Omri's family; she seeing all her artifices fail, and all her devices frustrated by the death of her kindred; resolved in her rage, with a more than diabolical malice, to extirpate the family of Judah, and really destroy'd the royal progeny. The youngest prince escap'd, with extreme difficulty, being hid in the temple, which inclines me to conjecture he was the son of another wife of Joram; not of Ahab's daughter; who can hardly be supposed to have deprived herself of all the means to be revenged on Jehu, by murdering her own grandchildren, and the only one that was left of her family. She herself was too far advanced in years for a second match, which certainly she wou'd have resolved upon, even without any other prospect than that of a future revenge.

Her own death proved at last as bloody as that of her relations. Joab in the seventh year of his age was proclaimed king by Jehoiada the high-priest, and Athaliah was slain with the sword. This merit of Jehoiada was ill requited to his family, for Zechariah his son having rebuked Joash for the idolatry into which he fell after Jehoiada's death, was stoned by order of the same king, who stood indebted to his father for his life and crown. He was punish'd by a terrible disease, and his own servants soon after conspired against him, and slew him on his bed.

At this time the former inveteracy revived between the houses of Judah and Israel. The rupture was occasioned by Amaziah, who challeng'd Joash, king of Israel; but was vanquish'd and taken prisoner. Joash took Jerusalem, and his son Jeroboam was made king or regent of Judah; but the Jews opposed him, and chose Uzziah, the son of Amaziah, who made however but a very indifferent figure whilst Joash was alive. After the death of Joash, Jeroboam set Amaziah at liberty, and contented himself with the kingdom of Israel. After this more troubles ensuing, Ahaz, king of Juda, sent to the king of Assyria to demand succours against the Syrians and Israelites. Tiglath-Pul-Asser came accordingly to his assistance, and went up against Damascus and took it; but Ahaz, as well as the Israelites, became tributary to him. The king of Israel endeavouring after this to throw off the Assyrian yoke, sent and contracted an alliance with So, king of Egypt; hereupon Salmanasser laid siege to Samaria, took it three years after, carried all away into Assyria, and put a final period to their kingdom.

Salmanassar, who is call'd Nabonasser in profane history, a king of great fame and power, conquer'd also Babylon. Probably he was call'd Nabonasser on his having taken Babylon, an event which might very well be the occasion of another name. Nabo and Adan are names which frequently occur in the list of the kings of Babylon, as Pul and Asser are given to those of Assyria. For instance, Merodach, king of Babylon, he that sent to Hezekiah, was son of Baal Adan, and his grandfather had the same name. There is a Nabon-Adan-Assar, a Nabo-Pul-Assar, and a Nabon-Adan, the last has been call'd Labynitus in Greek, which almost makes me believe, Adan or Eden was

was the name which the Babylonians gave to their territories. Be that as it will, he ruled over Assyria, Babylon and the provinces annex'd to it, and all Syria; and he had formed designs upon Egypt, the only kingdom able to resist him. So, king of Egypt, had encouraged the king of Israel to revolt against him. This prince was a hero and conqueror; at first he was no more than king of Ethiopia, for Egypt was a conquest of his own. His sons were princes of the greatest courage and valour; and the Ethiopians had the general reputation of excellent soldiers. Salmanassar therefore resolved to proceed cautiously, and to attack Tyre before that expedition: this was a town so advantageously situated, and of so great importance, that the siege of it was the first step taken by every prince, who entertain'd a design of conquering Egypt. Sidon and other towns having declared for him, and revolted against the Tyrians, this was a favourable opportunity for the execution of his scheme. The Sidonian fleet was defeated by the Tyrians, but these were besieged in their turn at land. Salmanassar did not live to see the end of the war, for he died the fifth year after the commencement of the siege. Sennacherib, or Nadius his son, succeeded to finish what was begun by his father, but he does not seem to have continued this siege in particular; probably he was tired with the tedious length of it, and intended after Hezekiah was become tributary to him, to invade Egypt, as the circumstances of this kingdom at that time seemed very much to favour his expedition. So, or Sabaco, king of Ethiopia, was a prince of great virtues, and an example to all conquerors; he had indeed subdu'd Egypt by force of arms; but proved a father to that country, neither oppressing the inhabitants with a numerous army, nor overloading them with taxes: On the contrary, he endeavoured to apply the public revenues to public uses, such as digging channels for the preservation of the land, and raising the walls of towns against inundations of the Nile. Being conscious that his public spirited designs could not be so successfully carried on by strangers, as by natives of the country, he appointed Sethos, who was priest of Vulcan, or high-priest of Egypt, to be his viceroy, he being a man of sufficient knowlege and authority, and clear of all suspicion of revolting against his sovereign. Sethos actually filled his station with integrity and wisdom, and executed the king's commands perfectly to his satisfaction. The militia of Egypt had heretofore been the hereditary privilege of particular tribes, who had certain established stipends. Sethos, being of opinion it was useless to maintain soldiers who were much inferior to the army of Sabaco, or thinking they might be better employ'd than in spending their pay in an idle way of life, order'd them to assist in digging channels, and in other public works set on foot by the king; they refused, and Sethos punished them by withholding their pay. Sennacherib knew this militia was disbanded, that very few or none of the Ethiopians were at hand, and the king himself absent at that time, he therefore resolved to surprise Egypt by hazarding a sudden invasion. However, Sethos was apprised of it in time, and order'd the militia to oppose him, but they had less inclination now to fight, than they had before to work, and were as resolute in declining the service as if they expected their stipend to be doubled for their refusal. Sethos in this extremity, collected as many of the people as he could; he encamped in a proper place, and expected the enemy, tho' with great anxiety of mind. As he was kneeling and praying before his idols, a sleep surprised him, as Herodotus was told by the Egyptians, and he was assured in a

vision,

vision, that the king of Assyria would never enter Egypt; the vision was verified; for a vast number of mice gnawed to pieces the strings of the bows, and the leather straps of the shields, and forced the enemy to an ignominious flight from the land of Egypt.

Sennacherib's intention to invade Egypt is mention'd in scripture; and that when he heard of Tirhaka or Tarakus, son of old Sabaco, who came to fight against him, he returned, summoned Jerusalem, and utter'd blasphemies against the God of Israel:. And the Lord sent an angel, which cut off all the mighty men of valour, and the leaders and captains in the camp of the king of Assyria: so he returned with shame to his own land.

This defeat occasioned a great revolution in the Assyrian monarchy. Sennacherib, as he was worshiping at Nineveh in the House of Nisroch his God, was smote with the sword by Adrammelech, and Sharezer his sons, called Porus and Chinzirus by Ptolemy, who says, they reigned five years, which is not improbable enough. According to scripture, they escaped into the land of Armenia, and Esarhaddon his son reigned in his stead; but probably, not immediately after his father had been slain. Those two sons of his who slew him, are barely mentioned in scripture, because their history had no connexion with the Jewish, as Esarhaddon's had, therefore he only is mention'd as king and successor of Sennacherib. Certainly they did not murder their father, merely with a view of residing in Armenia. Besides, as they slew him in public, in the temple, in the presence of the people, undoubtedly they were at the head of a numerous faction, and were strong enough to possess themselves of the crown. The fact was committed at Nineveh, and as they are placed in Ptolemy's list of the kings of Assyria, it is evident they must have been kings of that province and of Babylon. However, their reign

reign was attended with many and great troubles. Sennacherib being slain, the Medes revolted and chose Dejoces, a king of their own; and several other nations afterwards asserted their liberty, till at last, the Parricides lost all at once. Jugæus made himself king of Babylon, as mention'd in Ptolemy, and the Assyrians chose Esarhaddon whose youth and other circumstances render'd it difficult for him to support his claim to the throne of Babylon. Merodach, the successor of Jugæus, had nevertheless apprehensions that he might some time assert his right. He therefore sent ambassadors to Hezekiah, whose friendship he sought, being of opinion that the king of Judah wou'd prove a terror to his Enemies. Hezekiah, pleased with the Ambassadors overture, shewed all his treasures, in order to give them and their king an high idea of his power and greatness. Isaiah reproach'd him severely, for allying himself with a heathen nation after he had received the most evident proofs of God's immediate protection against Assyria, especially as alliances of this kind had been forbidden, and had always proved fatal to the Jews. In order to convince him of the blindness of human policy with respect to future events, he told him, the days were coming, when these very Babylonians, whom he now looked upon as the support of his kingdom, shou'd carry away all the treasures he had shewn them, and his sons become eunuchs in the palace of the king of Babylon; and this actually happen'd immediately after the death of this king. Asnaphar, king of Babylon, took his son Manasseh, and all the royal family prisoners. Brodach, or Merodach, is call'd in scripture a son of Baladan, and a grandson of a prince of the same name: consequently he was of the family of the kings of Babylon, who were dethroned by Salmanasser, and now recover'd their ancient right

right in the person of Merodach. This shews that Chinzirus, Porus, and Jugæus were Assyrians, and as such, they cou'd not send Ambassadors to Hezekiah, nor congratulate him upon Sennacherib's defeat. On the other side, this event must have given the greatest joy to Brodach, whose father had been deprived of the crown by the father of Sennacherib; especially as the Assyrians now having lost great part of their power, he had the opportunity of doing justice to himself by asserting his claim to the kingdom.

However, Babylon did not long subsist as a kingdom separated from the other provinces: great revolutions ensued after the death of Merodach, and the throne was vacant twice: till at last the Babylonians, tired of the confusions of war, surrender'd to Esarhaddon. Scripture takes no farther notice of these kings than by mentioning the captains of the king of Assyria, which took Manasseh, bound him with fetters and carried him to Babylon. Asnaphar is mention'd in Ezra, who carried away all the rest of the Israelites, and gave their lands to strangers: This, and Isaiah's prophecy, compared with chronology, answer to the time of Apharadan, or Apronadius. Manasseh, in his affliction humbled himself before God, who, after his repentance, brought him again to Jerusalem, where he became a blessing to his people.

After this, Esarhaddon endeavours to recover the ancient splendor of his monarchy, by subduing those nations that had revolted, especially the Medes. Saosduchetus, his successor, according to Ptolemy, slew Phraortes king of Media in a battle: Cyaxares, son of the latter, to revenge his father's death, laid siege to Nineveh. But a most unexpected accident changed almost the whole face of affairs in Asia. A numberless army of Scythians left Europe, forced the Streights near the Caspian sea, and

and conquer'd Media. Thence they went thro' Asia as far as Egypt, but Psammetichus, who was then besieging Asdod, persuaded them by presents and civilities to return. They did not depose any king, but levied contributions and taxes all over the country, and spent most of their time in Media.

Mean while new revolutions ensued in Assyria. Nabopolassar, probably of the family of the kings of Babylon, revolted, seized the crown, and left nothing to Chyniladanus but the single province strictly call'd Assyria. This scheme was laid in concert with Necho, king of Egypt, who came with a numerous army to fight against the Assyrians. This is plain from scripture, where it is said expresly, God commanded him to do so. Now according to the prophecy of Isaiah, God promised Nabopolassar, his son, and son's son, they shou'd be kings over all the nations: it is evident they acted in concert, and these prophecies must prove contradictory, if we admit any other explanation; a supposition altogether absurd and injurious to divine wisdom and providence. Whilst Necho was moving forwards with his army, Josiah, king of Judah, in order to convince the Assyrians of his fidelity to them, endeavoured with an ill-tim'd zeal to oppose his march, but he was slain in the battle near Megiddo; upon this, Necho subdu'd Judah, and return'd to Egypt, having given the kingdom to Jehoiakim the son of Josiah. Nabopolassar, or Nebuchadnezzar the 1st of that Name, provoked at being thus disappointed of the assistance of the Egyptians, had determined to revenge himself. However, Sarac, the son of Chyniladan, continued in the quiet possession of Assyria. This kingdom must have been but of a small extent in comparison with that of Babylon; as it joined to Media, the chief quarter of the Scythians, the Assyrians probably

bably were tributary to them, and they in their turn protected them against Nebuchadnezzar, who did not chuse to embroil himself with that nation. It appears from all circumstances, that the people of Asia were very indifferent soldiers compar'd to the Scythians: they did not even oppose them, tho' it would have been no difficult matter to raise a very numerous army, one that might have exceeded by far that of the Scythians, even supposing them to have amounted to an 100,000. Besides Cyaxares is said by Herodotus to have introduced in his army a different and better discipline.

To return to the history: Nebuchadnezzar went out to fight against Necho, defeated him near Carchemish, and forced the Egyptians to leave all the provinces they had before conquered in Asia. This victory proved fatal to Jehoiakim, who now became tributary to him, as formerly he had been to the Egyptians.

About the same time Cyaxares revolted from the Scythians; part of whom, it seems, were gone back to their country enriched with the vast spoils they had taken from so many conquered nations. The generals and captains of the rest being invited by him to a banquet were intoxicated and slain, and upon this disaster all left his country. After all this, he was unexpectedly engaged in a war with the Lydians. This however was soon finish'd by the interposition of Nebuchadnezzar, who thought proper to take hold of this opportunity, of inciting the Medes against the Assyrians, who were now destitute of the protection of the Scythians, and it was his design totally to extirpate this old and inveterate enemy. Accordingly Cyaxares married a princess of Lydia, took Nineveh, perhaps with the assistance of Nebuchadnezzar, and demolish'd that famous city, which was never after rebuilt.

The

Whilst the Babylonian army was near, and employed in driving the Egyptians out of Asia, Jehoiakim continued faithful to Nebuchadnezzar. But as soon as he was gone, he revolted, in hopes the Egyptians would not fail to assist him, and endeavour to recover what they had lost in Asia. He was deceived in his hope, and Nebuchadnezzar sent out against him bands of the Chaldeans, Syrians, Moabites and Ammonites, not willing to undertake the trouble of this expedition himself. Judah suffered dreadfully at this juncture, many thousands of the Jews were carried away captives. The beginning of this calamity was in the year 4105 of the Julian period, which is the more observable, as the Jews, tho' contrary to the words of the prophets, compute this to be the first year of their captivity, which of consequence must have been finished in the year 4174, the first after Cyrus had taken Babylon.

The incursions and the desolation of this country continued till Nebuchadnezzar came himself, and took Jehoiakim prisoner, who died before he could send him to Babylon, as was intended. At this time part of the treasure was taken out of the house of the Lord, and Jehoiakim was made king: but three months after, Nebuchadnezzar being displeased with him, came up against Jerusalem, and laid siege to the city; Jehoiakim surrendered, and was carried away to Babylon, and with him all the treasures of the temple, and of the palace; and they cut in pieces all the vessels of gold which Solomon had made in the temple, and destroyed all the men of might, and craftsmen, and smiths, all that were strong and apt for war, to the number of 10000: none remained except the poorest people of the land. Zedekiah obtained the kingdom in his stead.

It was natural to expect that this tragedy would have made some impression on Zedekiah: and for a considerable time he proved loyal, nay some years after

after he went himſelf to Babylon to aſſiſt at the ſiege of Nineveh, or to congratulate Nebuchadnezzar on the taking of that city, or for ſome other reaſons unknown to us. Soon after this, however, contrary to his oath, and tho' warned by the prophets, he made an alliance with Hophra, or Apries king of Egypt, and other princes, which deſervedly provok'd the king of Aſſyria to beſiege Jeruſalem; and having taken this city after an obſtinate ſiege, in order to inflict the moſt exemplary puniſhments on him for his perjury, the ſons of Zedekiah were put to death before his eyes, then he was deprived of ſight, bound with fetters and carried to Babylon, where he died a priſoner. The princes of Judah, and the captains and heads of the people were alſo ſlain: the mechanics and poor of the town were carried away to Babel, and none were allowed to remain in the country but vine-dreſſers and huſbandmen. They now plundered the temple, the king's palace, and the pillars of braſs, the baſes, and the brazen ſea in the houſe of the Lord were broken in pieces, and they carried the braſs of them to Babylon; in ſhort, every thing, not excepting the common implements. After they had done this, they burnt the temple, and the king's houſe, and in fine the whole city, demoliſhed the walls, and made Jeruſalem an heap of ruins.

Thus ended the kingdom of Judah, and this was the puniſhment inflicted by the Almighty on kings who had provoked him by their unparalelled idolatry, and diſobedience in other reſpects; and they had provoked the kings of Babylon, by revolting againſt them, contrary to all reaſon and hope of ſucceſs, notwithſtanding ſo many tragical examples to diſcourage them, and ſo many repeated warnings, intreaties, and menaces by the prophets.

To explain more clearly how this captivity happened, I ſhall endeavour to give a detail of the whole

whole matter, it being a period of great importance in history.

3023 Jews were carried away captives at the invasion, which happened 7 years after Nebuchadnezzar had begun to reign in Babylon, in the year 4105 of the Julian period. Jerem. lii, 28. 2 Kings xxiv, 2.

This was the beginning of the Jewish captivity, according to the calculation of the Jews; consequently they expected the end of it in the first year after Cyrus took Babylon, that is, in the year 4174 of the Julian period.

But this being only the 70th year from the beginning of their captivity, they obtained no more than the beginning of their deliverance, *viz.* permission to return into their own country, and the restitution of those vessels that had been taken out of the temple: for all the Jews did not now return, nor were those who actually did, able to build the temple, as the time was not yet come to begin the work.

10000 were carried away in the year 4109, of the Julian period, the city being taken, and Jehoiachin having surrendered. Probably, this number consisted partly of those that had been taken prisoners in the year 4105, the devastation of the country still continuing, and they were at last carried away to Babylon all together, in company with Jehoiachin. 2 Kings, xxiv, 14.

832 were carried away in the year 4115. when hostilities recommenced, upon the revolt of Zedekiah.

And again, 745 were carried away by Nebusar-Adan, the city being taken by assault, and a great many slain. These were the only persons of character and condition remaining. It is plain that no body was saved in the first heat of the assault; from

from hence, threescore men of the people of the land, that were found in the city, were slain by Nebuchadnezzar's order at Riblah.

In the same year the city was burnt, and with it the temple. From this event the prophets reckon the beginning of the 70 years: none being carried away afterwards, and all the punishments being fulfilled, with which they had been threatened.

This consequently is the true æra, the beginning of the 70 years, after the expiration of which Babylon was to be destroyed, the Jews to be set at liberty, and the temple to be rebuilt, agreeably to the prophecies. Daniel was aware of this; and therefore it is said; *In the first year of Darius --- I Daniel understood by books the number of the years, --- that he, the Lord, would accomplish* 70 *years in the desolations of Jerusalem.*

The term of the full expiration of these 70 years, is the year 4189, the first of Darius after he had taken Babylon. Then the walls and gates of Babel were destroyed, orders were given for rebuilding the temple, all the vessels were restored which belonged to it, and the building was actually begun the year after.

We see by this account that all the prophecies were fulfilled most exactly and punctually. This is a point of vast importance, and yet no author hitherto has attempted to explain it, without entangling himself in numberless difficulties, the consequences of a confused and most perplexed chronology. Some were even forced to plead, that the prophecies must not be taken too literally, nor according to the full number of 70 years; about 60 of them being sufficient for the whole. I flatter myself those enquirers will rejoice to find how punctually these prophecies have been accomplished in the most literal sense, and according to a calculation which may be freely exhibited to all who doubt or disbelieve, and the most artful adversaries may be defy'd to invalidate it. It will stand the nicest examination, the strictest enquiry imaginable, without giving these men an opportunity of trying it by the test of a lifeless ridicule, or of saving their own credit by trite evasions. To return to my history.

Nebuchadnezzar lived but a few years after the destruction of Jerusalem, during which he finished some other expeditions successfully. His son Nebuchadnezzar the second, or the great, inherited from him an extensive kingdom, and a formidable power. This was the same who dreamt the dream of the 4 monarchies.

This prince resolved to extend his dominions by the conquest of Egypt, which indeed was the only expedition left for him to engage in, the kings of the Medes and Lydia being his friends and allies. First he attacked Tyre, and after immense trouble and a siege of 13 years, all he obtained was a heap of stones and ruins; for the inhabitants of Tyre had, during the siege, begun to build another town in an island not far from the continent, to secure their treasure and their persons, at least the greatest part of them, and the conqueror having no fleet, was not in condition to attack them there. That town was taken in the beginning of the 27th year after Jehoiakim had been carried away to Babylon, as will appear from the xxixth chapter of Ezekiel.

After this, Nebuchadnezzar marched into Egypt. Hophra, then king of the country, was abominably insolent and proud: his language, as we read it in scripture, was, *The river is mine: I have made it!* and Herodotus informs us, that he thought himself so great, that neither the gods nor men had it in their power to take the kingdom from him: however, what had been prophecied by Jeremiah, was literally fulfilled: *I will give Pharaoh Hophra into the*

the hand of his enemies, and of them that seek his life; as I gave Zedekiah into the hand of Nebuchadnezzar, Jerem. xliv, 30. This is the prophecy, and how it was accomplished, we are told by Herodotus, who says, Apries became haughty and cruel at last: having once lost a battle, the Egyptians reproached him with having lost it designedly, in order to get rid of some who had been slain in it. This occasioned that country to revolt: they gave the command to Amasis, who defeated the foreign soldiers of Apries, took Memphis the capital, and carried him in chains to Sais, his residence. This proves a most literal accomplishment of the prophecy: for in the same manner Nebuchadnezzar had taken Jerusalem, the residence of the kings of Judah, and made Zedekiah prisoner, and sent him to his own residence at Babylon.---Apries was afterwards delivered into the hands of those who sought his life. Amasis treated him very kindly at first, in his palace at Sais; but at last he was necessitated to deliver him up to the Egyptians, who put him to death, as a prince whom Amasis, as well as themselves, had many reasons to destroy, and who was unworthy to live. This charge against him makes it probable he abused the favour of his benefactors, and perhaps entered into treacherous correspondence with Nebuchadnezzar, in order to recover the crown. This expedition of Nebuchadnezzar against Egypt, is confirmed by the testimony of profane historians, tho' they do not mention many particulars. Some think it contradicts Herodotus, who speaks of the reign of Amasis as attended with no calamities at all; but all this author says is, that according to the accounts given him, the Egyptians were in a flourishing condition, as far as concerned the advantages that country enjoys from the Nile, and the fertility of its soil: but this is not inconsistent with the attack of an enemy, who on the contrary is is most likely to invade a country, that is rich and plentiful.

Nebuchadnezzar having no more conquests to attempt, became a haughty, insolent and a cruel prince. Shadrach, Meshach, and Abednego refusing to fall down and worship his golden image, he was full of fury, and the form of his visage was changed against them, and he commanded to cast them into the burning fiery furnace: probably he gave more instances of his rage and fury, than this single one mentioned by Daniel. This prophet advised him to break off his sins by righteousness, and his iniquities by shewing mercy to the poor: but these pathethic admonitions had no effect. Then there came a voice from heaven, saying, *The kingdom is departed from thee*; and the same hour was the thing fulfilled, and he driven from men, till he blessed the most high, whereupon he was re-established in his dominions.

It wou'd be tedious to mention all the explications given of this history as related in the book of Daniel. Some pretend he really was transformed into an ox, others think it sufficient to suppose he fancied in his sickness, that he was become a beast of that kind: others make him delirious. For my own part, I do not see how this can be made consistent with scripture. Was there ever an instance of driving a man into the fields, who was out of his senses? and of giving him a fair opportunity of mischief? especially as he was a king so powerful and great, it is very improbable, that he should be suffer'd to expose himself so publicly. His queen, and his sons could not have suffer'd this. Not to mention Daniel, whose wisdom and power at court is sufficiently known from scripture? this wou'd have been a conduct too absurd to be encouraged by him? the prophet himself will prove his best interpreter.

Daniel

Daniel, when he was inculcating this particular instance of the nothingness of man to Belshazzar the king's son, he says, *The most high God gave Nebuchadnezzar thy father a kingdom, and majesty, and glory, and honour.---whom he would he slew, and whom he would he kept alive,---But when his heart was lifted up, and his mind hardened in pride, he was deposed from his kingly throne, and they took his glory from him.* Is not this informing us in as plain terms as possible, that the crown and kingdom were taken from him because of his pride? Daniel goes on, and relates what happen'd to him during his disgrace, *He was driven from the sons of men, and his heart was made like the beasts, and his dwelling was with the wild asses: they fed him with grass like oxen, and his body was wet with the dew of heaven, till he knew that the most high God ruled in the kingdom of men, and that he appointeth over it whomsoever he will.* I leave to any one to judge how rational the supposition is, that God almighty deprived a person of his reason, till he should be convinced of his being the governor of the world? how is this possible, whilst he continues delirious? The phrases and similes of scripture must be interpreted according to the subjects to which they are applied. Nebuchadnezzar lost his kingdom; he was banished into an uncultivated country, where he liv'd very miserably in comparison with the former splendor and majesty of a conqueror, and a sovereign; among barbarians, in deserts, even without a house to dwell in, feeding upon roots and other ordinary food: In short, he liv'd like a Russian exile in Siberia; for there were provinces enough like this in Assyria: Nations enough in the compass and under the dominion of that monarchy, as there are at this time, who spend their days in mountains, travelling from one wood and desert into another, and submitting to many inconveniences which custom familiarizes to them.

But what a life is this for a prince, and a prince like Nebuchadnezzar? Yet he was reduced to the necessity of bearing it for seven years together, till his pride abated. At length he was humbled, and own'd his dependance on providence; then he was recalled, and being replaced on his throne, he govern'd his people to their intire satisfaction.

History furnishes more examples of the same kind, of princes humbled in like manner, and restored to the use of their reason: there is one related by father du Halde, in his history of China, 'p. 1. of the emperor Tai-Kia, who begun his 'reign in such manner, as to incur the hatred and 'contempt of all his subjects; Yyn, a minister of 'great authority with his father, and much be-'loved by the people, made many remonstrances 'to him, and often reminded him of the judgments 'of heaven.' This proving ineffectual, he thought of an expedient which might have justly incurred the censure of rashness, had not his good intention and honesty justified it. He order'd a house to be built near the sepulchre of the late emperor: Tai-Kia was lock'd up there, and had time allow'd him to reflect on his past conduct. The monarch made a proper use of this state of humiliation, and spent three full years in meditating on the unhappy effects of a wicked life, and on the virtuous qualities requisite in the monarch of so large an empire. The minister being perfectly assured of his sincere Repentance went to see him; Tai-Kia was re-established on the throne, and he proved one of the wisest emperors.

While things were in the situation abovemention'd, Evilmerodach, or Ilvarodamus, was regent in the absence of Nebuchadnezzar, his father; which is plain from scripture, where it is said, it came to pass in the seven and thirtieth year of the captivity of Jehoiakim---that Evilmerodach, king of of Babylon, in the year that he began to reign, did lift up the head of Jehoiakim---and his allowance was a continual allowance given him of the king, as is ſtill uſual at the courts of eaſtern nations. Nebuchadnezzar reigned 43 years, conſequently, the 37th of Jehoiakim falls within his reign.

Evilmerodach probably made no great figure, and if we may believe the account given of him in Beroſus, he was a prince of a very weak underſtanding: Nitocris, his mother, for this reaſon took care of the government, and Daniel aſſiſted her, whom Nebuchadnezzar had made governor of Babylon. This prophet was in all probability, the chief cauſe and inſtrument of Jehoiakim's liberty, and of the amazing buildings erected in her adminiſtration, both for the ſafety and ornament of the kingdom, as mentioned in Herodotus.

The Median empire, ſays this author, was at that time very powerful, which occaſioned the ruin of Nineveh, and many other cities. Nitocris being aware of this, and of the continual increaſe of ſo formidable a power, thought of proper means for ſecuring Babylon. In order thereto, ſhe turned the courſe of the river Euphrates, ſo that it became neceſſary to paſs it ſeveral times in the way from Media to Babylon. The bed of this river, as far as it ran through the town, was bank'd with ſtones, encompaſs'd with walls of a conſiderable height; a bridge was built of ſtone, the paſſages and avenues were ſecured, and many other meaſures were taken conducing to the ſafety of the town, during her adminiſtration, at a prodigious expence, as well as infinite labour.

In order to underſtand this paſſage of Herodotus, it is to be remember'd, that Aſtyages, the laſt king of Media, married his only daughter Mandane, on account of a particular dream, to Cambyſes, a Perſian nobleman, which Nation was at that time very poor, and in low estimation among its neighbours. Cyrus, the son of Cambyses by this princess, was to have been put to death, according to the orders of his grandfather, but he was saved unknown to him, and educated secretly. Astyages became insupportable to his subjects by acts of the most enormous cruelty, and provoked them to make Cyrus king of Media. These troubles begun about the time of Nebuchadnezzar's being deposed, and the fourth year after he had lost his crown was the first of Cyrus's reign. Crœsus, king of Lydia, a wealthy and powerful prince, propos'd to assist his brother-in-law Astyages, and to re-establish him in his kingdom; at least he made use of this pretext, in making war against Cyrus. But Herodotus tells us, the enterprizing genius of Cyrus alarmed him so, that he determined to humble him betimes before his power became less resistible. Thus the balance of power was the great object even in those early times, and universal monarchy the great spring of action in the courts of the Asiatic princes. Crœsus was cautious enough in his undertakings: He contracted alliances with Lacedemon, Egypt and Babylonia; but he did not chuse to wait for his auxiliaries, for he thought himself powerful enough to oppose Cyrus, at least for some time: but the event proved otherwise. The first battle was fought without any considerable advantage on either side: But afterwards Crœsus retired to his winter quarters at Sardis, and was surprised by Cyrus, defeated and besieged in his own place of residence; he now sent to his allies to hasten their succours, but before they could arrive the town was surprised by night, Crœsus imprison'd, and Cyrus master of Lydia.

According to Herodotus, Labinitus was at that time king of Babylon, the same whose son was attack'd by Cyrus afterwards. This perfectly agrees

agrees with scripture, and with my chronology: for at that time Nebuchadnezzar had been restored to the crown. The administration of the government whilst the kingdom was taken from him, was according to the same author, in the hands of Nitocris; but it was now restor'd to Labinitus, or Nebuchadnezzar. Thus all circumstances agree with each other, a harmony not to be expected in any other system of chronology.

Nebuchadnezzar being re-establish'd in his dominions, *excellent Majesty was added unto him*; this passage of scripture cannot be interpreted of any additional wars and conquests; but must, I apprehend, be explained in the following manner. When he walked in the palace of the kingdom of Babylon, he said, is not this great Babylon, that I have built for the house of the kingdom, by the might of my power, and for the honour of my majesty? and then soon after this, the kingdom departed from him. When he was restored, he saw his residence much improved, and fortified by his queen, and the provinces secured by channels and castles to cover the avenues and passages: And this properly was the excellent majesty added unto him.

Nor was his power and authority diminished in any other respect. Cyrus did not venture to attack him, tho' he knew very well, how closely Babylon had been allied against him with the Lydians in former times. He was at this time employ'd in the conquest of other provinces, Ionia, Caria, Cilicia, &c. and in regulating his new established monarchy. But upon the death of Nebuchadnezzar, great revolutions ensued in the kingdom of Babylon. Evilmerodach, being an indolent and voluptuous prince, was very ill qualified to withstand a power like that of Cyrus; and he was soon slain by Neriglissar, his brother-in-law, who like-

wise

wise reigned but a few years. His son Laboroso-ardoch underwent the same fate, after a reign of nine months, and Nabonnadius succeeded. He was called Belshazzar in scripture, and Labinitus by Herodotus; tho' a son of the great Nebuchadnezzar, yet he proved as weak a prince as Evil-merodach his brother, preferring his debaucheries with wine and women, to conquest and majesty. This soon brought on his ruin. In the midst of all this confusion at Babylon, Cyrus enlarged his dominions on every side, and assumed the title of the great king, or monarch of Asia, in opposition to Nerocolassar, who had usurped the kingdom of Babylon, tho' a stranger, and not at all allied to the royal family. Soon after he conquered the Babylonian territories, and besieged the capital. According to the fortification then in use, the walls could neither be battered nor scaled. He therefore resolved to divert the channel of the river Euphrates, by which means his army having enter'd the town, surprised the Babylonians in the midst of their revelling. They never concerned themselves about Cyrus and his designs, till they saw him enter their conqueror. He treated them with great mildness, and left them to the course of life they were used to: nay, he continued Nabonnadius in the kingdom, being assured he had nothing to fear from him. It was indeed the custom of the Persians never to take the crown from any king, who did not seem of a disposition to revolt against his conqueror. Cyrus treated him with the greater kindness, as being, tho' undeservedly, a son of Nebuchadnezzar, a prince, whose memory he greatly respected, and Belshazzar continued at all times loyal to Cyrus, and Cambyses his son, kings of Persia.

Cambyses invaded Egypt, and took Psammenitus king of Egypt prisoner, he left him the crown

at

at first, intending to treat him like Belshazzar; but upon a discovery of his being engaged in deep designs against him, he was ordered to be put to death. The idolatry of the Egyptians was very offensive to this prince; he destroyed many of their temples and images, slew many of their priests, and spared not even Apis their sacred ox. The Egyptians resented all this to the highest degree, and stigmatized him with the character of a tyrant and an atheist. This last was extremely injurious, for it was a zeal for the religion of his own country, which prompted him to these outrages. All the nations of Asia, adored a Deity; and so did the Egyptians; each of them indeed, in a very different manner: some by an immediate address, as the Scythians, and as at this time several of the nations in Tartary, and the Chinese, who keep to their ancient form of religion, the emperor himself being their high-priest. These did not allow of any images, or symbolical representations of the Deity.---Others had their temples, or at least altars erected to that purpose, where they kept a perpetual fire. It is uncertain, whether this was intended as an emblem of the Deity, or the object of their devotion: but we may be sure they did not take this fire to be God himself. This was call'd the religion of the Magi, and was that of Cambyses, and all Persia. Others, altho' they worship'd one supreme God, the Lord of the universe, yet paid adoration also to some subordinate Deities, and Genii, whom they reverenced, as entrusted by him with the government of the whole. They had their temples, altars and images, to represent their power and other attributes; and address'd them kneeling in their prayers. They added to the number of these, such kings as had been distinguished by extraordinary exploits, whom therefore they deified, after death, or in modern language,

guage, they canonized them, and created them objects of worship; and this was called the religion of the Sabæans. But the Egyptians exceeded all other nations in this respect. This people, at least the greatest part of them, had a very odd hypothesis of the Anima mundi, which led them to worship and adore almost every thing; and their whole country was a temple as it were of a thousand strange divinities. It was for this reason Cambyses treated them as fools, and their idols with the greatest contempt. However he excepted one of them; the Egyptians, intending it perhaps by way of excuse, and in order to convince him of their worshipping one supreme God, in the midst of all their idolatry, shewed him the temple of Vulcan; a building hardly to be parallelled by any other in ancient and modern times. Cambyses did not violate either the temple or the image, but only burst out into a loud laughter at the sight of an impotent dwarf in this place, intended as a representation of the supreme Deity, all the other Gods being in the shape of enormous giants, tho' subordinate to him.

Cambyses died soon after, on his return into Persia, and left no issue. For a time one of the Magi usurped the crown, feigning himself to be a brother of the late sovereign. The imposture being detected, he was slain, and Darius was chosen a king. He was son of a governor of province.

The Babylonians did not think themselves obliged to acknowlege Darius, imagining their allegiance was due to none but those who were of Cyrus's family. They preferred Nabonnadius, the son of the great Nebuchadnezzar, to Darius, whose father had been only governor of a province. But he himself thought otherwise, and claimed the crown of Babylon in quality of one of Cyrus's posterity, and of the family of the kings of Media.

They

They persisted in refusing to acknowlege him, upon which he surprised the city, and treated them as rebels according to the full rigour of the Persian laws. Belshazzar being either at table, or drunk and asleep, was probably slain in this attack, notwithstanding his age, for he was sixty-two, and his dignity. He is no where said expresly to have been killed by Darius. If this had been the case, some notice would have been taken of it in history, especially as it is expresly related, that 3000 Babylonians of the noblest families, were put to death by his orders, under the pretext of rebellion and treason. The rest he pardoned. The gates of the town were demolished; part of the walls, which were of a prodigious height and thickness, was razed; the treasures were carried away; and the Jews recovered at this time the vessels of their temple and of the kings palace. This is another proof of that most exact harmony which there is between profane and sacred history, when the examiners of both make no mistakes in the chronology.

From this date the scripture reckons the years of Darius, confining itself only to such particulars in point of history, as are more immediately connected with the accomplishment of the threatnings and promises mentioned in the prophets. Now Jerusalem being destroyed by the kings of Babylon, is the reason, why in the sacred books particular notice is taken how the last of them was slain, and Babylon ruined, as well as of the rebuilding of the temple. All this actually happened, when seventy years were elapsed, as had been prophesied.

As the beginning of the captivity happened in the year 4105 of the Julian period, 3023 Jews being at that time carried away by Nebuchadnezzar's army; so the beginning of their deliverance was

70 years after, by order of Cyrus, in the year 4174, the first after the taking of Babylon.

Again; as the last of the Jews were carried away into captivity in the year 4120 of the Julian period, when the destruction of Jerusalem took place, so the last of the Jews returned, and the deliverance was completed in the year 4189, the first of Darius, after the destruction of Babylon, by his orders given in this 70th year of the captivity.

Thus in the year 4190, the 70 years of the captivity being quite expired, the Jews became again a free people, and laid the foundation of the temple, which was finished a few years after.

Some fix a third period, namely, the time of the Jews going into Egypt, in the 23d year of Nebuchadnezzar; from which time to the first of Cyrus, according to their computation, are 52 years, and thus they make up the sabbatical years mentioned, 2 Chron. xxxvi. 21.

According to the law, every seventh year was to be a sabbatical year, but the Jews were not very regular in the observance of it. Hence the interpreters think, the country was to be left waste and uncultivated as many years as had not been observed of the sabbatical. Now as they suppose, that after the Jews went into Egypt till the return of the captives, the country was quite desolate and not cultivated, at least not by the Jews, it must have continued in this condition 52 years; which multiplied by 7, make a number of years that reach back to the reign of Asa, in which the Jews begun to neglect religion. I beg leave to give my opinion of this hypothesis as far as it is intended for an epocha in chronology.

The sabbatical years mention'd here, or the land lying uncultivated, was in consequence of the word of the Lord, by the mouth of Jeremiah, as is expresly said in scripture; it is therefore to be be considered as a decree of God himself. But how can an event be the fulfilling of his will, which is quite contrary to his commands? He is said to have ordered the country's lying uncultivated; and yet he forbad the Jews to go into Egypt: Nay, he threatened them with sword, famine and pestilence, in case they were determined to go, which should force them to return into their own country. Consequently, it is contradictory to say, they went thither in order to fulfill the will of God; nor can their going into Egypt be considered, as the land's enjoying her sabbath, in lying desolate, which was mentioned by the prophet. For the same reason, it would be wrong to begin the account of the captivity with this event. This is plain and evident: nor is it unknown to those, who invented, or make use of this calculation; they only think the interpretation justified as a case of necessity. For if they had fixed the beginning of these sabbatical years before the period they have chosen, this would bring them as far as to the times of Solomon, David, or Samuel: all pious princes, who never would have permitted the people to trespass the law, in not keeping the sabbatical years, as they were there prescribed.

But suppose we were not to allow even the truth of their calculation, by proving the year in which they went into Egypt, to be the 19th of Nebuchadnezzar, and consequently that of the destruction of Jerusalem? This would necessitate them to go back as far as the reign of Solomon, tho' they should reckon but 52 years. A little attention in reading Jerem. lii. will shew the truth of this observation. In the fifth month, in the tenth day of the month, which was the 19th year of Nebuchadnezzar came Nebuzar-Adan to Jerusalem ver. 12. Then follows an account at large of what was done by him. He burnt the temple and the city, v. 13. He broke down

down all the walls round about, ver. 14. He carried away the poor of the people, and the residue that remained in the city, ver. 15. But left some for vine-dressers and for husbandmen, ver. 16. He carried away all the brass, and all the things of value, ver. 23. He took Serajah the chief priest, and several others, and brought them to Riblah, where they were put to death, ver. 24, 27. This account concludes with this observation: thus Judah was carried away captive out of his own land. Then follows a list of the people who were carried away captive: in the 7th year of Nebuchadnezzar, 3023. and lastly, in the 23, Nebuzar-Adan carried away captive from Judah 745 persons. Now Judah having been carried away captive already in the 19th year: this 19th and the other 23d, must be one and the same year, calculated according to two different epocha's. The first epocha begins with Nebuchadnezzar's having taken Babylon, the second a year after the death of Chyniladanus. It was a thing of the greatest consequence to fix the year of the captivity with certainty, and for this reason, the sacred writers took all possible care to remove doubts and objections, and in order thereto, they fix'd it according to a double epocha: one used by Nebuchadnezzar himself, and by all his subjects, *viz.* his accession to the crown; the other being that which probably may have prevailed with foreign historians. Agreeably to this, Ptolemy actually reckoned from the death of Chyniladanus, and he borrowed his memoirs from other and more ancient books. This double determination is therefore a character of divine wisdom, which is as plainly to be distinguished in point of chronology, as in all other particulars. This very year, in which Nebuzar-Adan was carrying away the Jews into captivity, was the same in which the Jews went into Egypt, as may be seen from Jerem. xxxix. xl. xli, and as they them-

themselves confess. Consequently they fled into Egypt that very year, when Jerusalem was destroyed; and they cannot avoid going back as far as the reign of Solomon, according to this account, tho' they should reckon but 52 of the sabbatical years.

I forbear alleging another circumstance, as I am unwilling to be too particular, *viz.* Nebuchadnezzar reigned but 21 years after the death of Chyniladanus, so that he could not order captives to be carried away in the 23d year of this epocha. A false hypothesis forced the chronologers to assert, that he was idle for 21 years together, and to attribute all to his son, Nebuchadnezzar the second, who reigned 43 years. This mistake made it impossible to discern the double epocha of 19 and 23: for the years of the reign of Nebuchadnezzar the second could not be reckoned otherwise than from the death of his father, which makes but one single epocha. From the same mistake, it was impossible to find out the sabbatical years. For the departure of the Jews into Egypt, and the destruction of Jerusalem, happened in one and the same year, from which they cannot commence their calculation of the sabbatical years, because the amount would be too great; at what period therefore are those years to commence? Nothing material happened after they went into Egypt, that looks like a desolation, or that could fix a period for the computation.

But suppose there was a possibility to go back as far as the reign of Asa, then I fear they will fall short in their calculation, the number of years not being sufficient: For it is said of the times of Rehoboam, 1 Kings xiv. 22. *Judah did evil in the sight of the Lord, and they provoked him to jealousy with their sins which they had committed, above all that their fathers had done.* And of his successor Abijam, xv. 3. *He walked in all the sins of his father, which he had done before him.*--On the contrary, of Abijam's successor Asa, it is written, *He did that which was right in the eyes of the Lord, as did David his father: Nay, he brought in the things which his father and he himself had dedicated into the house of the Lord, silver and gold and vessels.* How then can he be suspected of any neglect of the sabbatical year? Wherefore, supposing the neglect might be reduced as far as his reign I fear this will not yet prove sufficient to remove all difficulties. If it was allowed to make 52 years of 70, expresly mentioned by the prophet, just as a chronologer might think convenient for his hypothesis, then we need not regard difficulties in history. For this reason, I much wish to see the true meaning of the prophecies, and the case of the sabbatical years settled by proper judges of the subject, as it is neither my study nor my province. The controversy about the calculation of them being once removed, perhaps it may prove a new argument in favour of my chronology; which if true, must agree exactly. And in case it does not point out the year agreeably to the intention of the prophet, or if the interpretation should prove strained, unnatural, and far fetched, then it is as defective as all the rest, and I shall not make any scruple to acknowlege it erroneous. For this will hold for ever; any hypothesis in chronology, if true, must agree with scripture, and must point out the events successively in the very order in which they happened, so as to shew the accomplishment of prophecies with perspicuity and evidence, without forcing the text, and without any artificial explanation. In the same manner, it is required also that a true chronology should agree with profane history, which it may serve to distinguish from a romance. To give an instance in the history of Cyrus; some follow Xenophon's authority, others that of Herodotus. As these

great

great historians differ materially, the question is, which of them wrote truth? And suppose 3 or 4000 years hence, a chronologer was to prefer Madame Scuderi's Artamenes to both, in order to explain the ancient history of Persia, what would be the characteristical mark of truth to those, who then enquire into it? It is true, a chronology founded on the accounts of that lady could not boast much of connexion: But many things come to pass, that seem impossible and contradictory.

Scaliger, and others, thought it an impossibility to settle the chronology of the Jews from the small number of records handed down to us in scripture: The contrary, I think, is plainly shewn in this essay, and every competent judge I hope will draw this inference from it, that it must be as possible to regulate the chronology of the times preceding the term I have fixed upon; and as for those that follow it, the subject is still less liable to difficulties. Some think it impossible to connect the genuine records of profane history with scripture, they being corrupted and adulterated: But, with the leave of these gentlemen, I must ask them, what notions they have of God's providence and moral government of the world? By him scripture has been handed down to us without being corrupted, and it will be preserved in the same manner to the end of all things. Suppose no other records were extant of ancient history, what objections would not be made to scripture by unbelievers? How would they triumph in the question, Who knows whether any one was ever extant of all the persons mentioned in this book? How absurd is it to suppose a town like Babylon to be destroyed for the sake of Jerusalem, after having been the residence of the greatest conqueror in the universe, but 25 years before. Certainly it must be a very absurd piece of conduct in a conqueror,

queror, entirely to demolish a city of so vast an extent as Nineveh according to your account? All mere fictions of some idle Jews, in order to magnify their countrymen as a nation of great importance and authority. Shew us the place at least, the ruins of your Nineveh, and Babylon. Who can believe a book that contains such improbabilities and absurdities? These, and a thousand other objections, scripture would have been loaded with, if the records of profane history, their connexion with each other, and with the scripture, had not prevented the charge. The only means to prove this connexion, is chronology. God contriving every thing in such a manner, that men might be without excuse, took care to preserve as many of these records as would be necessary to give satisfaction in this respect. To know the names of all ancient kings, or the history of all the nations in antiquity, would be altogether useless; nor need we lament the loss of many hundred books, which perhaps might have given us the names of the Tyrian kings, their wives and children, the number of their ships, their cargo, and a thousand other circumstances of that nature. But all the particulars requisite to vindicate the truth of revelation against unbelievers we are amply furnished with, both in point of history and chronology. Faults may have crept in from the inaccuracy of those that copied the manuscripts: But the writings themselves never were designedly corrupted, on purpose to found a pretension to higher antiquity, or on any other account whatsoever. They are written with all the marks of authentic truth and honesty: They may be compared and connected, the sacred with the profane. For instance, let us consider the records relating to the Egyptian history; these never were corrupted with any evil intent, as may be proved beyond

yond contradiction. They seem perplexing and confused; this cannot be deny'd; but yet they are not without order and harmony, tho' not always exactly such as we expect, or such as we want to reduce them to. The Egyptians were singular in many other respects, as well as their history.

Travellers give an account of many fine pillars still to be met with in that country, but neither of the Corinthian, nor of any other order known to us. To what purpose would it be to criticise upon them according to the rules of art, or to form from the composition of several of them, one artificial Corinthian or Doric pillar? Providence has taken all possible care not to let us want what may be necessary towards our conviction in things relating to salvation: not only convincing and inviting us from afar, as it were by daily and continual benefits, but also by arguments both moral and historical, suited to captivate our understanding; these must remain unshaken, and will stand any attack of adversaries. This is the natural conduct of divine wisdom and goodness, attributes inseparable from the Deity; and this grounds a very strong presumption, that these historical arguments must be such, as not to be overthrown by any sophistry employ'd against them; they must admit of all proper conviction; and this strength must be evident, since it is merely on account, and in favour of our understanding and knowlege, that it is established. The complaints of some, who every moment think themselves in the dark, or place themselves there, are not owing to providence, nor to an impossibility of discovering the light, for every one may discover it.

All that has been now alledged, is only to shew the motives that induced me to an essay of this nature. Had I not been convinced of the intrinsic possibility, I never would have attempted a ſubject which has been eſteemed, in part at leaſt, impoſſible. I was as perfectly convinced afterwards by experience, of ſcripture being its own and beſt interpreter, as well in point of hiſtory, as in other reſpects; ſupplying us with arguments, which we look for in vain from any other quarter. I propoſe this as an inſtance of it, which, I hope is not attended with any material fault in the fundamentals here exhibited for a better ſyſtem of chronology. I ſhall be glad of any aſſiſtance in continuing to build upon it; or, if unaſſiſted, I ſhall go on myſelf, if it pleaſe God to allow me health and leiſure.

As for my taking notice of ſome errors and miſtakes committed by other chronologers, I hope no one will blame me for having ventured to mention them. I do not impeach the merit of any author in particular, and am very willing to own, that many of them have exerted amazing thought and induſtry: but what is all this, where the groundwork, the ſupport of the whole, is defective? Their ſuperſtructure is not without faults: But theſe are owing to the faults in the foundation which lay undiſcovered and unſeen by them: and I am the rather inclined to admire their ſkill in raiſing ſuch a building on it, as they have done, than to blame them for what they have omitted. I ſhould be glad if I could have avoided mentioning them at all: but without this, I could not prove the truth of my own hypotheſis. As I pretend to remove errors, and difficulties by it, I was neceſſitated to mention ſome of them at leaſt, before I made the experiment. After all, I appeal to thoſe, who are not unacquainted with ſubjects of this nature, whether I have exceeded the bounds of modeſty in this particular, and whether leſs or more ought to have been mention'd concerning it?

The

The years of each reign of the Egyptian kings before Psammetichus have not been specified; this being a subject depending on the connexion of the Egyptian chronology, and the proofs of its truth, it would have been to no purpose to insert them, as the reader could not be a proper judge of their authenticity: To annex the proofs themselves, would have been tedious and superfluous to my present design. These considerations have induced me to put it off to another opportunity.

I forgot to observe before, that in reckoning the years of the reign of a king who was deposed, scripture does not add the time during which he was dispossess'd of the crown, to the whole of his reign, before his deposition, and after his restoration; nor would such a calculation be strictly regular. This holds in the instances of all those three kings, who had the kingdom taken from them, Menahem, Hosea, and Manasseh. As for Amaziah, he never was restored, tho' he was set at liberty; yet scripture makes a proper use of his years, in order to determine some events more precisely; and intends the same in mentioning the 20th year of Jotham, tho' he died before; as this was the only means to determine the facts that happened about that time. Besides, the son of Amaziah administer'd the government for the most part in his father's name, notwithstanding he was king himself, and co-regent with his father, which was also the case in several other instances. This observation of mine, concerning the years omitted when a king lost the crown, has not to the best of my knowlege, been made by any other chronologer, nor would their system allow of it: It proves however an invincible argument for the truth of my hypothesis; which could not, unless it were true, agree in this particular, as it always does, and just in the very place where history requires it. Nay, others have been so far from observing this, that some attributed eleven years to Menahem, which is quite contrary to the express words of scripture; and Usher, a man of the greatest repute and authority, was necessitated to insert an interregnum of eleven years and a half before the time of Zachariah's accession to the crown. A contrivance very much approved of by those that came after him, as they thought it impossible without such an arbitrary insertion, to reduce the reign of Zachariah, and Shallum, to the 39 years of Azariah. But, according to this method, the possibility, nay, the necessity of this calculation is sufficiently plain. If there was but this one dilemma in the common systems of chronology, the necessity of inserting of 11 years and a half in a period of 219, without any proof and warrant for it, wou'd not this be an evidence rather more than sufficient to prove their inconsistency, and to put us upon a different method. Yet this has been the system of a chronology, which was to supply proofs for the accomplishment of the most important truths and prophecies: tho' with what success I need not mention here.

I cannot conclude, without repeating that there is such a profound wisdom apparent in the scripture, and so many arguments in behalf of its divine origin in points of chronology, that no tables, no explication or commentary is sufficient to give us a proper idea of it. Every one's enquiry and speculation must supply what is wanting here. Then the wisdom of the Almighty will appear the same every where, and will be justified by her children, to the shame and confusion of all blasphemers.

A

A

SYNCHRONISTICAL TABLE

OF THE

KINGS *of* JUDAH *and* ISRAEL.

PREFACE

TO THE

SYNCHRONISTICAL TABLES.

THESE Tables shew the true connexion and harmony in the years of the kings of Judah and Israel.

Arguments and proofs are added from scripture, as also a short explication of the manner in which these agree with the tables themselves, to the full satisfaction and justification of the history. The 1st of January has been chosen for the beginning of the term; the dates of days and months are to be understood according to this Hypothesis.

The whole period for the duration of the kingdom of Israel contains 219 years, as is proved in these tables without contradiction, which makes it plain, that the overplus of 36 years in the common systems of chronology is a mistake; and indeed the occasion of all the errors and confusion in history, and has made it impossible to shew either the connexion with profane historians, or the accomplishment of the prophecies.

It is to be observed, that when a king was dethroned, the years of his deposition are not in scripture added to the rest; as was the case in the reign of Menahem, Hoseä, and Manasseh; the two first of whom only are mentioned in this period of history.

Kings

Kings of Judah.	Years.	Kings of Iſrael.	Years.	Years after the Separation of the Tribes.
Rehoboam		Jeroboam		
Jan. 1.	1	Jan. 1.	1	1
		Dec. 21.	2	
	2	Dec. 9.	3	2
	3	Nov. 27.	4	3
	4	Nov. 16.	5	4
	5	Nov. 4.	6	5
	6	Oct. 24.	7	6
	7	Oct. 12.	8	7
	8	Oct. 1.	9	8
	9	Sept. 21.	10	9
	10	Sept. 9	11	10
	11	Aug. 28.	12	11
	12	Aug. 17.	13	12
	13	Aug. 6.	14	13
	14	Jul. 25.	15	14
	15	Jul. 13.	16	15
Abijam	16	Jul. 2.	17	16
Jun. 24.-1-	17	Jun. 20.	18	17
	2	Jun. 9.	19	18
Aſa. Jul. 1.-1-	3	Mar. 28.	20	19
	2	May 17.	21	20
	3	May 6.	22	21
		Nadab Jun. 1.	1	
	4	May 20.	2	22
		Baaſha Jun. 7.	1	
	5	May 26.	2	23
Jehoſhaphat	6	May 15.	3	24
born	7	May 4.	4	25
	8	Apr. 23.	5	26
	9	Apr. 11.	6	27
	10	Mar. 31.	7	28
	11	Mar. 20.	8	29
	12	Mar. 9.	9	30
	13	Feb. 26.	10	31
	14	Feb. 15.	11	32
	15	Feb. 4.	12	33
	16	Jan. 24	13	34
	17	Jan. 12.	14	35
	18	Jan. 1.	15	36
		Dec. 21.	16	

Scriptural Authorities.

1 Kings xiv. 20. Jeroboam reigned two and twenty years, and Nadab his son reigned in his stead,---in the second year of Asa, 1 K. xv. 25.

1 K. xiv. 21. Rehoboam reigned seventeen years---Abijam his son reigned over Judah in the eighteenth year of Jeroboam; he reigned three years, 1 K. xv. 1, 2.

1 K. xv. 9. In the twentieth year of Jeroboam king of Israel, reigned Asa over Judah.

1 K. xv. 25. Nadab the son of Jeroboam began to reign over Israel, in the second year of Asa king of Judah.

EXPLANATION.

In the 17th year after the Separation commences the 17th of Rehoboam, Jan. 1.
the 18th of Jeroboam, Jun. 20. the first of Abijam, Jun. 24, and consequently in the 18th of Jeroboam.

In the 18th year of the Separation, Jun. 24. commences the 2d year of Abijam.

19th	Jun. 24.	the 3d ditto
	May 28.	the 20th of Jeroboam.
	July 1.	the 1st of Asa.

consequently Asa began to reign in the 20th year of Jeroboam.

In the 20th year of the Separation, July 1, commences the 2d year of Asa.

21st	May 6.	the 22d year of Jeroboam.
	Jun. 1.	the 1st year of Nadab.
	July 1.	the 3d year of Asa.

consequently Nadab began to reign in the second year of Asa.

In the 22d year of the Separation, Jun. 7. commences the 1st year of Baasha.
July 1. the 4th year of Asa,
consequently Baasha began to reign in the 3d year of Asa, 1 K. xv. 28. and he reigned 24 years.

Joram

Kings of Judah.	Years.	Kings of Iſrael.		Years.	Years after the Separation of the Tribes.
	19		Dec. 10.	17	37
	20		Dec. 29.	18	38
	21		Nov. 17.	19	39
	22		Nov. 6.	20	40
	23		Oct. 26.	21	41
	24		Oct. 15.	22	42
	25		Oct. 3.	23	43
	26	Elah	Sept. 22.	24	44
			Oct. 1.	1	
	27	Zimri	Sept. 21.	2	45
			Nov. 1.		
		Omri	Nov. 7.	1	
	28		Oct. 27.	2	46
	29		Oct. 15.	3	47
	30		Oct. 4.	4	48
	31		Sept. 23.	5	49
Joram born	32		Sept. 12.	6	50
	33		Aug. 31.	7	51
	34		Aug. 20.	8	52
	35		Jul. 29.	9	53
	36		Jul. 18.	10	54
	37		Jul. 6.	11	55
	38	Ahab	Jun. 25.	12	56
Jehoſhaphat			Jul. 14.	1	
1 co-regent	39		Jul. 3.	2	57
2	40		Jun. 22.	3	58
3 Jehoſhaphat	1-41		Jun. 10.	4	59
4	2		May 30.	5	60
5	3		May 19.	6	61
6	4		May 8.	7	62
7	5		Apr. 26.	8	63
8	6		Apr. 15.	9	64
9	7		Apr. 4.	10	65
10	8		Mar. 24.	11	66
11	9		Mar. 12.	12	67
12	10		Mar. 1.	13	68
13	11		Feb. 18.	14	69
14	12		Feb. 7.	15	70
15	13		Jan. 26.	16	71
16	14		Jan. 15.	17	72

Scrip-

Scriptural Authorities.

1 Kings xvi. 8. In the twenty and sixth year of Asa king of
Judah, began Elah to reign over Israel two years.
10. Zimri killed him in the twenty-seventh year of Asa
king of Judah, and reigned in his stead seven days.
Tibni and Omri succeed him; Omri prevails and
is sole king.
23. In the thirty and one year of Asa king of Judah,
began Omri to reign over Israel twelve years; six
years reigned he in Tirzah.
24. After at Samaria.
29. In the thirty and eighth year of Asa king of Judah,
began Ahab to reign, and he reigned twenty and
two years.

2 Chron. xvi. 12. Asa in the thirty-ninth year of his reign was diseased in his feet--v. 13. died in the one and fortieth year of his reign, 1 Kings xv. 10.

1 Kings xxii. 41. Jehoshaphat the son of Asa, began to reign over Judah in the fourth year of Ahab king of Israel.--he reigned twenty and five years.

EXPLANATION.

In the 44th year of the Separation, July 1. commences the 26th year of Asa, and

	Sept. 22.	the 24th	of Baasha.
	Oct. 1.	the 1st	of Elah.
45th	July 1.	the 27th	of Asa.
	Sept. 21.	the 2d	of Elah.
	Nov. 1.	the 1st	of Zimri,
	Nov. 7.	the 1st	of Omri.

In the 31st year of Asa Omri becomes sole king, and reigned in all twelve years.

56th	July 1. commences the 38th year of Asa.		
	June 25.	the 12th	of Omri.
	July 14.	the 1st	of Ahab.

Asa being diseased in the 39th year of his reign, took Jehoshaphat into a share of the kingdom.

59th June 10. commences the 4th year of Ahab, and July 1. the 41st of Asa, but Jehoshaphat being already co-regent, his reign commences in the last year of his father's, i. e. July 1. begins also the 1st year of Jehoshaphat.

Kings of Judah.	Years.	Kings of Israel.		Years.	Years after the Separation of the Tribes.
17	15		Jan. 4. Dec. 25.	18 19	73
18	16		Dec. 14.	20	74
19	17		Dec. 2.	21	75
20	18	Ahaziah	Nov. 21. Dec.	22 1	76
21	19	Jehoram	Jun. 25.	1	77
22	20		Jun. 14.	2	78
23	21		Jun. 2.	3	79
24	22		May 22	4	80
25 Joram--1--	23		May 11	5	81
	2		Apr. 30.	6	82
	3		Apr. 18.	7	83
	4		Apr. 7.	8	84
	5		Mar. 27.	9	85
	6		Mar. 16.	10	86
	7		Mar. 4.	11	87
	8		Feb. 22.	12	88
Ahaziah-Joash-	1	Jehu	Feb. 7.	1	89
Athaliah assumes	2		Jan. 28.	2	90
the government	3		Jan. 16.	3	91
	4		Jan. 5. Dec. 25.	4 5	92
	5		Dec. 14.	6	93
Joash crowned	6		Dec. 3.	7	94
Feb. 8.	7		Nov. 21.	8	95
	8		Nov. 10.	9	96
	9		Oct. 30.	10	97
	10		Oct. 18.	11	98
	11		Oct. 7.	12	99
	12		Sept. 26.	13	100
	13		Sept. 15.	14	101
	14		Sept. 3.	15	102
	15		Aug. 23.	16	103
Amaziah born	16		Aug. 12.	17	104
	17		Aug. 1.	18	105
	18		Jul. 21	19	106
	19		Jul. 10.	20	107
	20		Jun. 29.	21	108
	21		Jun. 18	22	109

Scriptural Authorities.

1 Kings xxii. 52. Ahaziah, the ſon of Ahab, began to reign over Iſrael the ſeventeenth year of Jehoſhaphat, and reigned two years.

2 Kings iii. 1. Jehoram, the ſon of Ahab, began to reign over Iſrael the eighteenth year of Jehoſaphat, and reigned twelve years.

2 Kings i. 17. In the ſecond year of Jehoram, the ſon of Jehoſhaphat, king of Judah.

2 Kings viii. 16. In the fifth year of Joram, the ſon of Ahab, Jehoram the ſon of Jehoſhaphat, king of Judah, began to reign.

-- -- -- 25, 26. In the twelfth year of Joram, the ſon of Ahab, did Ahaziah, the ſon of Jehoram king of Judah, begin to reign; and he reigned one year. Both are ſlain at one time by Jehu.

EXPLANATION.

In the 75th of the Sep. July 1. commences the 17th year of Jehoſhaphat.

76th. June 1. Ahaziah is declared co-regent by Ahab, on account of the intended expedition. Jehoſhaphat viſits Ahab, is perſuaded to join him againſt the Syrians, they ſet out together in Sept. The 22d year of Ahab commences Nov. 22. The battle is ſoon after this. Ahaziah is ſole king from Dec. 1, to June 24. 77.

77th June 25. commences the firſt year of Jehoram king of Iſrael.

July 1. commences the 19th year of Jehoſhaphat.

81ſt Jehoſhaphat dies in the 25th year of his reign, and the 23d, ſince he became ſole king. Joram his ſon being already co-regent, his reign commences in the laſt year of Jehoſhaphat, July 1.-81. in the 5th of the reign of Joram, which year begins June 25.

88th July 7. Ahaziah ſucceeds to the crown of Judah, and attends the expedition againſt the Syrians. Joram is wounded in the battle, and healed at Jezreel; where Ahaziah viſits him. Mean time Jehu is anointed, and both kings go out to meet him, from whence may be concluded, that Joram was healed; and, conſequently, ſome time intervened between the battle and this day.

The 12th year of Joram expires Feb. 10.-89. Joram and Ahaziah were killed before this time. A year being attributed to Ahaziah, he muſt have reigned more than half a year; ſo that he was put to death in Feb. 89. being the ninth month. Joram died ſomewhat ſooner.

Kings of Judah.	Years.	Kings of Israel.		Years.	Years after the Separation of the Tribes.	
	22		June 6.	23	110	
	23	1 Jehoahaz	May 28.	24	111	
	24	2 co-regent	May 17.	25	112	
	25	3	May 6.	26	113	
	26	4	Apr. 25.	27	114	
	27	5	Apr. 13.	28	115	
	28	Jehoahaz	Apr. 2.	6	116	
Azariah born	29	sole king	Mar. 22.	7	117	
	30		Mar. 10.	8	118	
	31		Feb. 27.	9	119	
	32		Feb. 16.	10	120	
	33		Feb. 5.	11	121	
	34		Feb. 24.	12	122	
	35		Feb. 13.	13	123	
	36		{ Jan. 2. Dec. 22.	14 15 }	124	Years of Jeroboam's reign in Judah, before he acceded to the throne of Israel
	37		Dec. 11.	16	125	
	38	Jehoash	Nov. 29.-1-	17	126	
	39		Nov. 18.	2	127	
Amaz. Mar. 1-1.	40		Nov. 7.	3	128	
	2		Oct. 27.	4	129	
	3		Oct. 15.	5	130	{ Jan. 1 - 1
Jerob. K. of Ju.	4		Oct. 4.	6	131	Dec. 20 - 2
1 Azariah	5		Sept. 23.	7	132	Dec. 9 - 3
2 appointed	6		Sept. 12.	8	133	Nov. 28 - 4
3 king by	7		Aug. 31.	9	134	Nov. 16 - 5
4 the Jews	8		Aug. 20.	10	135	Nov. 5 - 6
5 instead of	9		Aug. 9.	11	136	Oct. 25 - 7
6 Amaziah	10		July 29.	12	137	Oct. 14 - 8
7 his father,	11		July 17.	13	138	Oct. 2 - 9
8 who was	12		July 6.	14	139	Sept. 21 - 10
9 deposed	13		June 25.	15	140	Sept. 11 - 11
10 by Joash.	14		June 14.	16	141	Aug. 30 - 12
11	15	Jeroboam	Mar. 7.	13	142	Aug. 18 - 13
12	16	king of Israel	Aug. 7.	14	143	
13	17		July 27.	15	144	
14	18		July 16.	16	145	
15	19		July 4.	17	146	
16	20		June 23.	18	147	
17	21		June 12.	19	14[illegible]	

Scriptural Authorities.

2 Kings x. 36. Jehu reigned over Israel twenty and eight years. ch. xi. 3. Joash, the son of Athaliah, was hid in the house of the Lord six years. v. 3. and the seventh year. ch. xii. 1. in the seventh year of Jehu, Jehoash began to reign, and reigned forty years. ch. xi. 3. six years Athaliah did reign over the land.

2 Kings xiii. 1. In the three and twentieth year of Joash, Jehoahaz, the son of Jehu, began to reign, and reigned seventeen years.---v. 10. In the thirty and seventh year of Joash, king of Judah, began Jehoash, the son of Jehoahaz, to reign over Israel, and reigned sixteen years.---ch. xiv. 1. In the second year of Joash, the son of Jehoahaz king of Israel, reigned Amaziah king of Judah.---v. 2. and he reigned twenty and nine years in Jerusalem.---v. 17. he lived after the death of Jehoash, son of Jehoahaz, fifteen years.---v. 23. in the fifteenth year of Amaziah, Jeroboam began to reign in Samaria, and reigned forty and one years.

EXPLANATION.

Athaliah having no right to the crown, the six years of her reign are computed among the forty of the reign of Joash, as if he had been the immediate successor of his father.

We read in the 2 Kings x. 32. that the Lord began to cut Israel short, and Hazael smote them in all their coasts; at this time probably Jehu admitted his son to a share in the government, in the 23d year of Joash, which began Feb. 8. and at that period the seventeen years of Jehoahaz commence; and as the latter was co-regent he enters immediately upon the last year of his father, Apr. 13. 115, which begins at once the 28th and last of Jehu, and the fifth of Jehoahaz. Jehoahaz likewise admitted his son Joash co-regent in the 37th year of Joash of Judah, which begins Feb. 8, 125. This Joash, or Jehoash of Israel, was probably the Saviour God gave to Israel against the Syrians. He being co-regent, his reign begins with the last year of his father's, Nov. 29, 126. and thus he reigned 16 years. The 40th year of Joash of Judah, begins Feb. 8. 128. therefore falls into the 2d of Joash of Israel, and nine months before the end of it, within which space the king of Judah was slain.

Joash of Israel dies Mar. 7, 142. in the 15th year of Amaziah, which began Mar. 1, 142. Jeroboam the son and successor of Joash, not having been co-regent with his father in Israel, but king of Judah, the years of his reign in Judah are continued in Israel, Amaziah having provoked Joash, was conquered, deposed, and taken prisoner by him, and Jeroboam was appointed king of Judah in his stead. A body of malecontents among the Jews chose Azariah, or Uzziah, who, like David in the time of Saul, might probably wander about till Jeroboam mounted the throne of Israel, when Amaziah seems to have been set at liberty, for we read that he lived fifteen years after the death of Joash, i. e. after his own deliverance. At last upon a conspiracy against him, he fled to Lachish, where he was slain.

Kings of Judah.	Years.	Kings of Israel.		Years.	Years after the Separation of the Tribes.
18	22		Jun. 1.	20	149
19	23		May 20.	21	150
20	24		May 9.	22	151
21	25		Apr. 28.	23	152
22	26		Apr. 17.	24	153
23	27		Apr. 5.	25	154
24	28		Mar. 25.	26	155
25	29		Mar. 14.	27	156
Azariah sole king	26		Mar. 3.	28	157
	27		Feb. 20.	29	158
Jotham born	28		Feb. 9.	30	159
	29		Jan. 29.	31	160
	30		Jan. 18.	32	161
	31		Jan. 6.	33	162
			Dec. 26.	34	
	32		Dec. 15.	35	163
	33		Dec. 4.	36	164
	34		Nov. 23.	37	165
	35		Nov. 11.	38	166
	36		Oct. 31.	39	167
	37		Oct. 20.	40	168
	38		Oct. 9.	41	169
	39	Zachariah	Feb. 27.		170
		Shallum	Sept. 1.		
		Menahem	Oct. 1.	1	
	40		Sept. 20.	2	171
	41		Sept. 9.	3	172
	42		Aug. 29.	4	173
	43		Aug. 17.	5	174
	44		Aug. 6.	6	175
	45		July 26.	7	176
	46		July 15.	8	177
	47		July 3.	9	178
Ahaz born	48		June 22.	10	179
	49		June 11.		180
	50	Pekahiah	Mar. 31.	1	181
	51		Mar. 20.	2	182
Jotham Feb. 1-1-	52.	Pekah	Mar. 3	1	183
	2		Feb. 11.	2	184
	3		Jan. 31.	3	185

Scriptural

Scriptural Authorities.

2 Kings xv. 1, 2. In the twenty and seventh year of Jeroboam, began Azariah king of Judah to reign, and he reigned two and fifty years.--v. 8. in the thirty and eighth year of Azariah did Zachariah reign over Israel six months.--v. 17. in the nine and thirtieth year of Azariah began Menahem to reign, and reigned ten years in Samaria.--v. 19. And Pul the king of Assyria came against the land; and Menahem gave Pul a thousand talents of silver, that his hand might be with him, to confirm the kingdom in his hand.--v. 20. So the king of Assyria turned back, and stayed not there in the land.--v. 23. In the fiftieth year of Azariah, Pekahiah the son of Menahem began to reign, and reigned over Israel two years.--v. 27. In the two and fiftieth year of Azariah, Pekah began to reign over Israel and reigned twenty years.--v. 32. In the second year of Pekah began Jotham, king of Judah, to reign,--v. 33. and he reigned sixteen years.

EXPLANATION.

The 38th year of Azariah begins Mar. 1, 169. and the 41st of Jeroboam, Oct. 9th. Jeroboam died, and was succeeded by Zachariah his son, Feb. 27, 170. consequently in the 38th of Azariah. Zachariah reigned six months, i. e. till Sept. 1, 170. Shallum one month, till Oct. 1. 170. and is succeeded by Menahem in the 39th of Azariah, which began Mar. 1. 170.

From 2 kings xv. 19. it appears, that Pul was for some time possess'd of the kingdom of Israel, and had deposed Menahem, but restored him as a tributary upon the payment of a certain sum. Pul staid not there in the land, i. e. as king, for it was very improbable he should fix his constant residence at Samaria. The time of his being in possession of the crown cannot be comprehended in the years of Menahem's reign. The same happened afterward to be the case with Hosea. The time of Menahem's deposition may be computed about nine months, by dating the beginning of Pekahiah's reign, Mar. 31. and supposing the last of Menahem to have been a whole year, and to have ended June 11 before.

The 2d year of Pekah, begins Feb. 11, 184. the first year of Jotham after the death of his father begins a few days after, for Azariah had almost reached his 53d year. But as Jotham reigned before the death of his father, (2 Kings xv. 5.) the 20 years, which determine the beginning of Hoshea's reign (v. 30.) are to be computed from Feb. 1. 183. and tho' Jotham was dead, his twentieth year is expresly mentioned to shew, that his own year was meant, not the 52d of his father, which began Mar. 1. for else this accuracy would have been needless. In short, Azariah was consider'd as dead on account of his leprosy, Jotham's reign commences Feb. 1, 183. Azariah dies after Feb. 11, 184. which is therefore the first year of Jotham's reign after the death of his father. Hoshea comes to the crown, Feb. 1. 202.

Kings of Judah.	Years.	Kings of Israel,		Years.	Years after the Separation of the Tribes.
	4		Jan. 19.	4	186
	5		Jan. 8. Dec. 28.	5 6	187
	6		Dec. 17.	7	188
	7		Dec. 5.	8	189
Hezekiah born	8		Nov. 24.	9	190
	9		Nov. 13.	10	191
	10		Nov. 2.	11	192
	11		Oct. 21.	12	193
	12		Oct. 10.	13	194
	13		Sept. 29.	14	195
	14		Sept. 18.	15	196
	15		Sept. 6.	16	197
Ahaz Sept. 1-1-	16		Aug. 26.	17	198
	2		Aug. 15.	18	199
	3		Aug. 4.	19	200
	4		July 23.	20	201
Feb. 1. the 20th of Jotham	5	Hoshea	Feb. 1.	1	202
	6		Jan. 21.	2	203
	7		Jan. 10. Dec. 30.	3 4	204
	8		Dec. 18	5	205
	9		Dec. 7	6	206
	10		Nov. 26.	7	207
	11		Nov. 15.	8	208
	12		Nov. 3.	9	209
	13				210
	14		Mar. 1.	1	211
	15		Feb. 18.	2	212
Hezekiah Dec. 1-1-	16		Feb. 7	3	213
	2		Jan. 26.	4	214
	0		Jan. 15.	5	215
	4		Jan. 3. Dec. 23.	6 7	216
	5		Dec. 11.	8	217
	6		Dec. 3.	9	218
		Samaria taken			219

The kingdom of Israel ended.

Scriptural Authorities.

2 Kings xvi. 1, 2. In the seventeenth year of Pekah, Ahaz began to reign, and reigned sixteen years.---ch. xvii. 1. In the twelfth year of Ahaz began Hoshea to reign over Israel nine years.---ch. xv. 30. Hoshea reigned in the twentieth year of Jotham.

2 Kings xviii. 1. In the third year of Hoshea, Hezekiah began to reign.---v. 9. in the fourth year of Hezekiah, which was the seventh of Hoshea, Samaria was besieged.---v. 10. and at the end of three years they took it, even in the sixth year of Hezekiah, that is the ninth of Hoshea.

EXPLANATION.

The 17th year of Pekah begins Aug. 26, 198. Ahaz began to reign Sept. 1. Jotham's 16th year commences Feb. 1. or Mar. 1. after which he died.---The mention of the 12th year of Ahaz shews, that Hoshea had then reigned nine years, after which he was deposed, and the time of his deposition is not reckoned. He is restored as a vassal, Mar. 1. 211. when his second reign commences. Feb. 7, 213, begins the third year of it, and Hezekiah began to reign Dec. 1. of the same year. The fourth of Hezekiah begins Dec. 1, 216, and the 7th of Hoshea, Dec. 23. After this Salmanassar besieges Samaria, (we may suppose) Mar. 1, 217. The second year of the siege ends Mar. 1, 219.---The ninth year of Hoshea ends Nov. 22, 219. and the sixth of Hezekiah, Dec. 1.

Samaria was taken, and the Israelites carried away captive, between Mar. 1. and Nov. 22, consequently in the third year of the siege, in the 9th of Hoshea, and the 6th of Hezekiah.

The remainder were carried away, together with Manasseh, in his 21st year, and in 4030 of the Julian period, by Apharadan, Apronadius or Asnaphar, and the land of Israel was filled with foreigners, sometimes subject to the kings of Judah. 2 Chron. xxxiv. The prophet Isaiah had foretold this second and total extirpation 65 years before, ch. vii. 8.

A

SYNCHRONISTICAL TABLE,

SHEWING

The Connexion *of* Sacred *and* Profane

HISTORY

From the Destruction *of* SAMARIA *to*

XERXES.

Jul. Per.	Olym.		Hezek.	Kingdom of Judah.		Assyrian Empire incl. Babylon.	
3986	15	1	6	Kingdom of Israel	7	Esar-haddon destroys	
		2	7	overthrown	8	Samaria	
		3	8		9	is overcome by the Tyrians	
		4	9		10	besieges Tyre five years	
3990	16	1	10		11		
		2	11		12		
		3	12		13		
		4	13		14		
	17	1	14	Sennacherib	1	Nadius or Sennacherib	
		2	15	defeated	2	is slain	
		3	16		1	Chinzirus and Porus	
		4	17		2		
	18	1	18		3		
		2	19		4		
4000		3	20		5		
		4	21		1	Jugæus	
	19	1	22		2		Esarhaddon
		2	23		3		
		3	24		4		
		4	25		5	Babylon	K. of Assyria
	20	1	26	Treaty with Babyl.	1	Mardokempad	
		2	27		2		
		3	28		3		
		4	29		4		
4010	21	1	1	Manasseh	5		
		2	2		6		
		3	3		7		
		4	4		8		
	22	1	5		9		
		2	6		10		
		3	7		11		
		4	8		12		
	23	1	9		1	Arkian	
		2	10		2		
		3	11		3		
		4	12		4		
	24	1	13		5		
		2	14		*	Interregnum	
		3	15		*		
		4	16		1	Belibus	

	Empire of the Assyrians over the Medes.		Kingd. of the Lydians.	Kingd. of Egypt.
	carries away the If-	3	Gyges	
	raelites to Halah, and	4		
	to Habor by the river	5		
	of Gozan and the	6		
	cities of the Medes.	7		
		8		
		9		
	goes into Egypt, and	10		
	before Jerusalem is	11		Tirhaka
	overthrown.	12		
	the Medes revolt,	13		
	erect a democracy,	14		
	then chuse a king	15		
1	Dejoces	16		
2		17		
3		18		
4		19		
5		20		
6		21		
7		22		
8		23		
9		24		
10		25		
11		26		
12		27		
13		28		
14		29		
15		30		
16		31		
17		32		
18		33		
19		34		
10		35		
11		36		
12		37		
13		38		
14		1		
15		2	Ardys	
16		3		
17		4		

4030

Jul. Per.	Olym.		Man.	Kingdom of Judah.	Assyr. Empire over Babylon.	
	25	1	17		2	
		2	18		3	
		3	19		1	Apronadius
		4	20		2	
4030	26	1	21	Manasseh is carried	3	takes Manasseh
		2		away to Babylon;	4	
		3	22	the year of his cap-	5	
		4	23	tivity not mentioned	6	
	27	1	24	in scripture.	1	Rigebelus
		2	25		1	Messessimor
		3	26		2	
		4	27		3	
	28	1	28		4	
		2	29		*	Interregnum
		3	30		*	
		4	31		*	
	29	1	32		*	
		2	33		*	
		3	34		*	
		4	35		*	
	30	1	36		*	End of the kingdom
		2	37		1	Assarhaddon king
		3	38		2	of Babylon
		4	39		3	
4050	31	1	40		4	
		2	41		5	
		3	42		6	
		4	43		7	
	32	1	44		8	
		2	45		9	
		3	46		10	
		4	47		11	
	33	1	48		12	
		2	49		13	
4060		3	50		1	
		4	51		2	Saosducheus
	34	1	52		3	
		2	53		4	
		3	54		5	
4065		4	55		6	

Assyrian Empire over the Medes.	Kingd. of the Lydians.	Kingdom of Egypt.
28	5	
29	6	
30	7	
31	8	
32	9	
33	10	
34	11	
35	12	
36	13	
37	14	
38	15	1 Psammetichus
39	16	2
40	17	3
41	18	4
42	19	5
43	20	6
44	21	7
45	22	8
46	23	9
47	24	10
48	25	11
49	26	12
50	27	13
51	28	14
52	29	15
53	30	16
1 Phraortes	31	17
2	32	18
3	33	19
4	34	20
5	35	21
6	36	22
7	37	23
8	38	24
9	39	25
10	40	26
11	41	27
12	42	28
13	43	29
14	44	30

Jul. Per.	Olym.			Kingdom of Judah.		Assyrian Empire comprehends Babylon.	
4066	35	1	1	Amon	7		
		2	2		8		
		3	1	Josiah	9		
		4	2		10		
4070	36	1	3		11		
		2	4		12		
		3	5		13		
		4	6		14		
	37	1	7		15		
		2	8		16		
		3	9		17		
		4	10		18		
	38	1	11		19		
		2	12		20		
4080		3	13		1	Chyniladan	
		4	14		2		
	39	1	15		3		
		2	16		4		
		3	17		5		
		4	18		6		
	40	1	19		7		
		2	20		8		
		3	21		9		
		4	22		10		
4090	41	1	23		11		
		2	24		12		
		3	25		13		
		4	26		14		
	42	1	27		15		
		2	28		16		
		3	29		17		
		4	30		18		
	43	1	31	Battle of Megiddo.	19	Nabopol. seizes	
		2	1	Jehoiakim	20	the kingdom	
4100		3	2		21	of Babylon	
		4	3		22	Exped. against Nec.	
	44	1	4	Jerusalem taken,	1	Nabopol.	Sarac
		2	5	under the Babylonians	2	drives the	king of
		3	6	3 years, then revolts.	3	Egyptians	Assyria
		4	7	beginning of the captivity, according to the Jews, 3023 car. away	4	out of Asia, lays Judah waste	

Assyrian Empire over the Medes.		Kingdom of the Lydians.		Kingdom of Egypt.	
15		45		31	
16		46		32	
17		47		33	
18		48		34	
19		49		35	
20		1	Sadyattes.	36	
21		o		37	
22	is slain by the Assyr.	3		38	
3	Cyaxares	4		39	
2	Nineveh besieged	5		40	
3	by the Scythians.	6		41	
4		7	War with the	42	
5		8	Milesians.	43	
6		9		44	
7		10		45	
8		11		46	
9		12		47	
10		1	Halyattes	48	
11		2		49	
12		3		50	
13		4		51	
14		5		52	
15		6	Temple of Diana	53	
16		7	burnt.	54	
17		8		1	Necho.
18		9		2	
19		10		3	
20		11		4	
21		12		5	
22		13		6	
23		14		7	
24		15		8	
25		16		9	overcomes
26		17		10	Josiah.
27		18		11	
28		19		12	
29		20	sends presents to	13	is defeated near
30	Cyaxares routs the	21	Delphi.	14	Carchemish.
31	Scythians.	22		15	
32		23		16	

Jul. Per.	Olymp.		Kingdom of Judah,		Aſſyrian Empire over Babylon.	
	45	1	8		5	
		2	9		6	
		3	10		7	
		4	11 Jehoiakim car. to Bab.		8 takes Jeruſ.	
4110	46	1	1 Zedekiah		9	
		2	2		10 makes	Solar
		3	3		11 peace	Eclipſe
		4	4 goes to Babylon		12	May 17.
	47	1	5		13	Nineveh
		2	6		14	deſtroyed
		3	7		15	
		4	8		16	
	48	1	9 is beſieged and		17 beſieges Jeruſalem	
		2	10			
			11 carried to Bab.		18	
4120		3	firſt of the	End of the	19 deſt. the temp. and cit.	
		4	captivity.	kingdom	20 ſubdues Elam, Me-	
	49	1		of Judah.	21 ſech, Thubal.	
		2			1 Nabopolaſſar II.	
		3			2 Dream. Expedition	
		4			3 againſt the	
	50	1			4 Tyrians.	
		2			5	
		3			6	
		4			7	
4130	51	1			8	
		2			9	
		3			10	
		4			11	
	52	1			12	
		2			13	
		3			14 Tyre demoliſhed	
		4			15 Expedition into	
	53	1			16 Egypt.	
		2			17	
4140		3			18	
		4			19	
	54	1			20	
		2			21	
		3			22	
4145		4			23	

Assyrian Empire over the Medes.		Kingdom of the Lydians.		Kingdom of Egypt.	
33	Lydian war	24		17	
34		25		1	Psammis
35		26		2	
36		27		3	
37		28		4	
38	Bat. with the Lyd.	29	Battle and peace	5	
39	Nineveh besieged	30	with the Medes.	6	
40	taken	31		1	Apries
1	Astyages	32		2	
2		33		3	Subdues the Sid.
3		34		4	War with the
4		35		5	Tyr. and Cyp.
5		36		6	
6		37		7	goes into Syria.
7		38		8	
8		39		9	
9		40		10	
10		41		11	
11		42		12	
12		43		13	
13		44		14	
14		45		15	
15		46		16	
16		47		17	
17		48		18	
18		49		19	
19		50		20	
20		51		21	
21		52		22	
22		53		23	
23		54		24	
24		55		25	is deposed
25		56		1	Amasis
26		57		2	
27		1	Crœsus	3	
28		2		4	
29		3		5	
30		4		6	
31		5		7	
32		6		8	

Jul. Per.	Olymp.			Kingdom of Babylon.
4146	55	1	24	Jehoiachin ſet at liberty.
		2	25	Nebuchadnezzar in exile, during which
		3	26	Evil Merodach has the title of king,
		4	27	Nitocris adminiſters the government.
4150	56	1	28	
		2	29	
		3	30	
		4	31	Nebuchadnezzar reſtored
	57	1	32	
		2	33	
		3	34	
		4	35	
	58	1	36	
		2	37	
4160		3	38	
		4	39	
	59	1	40	
		2	41	
		3	42	
		4	43	
	60	1	1	Ilvarodam
		2	2	
		3	1	Niricaſſolaſſar
		4	2	
4170	61	1	3	
		2	4	Laboroſoarchod, nine months
		3	1	Nabonnadius
		4	2	Babylon taken
	62	1	3	the kingdom tributary
		2	4	
		3	5	
		4	6	
	63	1	7	
		2	8	
4180		3	9	
		4	10	
	64	1	11	
		2	12	
		3	13	
		4	14	Nabonnadius rebels

King-

Kingdom of the Medes.		Kingdom of the Lydians.		Kingdom of Egypt.	
33		7		9	
34		8		10	
35	Astyages deposed	9		11	
1	Cyrus	10		12	
2		11		13	
3		12	sends to Delphi	14	
4		13		15	
5	subdues Lydia	14	is taken prisoner	16	
6	also Jonia, Caria, Cilicia		End of the	17	
7	and in time all the upper		kingdom	18	
8	Asia.		of the	19	
9			Lydians	20	
10				21	
11				22	
12				23	
13				24	
14				25	
15				26	
16				27	
17				28	
78				29	
19				30	
20				31	
21	takes the title of the great king, accord-			32	
22	ing to Ptolomy			33	
23				34	
24				35	
25	takes Babylon			36	
26	the first year of the Jewish deliverance;			37	
27	some of them return---they attempt to			38	
28	rebuild the temple but are prevented--- Daniel's vision, ch. x. 1.			39	
29	Cyrus's expedit. against the Massagetæ			40	
1	Cambyses			41	
2				42	
3				43	
4				44	
5	invades and conquers Egypt.			½	Psammenitus
6					End of the king-
7					dom of Egypt.
8	dies. Magus seizes the kingdom; is soon slain.				

Jul. Per.	Olymp.		Kingdom of Babylon.	
	65	1	15	
		2	16	
		3	17	Nabonnadius slain
		4		End of the kingdom of Babylon.
4190	66	1		
		2		
		3		
		4		
	67	1		
		2		
		3		
		4		
	68	1		
		2		
4200		3		
		4		
	69	1		
		2		
		3		
		4		
	70	1		
		2		
		3		
		4		
4210	71	1		
		2		
		3		
		4		
	72	1		
		2		
		3		
		4		
	73	1		
		2		
4220		3		
		4		

King-

Kingdom of the Medes.

1 Darius Hystaspis, or Medus
2 Babylon besieged
3 Babylon taken
4 Babylon destroyed. End of the Captivity.
5 The rebuilding of the Temple begun
6
7
8
9 The Temple finished
10
11
12
13
14
15
16
17
18
19
20
21
22
23
24
25
26
27
28
29
30
31 Battle of Marathon on the 6th of the month Boëdromion
32
33 Xerxes declared successor and king
34
35 Egypt rebels
36 Darius dies.

REMARKS

ON THE

Egyptian Hiſtory,

In the firſt Part of the

UNIVERSAL HISTORY,

By JOHN SOLOMON SEMLER.

THE CONTENTS.

RE-

REMARKS

ON THE

EGYPTIAN HISTORY, &c.

SECTION I.

LEST the reader ſhould expect more than is intended in this eſſay towards illuſtrating the Egyptian Chronology, it is neceſſary to premiſe, firſt, that it is not our deſign to examine or confute the different ſyſtems of Egyptian chronology.

2. That we are far from being perſuaded, that theſe obſervations place the Egyptian chronology in an unexceptionable light. We only pretend to treat the ſubject with the ſame freedom of ſentiment as Marſham, Newton, and others, have uſed in the ſame undertaking. We propoſe our conjectures, and ſubmit them to the readers free judgment, and though they may appear to claſh with the opinion of our ſuperiors in the learned world, we are not chargeable with preſumption, as we do not offer formally to confute them. All we intend, is only to pave the way for a more cloſe examination, and a more deciſive teſt of the current opinions; and tho' all the doubts we have raiſed ſhould be exploded, yet they will appear of ſome utility to this part of chronology. The more extravagant the errors are into which perſons of great erudition have run, in their endeavours to find a clue through all theſe intricacies, the leſs are theſe

obſer-

obſervations to be indiſcriminately rejected on account of any novelties they contain. We ſhall deliver them in the order obſerved by the authors of the Univerſal Hiſtory.

SECT. II.

Thot's Pillars.

As to the poſſibility of the events mentioned in the Egyptian hiſtory, and the preſervation of them, we ſhall avoid enlarging on them. In general they admit of no diſpute, and occur frequently in the ancient writers, in pillars, inſcriptions, and other hiſtorical monuments, and the Egyptian ſepulchres and art of preſerving dead bodies a thouſand years, are particularly well known; yet it is to be previouſly obſerved, that the celebrated pillars of Thot in the (A) land of Siriad, are not to be

(A) Amidſt the multiplicity of opinions (1) among the learned, none of them ſeem to have clearly made out, what country is meant by the land of Siriad; we ſhall not pretend to a greater perſpicuity than others, but only ſubjoin theſe obſervations, 1ſt, that Joſephus's account (2) relating the very ſame things of Seth which Manetho attributes to Mercury, is of no conſiderable uſe; for he not only delivers theſe things as antient Jewiſh traditions, but probably took them out of Manetho, from a conceit that they were more applicable to Seth; whereas the particular attachment of the Egyptians to aſtronomy, ſhews that any obſervations in that ſcience, rather belong'd to them than to the Hebrews, eſpecially in ſuch remote antiquity. At leaſt, that the Egyptians firſt received ſuch traditions from the Jews, is void of all foundation. The opinion therefore, that theſe pillars were in the land of Syriath or Syria, falls likewiſe to the ground, as it ariſes from that prejudice. 2. The opinion of M. Dodwell, that this name derives from the river Syris or Nilus, is no leſs improbable, it being uſed by none of the antient writers for any particular part of Egypt, contiguous to the Nile, but frequently denotes the whole land in general; nor would this point out preciſely

(1) *Univerſal Hiſt. Vol.* I. 7190. (2) *Joſephus, lib.* 1. *antiq.*

be reckoned among theſe without certain reſtrictions. Manetho aſſigns them a date beyond the deluge;

preciſely the ſituation of theſe pillars, as ſo large a tract of Egypt is watered by the Nile. 3. It likewiſe appears from hence, that Manetho did not mean the pillars which were to be ſeen near Thebes; as it is difficult to conceive why he ſhould omit the common name of this part of the country, and as thoſe were ſubterraneous paſſages, and walls with inſcriptions, which cannot with any propriety be termed pillars; beſides, theſe vaults were made long ſince the age of the pillars, and it is unaccountable, that Pauſanias and Ammianus in their account of theſe walls, ſhould have paſſed over ſuch a particular circumſtance, as that Mercury was the author of theſe inſcriptions, which the Egyptians would not have failed to have conſtrued as a divine proof of that antiquity on which they ſo highly valued themſelves. 4. The conjecture of father Goar will appear likewiſe equally groundleſs, (3) that this appellation belongs to the iſle of Seria, if we conſider how improbable it is, that Mercury ſhould have compoſed theſe inſcriptions in an iſland of Ethiopia, and that the Egyptians ſhould not appropriate them particularly to themſelves, and remove ſuch valuable monuments into their own country. As therefore it is highly probable, or rather certain, that theſe pillars have been preſerved in Egypt, and as neither the Greek, nor the other geographical names of Egypt are applicable to them, we take the liberty to offer the following conjecture. In the Coptic tongue, which may very naturally be uſed here, *Ri*, *ſignifies the Sun*, and is often altered to *Cheri*, *Sari*, or according to a common dialect in Egypt, *Seri* or *Siri*; and from hence Manetho adding to it a Greek termination, gives the name of *Sirikos* or *Siriacos*, and Σειριακὴν γῆν to that diſtrict or *Nomos* of Egypt, which being the name of the Sun was called Heliopolis. ---This obſervation might be corroborated from that of de Pinedo, a learned Jew, (4) were it true, that the city Heliopolis was by the Greeks called Thebes; and likewiſe from Stephanus (5) according to whom there was in the Nomos of Thebes, a city of the name of Mercury, and

(3) *Goar ad Syncell. p.* 12.
(4) *De Pinedo ad Steph. Byzant*, Ἡλιούπολις n. 6, *et* 8.
(5) *Stephanus in* Ἑρμούπολις.

deluge, when Thot is ſuppoſed to have inſcribed ſeveral matters on them in *ſacred letters*, but which another hand has tranſlated into the preſent characters (B). As to the contents of theſe inſcriptions, there are no circumſtantial accounts of them extant, but we are inclined to think them ſomething

thing

and, poſſibly, from its having in it ſuch a famous memorial of him; but that is an overſight of thoſe writers, for Herodotus and all geographers, make Thebes and Heliopolis two different places. The different readings of this word may be accounted for from its occurring ſo ſeldom, and its affinity with other words, thus by an eaſy miſtake of Δ for Α, Σειριακὴ has been altered to Σειριαδὴ.

(B) The compilers of the univ. hiſt. have given a more explicite account of this tranſlation (6) and in their notes endeavoured to illuſtrate it with ſeveral obſervations. It is certain, that the expreſſion εἰς τὴν ἑλληνίδα φωνὴν muſt be erroneous, for the uſe of Greek in Egypt could not be ſo early, and it is inconceivable on what account that tongue ſhould be preferred to the Egyptian, but the alteration propoſed by the compilers of εἰς τὴν ἐλλειοχον for ἑλληνίδα, ſeems to us inſufficient for rectifying the miſtake; it is ſomewhat too forced, and the reſemblance of the letters, and the propriety of the alteration of the words are not very apparent. We apprehend therefore, that the true reading may be diſcovered by ſubſtituting in lieu of the former expreſſion, εἰς τὴν ἄλλην ἴνθα φωνὴν where poſſibly the junction of the two words according to the ancient mode of writing, occaſioned a copiſt to miſtake them for ἑλληνιθα. But the following reading, may perhaps appear ſtill more eligible, εἰς τὴν ἄλλην διάφωνον, i. e. διάλεκτον, for the preceding words are ἑρμηνευθεισῶν ἐκ τῆς ἱερᾶς διαλέκτε, εἰς τὴν ἄλλην διαφωνον, a connection quite regular and uſual, and at once ſhews the propriety of the alteration. This different dialect is then contraſted with the ſacred, and meant to ſignify the moſt current. And it is well known that Thebes, Alexandria, and many other places in Egypt had their peculiar idioms, at leaſt, it is undoubted, that the Greek is quite out of the queſtion here, theſe books being accounted by the Egyptians prior to any knowledge they had of the Grecians.

(6) *Part* 1. *Univ. Hiſt.* §. 605.

thing very different from a liſt of kings, and the years of their reigns; not the former for two reaſons, *firſt* on account of the time when they were compoſed, that is, according to the Egyptians themſelves, before the deluge, when their country could have but few kings; and neither the tranſlators, nor the Egyptian prieſts give the leaſt intimation, that they have continued ſuch a pretended table of the ſucceſſion of kings; and it could have been neither neceſſary, nor on many accounts intelligible. *Secondly*, the title which Syncellus (C) gives to the extract which Manetho made of theſe inſcriptions, contradicts any ſuch idea of them. Speaking of Manetho, he ſays, χρηματισας, which rather imports a prediction than a narration of events; to which may be added, that Manetho's letter which the ſaid monk has cited, betrays the contents of the book *Sothis*, and what end Manetho chiefly propoſed to himſelf in theſe inſcriptions, for in his dedication to Ptolomy Philadelphus, he declares that he had a ſtrong deſire of ſearching into futurity. We are therefore of opinion, that the ſubject of theſe inſcriptions were ſome aſtrological predictions relating to this world, and according to Abulpharajus, (D) one of them came to paſs in the deluge which a little preceded the times of Thot; and another part of theſe inſcriptions is ſaid to have been the ſciences then cultivated.

SECT. III.

The ſacred books.

The Egyptian hiſtory makes frequent mention of the ſacred writings or books. We cannot ſuppoſe the contents of theſe to turn wholly, or chiefly on their civil revolutions and ſtate affairs; for the prieſts

(C) P. 31. Edit. Venetæ.
(D) Abulpharaius hiſt. dyn. p. 6, 7.

priests had the superintendency of these sacred writings, to conduct and continue them; and it is certain, that under this appellation were also included the writings of Mercury, which chiefly consist of theology, astronomy, physic, and natural philosophy. These histories of their kings were composed in the Egyptian language, but not without a considerable mixture of the hieroglyphics or emblems, as may be inferred from a passage in Plutarch (*c*) where it is said, that the Egyptians in their monuments have expressed Ochus the cruel king of Persia, under the representation of a sword. These two kinds of sacred writings are distinguished here in order to enable us to form a better judgment of the supposed destruction and interpolation of the Egyptian records, which is said to have been first introduced by Cambyses. This seems a groundless supposition, or at least matters have been exceedingly exaggerated. Cambyses, indeed, having plundered the temple, carried away the sacred books, but it doth not follow therefore, that the Egyptian priests in compiling a fresh set of annals inserted abundance of fictions, tales, and dubious matters, which produced the obscurity and inextricable perplexity of the Egyptian chronology. It is besides, here taken for granted, that these writings could not possibly escape the king's hands, that there was but a copy or two of them, that both kinds of sacred writings were equally involved in the calamity, that one of them corresponded with the Bible in point of chronology, more than the other, and that the inconceivable antiquity of the world, and of the Egyptian monarchy, hath not been equally maintained in both. All this is highly improbable, and void of any satisfactory proofs; at least, it cannot be inferred from thence, that these memorials were of

(*c*) De Iside, p. 332, edit. frobeniam.

of two kinds, that the ancient were the genuine authentic ones, and thoſe that were compoſed after were imperfect and erroneous. But allowing theſe conceits to be true, yet the prieſts have ſupplied all theſe loſſes, from the innumerable old pillars, edifices, and eſpecially the ſepulchres, where are preſerved the corpſes and images of the deceaſed monarchs.

SECT. IV.

I come now, with all poſſible brevity, to give an account, or rather liſt of the writers of Egyptian hiſtory, or whoſe works have contributed towards the illuſtration of it, but of whom little more hath been tranſmitted to us, than a bare mention of their names, or a few fragments of no great utility. Sanchoniatho, whoſe αιγυπτιακα, and a treatiſe on the natural philoſophy of Mercury, is mentioned by Suidas, would be indiſputably the moſt ancient, were not the antiquity of this writer, and of all the works attributed to him, expoſed to objections not eaſily ſurmounted; and eſpecially with reſpect to the laſt compoſition, few ancient writers making mention of it; and it being not very clear from whence Suidas drew his authorities, or what credit they deſerve. Hellanicus, Hecatæus, and Eudoxus, are entitled to our firſt notice. (C) As the authors

(C) To ſpecify all the writers who make mention of theſe hiſtorians, would carry us too far, and be of no great uſe; for thoſe who are curious of knowing them, may conſult Voſſius's diſſertation on the greek hiſtorians, and Fabricius's bibliotheca Græca. However, ſome notice muſt be taken of the more eminent; the firſt is Hecatæus, of this name there were two celebrated writers, one of them diſtinguiſhed by the ſurname of Mileſius, from the city Miletus, by way of diſtinction from the other called Abderitanus, from Abdera a city in Thrace.

thors of several historical and geographical accounts of most of the then known countries,

Thrace. The Milesian is of great antiquity, relating the events or rather the fables of the remotest times, being by Herodotus, nicknamed the fabulator; he lived in the time of Darius Hystaspis. We cannot agree with Vossius Fabricius and others, who attribute to him, the famous descriptions of the earth; Stephanus would not have made so frequent use of such a fabulous writer, nor can we suppose that the three parts of the world were so throughly known in the early times in which he lived; so that all that seems of right to belong to him, are some genealogies and histories which he doubtless took care to intermix with his fables. But the second is the person here mentioned, he lived in Egypt in the time of Ptolomæus Lagus, and he it is, in all probability, who wrote the Περιηγησις Αιγυπτω the contents of which are geographical and historical. Hence it was, that Plutarch drew his intelligence, and thus, beyond all question, the book mentioned by Laertius, is an extract from this. He likewise gives an account of the Jews, on occasion of his journey through Palestine. Altho' Stephanus, in his Geography, expresly calls him *Abderites*, yet he is sometimes, by mistake, called *Miletus*.

Instead of *Cosmes*, Vossius has *Cosme*, which is wrong; Alexander the grammarian is mentioned by Stephanus; as is Aristagoras by Plutarch in his book of Isis, and by Laertius and Stephanus. The four following occur among others in Athenæus, and Ptolomy is cited by Clemens Alexandrinus, and Syncellus. To these may be added Palæphatus, an Egyptian, who wrote of the history and Philosophy of his country; Appianus himself makes mention of his own Αιγυπτιακα; Aratus Cnidius, to whom the unknown author of the life of the poet Aratus, attributes an Egyptian history; Charon, who wrote of the most remarkable actions of the Egyptian priests and kings; Evagoras, surnamed Lindus, in the isle of Rhodes, Lysimachus of Alexandria, mentioned by Josephus contra Appion. Likewise many illustrations of Egyptian history, as Leo of the gods of Egypt, Nicomachus of the festivals, Ister of the colonies, Istrus of the city of Ptolemy, &c.

especially

especially of Egypt, and frequently quoted by Plutarch *(e)* and others, as authorities in Egyptian history. Laertius *(f)* mentions a treatise of Hecatæus on the *Egyptian Philosophy*, which we imagine may be a piece of the Περιηγησις Αιγυπτυ so often mentioned by Stephanus. We omit a multitude of ancient historians, mythologists, and geographers, who all mention the Egyptian affairs, many of them indeed but cursorily; and shall confine ourselves to the chief of those who treat professedly upon the history of this nation. These are Cosmes, Alexander, surnamed Polyhistor, Appion; in confutation of whose Αιγυπτιακα Josephus has purposely written two books; Aristagoras, Asclepiades, whom we shall mention in speaking of the Theban kings; Apollonius of Rhodes, Asclepiades, Lycias, Lynceus of Samos, Ptolomy Mendesius, together with other writings, the authors of which are not known. Such were the Genethlia of Horus, the Κυρανιδες (D) and γενικα

(e) Plutarch de Iside passim. *(f)* Laertius in proemio.

(D) Various are the opinions of the learned concerning this word. Scaliger, Reinesius, and others (7) derive it from the Arabic *Karaa*, which signifies Koran or κυρανις, i. e. a collection. Others suppose this name to be no other than that of the author of the book, Kyrannus or Kyrannides. a Persian king; but this indeed seems very far-fetched. Father Goar, who is apt to contradict Scaliger too boldly, will have the origin of it to be from the island Kyranis, and pretends that the Egyptian mercury gave this apellation to these writings, as Hippocrates gave to his that of his native island of Cos. But this island belonging to Lybia, it is not very probable that the Egyptian Mercury would give the name of a foreign island to his works.

This word κυρανιδες is mentioned twice in Syncellus (8), and in such a manner as shews the contents of these writings

(7) *Scaliger ad Euseb. Reines in var. lection. lib.* 1. c. 2. *Goar in notes ad. h. l.* (8) p. 12.

γενικα of Mercury, the Phrygian narratives, the ἑρμαϊκα, or the writings of Hermaius and several others.

SECT V.

Observations from Herodotus and Diodorus. Of the other writers relating to the Egyptian history, authentic and sufficient information may be had in the first volume of the Universal History. We shall not repeat any thing from thence, but

ings to have been astrological, for they treat of the circumvolution of the whole zodiac, in a space of more than 36000 years. Now Hermes being reputed the author of it, this piece which is divided into four κυρανιδες, seems to be a distinct work, as it doth not treat of astronomy, but of physic and chemistry; it cannot therefore, be a translation from the Arabic, but was written originally in Greek, which the date of it likewise evinces. It is, besides, well known, that a great many writings, especially medical, were attributed to Hermes. The γενικα were of the same kind, (9) and the word is of the same import as γενεθλια, this science being in great vogue among the Egyptians, no less than the Babylonians, grounded on a pretended influence of the stars on this world; therefore the opinion of Scaliger (10) who compares the תולדות of Moses with these γενικα, has little probability either in respect of the contents, or of its meaning in the Greek language.

The Phrygian memoirs were in great repute among the ancient writers, and the Egyptians made the author of them to be no less a person than Hercules, the son of Nilus, one of their most ancient kings. (11) Plutarch in his dissertation on Isis, cites a passage from them; according to which, Typhon was a son of Isæacus, and he of Hercules. These Phrygian chronicles must not be confounded with those which Stephanus (12) and Plutarch attribute to the abovementioned Alexander, which related to the ancient history of Greece.

(9) *Syncell. p.* 28. *et p.* 41. (10) *Scaliger ad Eufeb.* (11) *Cicero de nat. Deor. l.* 3. c. 16. (12) *Stephanus voce* Γαλλας. (13) *Plutarchus de musica p. m.* 549. *edit.* Froben.

but only offer a few observations which may direct to a right judgment of Manetho's Dynasties; such are the following upon Herodotus.

I. That he obtained his list of the Egyptian kings from the priests at Byblus.

II. That they informed him of 365 in all, who had reigned over that country; so that there are no vestiges to be found in him of the subordinate governments of lieutenants, who were reckoned, as some believe, among the kings, which swells them to so great a number. This conjecture is ill founded, as the vice-roys could not be put on a level with the actual kings in these records, without a considerable diminution of their honour; whereas the Egyptians had a fairer plea for their pretended antiquity, from the pretence of a succession of real kings through such a prodigious length of time. More shall be said on this head, when we come to treat on Manetho's Dynasties.

III. That Herodotus has given an account only of those kings, of whom something remarkable, and at the same time probable, was transmitted; therefore he makes no mention of 330 kings betwixt Menes and Sesostris, nor of the 12 kings who reigned at one time; so that we cannot conclude that the kings he mentions were the only series in the Egyptian rolls of his time.

IV. That according to the computation of those times, Menes was 11340 years before Sethos, and that from the admission of the 12 Gods among the 8 old ones, to king Amasis, was 17000 years; and from Myris to the coming of Herodotus into Egypt, not quite 900. This observation serves to shew what conformity there is betwixt Herodotus and Manetho, in these excessive numbers.

N Of

Of Diodorus Siculus it may be remarked.

1st, That the contents of his 3 first books are very fabulous, even in his own opinion, consequently that the most ancient Egyptian memorials are of the same kind.

2dly, That these 3 books reach to the Trojan war, which, in respect to the Egyptian history, is only to be understood of the greatest part, and reaches to the time of king Proteus, consequently in all the accounts preceding this time, little certainty is to be expected.

3dly, That from Menes to the 180th olympiad, includes 18000 years, in which space are computed 470 kings and 5 queens.

4thly, That he, like Herodotus, has given an account only of the most distinguished kings, tho' his number exceeds that of the former, and he has punctually set down the intervals of the unknown kings. So that he also agrees pretty well with Manetho in the multitude of kings, and exorbitant computations, of which, as from Herodotus, we have cited but a few.

SECT. VI.

Of the Egyptian Chronicles.

We now come to the table of Egyptian kings as digested by Christian chronologers. As the Dynasties of Manetho in point of time and accuracy precede others, we shall first examine them, but so as previously to justify our disposition; since some follow Syncellus and adopt an old Egyptian chronicle, as prior to Manetho's Dynasties, and consider the latter as struck out from the former. Marsham (E) is of opinion, that the Dynasties of Manetho, were not very different from the method of this old pretended chronicle; and this manifest congruity, has induced the learned Des

(E) Marsham, canon chronic. p. 2. §. 2.

Des Vignoles (F) to think, that this Egyptian chronicle was firſt compoſed in Euſebius's time from Manetho, and publiſhed as a diſtinct Egyptian annal. We apprehend, on the contrary, that this is not ſo much a modern, and a groſs impoſture, as an error of Syncellus. As Manetho himſelf, in Africanus or Euſebius has either cited theſe Egyptian annals, or they have given this name to his preceding regiſters: this monk who was in other reſpects ſo diligent and ſagacious, could not well avoid judging theſe two accounts to be different, not having Manetho at hand to compare them. We ſhall firſt exhibit their perfect agreement, and then point out the occaſion of Syncellus's miſtakes.

Manetho according to Syncellus (G) contains 30 Dynaſties, ſo does this chronicle.

Manetho has given an account of 113 generations; ſo has the chronicle.

This chronicle includes 36525 years, the exact number included in Manetho. If we only take the trouble to reduce the years of Manetho's reigns of the Gods to days, as ſome Chriſtian chronologers account them no other and ſo make their amount conſiderably leſs, the deficiency will appear very ſmall, and what difference there is, will be found unavoidably to have proceeded from the copyiſt's miſtaking ſome ſimilar numerical letters by which the years and numbers were expreſſed.

Manetho treats of Gods, demi-Gods, and Men, and the chronicle of *Auritæ*, *Meſtræans*, and *Egyptians*, which gradations anſwer to the former. In this chronicle the computation of time is regulated by the cynic cycle, ſo it is likewiſe in Manetho(H). Here

(F) Chronolog. tom. p. 659. §. 4.
(G) Syncell. p. 41. et ſæpius.
(H) Syncell. p. 82. The 10th Dynaſty being in Manetho according to the cynic cycle.

Here we shall remove an objection, and at the same time detect the cause of Syncellus's mistake. This chronologer writes thus, " the computation of the Egyptian chronicle runs to vast numbers, and not the same that are assigned by Manetho, " and soon after he says, " Manetho who recorded 30 Dynasties," to which, as we apprehend, he was induced by the old chronicle, is very different in his numbers, all his 30 Dynasties including only 3555 years. However this objection may seem to make against us, it is of little weight. The last clause clearly shews Syncellus to have committed an oversight, and so to have imagined these writings to differ. He forgets what he had before observed (I) that Pannodorus, Annianus, and other chronologers, in order to remove the difficulty of the immense numbers had reckoned them but as days, and by that means considerably reduced the numbers in the years of the reigns of the gods, and thus at last reconciled the whole sum: and here he supposes 3555 years to be the number assigned by Manetho, and thinks that this chronicle differs very widely from it, because it consists of 36525 years, Manetho only of 3555 years; whereas only one of the reigns of the Gods is by Manetho computed at a much larger number. This is the source and principle of Syncellus's judgment, which being erroneous, the judgment of course cannot hold good; and we are the first that maintain, these two pieces, however distinguished by Syncellus, not to be different. Not to mention the utter improbability that Manetho should have made no use of these annals, and yet have agreed with them in the numbers. The learned Marsham (K) was well aware of such an evident harmony, but being at a loss to reconcile it with the words

(I) Syncell. p. 15, 27, 32.
(K) Marsham, canon. chron.

words above quoted, and Syncellus's opinion, he imagined an error in the reading, which he alters to και τον αὐτον (χρονον) τον Μανεθω; in opposition to all the editions, which rightly have it και ου τον αὐτον κ. τ. λ. this also led P. Goar (L) to animadvert on these words with the note *redundat* in the margin, but with so little reason, that the pretended mistake is the only foundation for it, and it is amply exploded by the last passage of Syncellus himself (M).

SECT.

(L) Goar in Syncello, p. 41.

(M) In this chronicle are three generations or titles, concerning which the learned vary. We shall therefore set down the words of Syncellus * who makes mention of them, that a judgment may be more easily formed.

"The Egyptians have an old chronicle (by which I "am apt to think, Manetho has been misled) which con-"tains 30 Dynasties or 113 generations, in a prodigious "course of years, namely 36525, wherein it differs from "Manetho; these generations are 1 the Auritæ, 2 the "Mestræans, and 3 the Egyptians." The title runs thus, The reign of the Gods according to the old chronicle.

"No time is assigned to Vulcan, being seen day and "night; the Sun, his offspring, reigned 30,000 years, "after him Saturn, and the remaining 12 gods 3984 "years; then 8 demy-gods during 217 years; these were "succeeded by 15 generations, who according to the cy-"nic cycle reigned 443 years; after these came the 16th "Dynasty of the Tanites."

We have already signified, that we apprehend these names to be the same with those mentioned by Syncellus from Manetho, as gods, demi-gods and heroes, and men. The Egyptians in Manetho are men. Now there must be a reason for distinguishing the Auritæ and Mestræans from the Egyptians; therefore the opinion of Fourmont (14) that these were a people dwelling near Abaris, seems to be invalidated by this account of Syncellus, who expressly places the gods first, who begin with the Auritæ, as undoubtedly the Egyptians do from the Tanites, and the

* *Syncell. p.* 40.

(14) *Fourmont reflex. critiqu. upon the history of the ancients l.* 2. *p.* 104.

SECT. VII.

Of the former state of these Dynasties.

As to the Dynasties of Manetho, as we find them extracted by Eusebius and Syncellus, it is hard

the Mestræans in the middle must be the heroes, to which rank the founders of a nation were usually exalted. Besides the opinion that the Auritæ and Mestræans derived their name from a certain territory in Egypt, is unsupported by any ancient geographers or other writers, as having never heard of such a name, neither do the historians mention any such kings. The etymology of the name Auritæ is by Marsham, Goar (15) and others attributed to the city Abaris, as the supposed residence of these governors and kings. Against this conjecture Perizonius objects (16) that it is not to be conceived, why this appellation of the most ancient kings should be taken from this town, being smaller than any other, and universally detested by the Egyptians, as the residence of the shepherd kings, as likewise being, from the account of Manetho himself, a town of Typhon where men were sacrificed to that tyrannical god. The compilers of the universal history (17) object farther, that this town was built late, and by the shepherd king Salatis, which together with the objection of Perizonius, remains as yet unanswered. To this we add, that the alteration of β and υ in the Greek language is not usual, or rather without a precedent, and likewise the vowel α which forms the other syllable must be omitted without any apparent reason. It is likewise evident, that these names refer to the sequel which Syncellus himself endeavoured thereby to render more intelligible. We should readily close with Perizonius's derivation of this name from the Hebrew אירדת if it could be shewn, that the Egyptians in giving names to things of their own country made use of the Hebrew language and not rather of the Coptic, which as to any affinity of derivation differs greatly from the Hebrew. This analogy in times so late is still less conceivable, as most of the accounts of the reigns of the Gods, may be accounted

(15) *Marsham canon. chron. secul. Goar in notis ad Syncellum.*
(16) *Pergon orig. Egypt. c. 11. p. 27.*
(17) *Universal History, v. 1. §. 208.*

hard to determine, whether the opinion hitherto entertained of them be a miſtaken one, or whether we

accounted the reſult of their doctrines concerning the world, and of the influence of the ſtars, things of a poſterior date. The Auritæ therefore being gods, and indeed conſtellations, we believe their name to relate thereto, but ſo as that the idea of their government remains. If inſtead of αὐρίτων, by the alteration of a ſingle letter, which has often led the antient writers into many errors Κυρίτων be ſubſtituted, there's an end to all objections. This word, and ſtill more its derivatives, Κυρανίδες and Κυρανις are well known among the Egyptians, and by them applied to the heavenly bodies, their power over the earth, and the viciſſitudes and mutations ariſing from thence. The moſt ancient writers attribute the invention of the Zodiac to the Egyptians (18) and an accurate Grecian annotator (19) obſerves, that from it they formed their 20 gods as a *ſupreme council*, giving them the 7 planets as their ſatellites or guards. Thus the Egyptians repreſented their country under the protection and government of the conſtellations, agreeably to the influences which they attributed to them. As to the name of Meſtræans, we account it to mean the deſcendants of Meſtrem or men, who after death were deified, and thus are to be diſtinguiſhed from thoſe who were originally gods, and from the kings on whom this honour was not conferred; ſuch were the kings after Menes. That the Egyptians ſhould know nothing of their own founder ſeems the more difficult to conceive, as it was the general practice of thoſe times, to confer the apotheoſis on the founders of nations. Fourmont (20) in deriving this name from a part of Egypt peculiarly called Meſtræ or Mitzraim is not better grounded than we, no ſuch diviſion of Egypt, or obſervation of the difference of ſuch appellations being demonſtrable from any old writers; neither does the authority of the Bible reach this caſe, as theſe kings muſt have reigned not over a ſingle part but over all Egypt; of which we ſhall ſpeak more largely hereafter. However, as Manetho muſt alſo have treated of the Meſtræans, but the Chriſtian chronologers omit them, they cannot

(18) *Mairot in ſomn. Scip. l.* 1. *c.* 21.
(19) *Scholiaſtes Apollonii ad l.* 4. *v.* 262.
(20) *Fourmont loc. cit.*

we only conceive an opinion not founded in fact. We submit it to the reader's judgment, and shall only lay before him the reasons of our singularity. The ancient Christian chronologers who had the use of Manetho, agree that he has composed his Egyptian history of 30 or rather of 31 Dynasties, but these chronologers themselves begin the first Dynasty with King Men or Menes, who, according to their own accounts, was the first of the merely human kings, who obtained the government, after the gods, demi-gods, and heroes. So that they exclude the reigns of the gods and heroes from the Dynasties, as if Manetho had treated of them in a particular, or at least certainly not in this method. This inference is just, tho' not expressly mentioned by them. But we are at a loss to reconcile, that in several places they plainly and expressly say, that Manetho in the first Dynasty, has treated of the reigns of the gods and heroes, as a part of the Egyptian history. We shall quote the

cannot have been kings over a part of Egypt, for if they had, these would not have failed to have inserted them, as the omission would have been entirely without cause. But being heroes and demi-gods, these writers looking upon them to be no more than fictitious, omitted them. Manetho indeed has assigned an extravagant length of time to these demi-gods, filling up with them 217 years, according to the computations of Christian chronologers; so that it admits of a conjecture, whether it be not on this account that Eratosthenes's kings begin in the year of the world 2900, whereas the other chronologers begin their Egyptian kings in 2776, from Mestrem, and that he chose the compleat number 2900 instead of 2917. To this may be added, that the first kings in Syncellus's table occurring no where, may be concluded to be utterly unknown; as Mestres, Kurides, Aristarchus, whose name appears to be corrupted, Spanius and the most antient Sesonchoses, who must have belonged to the heroic ages. But concerning this, we will not take upon ourselves to advance as certain, that these were of the Mestræans.

the principal paſſages, they being eſſential towards knowing the proper form of theſe Dynaſties and how they were left by Manetho. Syncellus (*o*) has preſerved to us the following extract from Africanus, relating to Manetho's hiſtory.

" Manetho, who lived ſince the time of Beroſus, " and was high prieſt among the idolatrous " Egyptians in the time of Ptolomy Philadel- " phus, writes in the hiſtory which he dedicates " to that king, exactly in the ſame method as " Beroſus, of 16 Dynaſties (N) or 7 Gods, who " never were in being, and yet, who, as he pre- " tends, reigned during 1985 years; the firſt of " theſe was Vulcan, and his reign is made to be " no leſs than 9000 years, which, however, ſome " chriſtian chronologers, have turned into lunar " months, and divided this number in ſuch a man-

(*o*) Syncell. in chronogr. p. 14.

(N) Here an error of the tranſcriber muſt be rectified, to give this place its true meaning. That Manetho ſhould have treated of ſeven gods in ſixteen Dynaſties, is ſomething enigmatical and flatly contradicts the other before-quoted places; according to which, ſeven gods reigned in ſix dynaſties. The firſt of them, Vulcan, being omitted, as according to the chronicle, no peculiar time is aſſigned to him; therefore, in this place of Syncellus, inſtead of ἑκκαίδεκα, the reading muſt be only ἓξ as it manifeſtly ſtands in the other places. Likewiſe, here is a miſtake in the Latin tranſlation to be adjuſted; *de ſex decim Dynaſtiis, hoc eſt de ſeptem, qui nunquam exſtiterunt, contextis mendaciis ſcribens*, where after *exſtiterunt*, *Diis* muſt be inſerted. Further rejecting the number 1985, as the amount of the reigns of the gods, the reading muſt be 11985, or as Goar 11988. From the moſt exact calculation, of the gods, demi-gods, heroes, and men, no more than four generations can be made; ſo that in the Greek, inſtead of πέντε the letter Ε denoted the number, but as has not ſeldom been the caſe, was confounded with Γ. Likewiſe, thoſe 3 generations are to be underſtood of the Auritæ as the reading hitherto has been of the Meſtræi and the Egyptians.

" manner as to make them anſwer to 365 days; " and thus, by a very extraordinary performance, " as they imagine, bring it to 724 years 6 " months and 4 days.

After this comes the table of the gods and demi-gods, with this plain inſcription πρώτη δυναστεία, as is mentioned in the *Univerſal Hiſtory*, with an account of the years of each reign, according to that computation. We will add another paſſage, which Syncellus tranſcribes from Euſebius, of the ſame import, but more explicit than the former (21).

" After this Manetho begins his hiſtory in " 30 Dynaſties including the 5 Egyptian gene- " rations, namely the gods, demi-gods, departed " heroes, and mere men, of whom Euſebius alſo " makes the following mention in his chronicle; " the Egyptians ſhew a moſt extravagant and fa- " bulous hiſtory of their gods and demi-gods, and " next of their heroes and common men; for the " moſt ancient Egyptians called a month, that is, " a ſpace of 30 days, but the demi-gods, or thoſe " who lived after them, called the *Horos*, a year, " that, is a ſpace of three months."

Syncellus proceeds in the following manner; Pannodorus has cenſured this opinion of Euſebius, but without foundation, and maintains that neither the number of days belonging to a year or to a month were known 'till the Egregori had taught them this as well as other calculations of time, from whence it proceeded that among the Egyptians, the reigns of the ſix Dynaſties of the gods comprehended each but 30 days or a month, and thus altogether made 11988 lunar months or 969 ſolar years. If theſe be added to 1058 other ſolar years of the preceeding reigns of the

(21) Syncell. Chronogr. p. 32.

the gods, (O) the total is 2027; ſo likewiſe, he makes the two dynaſties of the nine demi-gods, who never exiſted, but are admitted by him as real, amount to 214 and a half years, in lieu of the 858 *Horoi* or *Tropoi*, according to his interpretation of the years alledged, ſo that with the above 969, the total becomes 1183½.

SECT. VIII.

Continuation thereof.

From theſe paſſages Manetho appears to have aſſigned at leaſt 6 Dynaſties to ſix gods, and to have compriſed 9 heroes in 2, and ſo eight of theſe 30 Dynaſties in no wiſe relate to the reigns of men. Let us therefore compare them with that Egyptian chronicle which Syncellus diſtinguiſhes from Manetho. According to this, 8 demi-gods reigned 217 years, agreeably to the laſt cited place, where it is ſaid, that 9 demi-gods reigned 214 years, ſo that the numbers η and θ are exchanged for each other, elſe 8 or 9 would have been the numbers of both paſſages, and from this alteration proceeds the difference of years. Next the chronicle recounts 15 generations according to the cynic cycle who reigned 443 years, and after theſe the 16 dynaſties of the Tanites. Father Goar (Q) in his notes upon Syncellus, inſiſts, that the reading ſhould be δυναστειαι ιε inſtead of γενεαι ιε fifteen generations;

(O) The Greek text here, is as follows, ταυτα δε συναριθμημενα τοις προ της τουτων βασιλειοις ηλιακοις κ. τ. λ. which muſt be rectified thus, προ της τουτων βασιλειας; and this is to be underſtood of the 9000 years, attributed to Vulcan or likewiſe of the Sun, but the tranſlator not knowing what to make of it, has omitted it, and only ſet down *iidemque alijs mille quinquaginta octo ſolaribus adjuncti* where ſhould be inſerted, before *adjuncti*, *Regni ſuperioris* or ſome ſuch words.

(Q) Goar in notis ad Sync.

tions; and herein he is seconded by the learned des Vignoles, (P) but we cannot see the necessity of this alteration; for 1*st*, the variation and difference of the words is too great to be mistaken. 2*dly*, We have already shewn, that a certain number of the Dynasties relate to the gods, and demigods, and that therefore, the first 149 cannot be understood of the mere men. 3*dly*, It is no small difficulty these chronologers bring upon themselves, to fill up 15 entire Dynasties with 15 generations or persons, and 443 years, and amidst such a general and manifest congruity of this supposed chronicle; it shocks all probability, that Manetho should have run into such an excessive difference. So that the words 15 generations, must be understood agreeably to our opinion of the first reigns of the mere men who succeeded the heroes, though it cannot be punctually decided, to what Dynasty they properly belong, whether to the 15th or 14th, or to both. All this makes us at a loss to conceive what could induce Africanus, and Eusebius in their epitome's to introduce the mere men from the very first Dynasty. The only conjecture we can form about it, is, that these chronologers have filled the dynasties of gods with men, for want of gods, of whom to compose a regular history, as Syncellus affirms. It is something unheard of, that amidst so many arbitrary alterations of the order of the Dynasties, these chronologers should be charged with such an irregular procedure; which if true, must have caused very confused alterations in Manetho's dynasties (Q).

SECT.

(P) Des Vignoles, tom. 2. p. 661.

(Q) Towards the better understanding of the ancient texture of Manetho's history; we take the liberty to subjoin the following remarks. 1. The book Sothis, which is also attributed to Manetho, must not be distinguished from his history; it having relation to these Dynasties: and this

SECT. IX.

We now come to another disquisition concerning these Dynasties, that is, whether they follow after *Whether they are successive*

I. Proof.

this we conclude from a passage in Syncellus, where he cites from the book Sothis, a dedication of Manetho's to king Ptolomy, and immediately after proceeds thus, "Thus much Manetho says of the translation of the said "books of the other Mercury, and here begins his Egyp-"tian history in 30 Dynasties." Sothis therefore appears to be the name, which Manetho gave to his memorials, this word among the Egyptians importing, the rising of the Dog-star, from whence the cyclus Cynicus, a usual method of computation among them had its origin. This Star being by the Egyptians peculiarly attributed to Isis, it is probable, that Manetho has kept to the usual order, treating first of the gods, then of the demi-gods, of which number were Osiris and Isis, and to the history of Thot has annexed these prophecies, astrological remarks, and most of their speculative theology. This is apparent from a passage in the Alexandrian chronicles, (21) where it is said, Manetho has given the stars quite different names from the common ones. 2. That the Christian writers expresly make him to have composed six or seven dynasties for a like number of gods. This is farther confirmed by the title we find in Syncellus to the register of the catalogue of gods, as *the 1st* Dynasty which should have been repeated at each god, as the *2d* the *3d* &c. These Dynasties of gods followed one another in a different order from that observed in the Alexandrine chronicle and Syncellus, where the new grecian divinities are intermingled with the ancient from whom they were distinct. 3. The generations noted according to the cyclus cynicus, may possibly have been the real Egyptian kings, no such limited numbers being assigned to the preceeding reigns of the gods, and demi-gods, but a more extensive and extravagant space of time, a long succession of ages as became their dignity: At least, the mention of such a computation seems to intimate it, and there is no other apparent reason, but that the reigns of the gods may have been regulated by

(21) *Chronicon. Alexandr. p.* 38. *edit. Venetæ.*

after one another as they ſtand ſucceſſively in theſe abſtracts, or whether more than one of them exiſted at

by that cycle. 4. That Manetho, the author of three books, unqueſtionably compriſed 10 Dynaſties in each book or tome, as they were anciently termed, and inſerted in the firſt, thoſe Dynaſties which relate to the gods, demi-gods, and the celebrated ancient heroes. 5. That the chriſtian chronologers appear to have greatly curtailed the numbers of the human reigns. Many exorbitant computations are found in Herodotus and Diodorus, as of 11000 years from Menes to Sethos, and Manetho certainly was not for diminiſhing the antiquity of his countrymen. 6. Manetho himſelf appears to have made a difference betwixt his kings, and only to have recorded and enumerated the years of ſuch kings, the events of whoſe reigns were both important and uncontroverted; naming indeed the others, but giving no further account of them, than the prieſts did to Herodotus and Diodorus. This we infer from a paſſage in Syncellus, (22) who obſerves that the 113 generations of whom Manetho gives an account in his 30 Dynaſties, to the time of Alexander, includes a ſpace of no leſs than 3555 years. Upon examination of the meaning of the word γενεα or generation, it will be found, that it cannot here be any ſpace of time, as in Herodotus and other writers, in whom it denotes 30 years; for, beſides that this contradicts Herodotus and other Egyptian accounts, who compute above 340 γενεας, only from Menes, it alſo diſagrees with Manetho himſelf, who includes 30000 years in his account, and conſequently ſhould have greatly increaſed the number of γενεαι: It accords as little with the ſhorter years of Syncellus; but what more eſpecially manifeſts the impropriety of taking it for a computation of time, is, that the numbers were otherwiſe particularly ſpecified. Further it is irreconcilable with the Egyptian chronicle of which we have been ſpeaking, where 15 generations of the Cynic Cycle, are ſaid to have reigned 443 years, 8 generations 190, &c. Conſequently this word, γενεα muſt here be differently underſtood to bring it to a congruity with the

(23) *Dionyſius Halicarn. vide indicem Sylburgii.*

at the ſame time. The latter opinion has hitherto moſtly obtained, ſince Marſham firſt ſtarted the chronology which admits of ſeveral kings in Egypt at the ſame time. (R) What occaſioned it was, that the

the paſſages cited. And the only ſenſe it can be taken in, is, that of a perſon, a monarch or king, of whom all reigned during the terms aſſigned to them; and in this ſenſe it is frequently uſed by other writers, among whom it imports a ſucceſſive ſeries of ſingle perſons; thus Dionyſius ſays, (23) that the empire of the Medes came to a period, ἐπὶ τεταρτης γενεας, where agreeably to Herodotus, he admits of only 4 Median kings: he likewiſe fixes the building of the city of Rome at the 17th generation, meaning Numitor the 17th latin king. The abſolute neceſſity of this conſtruction renders it needleſs to give any more inſtances of it. Now let the γενεαι of the Egyptian chronicle be computed, and they will appear, including the Demi-Gods, to amount to 92, beſides thoſe numbers which are loſt in ſome Dynaſties, which, together with the Gods, might have completed the 113 generations mentioned by Syncellus. This appears to be the reaſon why Eratoſthenes has ſet down but 95, and Syncellus no more than 93 kings, for leaving out the Gods and Demi-Gods, they could find no more real kings even amongſt the Egyptians. This remark being proved, and acquieſced in, will, in our opinion, ſave the trouble of dividing this great number of kings into many kingdoms, contrary to the reſt of the Egyptian hiſtory; and thus of courſe this ſtructure of Egyptian chronology muſt fall to pieces.

(R) Among the many ſticklers which Marſham's opinion has every where met with, ſome have gone further than himſelf, launching out into conjectures far more bold and extravagant than their leader. Marſham allows but 4 kingdoms to have ſubſiſted at the ſame time; thoſe of Thebes, This, Memphis, and the lower Egypt: But father Pezron (24) doubles their number, adding Heracleopolis, Xois, Elephantis, Dioſpolis, and Thanis. But theſe fanciful and arbitrary diſquiſitions tend to ſubvert all hiſtorical probability and argument, which are the only grounds of a

(23) *Dionyſius Halicarn. vide indicem Sylburgii.*
(24) *Pezron. in antiq. des tems retablie.*

the other chronology far exceeds the real age of the world. But as this objection may be obviated in a different method, and when the difficulty is removed, others of more conſequence remain to embarraſs us; therefore for aſcertaining this point with the greater clearneſs and ſolidity, we take the liberty to exhibit them.

Our firſt reaſon, why we cannot abſolutely agree to the received opinion is this; had Manetho intended this multiplicity of collateral reigns and kingdoms, he could not have reduced them into one number and computation, yet he certainly does this in theſe Dynaſties, there being not only the computation of the years, which in every part of his hiſtory he treats of, ſummed up at the end of every part, but alſo at the concluſion, the ſum of all the 30 Dynaſties, of all the three parts.

To this, the learned des Vignoles (S) objects, that theſe ſums are the work of Syncellus, and not of Manetho, becauſe Syncellus was of the erroneous opinion, that theſe Dynaſties follow one another, and farther adds, that Scaliger himſelf fell into the ſame miſtake. This celebrated chronologer

a rational belief; and yet Caſpar Abel (25) inclines to ſide with them. The opinion which adds 2 kingdoms within leſs than 30 years to thoſe of Marſham, is equally improbable, that the Tanaites, and the ſhepherd kings, without any proof, that Egypt afforded territory enough to form ſo many ſovereignties, for according to Manetho's account, theſe ſhepherds ſubdued the whole country, and maintained their dominions above 500 years. As all theſe ſeveral opinions reſt only upon unſupported conjectures, without any regard had to accounts of which the truth hath not yet been diſproved, our argument ought the rather to preponderate againſt them, and the meer aſſertion of ſuch different kingdoms, tho' poſſible, cannot claim the weight of a proof, eſpecially as it is abſolutely ſingular.

(S) Des Vignoles, tom. 2. p. 787.

(25) *Abel. in Hiſtor. monarch.*

ger has his eye upon a paſſage of Scaliger, which had been obſerved by Perizonius (T) and the Dutch tranſlator (U) and hence Perizonius agrees with our opinion, though here and there he ſeems to deviate to the oppoſite ſide. But the objection is very eaſily refuted. We aſſert not only, that Syncellus is not the author of theſe aggregated ſums, but that if he were, it is yet impoſſible he ſhould have been miſtaken. Manetho himſelf, as is obvious, added thoſe computations which we ſee in the Dynaſties of the Gods, and the immenſe numbers of years through which the Egyptian hiſtory is made to extend itſelf. Now the total of all the reigns amounting to above 36000 years, and this computation being confirmed by Herodotus and Diodorus, theſe ſums appear not to proceed from any miſtake of the Chriſtian chronologers. Such an error was beſides utterly impoſſible; the Chriſtian writers, from whom Syncellus tranſcribed theſe ſums, had Manetho himſelf before them when they were digeſting this abſtract, and thus could not avoid ſeeing whether the reigns he recorded were collateral or ſucceſſive. So that this objection furniſhes nothing farther for invalidating our firſt argument.

SECT. X.

The ſecond argument is this; there is no ſuch conſtitution of Egypt recorded in any one writer of antiquity; they are, on the contrary, all unanimous that all Egypt was governed by one ſingle king. No leſs than four kingdoms are ſaid to have ſubſiſted in Egypt at the ſame time; the firſt at Thebes, the ſecond at Memphis, the third in This, and the fourth in the lower Egypt. This hypo-

(T) Univerſal Hiſtory, 1. § 607.
(U) Perizon. orig. aeg. c. 5. p. 66, 67.

hypotheſis implies many revolutions at the erection and diſſolution of theſe kingdoms, in all which ſo many remarkable events muſt have occurred, that it is impoſſible they ſhould have been entirely unknown. If it be objected that theſe writers, paſſing over the cotemporary kingdoms, treat only of the ſupreme ſtate, we cannot account how they could juſtify the omiſſion, after having taken notice of ſo many inſignificant things, eſpecially as theſe collateral kingdoms muſt have been as famous as the chief kingdom, on account of the many changes and remarkable events to which they were expoſed, from their relation to the ſupreme ſtate. There are two circumſtances which ſtrongly confirm this; *Firſt*, Herodotus, Strabo, Diodorus, and others who went into Egypt, are explicit in their accounts of Thebes and Memphis, yet ſilent as to any kingdoms denominated from thoſe cities. Of *This* they make hardly any mention, and when they ſpeak of the diviſion of Egypt, the lower Egypt does not appear, by their accounts, to have been a diſtinct monarchy from the reſt; inſtead of this, it appears, from the ſhort tranſition they make from upper Egypt to lower, that they were never diſtinct kingdoms. *Secondly*, Herodotus and Diodorus, mention it as ſomething extremely particular, that once 12 kings governed at the ſame time, dividing Egypt among themſelves; hence it follows, that they had heard nothing at all of ſo many kingdoms which had continued together through ſeveral ages, and undergone ſo many viciſſitudes amongſt one another, which implies that ſuch kingdoms never exiſted, it being quite incredible, that tranſactions of ſuch moment ſhould have lain hid from them, eſpecially having the annals of Egypt at hand, and being ſo ſo very minute in the relation of matters much leſs intereſting. (X)

SECT.

(X) Theſe Grecian writers, who yet had all poſſible acceſs to the Egyptian accounts, appear utterly to explode this diſtribution of ſo great a number of kings, as appear in the extracts of Manetho, into thoſe four kingdoms, from one time to another. Herodotus omits above 300 kings, and merely, as he ſays, for want of matter to relate of them. Diodorus likewiſe ſays, that of a vaſt number of kings, nothing could be ſaid, but that they ate and drank, and therefore omits them. Now if this great number of kings ſtood in the relation of cotemporaries to each other, then this ignorance is not poſſible. Upon the extinction of a Dynaſty in Manetho, as of *This*, *Dioſpolis*, &c. the modern chronologers maintain that it was incorporated with another, under another kingdom. Not to mention the many other circumſtances inſeparable from ſuch revolutions, this alone was ſo remarkable, that the Egyptian prieſts could not want accounts of it; conſequently neither Herodotus nor Diodorus would have omitted it, or complained that they wanted intelligence; conſequently the Egyptians muſt have been without the leaſt knowledge of this ſuppoſed conſtitution of ſo many cotemporary kingdoms. It is moreover a mere prejudice to affirm that the above hiſtorians concerned themſelves only with the kings of the ſupreme monarchy, and ſtill a greater to place many of thoſe kings at Memphis, Thebes, &c. becauſe, in Manetho's Dynaſty, they are diſtinguiſhed by thoſe appellations. There is not the leaſt trace of this to be found in them; and the more ſtreſs is laid upon it, and the more important the concluſions from it, the more fully ought it to be evidenced, So many particular diſtinctions are aſcribed to kings, whom Herodotus and Diodorus did not think worth naming, as not having any merit characteriſtical to kings, that hiſtory cannot well deſcend to more circumſtantial accuracy; and all this ariſes from the titles of the Dynaſties, without being able to defend ſuch interpretation by hiſtorical proofs, as we ſhall maintain more at large. It is equally groundleſs to attempt to convert many of theſe kings into vice-roys; Herodotus and Diodorus having

SECT. XI.

Third Proof. Our third argument is drawn from Moses's history of the Israelites, in which omitting other circumstances, we shall only examine the seven years of famine and distress in Egypt. Who can imagine that after so many repetitions of this plain expression, *all the land of Egypt* (Y)

accurately distinguished such governors and subordinate officers from the kings; and the Egyptians themselves were under no necessity of contriving a fraud which might be detected without a close scrutiny. Herodotus also affords us another argument; his account of the kings, as observed before, he had from the priests of Byblus. If then, there were so many distinct kingdoms in Egypt, how could these priests give so just an account of the other kingdoms to which they must have been ver y great strangers. Is it credible that at Thebes, This, Memphis, and other supposed royal residences, they had no records, and especially of their respective monarchs, this having been one of the first institutions of their kings. But if it be objected that all these records were compiled together at the time of Herodotus, we ask how is this possible? for each must have been separated and separately preserved, and the histories of the first kings could not have been related like that of the last, to whom all Egypt was subject; therefore, either the Egyptians themselves must have been ignorant of this, or no kingdoms could jointly subsist among them for so long a time.

(Y) Our proof seems to us sufficiently to shew that it is an error to limit the Hebrew expression to a certain part of Egypt, and this was the opinion of Meier (26) and Stillingfleet, (27) at least Perizonius (28) has not proved the contrary, when he says there is no reason for understanding this of all Egypt, this being rather more applicable to the opposite opinion, as it is insufficient to supply the immaginary impossibility of the chronology; these passages are the following. Genesis, xli. 41, 43, 44, 46, 55. chap. xlvii. 21.

(26) *Meir ad Seder Olam p.* 126. (27) *Stillingfleet in Orig. sacris l.* 5. (28) *Perizon. orig. Ægyp. c.* 5. *p.* 75.

can

it is to be underſtood only of a ſmall diſmembred kingdom; and beſides, the famine is repreſented to have been ſo extenſive as to reach Canaan and other adjacent countries. Either the reſt of the Egyptian kingdoms were exempt from this calamity, or they were not; if they were exempted, let it be ſhewn how Moſes diſtinguiſhes the other Egyptians; and this diſtinction was ſo far neceſſary, that without it, his hiſtory muſt be vague and uncertain. As no ſuch diſtinction appears, let a reaſon be produced, why the inhabitants of Moſes's Egypt did not ſeek refuge among thoſe Egyptians who were under no ſuch diſtreſs. But if they were not exempted, it is inconceivable how ſuch a ſmall kingdom as that of *This* or of lower *Egypt*, which ſome will have Moſes to mean, could afford ſuch a proviſion of corn, as to ſupply, not only themſelves and the Canaanites, but alſo the other vaſt kingdoms of Egypt.

Further, Moſes calls his Egyptian kings *Pharaoh*, without any diſtinction. Now the Egyptians themſelves allow this name to have been peculiar to their kings. Had there been more kings than one at a time, they either bore this name, or did not; if they did, Moſes has been extremely deficient in correctneſs and perſpicuity; as then it may be equally underſtood of a king of Thebes, This, Memphis, or any other king; therefore, there would be no knowing particularly on whom this divine chaſtiſement fell, and this was the more neceſſary, as the Egyptians themſelves would have rather buried it in ſilence. In a word, upon reading the books of Moſes, in events which relate to Egypt, and examining them according to the moſt natural rules of conſtruction, there are no appearances of more than one kingdom at the ſame time. From the importance of knowing whether other kings ſhared in the tranſactions of Pharaoh, we may preſume, this would not have been omitted; and without theſe extracts of Manetho, or more eſpecially the different titles of the Dynaſties, it is impoſſible that a ſingle imagination of any ſuch thing could ariſe from Moſes's narrative. The objection which ſome are for drawing from hence, ſhall be more largely conſidered in the ſequel.

SECT. XII.

Fourth Proof.

Our fourth argument is, that Joſephus's extract from Manetho relating to the ſhepherd-kings, is ſo far from being reconcileable with the oppoſite opinion, that it directly contradicts it. Manetho (*x*) writes thus, *Under our king Timæus, it was the appointment of God that an unknown people invaded the land.* We cannot enter into the reaſon why he ſhould diſtinguiſh this revolution by the name of one king, and make him ſovereign over all Egypt, by the addition *our*, had there been ſeveral kings and kingdoms at that time; nor why he is ſo inaccurate in his account, and does not particularly name what kingdom theſe unknown people firſt invaded. Marſham (*y*) indeed is for obviating this objection, as it doubtleſs occurred to him, and ſays, this Timæus was a king of Heliopolis; but as he alledges no authority from whence he took this, nor can produce any, we muſt be excuſed from acquieſcing in it on his bare word. Manetho further ſays, that the firſt ſhepherd-king *Salatis*, impoſed a tribute on upper and lower Egypt, and committed great outrages on the temples and towns, and treated the inhabitants very cruelly. This plain account of Manetho

(*x*) Apud Joſeph contr. ap. lib. 1. (*y*) Seculo 8. p. 105.

can-

cannot be underſtood otherwiſe than that the ſhepherd-kings ſubdued all Egypt; and how can we, at the ſame time, admit the kings of *Thebes*, *This*, *Memphis*, *Tanais*, and the *Shepherd-kings*; when the latter ruled over all upper and lower Egypt? Now as this muſt have been ſomething extraordinary, that one king ſhould reign over all Egypt, after it had been under the government of ſeveral kings 'till then; certainly ſo ſudden and ſingular a change would not have eſcaped Manetho's obſervation. Undoubtedly, the explicit authority of an Egyptian writer, muſt outweigh any meer conjectures, and any ſyſtem of chronology, however ſpecious and poſſible, founded thereon. Manetho further obſerves that this Salatis, under an apprehenſion of being attacked by the Aſſyrians, built fortreſſes in ſeveral places, and every where put the country in a poſture of defence. Would not an obſervant reader, here naturally aſk, why not againſt the Theban, the Thinite, the Memphian, and other kingdoms, of which Egypt at that time conſiſted, for had they ever actually been independent ſtates of Egypt, the ſhepherd-kings would have had cauſe to apprehend an inſurrection from them, as the Egyptians under their new yoke would not have failed to have ſeconded them; thus is it totally improbable that theſe ſhepherd-kings, content with their conqueſts, ſhould forbear ſubduing the other kingdoms, who were very incapable of reſiſtence, if ſuch kingdoms had actually exiſted.

SECT. XIII.

Anſwer to the firſt objection.

We now come to anſwer the objections which may be made in defence of the current opinion; the firſt objection we ſhall take from the laſt mentioned

tioned abstract of Manetho in Josephus. Manetho there writes, "that the kings of Thebes and upper Egypt had began to make an attempt to deliver their country and drive out the shepherds," consequently there must have been other kings besides the shepherds; but this is a conclusion far beyond what the objection will bear. Either Manetho must contradict himself by admitting other kings besides the shepherds, who, he says, had conquered upper and lower Egypt; or this must be differently understood, namely, that in the declension of the shepherd-monarchy, there was a general insurrection both in upper and lower Egypt. The several leaders represented the former kings in respect to those Egyptians whom they headed, to their commands and their conquests; but at length, these different parties of the revolted Egyptians united, the weaker submitting to the stronger, and in order to attain the freedom which was the end of their insurrection, put themselves under the most fortunate chief. It is clear from what Manetho says, that the expulsion of the shepherds was not effected 'till after a long and vigorous war, in which the Egyptians at length, after many vicissitudes in the field and different commanders, gradually obtained the advantage; but that at last they set up one general sovereign, appears in that Manetho attributes the accomplishment of their delivery and the subsequent government of the whole land, to but one king, after whom follows a regular succession; now this could not have been done, had there been different Kingdoms at this time.

SECT. XIV.

Of the second objection.

The second objection is taken from some passages in writings, which either make mention of, or or seem to imply several kings; of the last kind is particularly alledged, 1*st*, Genesis x. 14. where it is said, Misraim begat Pathrusim, concerning whom Bochart (Z) proves their capital city Pathros, to be the same with that called Thebes, likewise that Misraim, the name of Egypt, manifestly denotes the plural number. To this we answer, that all together shews no more, than Egypt, so early as Moses's time, was divided that into *upper* and *lower*, not that it can follow from thence, that there were also at the same time two or more kingdoms distinct from each other. This division of Egypt, was partly occasioned by the natural situation and variety of the country, partly by the greater conveniency of civil government as in other nations, but not by the existence of several independent kingdoms. As it cannot be inferred from the division of Media, Arabia, Persia, and Egypt itself, into 36 districts or nomes, that these several parts of the division were so many kingdoms; so neither does it follow from the aforesaid passage.

2*dly*, Exodus i. 9. the Egyptian king says, that his subjects are fewer than the Israelites, which cannot be understood of all Egypt. This objection, besides its weakness, proves nothing; the words only intimating the king's apprehension, that

(Z) We cite this opinion of Bochart's, and of others after him, without canvassing the general solidity of the proof advanced by him, or admitting the opinion of Hiller, who construes Pathros to be not Thebes, but the limits of lower Egypt on the other side of the Nile, and betwixt the Mediterranean and the red Sea, towards Arabia. Much less shall we follow the fantastical far-fetched Etymon of Lydiat, who derives the appellation of Ethiopians from *Ai* an island, or according to him, any piece of land, and Thebes; and accordingly joins Thebes to Ethiopia, and conceits that the former was usually comprehended in the latter.

that the Jews might in time become able to make a powerful inſurrection, which apprehenſion the king might entertain, tho' he was at the head of all Egypt, for the armies of thoſe times were not ſo very numerous. Not to mention other circumſtances with which this objection may be invalidated.

3dly, It is further alledged, that the magick arts which the Egyptians exhibited in defiance of Moſes, are quite unaccountable, if ſuppoſed to have been done out of the kingdom of Zoan, conſequently the kingdom where the Iſraelites were oppreſſed, muſt at that time have been diſtinct from other Egyptian kingdoms, ſince theſe magicians muſt elſe have travelled as far as Lybia, and Arabia, where a wanton deſtruction of the country would not have been tolerated. But this objection is very far from evincing, that on this account more Egyptian kingdoms muſt be admitted, to which the magicians travelled, to counterfeit Moſes; for the paſſages cited do not mention the time how long the waters of the Nile remained blood, therefore the magicians may have counterfeited him, and they, when this miracle had ceaſed, might have made the experiment on other waters, as in ſprings and veſſels. As to the firſt kind of paſſages, ſuch as the 2 kings vii. 6. in which Egyptian kings are mentioned in the plural number, they cannot be made to ſhew more, than that, at that time, there were more than one king in Egypt, which muſt oft have happened amidſt the conteſt for the ſucceſſion, but there are many more paſſages in which mention is made of only one king. Beſides, the circumſtances, and the connection of theſe places, account for the uſe of the plural number. After all, ſuch proofs are of too weak a nature, to eſtabliſh the contrary opinion, in oppoſition to the force of thoſe reaſonings which we have brought againſt it.

The

SECT. XV.

The third objection, upon which Marſham, and other moderns who follow him in moſt points, lay a very great ſtreſs, is, that theſe Dynaſties having various inſcriptions, always denoting a royal reſidence, conſequently more kings than one, muſt have reigned at the ſame time. But 1*ſt*, this conſequence is forced, and exceeds its premiſes. The Egyptian kings might in time have altered their reſidence, as Diodorus informs us was the caſe of Thebes and Memphis, without making as many different kingdoms as there were different capitals. Beſides, it muſt be ſhewn, that there were ſeveral kingdoms in Egypt. before any argument can be formed upon the reſidence of the kings. 2*dly*, This interpretation of the inſcriptions that they ſignify reſidences, is merely imaginary and impoſſible to be proved; we affirm theſe inſcriptions univerſally to denote the origin, deſcent, and family of the kings (A) named in them, as is evident from the inſcriptions of the Dynaſties of the Ethiopians, the Perſians, the ſhepherd-kings, the Saites, and others. Therefore, if a king be a Memphian, that is, a native of that city, it was not a neceſſary conſequence that he muſt reſide there, any more than the Saites did at Sais, or the Phenician ſhepherds in Phenicia. *Laſtly*, We deny that explanation, as contradictory to other circumſtances. Let it be conſidered that Athotes, who has been ever accounted a king of *This*, built, as Africanus informs us from Manetho (B), a palace at Memphis; how can the chronologers reconcile this with their opinion, that the Mem-

The third Objection.

(A) Poſſibly here ſome may object to us, that this Menes may be both a Thinite and a Theban, for Manetho places him in the former liſt, and Eratoſthenes among the Theban kings; but we ſhall ſhew, that the latter appellation is fully applicable to him, as an Egyptian.

(B) Univerſal Hiſtory, I. §. 586.

Memphian was one of the ſeparate kingdoms of thoſe times; would Toſorthros, who, according to Marſham, and others, reſided at that time at Memphis, have permitted ſuch a thing in his dominions. In like manner Cæacus is a Thinite; that is, a king of *This*, according to the received opinion; and yet a remarkable event which concerns the Memphian kingdom, is related in his reign, the deification of Apis; from all which, it is a certain inference, that the explanation of theſe inſcriptions is erroneous, and the conſequences drawn from it ſtill more ſo.

SECT. XVI.

Further Objections. Laſtly, we proceed to remove one more objection which may poſſibly be brought againſt us; that it appears from ancient writers, that the opinions, uſages, and religious ceremonies of many parts of Egypt were generally very different, which could ariſe only from a diſtinct, and different civil conſtitution; but this objection will prove too much, and introduce a multitude of Egyptian monarchies; for the leſſer tribes of Egypt, as the Oxyrynchitæ, the Lycopolitans, Cynopolitans, and the like, and almoſt all the nomes had different, and often oppoſite (C) cuſtoms. We need not therefore aſſign any other cauſe of theſe cuſtoms, than that which ſome have conjectured, not without probability, that they were firſt inſtituted by the prudence and policy of the ancient governors; tho' we muſt admit, that ſeveral of them take their riſe from ancient traditions and hiſtories, which are not of equal weight and authority (D).

SECT.

(C) Plutarch. de Iſide et Oſiri. Strabo. Pliny.

(D) An objection like this is drawn from that paſſage of Artapanus in Euſebius, where he ſays, that in the time of Moſes there were many kings in Egypt, who all exceedingly oppreſſed the Jews: an objection of ſo little force, that

SECT. XVII.

Of the ſhepherd Kings.

In Joſephus's abſtract from Manetho, which has already been mentioned more than once, an account is given of the famous ſhepherd-kings, and of ſome of their ſucceſſors after their expulſion. The ſeveral opinions of the learned concerning what people are to be underſtood by theſe ſhepherds, being accurately ſet forth by other hands, we ſhall forbear repeating them (E). In the mean-time, both the opinion, which ſuppoſes them to be the Iſraelites, and that which maintains the con-

that the following ſhort anſwer will be ſufficient for it. If this writer, who here affects to be wiſer than Herodotus, Diodorus, and Manetho, and many others, had been known not only to the Chriſtian, but alſo to other foreign authors; if the few fragments of him did not betray a mixture of the true hiſtory of the old teſtament with the Pagan, to which are added, many circumſtances utterly fabulous; if his age were both more demonſtrable, and ſufficient to verify and explain this account of his, and if it could be ſuppoſed, that he has taken a great deal of pains in the ſearch of old records, tho' none appear in confirmation of this account, we then ſhould be willing and obliged to pay ſome deference to his aſſertion, and endeavour to reconcile it to our principles. But he being in general of little repute, all the remains we have of him ſerve only to prove at firſt ſight the rectitude of the judgment we have paſſed upon him. Whoever will take into conſideration the paſſages concerning Moſes, preſerved in Euſebius (29) and Clemens Alexandrinus (30), will cloſe with our opinion. But abſtractedly from all this, nothing can be concluded from his information, but that he was of the opinion of Joſephus, who held the ſhepherds and Iſraelites to be the ſame people, and the ſeveral kings to be thoſe who ſucceſſively made head againſt them, and drove them out.

(E) Univerſal Hiſtory, part 1.

(29) *Euſeb. de praep. evangel. lib.* 9. 27.
(30) *Clemens Alex. l.* 1. *ſtromaten.*

contrary, ſeem to be ſo balanced that it is not eaſy to determine in favour of either. To the advantage of the former it may be obſerved, 1. that it is quite inconceivable, that no veſtiges of the great changes which the Egyptians underwent from the Jews, ſhould occur in the Egyptian hiſtory, if this abſtract be not admitted, which in ſo many circumſtances, harmonizes with the hiſtory of the bible. 2. That the other opinion of an invaſion of the Amalekites, or of any other nation, is improbable, becauſe ſuch a ſuperiority of the Amalekites, in thoſe ancient times, is no leſs difficult to be conceived than their appellation, Hyxos, however, interpreted; and among all the ancient Greek writers not one makes the leaſt mention of this long ſubjection of the Egyptians; on the contrary, there is the higheſt probability, that the Egyptians have altered this paſſage of their hiſtory in ſome circumſtances which were thought diſgraceful, or of ill conſequence, thereby obviating the oppoſite narratives; and this wilful corruption hath been accidentally increaſed by defective traditions, and an actual ignorance of many circumſtances. Add to this, that they exalted Joſeph and his brethren, or other Iſraelites, to the rank of kings, to which the power and dignity of Joſeph might greatly contribute, but as to the other Iſraelites, it can be no more than an ignorant conjecture. Theſe Egyptian accounts, therefore, do not relate to another people diſtinct from the Iſraelites, becauſe theſe were not kings; on the contrary, Hyxos being interpreted captives, and enſlaved ſhepherds, as it ſtands tranſlated in Joſephus, and is ſupported by the opinion of many Egyptians, cannot be applied to the Amalekites, Kenites, or any others, but abſolutely quadrates with the condition into which the Jews fell upon Joſeph's deceaſe.

The

The shepherd Dynasties in Africanus (F) serve to complete the abstract of Josephus (G) where the shepherds are only said to have maintained their sovereignty in Egypt 511 years, but Africanus recites the number of the kings. They were called Phœnician shepherds, or a people coming from Phœnicia and Arabia, as is mentioned in Josephus. Africanus places them in the 15th, 16th, and 17th Dynasty, and the inscription of the last of these is, *other shepherds*, that is, distinct from those Phœnician or Arabian shepherds which they were reputed to be. We have therefore, with good reason, given another appellation to these *Greek* shepherds, as they were hitherto imagined to be (H). Syn-

(F) Universal History, part 1.

(G) lib. 1.contra. Ap.

(H) We shall here subjoin an observation or two towards throwing some light on those shepherd-kings; first, that some have ventured too far, and have alledged more heads of similarity betwixt these shepherds and the Jews, than can be proved: one instance of this is the conceit of a late writer, (31) that Salatis is the Arabic appellation Sultan, or the Hebrew Schallith, which was conferred on Joseph as the title of his exalted station in Egypt; and that Bæon may be applied to Joseph's brother Benjamin; which etymologies, ridiculous as they may appear, are not the only ones to be met with in his work. 2. That hitherto the strangest ideas have been entertained of the Greek shepherds mentioned in Africanus's 15th Dynasty, which are rejected by Marsham and his followers as fictitious and absurd, whilst the reality of them is asserted by This hath been chiefly done, but with very little success, by the above-mentioned writer, who divides Africanus's 15th Dynasty so as to make the three first Phœnician and the three last Greek shepherds, which he infers from the affinity of the names, *Aphophis* and *Epaphus*, who returned again from Greece into Egypt; likewise of *Janias* with *Jonia*, or if it be read *Tanias*, then it answers to *Danaus*; of *Asis* or *Aseth* with *Asterius*; lastly, of *Archles* with *Her-cules*

(31) *Abel lib.* 1. *c.* 4. *in histor. monarch.*

Syncellus and Euſebius have omitted moſt of the ſhepherds, and admitted only the firſt ſix or four of

cules: and theſe with him, are palpable proofs. This ſingular fancy has many difficulties to combat; ſuch are the expreſs inſcription, *Phenician Shepherds*, the impoſſibility of the Greeks being then ſo powerful and renown'd, and the greater incongruity of the name of *Shepherds*; likewiſe thoſe derivations, which are ſo wild and arbitrary, as not to deſerve a confutation at large. All the opinions of theſe Greek ſhepherds, which have hitherto obtained, vaniſh at once upon reſtoring the true Greek text, and, inſtead of ποιμενὲς ἴλληνὰς βασιλεις reading ποιμενες ἀλλοι βασιλεις, which inſcription ſtands right in the very following 17th Dynaſty, but the miſtake aroſe from the ſimilarity of the letters and the inadvertency of the tranſcriber, and had not been made in the times either of Euſebius or Syncellus. 3. We obſerve that either Joſephus or Africanus have been miſtaken, for the latter in the 16th Dynaſty, allows the remaining paſtor kings to have reigned 518 years before the inſurrection of the Egyptians againſt them, excluſive of the firſt ſix, whom Joſephus has included. That Joſephus makes the number above 500 to be 11, and Africanus 18, proceeded from the reſemblance of the Greek characters IA and IH, and one number muſt be wrong. 4. That *Euſebius* and *Syncellus*, when compared with Manetho, have exceedingly erred in placing Aſeth and Amos of the 18th Dynaſty immediately after the 6th ſhepherd king, though there was an interval of above 300 years, betwixt the immediate ſucceſſors of the latter and thoſe princes; not to mention the alteration in the name and ſucceſſion of theſe firſt ſix kings and of their years, Syncellus dividing the laſt reign into two. 5. That the Greek in Euſebius is faulty in rendering the inſcription of his 17th Dynaſty unintelligible; in Syncellus's extract it ſtands thus, (32) 17 δυναστεια ποιμενες ησαν αδελφοι φοινικες ξενοι βασιλεις οἱ και Μεμφιν ειλον, now 'tis a myſtery what αδελφοι, brothers has to do there; therefore, it is not unlikely that the original ran thus, ποιμενες. Ησαν δε ἀυτοι φοινικές, &c. 6. *Laſtly*, if by them the Jews are to be underſtood, it ſeems not altogether abſurd to ſuppoſe the tranſpoſitions in the ancient Jewiſh, and particularly the Egyptian hiſtories, to have begun in the time of Manetho, when

(32) *Syncell. p.* 48.

of them, holding according to the opinion of Joſephus, the others as ſuppoſititious.

SECT. XVIII.

We now come to that table of Eratoſthenes, intitled *the Theban kings*; in the illuſtration of which moſt chronologers have followed Marſham, who is of opinion, that this table was compoſed to rectify an error of Manetho, ariſing either from his negligence or prepoſſeſſion. They pretend that the kings contained in it were quite different from thoſe in Manetho, that they were omitted by him, and belonged to a ſeparate kingdom. In anſwer to this it is alleged, *1ſt*, That it is ſcarce conceivable, that Manetho ſhould have paſſed over a kingdom of ſuch antiquity and extent as that of Thebes was in compariſon with the other ſuppoſed kingdoms, and not rather have exerted all his abilities on thoſe kings whoſe reſidence had in all times been ſo famous, and who had furniſhed the antient writers with ſuch intereſting materials. *2ly*, That tho' Manetho, as may be ſeen in Joſephus (I), mentions the Theban kings, and makes them the firſt promoters of the deliverance of their country from the ſhepherds, yet he ſays nothing as to the duration of their royalty, whether their kingdom was diſtinct from others, or whether they incorporated them with theirs, as appears from this very account of Manetho, who after the expulſion of the ſhepherds, ſpeaks only of one king. And ſeveral of the Dynaſties are of Thebes and

Theban kings.

when under Ptolemæus Philadelphus, the books of Moſes were not unknown in Egypt; and they might diſguiſe and ſoften whatever was offenſive in them. This might account for the ſilence of Herodotus, for there was in his time no account of the ſhepherd-kings in the hiſtory of Egypt.

(I) Joſ. loc. cit.

Dioſpolis; ſo that Manetho did not totally omit the kings of Thebes, but gives a broken ſucceſſion of them, recording only ſome of the moſt diſtinguiſhed; which is equally unaccountable if Thebes was a monarchy of ſuch antiquity, whoſe kings are found in Eratoſthenes. *Thirdly*, This opinion is combated by all the preceeding arguments brought againſt the plurality of Egyptian kingdoms.

SECT. XIX.

Confutation of Marſham. Marſham, who in general ſeems to think he has proved his point, paſſes this categorical deciſion, (K) " If theſe kings had been recorded by Manetho, Eratoſthenes would have given himſelf an " unneceſſary trouble." We ſhall conſider this as his firſt and capital proof, for he advances but very few; and this will by no means anſwer his purpoſe. It might with equal reaſon be inferred, that after Africanus's epitome of Manetho, there was no need that Euſebius ſhould ſet about the ſame work. But how abſurd is this concluſion? It holds againſt every writer who is not original in his ſubject: Therefore it fails, even if Eratoſthenes had only given a bare liſt of the Egyptian kings; but he has further recorded and explained their proper Coptic names, and what is ſtill more, we affirm his liſt to be more credible and exact, than that of Manetho; which entirely ſubverts the above principle. Beſides, Manetho as an Egyptian, may be ſuſpected of prejudice, an imputation which cannot lie againſt Eratoſthenes, a learned and judicious Grecian.

The 2*d* proof with which Marſham, and many others ſupport this opinion, is, that the names of the kings in this table, are very different from thoſe in Manetho, conſequently, they muſt be a different ſucceſſion of kings omitted by him. But this

(K) In proparaſc. §. 3. p. 3.

this objection is demonſtrably ill-grounded, and withal does not authoriſe ſuch an inference. The firſt is evident, from the identity of ſeveral names in Manetho and Eratoſthenes, as *Menes*, *Athotes*, *Suphis* or *Saophis*, *Pſammus*, *Mares*, *Maris*, and *Nitocris*; and as to thoſe names which are different, 'tis certainly carrying the concluſion too far, for the names may differ and the perſons denoted by them be the ſame. The natural conjecture, that poſſibly a king had more names than one, is manifeſtly confirmed by the expreſs words of Syncellus (L) who affirms, that a king had uſually 2 or 3 names. Were it not ſo, theſe Egyptian kings muſt be the ſame in all writers who make mention of them. And this appears from a paſſage of the moſt accurate and indefatigable Clemens of Alexandria, (M) who expreſsly obſerves, that every Egyptian, upon his becoming a myſtes, or being initiated into the religious myſteries, received a new name; and all the kings of Egypt were *Myſtes*. Now this difference of names, even if admitted with ſome limitations, is eaſily accounted for; Eratoſthenes having, as Apollodorus explicitly ſays, and Syncellus (N) from him, recorded them in their proper Coptic names; whereas the other tables follow their more uſual names, as they were altered and terminated, to adapt them to the Greek pronunciation. All this is only alleged to ſhew, how eaſily the objectors might be anſwered, even if the judgment formed of theſe names at firſt ſight were indiſputable.

The 3*d* objection which may be drawn from the titles of the Dynaſties, that thoſe of This, Memphis, and the like, indicate each a diſtinct kingdom, hath been already replied to in our arguments

(L) Syncell. p. 33.
(M) Clemens Alex. ſtromat. lib. 1.
(N) Syncell. p. 73.

againſt the interpretation of thoſe titles, which we would hope are ſufficient for the confutation thereof.

SECT. XX.

Our Opinion.

As to our opinion of this table, we ſhall endeavour to ſhew, with more probability, if not certainty, that this appellation of *Theban* kings, means no other than kings of *Egypt*, and in ſupport of this conſtruction, we conceive ourſelves furniſhed with ſufficient proofs from ſome of the moſt celebrated writers of antiquity. The firſt is Herodotus (O), whoſe very words are, that *Egypt* had formerly been called *Thebes*. Our ſecond authority is Ariſtotle (P), who affirms, that under the name of *Thebes* all *Egypt* was formerly underſtood (Q). This

(O) Herodot. l. 2. c. 15.

(P) Ariſtot. Meteorol. lib. 1. c. 14.

(Q) It will not be without ſome utility, and, at the ſame time, add conſiderable weight to our opinion, if we ſubjoin a remark or two on ſome ancient names, which have at times been applied to Egypt, and the Egyptian hiſtory. A paſſage of an old, but unknown writer, which the induſtrious Suidas has preſerved, (33) runs thus, "Aſclepiades, an Egyptian philoſopher, has wrote a hiſtory of "the Ogygian Egyptians, comprehending a ſpace of "30000 years, rather more than leſs." We know not of any chronologer who, in his account of Egypt, has made uſe of this paſſage, elſe Marſham and all the maintainers of the Theban kingdom, would have been ſomewhat diffident of the meaning of that name, upon which they ſo poſitively inſiſt. We muſt either erect a new kingdom in Egypt, and call it the Ogygian, or ſuppoſe this to have been one of the ancient appellations of Egypt in general. But Stephanus (34), and many other writers, ſhew the name of Ogygia to have belonged to *Thebes* in *Greece*. Now *Thebes* in *Bœotia* having unqueſtionably received its name from the more ancient *Thebes* of Egypt, it is probable that from

(33) *Suidas in* Ηραισκος. (34. *Stephanus in* Ωγυγια.

This certainly arose from Thebes being the oldest, and by the accounts of some writers (R) the principal city in Egypt, and the residence of its kings, till in succeeding times their seat was removed to Memphis: Therefore Eratosthenes, being consummately versed in antiquity, might very well give his Egyptian history the name of the most ancient and famous city of *Thebes*. But as this proves no more than the possibility of our explanation, we shall allege some further reasons to evince the truth and propriety of it, exclusive of any other. 1. The consonance of the names of these kings is much greater than has hitherto been imagined, as may be seen in the instances hereto annexed (S). 2. It

from Egypt also derived that of Ogygia; why then should the import of *Thebes* and *Theban* kings in *Eratosthenes*, be different from, and much more limited than *Ogygia*, which is synonymous to *Egyptian?* But if *Ogygian* be taken in the same contracted sense, as *Theban* usually is, and made the appellation of a kingdom distinct from the rest, it will be necessary previously to prove this; and it would be a point of difficulty, thus to limit the signification, whilst the proofs are so clear, that *Ogygia* no less than Thebes did include all Egypt. This passage likewise agrees with Manetho, he having, in his history, comprehended above 30000 years.

(R) Geographi et historici apud Schol. *Apoll Rhodii* ad lib. 4. Argon v. 260.

(S) It is necessary before we compare Eratosthenes with other writers, to observe 1. that he uses the peculiar Coptic names, which are not so accommodated to the Greek language as those in the other tables; therefore, a small difference in syllables and letters, affords no grounds for a particular objection against him. 2. It is not to be expected, that every member and succession in Eratosthenes's table, should exactly correspond with the numbers and successions in Herodotus, Manetho, and Diodorus; since the admission of such kings in a table, depends only upon the compiler's judgment, and one might account this another that king real and worthy to be re-

 corded.

2. It is the only possible construction excepting one, that is, that they are called Theban kings in distinc-

corded. Hence it may easily be conceived how little the case admits of a perfect universal agreement in every particular king and succession, as will appear from a comparative view of *Herodotus* and *Diodorus*.

Menes is the first king in every table, and without any great difference of name, except that in Herodotus he is called *Men* without a Greek termination, Eratosthenes interprets that name by Διονιος, which La Croza and Jablonski read Αιωνιος, *eternal*, which better agrees with the Coptic word *Meneh*; and as the great similarity of the words renders them very liable to be mistaken; it is the more probable that the latter is the true reading.

Athotes I. is next, and also mentioned by Manetho; being the son of Menes, his proper place is among the descendents of that prince, who are not recorded by name either in Diodorus or Herodotus. The years of his reign would correspond with Eratosthenes, if Eusebius had not mistaken K for N, 20 for 50. This name is, by *Eratosthenes*, construed to signify ἑρμογενης, or one issued from Mercury.

Athotes II. is not to be found in Manetho, who places Cencenes next, but the number of the years of both reigns appearing to be the same, though falsified in *Africanus* and *Eusebius*, or in *Eratosthenes* through the affinity of θ or ϑ and β, we imagine them to have been one king. If, instead of the Greek Σεναῦς in Manetho, we take a liberty very common, and suppose the Σ to have been changed from K and A, it would then signify in the Coptic, the *second*, *i. e.* of that name.

Diabies, as Eratosthenes names the succeeding king, may be reputed the same with the 6th in Manetho, and our opinion that the names in both are corrupted, is not without probability. *Diabies* is a word, which, with respect to the first syllable of it, does not occur throughout the Coptic language; and *Diabio*, which the learned *Jablonski* compares with it, cannot, according to the interpretation thereof, *rich in honey*, *sweet*, be reconciled with the φιλεταιρος or φιλεταιρος of *Eratosthenes*; and has also this further difficulty, that the last syllable must not be Διαβιης but Διαβιως. If we compare this name with that of *Manetho's*

diſtinction from others, the Memphian, the Thinite, and the like, which however has been before con-

netho's 6th king, *Miebidus* or *Miebes*, as *Euſebius* has it inſtead of *Niebes*, it will then be clear, that the original word was *Miabies* and not *Diabies*. The years of the reigns indeed differ, but the difference is only imputable to an alteration in the numerical letters. As to the explanation of the Coptic word, by the Greek φιλεταιρος, it is ſo extremely obſcure, that Scaliger and others, have, in lieu of it ſubſtituted φιλιταιρος without any proofs from the Coptic in favour of ſuch a conſtruction. We ſhall take the like liberty, and propoſe the change of only a ſingle letter, φιλαιτερος, of which ſome traces occur in the Coptic tongue. So that here Eratoſthenes omits two kings, *Venephes* and *Uſaphanes*.

The fifth king in *Eratoſthenes* is called *Pemphos*, but rather *Senphos*, as we before conjectured, and is confirmed by the abovementioned Jablonſki. There is no doubt but that he is the ſame with Semempſis, who is the next in Manetho, as not only the years of the reigns tally, but an alteration might eaſily happen in the laſt ſyllable, as by an overſight, there is, in the middle, a repetition of two letters.

The ſixth king in Eratoſthenes, has a ſtrange name conferred on him by the tranſcribers; which the learned Jablonſki is for rectifying in this manner, Τοιγαραμ ἀχος ρονχειρι, or rather Τοιγερεμ, σνωφ μαι ρωσχηρι, which he tranſlates Σωσανδρος, a benefactor to mankind, and a remarkable giant; and ſo amends the της ανδρος in the tranſlation of Eratoſthenes. As he is, by this laſt hiſtorian, expreſsly called Μεμφιτης, we may ſafely look for him in the third Dynaſty. Poſſibly he is the firſt king Necheropes or Necherophes, inſtead of which, according to *Eratoſthenes*, *Techerophes* may be the beſt reading; in the reigns indeed there is ſome difference, but that is not a ſufficient ground for exploding this conjecture. However, as the compariſon may ſeem too remote, we ſhall dwell no longer on this uncertain king.

The ſeventh king is *Stoechus*, ſon to the former; his name imports Ἀρης αναισθητος *without underſtanding*, or of weak parts, as Jablonſki has rightly rendered it. The order of the kings in the Dynaſties having been greatly tranſ-

confuted. 3. There muſt have been ſome cauſe for the king of Egypt's diſlike of Manetho's accounts, that

transſpoſed by the chriſtian chronologers, we may venture to compare Tyris with him, and to alter the name of the latter to Ἀϱις, as the ſaid chronologers muſt have obſerved this Greek name, Manetho having unqueſtionably taken notice of his weakneſs, and the ſur-name which it occaſioned. Their reigns agree except in the alteration of ϛ 6 for ζ 7.

In Eratoſthenes follows the eighth king, under the name of Goſormies, whom we hold to be the ſame with Toſorthrus the ſecond king in Manetho's third Dynaſty; which will appear not improbable, *1ſt*, If the name in Eratoſthenes is reſtored from Goſormies to Toſormies, the miſtake having been eaſy from the near ſimilarity of the initial letters Γ and Τ. *2dly*, If the falſe and corrupt reading in the explanation of Eratoſthenes is amended. In the ſeveral editions of Syncellus he has been called ετησιπαντος, a word without meaning. It were to be wiſhed the ſagacious *Jablonſki* had favoured us with his thoughts on it, for they would have rendered ours ſuperfluous. However we ſhall try to rectify this error by αιτιος παντος; Scaliger has it ἀιτησις παντος, but this, as it affords but little light, ſo it doth not come up to the Coptic word, which we would explain. *Toſi* in the *Coptic*, is equal to the Greek φυτευειν, but *eramahi*, the laſt part of the word, ſignifies *to communicate ſtrength*; ſo that *Toſormies* with a ſmall change of the enunciation, very properly ſignifies an author of the productive or creative power, which is alſo very well expreſſed by the Greek ἀιτιος παντος, or the cauſe of all created things. This, in the Egyptian religious accounts, is the predicament both of *Mercury* and *Oſiris*. Now *Toſorthrus*, as it ſtands in *Manetho*, is a name among the Egyptians both for *Eſculapius* and *Mercury*, for they hold the latter to be eminently ſkilled in phyſic and natural knowledge: all the difference in the years of their reigns, is, that Manetho makes them 29 and Eratoſthenes 30. Further, Syncellus informs us that Toſorthrus left ſome writings behind him, as the Greek expreſſion γϱαφης επιμεληθη, is better rendered than *that he improved the letters*, as the Engliſh compilers have it. (35) The

(35) *Univerſal Hiſtory, part* 1. § 588.

that he ſhould appoint a Greek to compoſe other tables. The improbable conjecture which Marſham

The ninth king in Eratoſthenes is called *Mares*, or, *the gift of the ſun*, as he renders it; and were not the name corrupted he would tally with the following king in Manetho. If, inſtead of *Meſochris*, be read *Moſcheris*, tranſpoſing a letter or two, the word will be of the ſame import, and occurs again in Eratoſthenes's 17th king. He allows 26 years to this reign, but Manetho only 17, by an alteration of K and I ζ and ϛ.

The 10 Anoyphes is the ſame with Soiphis, who follows in Manetho, as will be manifeſt, 1. If we conſider that there is an error in the name in Eratoſthenes, which we infer from the Greek tranſlation thereof, υιος επικοινος. Jablonſki is for altering it to επικλεινος *famous*, as coming nearer to the Coptic, but as our conjecture requires leſs alteration we beg leave to differ a little from this great man. We read the Coptic word, Μωϋφης, an A and N having been made from the M, as might very eaſily happen. Of this the proper meaning is a *given ſon*, or επικοινος as ερμης κοινος, in which all have a right and ſhare as in a gift. 2 In Manetho we alſo read Moiphis which ſhews M to have been turned into Σ, poſſibly from its leaning poſture in ſome copy, admitting that ιϛ has been made from K 20, the years of their reigns alſo agree.

Sirius follows in Eratoſthenes, with whom Soris, in Manetho's 4th Dynaſty is identical; therefore we ſhall only make an obſervation upon the meaning of the name. Eratoſthenes renders it υιος κορρης, or αβασκαντος, the former being the literal tranſlation, it is the more ſurpriſing that the learned Jablonſki could neither reconcile nor underſtand it. *A ſon of the cheeks* denotes a very beautiful ſon, the countenance being more eſpecially the ſeat of beauty; 'Αβασκαντος is but a nearer tranſlation, and properly means one who is proof againſt incantations, alluding to the well known ſuperſtition of ancient times, that comely perſons were to be prejudiced and bewitched by an envious malevolent look. But his beauty was ſuch that he had nothing to fear from ſuch practices.

The twelfth king in Eratoſthenes is Gnubus or Gnubis. it has been already noticed that both in the order of the Dynaſties, and the ſucceſſion of the kings in Manetho, there have evidently been ſuch various and manifeſt alterations

sham endeavoured to establish, that Manetho had omitted the succession of Theban kings, being thus ex-

terations, that they cannot defeat our comparison; therefore if Obnus of the fifth Dynasty is not the duplicate of him, we conceive the Coptic name in Eratosthenes to be erroneous and consequently unknown.

Rhavosis the succeeding king, is, by a slight alteration, the same with Rhatoses, in the fourth Dynasty, but in which the error lies, is uncertain. The difference is much the same betwixt Biyris and Bicheris, who is the next in Manetho.

Saophis, the fifteenth king, is evidently one with Suphis in Manetho, Sensaophis or Suphis the II. falling next in both. The right interpretation having hitherto not been hit upon, we shall attempt it from Manetho, by means of a short account of this king, which Syncellus has preserved. It is there said (36) that this king had seen the Gods, but that he afterwards repented of it, and wrote a book, which was held in great veneration by the Egyptians. Thus the English compilers have translated the words. Others, instead of ὑπεροπτης, have substituted περοπτης, from whence comes *Peroptes* in the Latin translation, though so faulty that no Greek word can be made of it; but the true reading will be restored by ἐποπτης, not a contemner, but one admitted into the intimacy of the Gods, this word, together with ἐποπτευειν being frequently used in this sense by the Greek writers, and the primitive fathers. But here appears no cause for sorrow and repentance, therefore μεταvοήσαντα must be altered into μεταμυησαντα; the knowlege which he had acquired, he formed into such a system, as to require several preparatives, μυησεις, towards a full participation of it, which accounts both for the composure of the book, and the veneration paid to it. This clears up the words κομαςης, or χρηματιςης in *Eratosthenes*; for the last word is very erroneously rendered *negotiator*, one who deals in money and traffic; and must be explained by the known signification of the verb χρηματιζειν χρηματισθηναι, which means one who has intercourse and converse with the Gods, obtains oracles and intelligence from them, or is a mediator in those cases, and promulges the divine decrees, &c. As to κομαστης, that it should be read κοναστης, is supported only by a bare

exploded, the true cauſe indiſputably was, that the former table appeared to the king ſo extravagant and

bare conjecture of its alluding to the building of the greateſt pyramid, attributed to him by Manetho. The other tranſlations which have hitherto obtained, are not very deſerving of that name, and leaſt of any the latin tranſlation *Comatus*, as contrary to the rules of ſpeech and ſtruck out of its ſuppoſed derivation κωμᾶν.

Moſcheris, who follows in Eratoſthenes, is the ſame with the next in Manetho, falſely called *Mencheres*, inſtead of *Mocheres* or *Moſcheres*; ſuch ſmall alterations frequently happening through the ſimilarity of letters. The ſucceeding two we ſhall omit, as we cannot ſo clearly match them, and proceed to Apappus who is the ſame as Aphiops in Euſebius, and Phiops in Africanus; the former agrees to the hundred years attributed to their reigns, the latter makes them only 94. The occaſion of this is not any alteration of the numerical letters, that being ſcarce poſſible, it is to be looked for in Eratoſthenes, who ſays that the hundred years fell ſhort, ὥρα μία. Hitherto it has been generally rendered by *hora* an hour, but we are of opinion that ὥρα is rather equal to ὧρος, which, in the Egyptian computation, was a ſmall number of years, as may be ſeen in Syncellus; beſides, this ſignification *hour* had not obtained in the Greek language, in the early times of Eratoſthenes, but is later by no leſs than ſome hundreds of years.

Acheſcus Okaras follows in *Eratoſthenes*, and although his name be ſo ſtrangely corrupted, he appears to be the ſame with Mentiſuphis in Africanus and Euſebius, from the ſingle year of his reign, and from Nitocris being in both authors placed as the next ſucceſſor. Chronologers have hitherto given themſelves unneceſſary trouble in clearing up and dividing the years this princeſs reigned, which Eratoſthenes makes ſix, Africanus twelve, and Euſebius three. Euſebius's number Γ, ariſes from a miſtake of the character ϛ 6, as does that of Africanus. Her different reigns at Memphis and Thebes, admit of no manner of proof, and the ſuppoſition of them ariſes only from the difference of the numerical letters.

The names in the following Dynaſties not being preſerved, any farther comparifon muſt fail, or at leaſt be at-

and incredible, as to shock his Grecian taste, which considering the time, was not a bad one. This inclined him to order a more accurate table of the real Egyptian kings to be compiled, suppressing the many interpolated names which were meant to fill up an inconceiveable space of time, and give it the greater air of probability: All this is manifest from this very table, where Eratosthenes extremely curtails the antiquity which the Egyptians arrogate to themselves, regulates their kings by the common age of man, very different from the exorbitant length of their reigns in Herodotus's computation, and says not a word of their gods and heroes (T).

SECT.

attended with great difficulties and uncertainties. Omitting Amyrtæus or Myrtæus, we compare Usimares (not Thyosimarus, as it has hitherto been falsely read) with Osymandyas in Diodorus Siculus, Maris and Mendes or Mandes being the same.

Stamenemes the 32d, may be compared with Ammenemes according to the 11th Dynasty, where, being called the second, another of that name must have preceeded him.

Sistosi-Chermes is the same as Seson-Goses or Seson-Choris, as Maris and Ammeres and Ammenemes differ but little in their signification. We shall carry the comparison no farther to avoid perplexity, the premises also being sufficient to shew how many kings, both as to their names and successions in the tables of Manetho agree with those of Herodotus and Diodorus. It is a very insufficient answer to say, that all the kings, whose names likewise occur in Eratosthenes, were also possessed of the kingdom of Thebes, since this requires proof, and it is not easily demonstrable, that the term *Theban kings* is to be taken in this sense.

(T) Although we grant that the omission of such incredible events in this short epitome does not certainly prove that Eratosthenes has said nothing of them, yet we are much less warranted to draw the contrary conclusion from thence. This very concise and probable account, rather

SECT. XXI.

Comprehends more than 38 kings.

Here it is proper to take notice of a miſtake of ſeveral chronologers in the uſe of this table. Of theſe the *1ſt* is Marſham (U), and poſſibly his is rather deliberate than owing to ignorance. He would perſuade us, that Eratoſthenes has enumerated only 38 kings, and that the remaining 53 attributed to him by Syncellus are none of his; but Perizonius (X), furniſhes every impartial reader with an objection againſt this groundleſs opinion taken from the expreſs words of Syncellus; for he ſays peremptorily (Y), Eratoſthenes has recorded 91 Theban kings, and after ſetting down 38 with the years of their reigns, he adds, 'the remaining 53 we omit, their names being of as little uſe to us as the preceeding 38.' What clearer expreſſions could Syncellus, or rather Euſebius uſe, to ſignify that Eratoſthenes had included 91 Theban kings in his memoirs? But this not ſuiting Marſham's opinion, and being at a loſs what uſe to make of the remaining 53 in his ſyſtem, he has recourſe to an aſſertion utterly groundleſs. Others likewiſe have fallen into the ſame error, and form their tables of the old kings, as if that of Eratoſthenes conſiſted but of 38. Thus as theſe opinions are here ſhewn to be unſupportable and groundleſs, ſo likewiſe that plauſible connexion of ſeveral kingdoms vaniſhes; the 53 Theban kings moſt wrongfully expunged, have a right to be replaced, and

rather ſhews the caution, judgment, and good ſenſe of the author, every where avoiding any thing of the marvellous, elſe he would not with ſuch preciſion, have moderated the number of kings, and the names and years of their reigns.

(U) Marſham can. chron. proparaſceve p. 3. § 111.

(X) Perizon. orig. œg. c. 6. p. 90, 91.

(Y) Syncellus, p. 117. ed. venet.

and thus these systems, are, till some further modification, annihilated.

SECT. XXII.

Syncellus's Table. It remains that we consider the Grecian table extant in Syncellus. Various are the opinions of the learned on its value and form. Marsham has a very high opinion of it (Z) and believes it of great use in regulating the Egyptian chronology; but supposes those kings to have reigned in Lower Egypt jointly with the other kings. The learned English compilers (A) side with Perizonius, and others, who esteem it of very little use, from the uncertainty of the kings, most, or many of which he seems to have set down at pleasure, where he thought they would best come in; other opinions we shall pass over, We would the rather preserve this account in all the regard due to it, as we have very few remains of these sort of memoirs of such ancient times; therefore after previously proposing our own opinion of it; we shall endeavour to invalidate the objections brought against it. This catalogue we believe to contain Egyptian kings, as the like occur in Herodotus, Diodorus, Manetho, and other writers, that is, such who were sovereigns of all Egypt exclusive of all other kingdoms, which we prove thus; 1*st*, It is not to be conceived, why Syncellus should select one of the 4 pretended kingdoms in Egypt in order to connect the chronologies of all, and yet make no kind of mention why he preferred this of Lower Egypt, and that he should not even know any thing of it himself, for to these kings he assigns transactions which concerned the other kingdoms, and most of his kings he took from Manetho. So according to Man-

(Z) Marsham, p. 7.
(A) Universal History, part. 1.

Marsham's opinion, has assigned Theban and Memphian kings to Lower Egypt; all this without the least shadow of any intimation of his procedure. Now it is impossible that a mere conjecture of Marsham, can have weight enough to limit these kings to Lower Egypt, when Syncellus, like all ancient writers, speaks of them as kings of all Egypt. 2*dly*, Syncellus expresly assures us, that in the prosecution of his history, he shall consult only writers of the best repute, but this predicament is not applied in this case to Christians, for he often censures and rejects Africanus, Eusebius, Pannodorus, and Annianus; it rather extends to Pagan writers, and their more credible and clear accounts of the Egyptians. Consequently, this table is the more worthy of attention, as it is quite unaccountable where he could procure a series of kings of Lower Egypt, no vestiges or mention of more kingdoms than one occurring in any ancient writers; much less any circumstantial narratives of the successions of those kingdoms, or any other proofs of their existence in those times. So that even the possibility of such a list ought to be demonstrated; and the rather, as all our before-mentioned arguments militate against this plurality of kingdoms. 3*dly*, We believe that Syncellus in his account of the number of real Eygptian kings takes Eratosthenes for his guide, the latter having entered upon this disquisition by the king's command. At least, it cannot be merely accidental, that Syncellus's number of kings tallies so exactly with that of Eratosthenes. We refer the reader to what we have before observed concerning the 113 generations which Manetho reckons. Syncellus has in this adhered to the opinion of Herodotus, and Diodorus, who consider most of those hundreds of Egyptian kings as supposititious. And this is the less exceptionable, because it is difficult or rather impossible to prove, that to admit of the collateral existence of many kingdoms, is the only true way of bringing this chronology into any order; yet upon this argument, or prepossession, are founded the reproaches cast upon this table. And it may farther be rationally concluded from the frequent censures of Syncellus on the many arbitrary corrections of Africanus, Eusebius, and others, that he himself would strictly guard against such, or any other faults; and that both the choice of the kings, and their names, were entirely left to his judgment.

SECT. XXIII.

Objections against him.

The most usual objections against this regal table, are, 1*st*, That some of the kings contained in it are both unknown, and manifestly false and imaginary, such as the Greek and Latin names. As to the first article of this objection, it may be granted, that there are in it some names so far unknown, that they are not to be met with elsewhere; but this does not absolutely conclude them to be fictitious; for in that case, many proper names in history must fall under the same charge. It has already been noticed, that the kings had more Names than one, some of which were, doubtless, more common than the rest. It is besides indisputable, that the obscurity, or strangeness of these names is generally to be imputed to the oversights, or ignorance of the copyists who have corrupted them. The same answer will suffice for the other part of this objection; for that Syncellus had no Latin names among his Egyptian kings, as some, but on very weak grounds, account *Certus* to be, is self-evident; and that he must have known, that no Grecian name could belong to the ancient kings of this country; it is therefore deciding with too much precipitancy,

and

and injuring Syncellus, to reject his table as useless and erroneous on account of alterations, in which he had no hand. And though the true reading were not to be restored, yet is not this diligent monk chargeable with the least fault. 2*dly*, It is objected, that the places and successions of many kings are exceedingly transposed, and utterly irreconcileable to Manetho, but nothing further is deducible from hence, than that Syncellus used the greatest attention and diligence to dispose his kings in the most probable order, which the authorities he was furnished with would allow. It must previously be proved, that the epitome of Manetho exhibits the Dynasties in the right order; which would be very difficult amidst the many manifest alterations of Africanus and Eusebius. So that this table cannot, upon their authority, be censured with any propriety or justice. 3*dly*, It is objected, that Syncellus has omitted the Persian Dynasties, but what prejudice this does to the Egyptian kings cannot be shewn, and his computation reaches to king Amasis, whom Cambyses conquered.

In order the better to prevent any hasty rejection of Syncellus's table, we shall add a few more observations. Syncellus quotes several fragments from Manetho, which are of use in this chronology and history, and are not to be met with elsewhere. He observes, that the 700 years of the cynic cycle terminate under Concharis, the 25th king. Here it must be noticed, that these 700 years are to be understood according to the received, and already mentioned opinions of the Christian chronologers, for the computations of the Egyptians, as appears from Manetho, and particularly from Diodorus, Herodotus, and others, are much larger, and this cycle is the same with that of Sothis, or the *Periodus*

dus Sothiaca, for Sothis (B) is the same with the Dog Star among the Greeks, the Greek word κυων being but a translation of the Hebrew (שדר) which signifies *pregnant* or *faithful*. Hither also may be referred the computation of Clemens Alexandrinus (C) that the Jews went out of Egypt 345 years before the conclusion of this period; which computation does not agree with Syncellus, and possibly from hence, that Clemens did not understand this space of time in the contracted sense to which the Christian chronologers afterwards reduced it. Of his 32d king, Aseth, he observes, that he added 5 intercalary days to the year, which before him consisted of but 360, and that under him Apis was deified; particulars, which he certainly borrowed from Manetho; therefore, we are rather inclined to credit him, than the extracts of the Dynasties, in what is said concerning Cæacus in the 1st Dynasty, that under him was the Apotheosis of Apis, and of the Goat at Mendes; for the Egyptian Mythology, which join these deifications to the institution of the intercalary days, confirms those facts. So many more such observations are to be found in Syncellus (D) that we are persuaded the contempt of his table in general, is an ill-grounded piece of injustice to him.

SECT. XXIV.

Of the Arabick and Jewish accounts.

We shall now, but briefly, treat of the accounts of the Egyptian kings to be met with in Arabian and Jewish writers, and of the former from the extract, for which we are indebted to the compilers of the Universal History (E). The remoteness of the

(B) Porphyr. de antro Nymphar, Plutarch de Iside.

(C) Clemens, Alex. lib. 1. Stromat. p. 335. ed. Colon. 1688. (D) Plutarch de Iside.

(E) Universal History, part I.

the time in which theſe Arabian writers attempted this hiſtory, from the facts themſelves, ſcarce permits us to expect any thing of real utility from them; it being difficult to imagine from what ſources theſe hiſtorians could draw any ſolid, uſeful and intereſting informations. They themſelves indeed, pretend to have taken the materials of their hiſtories from the Coptic annals (F); but from the manner and contents of them, this can be underſtood only of the ſubject and ſubſtance thereof; how can it be imagined, that the Copts or Egyptians ſhould have preferred the books of Moſes, and other writings to their own traditions, and the hiſtories formed upon them? Noah, Abraham, Sarah, Hagar, and Joſeph, appear in every particular here as in the book of Geneſis, and their account of the religion of theſe Egyptian kings, differs in nothing from that of Moſes, without any traces of the idolatry and ſuperſtition which are known to have prevailed in Egypt. Theſe Copts muſt have been Coptic Chriſtians, and their narratives conſequently a mixture of Chriſtian and Pagan traditions, beſides what the Arabian writers themſelves muſt have added; for nothing can be plainer, than that they connect the hiſtory of the bible with traditions from old and ſpurious writings, and fragments of ancient Grecian accounts of Egypt, and with their private conceits. This appears too plainly in the accounts of magic and other arts, and the angels Harot and Marot, who alſo occur in the Koran. It is likewiſe manifeſt from the threefold diviſion of the kings of Manetho, and from circumſtances which peculiarly belong to Egypt, ſuch as the fences againſt the inundation of the Nile, and the like, that they were collected from Greek writers, but with many alterations. Of the laſt they have not, nor could make any great uſe;

(F) Ibid. §. 696.

the Greek writings having been at times but little known among the Arabians, or judged very useless, as they imagined their own language sufficiently furnished with tracts on most points of history, but which were indeed, very defective, trivial, and erroneous. This defect, however, the Arabic writers were very skilful in supplying, by pompous additions suited to the oriental taste, and favouring rather too much of the marvellous. From such sources as these nothing useful or instructive can be expected, either in point of chronology, or history.

The Jewish accounts do not deserve a much more favourable idea; tho' they are drawn up with more circumspection than the former, and omit all the early kings that were said to have lived before and after the deluge, and who performed so many wonderful exploits. The reason probably was, that they found there was no reconciling these things with the accounts of Moses, especially, as it is very late before he makes mention of Misraim: but another reason might be this, that they concerned themselves less than the Arabians about foreign transactions. As to the kings since the deluge, Rabbi Abraham Zacut in his Juchasin, agrees pretty well with what has been mentioned in the first Vol. of the *Univ. Hist.* from the Arabian writers, and as he himself informs us (G) he has taken these accounts from an Arabic book, which contained the history of these kings, and is known to have made use of more such Arabian materials in the work abovementioned (H) (I).

SECT.

(G) In Juchas fol. קלח edit. Cracoviensi.

(H) Pocock in præf. ad Abulpharaij Dynastias.

(I) If these accounts deserved any degree of regard, it might be worth while to endeavour to compare them with others; but being an ill-digested mixture of all kinds of in-

SECT. XXV.

Having thus proposed our doubts and sentiments on the several accounts of the Egyptian kings still extant, we shall now add some observations, which may conduce to a right use of them as we do not undertake to give an actual plan of this chronology, whilst we cannot propose our opinions otherwise than as dubious, at least not as certain and uncontrovertible. It would indeed, be no very arduous point, if after the example of many chronologers, we should build much on conjectures. Therefore, deferring this attempt to another time, we shall first wait to see what judgment will be formed on these positions, and consequently what reception such an attempt may *Of the right use of these accounts.*

informations, it would be but a fruitless labour; however, we shall bestow the following short remarks upon them.

Kraus perhaps is taken from Manetho's Kirites and by the Christian Copts, transferred from among the gods into the fifth descent from Adam, in order to give a better appearance to this account.

Esmun, or Aschmun, seems to have been taken from the pretended Phenician accounts, (37) where he is set down as the eighth son of Sydis, and is also called Esculapius.

Budesir may be compared to Busiris, unless the contradiction of other accounts is allowed to have weight against it.

Gad, or the Hebrew [illegible] Ath, is the Grecian ὧρος Horus; and Sedeth seems not to be different from Seth or Typhon. If the Hebrew Etymology may be permitted, Asmar or the vigilant, might represent Anubis. Tulis is the [illegible] in the Alexandrian chronicle, and in Syncellus, Totis, Tithoes or Mercury. This comparison might be carried to a much greater length towards the elucidation of several particulars, were it not from an apprehension of being too prolix, and that after all, amidst such intricacies, nothing can be advanced but conjectures, and consequently uncertainties.

(37) *Damascius in vitâ Isidori ap. Photium.*

expect from the public. The end of theſe reſearches being to reconcile theſe hiſtories and their chronology with that of the bible, and of other nations, therefore, the greater precaution is requiſite, as conjectures muſt frequently ſupply the want of hiſtorical authorities. It is true that the abſolute truth of theſe will not admit of any formal demonſtration; yet even conjectures may have ſome foundation and veriſimilitude. Where this is wanting, or, unequal to the conſequences drawn from them, ſuch a chronological ſyſtem muſt, at leaſt be uncertain, or rather imaginary and deſtitute of proofs. Therefore we ſhall only exhibit a few obſervations relating to the Egyptian chronology, which may lead to a juſt idea of the ſeveral ſyſtems, and the uſe to be made of them.

SECT. XXVI.

Of the choice of authors.

First as to the authors, who, beſides the plaineſt and fulleſt informations, contain ſingle and ſeparate pieces relating to Egyptian affairs, thoſe only deſerve notice, who are of eſtabliſhed authority.

This authority partly depends upon the diſtance of their own time from the facts they relate; or, if they labour under difficulties in this, their next qualification is an extenſive uſe of other writers, as well as great caution, judgment, and taſte, in the accounts they embrace. Writers, who are deficient in all theſe points, are not to be conſulted for any inſtruction either hiſtorical or chronological; their works have not the leaſt title to the name of hiſtory, ſtuffed as they are, with the moſt monſtrous and incredible relations; which with the endleſs train of fantaſtical inferences from them, would

would totally adulterate all real hiſtory, and embarraſs it with inextricable confuſion (K).

SECT.

(K) Among theſe are, not only the ſuppoſititious narratives of Annius of Viterbo, theſe ſeldom having the undeſerved honour of being cited in hiſtories, though as to Egyptian affairs, Chevreux has given them a place; but more eſpecially the later hiſtorians, chronicles, and ſuch compoſitions as uſually begin with the old fictitious gods and heroes who are ſuppoſed to come into Europe from Aſia and Africa. Thus Oſiris and Iſis, (38) are ſaid not only to have gone into Germany, but likewiſe to have made a viſit to Mars, at the place now called *Merſeburg*, and, among other arts, introduced that of brewing; likewiſe the writers of the northern kingdoms, ſuch as *Saxo Sialandicus*, *Torfæus*, *Ericus*, *Adamus Bremenſis*, and others. Many alſo who have treated on the German affairs, are not free from relating prodigies and miraculous actions, and extolling the atchievments of their ancient monarchs beyond all belief, whom they never fail to make perſons of the moſt remote countries; inſomuch that one knows not whether to pity or expoſe them, it appearing that they had heard or read ſomething of ancient hiſtory, but from the ignorance of their times, were incapable of making a right uſe of ancient writers, and wanting materials in the firſt periods, which their volumes are made to comprehend, they decked their hiſtory with products of their own fruitful invention. But theſe narratives, conſiſting of conjectures accommodated to the taſte then in vogue; it would be very unwarrantable to allow them the credit of hiſtory, in clearing up the abſurdity of ancient times, and to go about to ſupport them by other far-fetched conjectures and forced compariſons with ancient hiſtory. Without a previous ſearch into the perplexed memorials of antiquity, ancient hiſtory will appear to be more fabulous than mythology itſelf. Thus Ninyas or Seſoſtris would be the only repreſentative of all the great perſonages of antiquity, his fame alone would fill every part of the world, he would be the ſole god of all nations, his journies and exploits would far exceed thoſe fabulous ones of Hercules; ſince an hiſtorian of this ſort would attribute to Ninyas, or to any ancient king in his hiſtory, every great exploit or adventure he meets with, or, by a very ſlight interpretation

(38) *Spangenberg's ſaxon Chronicles.*

SECT. XXVII.

The second and third Observation.

Secondly, in the use of all authorities, great caution is requisite, that they be not limited or stretched beyond what the circumstances of the point itself, or the times when they were written will bear; and so far the judgment is free and ought to carry them: whereas it is the practice of many chronologers, in explaining the accounts of antient history, to consult their own particular opinions, more than the connexion with the course of those times. This is the case when they go about to demonstrate that this or that king in Herodotus or Diodorus must properly have been of Thebes or Memphis, without considering that these writers manifestly speak but of one set of kings, without the least intimation of any lesser kingdoms.

Thirdly, these authorities must be such as are of undisputed credit. If every conjecture, however far-fetched, be a warrant for depreciating ancient accounts as erroneous, the whole ancient history would be exposed to the most outrageous abuses; and such instances we see, when upon an imaginary resemblance, some will take upon them to withstand the concurrence of many ancient accounts and decry them as erroneous, corrupted and falsified. It will necessarily happen in history, that many similar adventures may be related of persons quite different; so that if the time and places, and other circumstances by which only they could be distinguished, be slighted and accounted fabulous disguises, one may, with Gerrard Crusius, hold the Iliad to be a history of the

tation, he would shew that they were originally the acts of Ninyas, or at least he would think himself justified in attempting to shew it. In short, all these late ignorant historians might have enriched their histories, at least, with short digressions and a judicious use of their materials, beyond all the ancient writers.

Patri-

Patriarchs and primitive Jews, or with Franc. Bianchini, of the Æthiopians, Egyptians and Assyrians; and from Plutarch's comparisons of the lives of several illustrious Romans and Greeks, one may upon this plan, suppose that he invented the one to be a contrast to the other.

SECT. XXVIII.

Fourth observation.

Fourthly, the Grecian history and chronology are by no means to be looked upon as contemptible, uncertain, and useless; nor let it be concluded that because they interfere with many conjectures, therefore no instruction can be drawn from them. But the most indefensible practice, is an endeavour to amend these chronologies by ones own researches and conjectures. It will be pleaded in answer to this, that there is no knowing from whence the Greeks had their informations; but, were this a conclusive objection, it must likewise affect all ancient history, the Jews only excepted. But tho' the sources whence the Grecians drew their informations, be at present unknown, it does not absolutely follow, that they had none. Oral traditions, and very short and imperfect remarks, might answer the end of determining a Period from some certain and memorable circumstances. It would likewise be an egregious mistake to account Homer's writings the most ancient among the Greeks, for the perfections of those writings, is a proof of the contrary, and several ancient authors expresly mention others as prior to them. Were we possessed of those Grecian writers cited by Dionysius of Halicarnassus, and by Stephanus of Byzantium, they would furnish us with further anecdotes of the transactions in the old Grecian history, and remove any scruples about the possibility of their having been preserved in their

their original truth. It is besides observable, that any fabulous insertions in history are no impediments to the justness of the chronology, as the former may be filled with the most extraordinary and incredible events, without a necessary consequence that the latter must be irregular and fictitious, and the Chaldeans and Egyptians give much greater cause of complaint on the confusions of their chronology than the Greeks. So that it is wrong to represent the most known Grecian epochas as uncertain and false, because they do not correspond with many new discoveries, or rather conjectures.

SECT. XXIX.

[illegible]. *Fifthly*, the superstructure erected upon a principle must bear a proportion to its evident strength. Thus Ninyas, one of the first Assyrian monarchs, did, according to some old accounts, subdue almost the whole earth; and the same conquests being related of the Egyptian king Sesostris, therefore these kings are made to be but one person; we are told that they must be sought for amongst the ancient heroes of the Greeks, among whom they are disguised, and that they were the authors of many revolutions, and the founders of ancient cities even in Europe. Now, in our opinion, the premises are unequal to the support of any such inference, consequently the oldest accounts must be admitted, which place this Sesostris in the fabulous ages. For who will take upon him to shew, that the Egyptian monarchy, when in its infancy, rose to such a degree of power, as to master, not only Assyria, but all Asia and Europe, together with a part of Africa? it must first be shewn that they had any knowledge in those times, of other parts of the world, and further that a com-

communication was opened with them. It is even probable that many nations of Europe, where Seſoſtris is ſaid to have carried his arms, did not ſo much as exiſt at that time. Beſides, the Egyptians themſelves are the authors of this pretence, but as their word is not to be taken in regard to the antiquity, which they arrogate to themſelves, ſo but little credit can be given to theſe accounts of their prodigious conqueſts; yet merely on ſuch oſtentatious relations are grounded all the revolutions of the Grecian hiſtory, even of the modern part of it. The caſual and very remote reſemblances, which are ſuppoſed, in the caſe of ſome perſons, will, by no means, juſtify ſuch diſquiſitions, as we have ſhewn above. To render therefore theſe accounts of Seſoſtris in any degree tolerable, we muſt ſuppoſe Herodotus either to have miſtaken ſome more ancient prince for him, or to have attributed to him many of the other's heroic exploits.

SECT. XXX.

Sixthly, and *laſtly*, it is neceſſary, that in all conjectures and ſuppoſitions, a moſt cloſe attention ſhould be had to the different degrees of their poſſibility. The poſſibility and probability of a conjecture, which is to ſupply the defects of informations, depends particularly on the effects of the ſuppoſed revolutions and their conſequences in the nations and countries whom they muſt have concerned. If theſe events are great and general, or if they affect a whole people, or ſeveral nations, then their conſequences are more important and remarkable; a total ſilence or ignorance, or even a wilful miſrepreſentation of ſuch, is not in the leaſt probable: And in that caſe, conjectures which are advanced as expedients under the ſuppoſed defects of hiſtories, will fall ſhort in probability *Sixth and cloſe.*

bility, at least cannot be accounted satisfactory illustrations. Of this we shall produce an instance from that part of the history of Egypt, in which that people are said to have taken Troy and possessed themselves of Greece. As this is not confirmed by any one ancient writer, it might be imputed to the deficiency of ancient histories, and every conjecture concerning some obscure memorials, seemingly applicable to it, might appear not altogether void of truth and possibility; but upon considering how totally silent the Egyptian histories are on that head, and that it is the more unaccountable, because this dominion in Greece is said to have been of long duration, and been attended with so many vicissitudes, and because the Egyptians were apt to arrogate superiority above all other nations, and all these changes are of a very late date, these things will sink many degrees below probability. Whoever examines the Egyptian accounts in Herodotus of the Trojan war, under king Proteus, cannot but wonder exceedingly, that not the least vestiges are to be found of the share which the Egyptians are said to have had in it, which is sufficient to explode such a fact, however speciously it may be represented. It is equally improbable, that the Greeks should have been totally ignorant of, or should have disguised this event; as the final shaking off the yoke of so powerful a nation must have greatly redounded to their honour, and as they must have apprehended any misrepresentation to be detected by the Egyptians, to whom the writings of Homer and other Grecian narratives were not unknown; and indeed no instances are found that the Grecians took any pains to conceal such revolutions in their state from posterity.

Here we conclude our observations on the opinions which have hitherto prevailed of the Egyptian

tian hiſtory, and the manner of treating it, and would have them conſidered only in this view; for to have given a full analyſis of this chronology, would have ſwelled this eſſay to twice its preſent bulk, and though not ſo in reality, would have given us the appearance of all the temerity and conceitedneſs charged upon too many other chronologers.

REMARKS

REMARKS

ON THE

INTRODUCTION

TO THE

UNIVERSAL HISTORY.

Which contains

The Cosmogony or Creation of the WORLD.

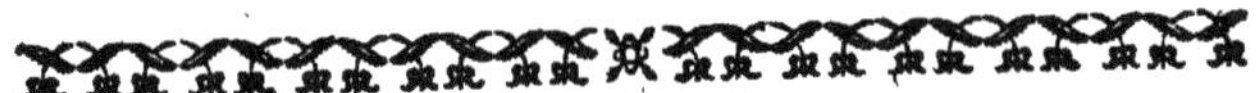

REMARKS

ON THE

INTRODUCTION

TO THE

UNIVERSAL HISTORY, &c.

THIS Introduction is not intended as an essential part of the *Universal History*, nor absolutely necessary for the understanding or use of it. So that the reader, who has no taste for enquiries of that kind, may safely overlook it. But many will find it both entertaining and useful. For besides illustrating the history of philosophy, it serves to dilucidate the first of all events, consequently the beginning of all true history; to confirm the credibility of the scriptural accounts of it, and to shew the great use and expediency of a divine revelation. The learned and thinking reader will easily observe, that the whole will admit, and in many parts require, a further and more accurate examination. He will not acquiesce implicitly in the judgment of others, nor in the authorities alleged, nor in the confutations here cited. He will observe, however, in perusing the accounts and recital of the several opinions and systems, how dark and intricate is the history of human opinions and doctrines, particularly those of ancient times, and how various the opinions of the learned are, upon the subject of learned opinions. In order to examine these more at large, the following authors may be consulted, besides those quoted in the introduction itself; *Gale*, *Stanley*, *T. Burnet*, *Grotius*, *Gassendus*, *Lescalopier*, *Thomasius*, and particularly *Cudworth* and *Bayle*, which the compilers of this introduction consulted; and they seem to have followed the two last too closely. See likewise *Brucker's Hist. crit. Philos. Mosheim's* notes upon *Cudworth*, and a dissertation of his subjoined to his *Latin* translation of *Cudworth*, upon the question, Whether any of the heathen philosophers maintained the world to have been created by God out of nothing? where many passages of this introduction are examined; *Banier's* mythology, *&c. Beausobre hist. critique de Manichee & du Manicheisme*, *Crenii fasciculus dissert.* tom. 1. *Morgues plan theologique du Pythagorisme*, &c. *Sam. Parker's cogitationes de Deo*, *Dickenson's physica vetus & nova*, *Vossius de Theol. gentili*, &c. *Huetii demonst. evangel.* and his *Quæstiones alnetanæ*, and *Buddei Theses de atheismo & superstitione.*

Pag. 4. Of the non-existence of matter.

The opinion of the non-existence of matter is exploded by *Christ. Wolf.* in his *Theol. natur.* part 2. and by *Carpzov.* in his *Idealismus ex concessis explosus.*—The necessity here asserted of an infinite divisibility of matter, and of a vacuum, will hardly be universally admitted. Nor can it be taken for granted, that we have no clear ideas of extension and space, or that the difficulties objected by the idealists are unanswerable, for which, in point of discretion, *Bayle* was not the author to appeal to.

Pag. 4. Third Opinion of the origin of the world.

The third opinion, being placed in opposition to the other two, must import, as it is afterwards explaned, that the world had a beginning both as to matter and form; else the advocates for the second opinion might admit a change of the present form of the world, without prejudice to their doctrine of the eternity of matter; as those may be ranked under the third class, who maintain the beginning of the world, tho' they should not admit the dissolution of it.

Here seems to be a mistake in confounding two persons of the same name who both taught at *Alexandria* with considerable reputation, and were highly revered among the latter *Platonists*, or rather *Eclectic* philosophers. The younger *Ammonius*, who was the scholar of *Proclus*, and the master of *Simplicius*, of *John Philoponus*, and *Damascius*, florished in the sixth century, and is vindicated against *Zacharias*'s charge of atheism by *Reimman* in his *Hist. atheismi*; but he was neither the first assertor of this doctrine of the eternity of the world, nor the person who first introduced it into the christian church, for in both respects he had great predecessors, particularly *Ammonius Saccas*, the teacher of *Origen*, to whom both are more justly to be attributed. See *Brucker*'s account of both in his *Hist. phil.* *Pag. 8. Ammonius, the scholar of Proclus.*

When the compilers here seem to insinuate, that the creation of the world out of nothing, and in time, is not easily demonstrated by mere reason, it is to be observed, that they mention this only as the confession of some eminent men, which is not to be interpreted to the prejudice of others, who have defended that doctrine upon rational principles, even as the confession of many men of tolerable abilities, that it is not demonstrable from scripture, doth not supersede the scriptural proofs of it. This last was a strange confession made by *Beausobre*, and laboriously maintained, in contradiction to the passages of scripture, which are alleged to support it, and to the testimony of *Petavius*. However, the consequence drawn by the compilers is true from other premisses; that the heathen philosophers, *Pag. 9. The creation of the world in time.*

who had no immediate revelation from God, are more excusable, in this respect, than Jewish or Christian philosophers, who have maintained this error.

Pag. 10. *Opinion of the* Socinians *about the eternity of matter.*

The opinion of the eternity of matter is commonly imputed to the *Socinians*; but *Beausobre* proves, that it is no general tenet of theirs, and shews, against the conjecture and insinuation of *Bayle*, who affirmed it to have sprung from the impossibility and incomprehensibility of a creation from nothing, that those among the *Socinians*, who disputed the creation out of nothing, were led to it merely by the difficulty of proving the same from scripture, which difficulty was all they meant to maintain. Thus much is certain, that in later times several philosophers, from their unbounded veneration for the doctrines of some erroneous sects among the ancients, have fallen into the suspicion, at least, of this error. *Beausobre* interprets some passages in the fathers in favor of this error; but this is an accusation not easily supported.

Pag. 11. Bayle's *opinion of the eternity of the world.*

It being matter of doubt, whether *Bayle* is the opposer or the advocate of the eternity of the world; it being certain, at least, that he hath endeavored to render both sides doubtful; one would suspect that he did not, in earnest, esteem this argument against the eternity of the world a sufficient confutation of it; but from his opinions and conclusions in other parts of his philosophical works, we may judge, that his way of thinking may very well admit of an inconsistency. But the compilers are excusable in their seeming approbation of it, since those who compile historical accounts of opinions and the refutation of them, are not always judges of their strength or weakness, or capable of discerning and correcting the errors of others. A judicious enquiry into past events, and a knowlege of of abstract subtil truths, are very distinct talents, tho' very consistent, and of reciprocal use to each other. The principal errors of *Bayle*'s doctrine are the following; 1. He represents the divine decree of creation as subsequent to several other acts and decrees of God, even the pretended creation of time, whence it ceases to be an eternal decree. 2. He supposes the possibility of a successive duration without beginning and end, which is not only void of proof, but absolutely false and absurd, and therefore God could neither conceive nor actually form it. As no number can be imagined without unity and beginning, tho' it may be multiplied to infinity, so we cannot conceive a series of successive beings, without supposing a first or beginning. 3. He supposes a creation of time without successive beings, which is as absurd as the actual existence of a quality or accident without supposing the existence of a substance to which it belongs; or as it would be to maintain, that God transferred a number from a state of bare possibility to a state of actual existence, without creating things numbered or numerable.

Pag. 11. *Restriction of the word* unintelligible, *as applied to the divine nature.*

The word *unintelligible* is ambiguous. If it be meant to express the want, or the impossibility, of a sensible representation of a thing, or of a clear idea and explanation of the entire possibility of it, this is no argument against any thing supported by other proofs. And that the eternity of God, and every idea of infinity, is, in this respect, incomprehensible, will be readily admitted. But if the word be meant to signify a contradiction, which cannot be conceived, in this sense it is not, with any proof, applicable to the eternity of God, unless we make the authority of learned and ingenious men pass for an argument, which is here the case; or unless we so change a doctrine by misrepresentation, as to render it contradictory and absurd. If we avoid the latter abuse, then the two objections here made lose their force. For when the eternity of God is called an instant, the expression is comparative, not meant to signify literally a moment, but only an exclusion of all dependent successive beings, or to express his indivisibility. But when it is affirmed of the necessary being of God, that it exists together or at once, and therefore admits no internal succession, this doth not affect the relation of successive beings to God, which exist without him; for in that relation coexistence takes place, tho' it produces no internal succession in the essence of God, and his necessary existence or duration, but rather implies, that God continues unchangeable, and co-exists with all successive beings.

Pag. 12. *and* 13. Bayle *and* Cudworth *on* Xenophanes.

The compilers were not willing to decide, but only to state, the very different opinions of *Bayle* and *Cudworth* concerning the eleatic sect. Both sides are espoused by learned men, some, like M. *Bayle*, taxing *Xenophanes* with being the predecessor of *Spinoza*; others, among whom are *Fabricius* and *Mosheim*, disculpating him, and representing his doctrine in a more favorable and rational light. *Brucker* has chosen a medium, and whilst he admits and proves *Xenophanes*'s doctrine to be distinct from *Spinoza*'s, he, at the same time, charges *Simplicius* with having perverted his real opinion, which, considering the prejudices of this last, and how strangely he reconciles the most contrary opinions, is not at all improbable. See *Brucker*'s *Hist. Phil.*

Pag. 14. Strato *of* Lampsacus.

The real doctrine of *Strato* is not more precisely determined, than that of *Xenophanes*. *Bayle*, *Leibnitz*, and others, more than once, charge him with *Spinosism*; and *Leibnitz* calls the *Spinosists* by the name of *Stratonicians*. But others refute the charge. It is generally agreed, indeed, that he

was

was one of the atheists of antiquity; but *Brucker*, among others, shews his errors to have been very different from those of *Spinoza*.

Pag. 15. Alexander the Epicurean.

The account of the person and doctrine of *Alexander* is very defective and suspicious. *Thomasius*, in the passage referred to, appeals only to the passage here cited, of *Albertus Magnus*, whose ignorance in the history of philosophy was so great, that he stiled all erroneous philosophers *Epicureans*. *Thomasius*'s addition, that he was cotemporary and intimate with *Plutarch*, is groundless, especially as *Plutarch* made use of fictitious names in his dialogues, and no other traces occur of an *Epicurean* of this name. It is besides probable, that *Albertus* meant neither *Almaric*, the teacher of this *David* of *Dinant*, nor *Alexander Aphrodiseus*, whose expositions of *Aristotle*, as well as the writings of *Aristotle* themselves, were at that time esteemed the fountain of these errors; and perhaps the whole may be invention.

Pag. 15. Almaric.

Almaric is the name of this famous teacher, rather than *Amalric*. The *French* call him, upon still better authority, *Amauri*. The synod held at *Paris* in the year 1209, which condemned this *Almaric* and his followers, at the same time order'd the works of *Aristotle*, which had occasioned these heresies, to be burnt, and prohibited the reading, or transcribing, or possession of them, under pain of excommunication. This decree was confirmed and recommended strongly to the university of *Paris* by the pope's legate in 1215, and by pope *Gregory* the ninth himself in 1233. We may conjecture, from hence, that this sect taught the *peripatetic* doctrine, to which they might add some *platonic* tenets and expressions, taken from the writings of the spurious *Dionysius* the *Areopagite*, and *Joh. Scotus Erigena*, without supposing them to have been the direct predecessors of *Spinoza*.

The

Pag. 15, *and* 16. Japonese *and* Mohammedan *opinions.* The sects and doctrines among the *Japonese* are derived from *China*, of both which more will occur in the sequel. The whole account here given of the *Spinosism* of the *Mohammedans* is taken from *Bayle*, who, in the article of *Spinoza*, and that of *Abumuslimus*, is very copious on this subject, but should be compared with *Sale*'s preliminary discourse to his *Koran*, § 8. p. 176 and 182.

Pag. 17. Pliny. The opinion of *Pliny* the elder is not to be gathered from here and there a passage, as he frequently proposes very different and contrary opinions, without declaring his own. So that this passage, which savours of *Stoicism*, doth not prove him a follower of that sect, for he was generally reckoned an *Epicurean*.

Pag. 17, *and* 18. *Confutation of* Spinoza. The confutation of *Spinoza* is chiefly taken from *Bayle*, and will hardly satisfy a sagacious adversary, as it consists partly of consequences drawn from premisses, whose absurdity is taken for granted, and partly of principles, which, if some of them are demonstrable, do all require much proof, and will not easily be admitted by the other side. However those, who are convinced of these principles, may see enough here to discover the falsity and wickedness of this system.

Pag. 19. Bayle *mistaken in his confutation of the second opinion.* The position of *Bayle*, that those who suppose two or more eternal beings are more inconsistent than atheists, may appear very specious, but, if narrowly examined, will prove mistaken and groundless. In order to form a judgment in the comparison of false doctrines, which of them are more or less consistent, we must examine the arguments for, and deductions from, their principles, their mutual connexion with each other and with their consequences, and the number, weight, and solidity of the other difficulties that attend them. In all these respects, those who totally exclude God from the disposition and government of the world, are charge-

chargeable with more internal contradiction and abſurdity. The difficulty here ſtarted concerning the power of God over matter, is founded in the miſtake, that matter has any rights like thoſe of a rational being, of which it is as incapable as it is of obligations. It is true, the doctrine that God is the full and neceſſary proprietor of all things is much better eſtabliſhed, by ſuppoſing the exiſtence of matter, and the whole diſpoſition of the world, to be grounded in him, and derived from him; and the neceſſary ſubjection of all rational creatures, or God's neceſſary ſovereignty over them cannot be demonſtrable without deriving their origin and exiſtence from God. But ſtill the formation of mere matter, which is here ſuppoſed to be neither living nor rational, cannot be deemed an unjuſt *uſurpation*, contrary to the law of nature, ſince property may ariſe amongſt men from merely taking poſſeſſion of things, which were not before the property of another, nor capable of any property in themſelves.

Pag. 22. Hiſtorical proofs of the beginning of the earth.

The hiſtorical proofs of the beginning of the earth are drawn either from natural hiſtory, or from the hiſtory of mankind. The former require much caution, that our obſervations be true and demonſtrable, and that we place no ſuch changes of the earth to this account, as may affect the doctrine of its creation in time, and of its future diſſolution, in caſe it ſhould appear that the loſſes it has ſuſtained have been repaired. For the conſumption of water by plants is repaired by the inceſſant exhalations of plants and animals, and the waſhing away of land and ſinking of mountains is compenſated by the increaſe of land in other parts, and the appearance of whole iſlands. The ſame caution may be given with reſpect to Dr. *Halley*'s asgument in the philoſophical tranſactions, drawn from the perpetual increaſe of the

ſalts

ſalts in the ſea, where it is ſuppoſed that theſe ſalts have no waſte in proportion, tho' the contrary is indiſputable from the exhalations and the number of animals. The hiſtory of mankind proves no more than the impoſſibility of an eternal ſucceſſion of the human race upon earth, by obviating all poſſible evaſions of the adverſary, in ſhewing the improbability or impoſſibility of the frequent deſtruction of the far greater part of mankind, without deſtroying them all.

Pag. 23. Sanchoniatho. *His antiquity.*

The learned differ in opinion about the authenticity of the fragment of *Sanchoniatho*, as well as about the ſenſe and merits of his coſmogony. The chief of thoſe who diſpute the antiquity of it are *Urſinus*, *Van Dale*, and *Dodwell*, whoſe arguments being drawn from the ſilence of all ancient writers till the ſecond century, from the miſtakes in chronology, and from the mention of later opinions and facts, are of ſome weight, and prove, at leaſt, an interpolation. The advocates for the antiquity of it are biſhop *Cumberland*, the *Memoires de Trevoux*, Jan. 1714. and *Tourmont* in his *Refl. ſur les anciens peuples*. It is to be wiſhed, that ſome one would vindicate the authenticity of this fragment, by ſolidly refuting the objections made to it. It ſeems incredible that a piece of ſuch conſequence ſhould be unknown to every writer before *Porphyry*; that it ſhould be forgot by *Joſephus*, eſpecially in his books againſt *Appion*, and by all the polemic writers, both of the chriſtian and heathen party, till the fourth century, and be firſt produced by the younger *Philo* in the ſecond. It is poſſible, on the other hand, that, at a time which abounded more than any other in ſpurious pieces, the heathens might forge a writing which gave their theology a more tolerable appearance, and reconciled it better to true hiſtory, than any of the *Greek* poets; and that *Euſebius*, and other chriſtian writers after him,

par-

particularly *Theodoret* and *Cyril*, might be apt to receive it as genuine, from their zeal in applying to their own advantage, ſomewhat indiſcriminately and incautiouſly, all the domeſtic authorities of their adverſaries; eſpecially as this fragment ſeemed favourable to them in ſeveral inſtances, where it corresponds with the ſcriptural hiſtory, or at leaſt as it was an admirable tract againſt the fabulous theology of the *Grecians*. As to the interpretation of this coſmogony, ſome have conſider'd it as agreeable to *Moſes*'s account; theſe are *Cudworth*, *Grotius*, *Bochart*, and *Huetius*. Others rightly oppoſe them, and either interpret the whole of the doctrine of atoms, which has been done by *Godf. Olearius*, or diſtinguiſh it from that, becauſe it ſuppoſes two, tho' material, principles; which is done by *Cumberland*, *Moſheim* upon *Cudworth*, *Brucker*, and *Banier*. This interpretation would be more uniform and conſiſtent, if *Zophaſemin* were not underſtood to be the heavenly bodies, but rather the animals of the earth, who were ordained to enjoy, perceive, and contemplate the heavens; and the latter part of the doctrine authorizes this, where the intelligent animals are repreſented to have been awakened and terrified at the ſound of thunder, long after the exiſtence of the ſun and ſtars. The uſe which *Porphyry* makes of this fragment ſhews, that he thought it of ſervice to the heathen cauſe; and *Euſebius*, upon the ſame principle, diſputes both the contents and the pretended antiquity of it. See *Fabricii Bibl. Græc.* and *Cuper*'s Letters, and a diſſertation upon *Sanchoniatho*, addreſſed to *Heineccius*. *His coſmogony.*

The *Egyptian* coſmogony has been treated like the *Phenician*. Thoſe who allege that it agrees with *Moſes*'s hiſtory of the creation, ſeem to have been encouraged by the hopes that the ſcriptural hiſtory would derive particular advantages from this *Pag. 25—28. The* Egyptian *coſmogony.*

this confirmation of it, and have, on that account, been extremely well received. These authors are *Grotius*, *Huetius*, *Cudworth*, *Dickinson*, and *Witsius*, in his *Ægyptiac*. But as such foreign confirmation of scripture ought, in general, to be applied with the utmost caution, so with respect to the *Egyptian* doctrine it has, in general, been carried to an extravagant height, particularly by *Kircher*; and in treating of this cosmogony the true meaning of it has been misrepresented, and a new, corrupt, and spurious, has been confounded with the ancient genuine *Egyptian* system. Our compilers have therefore very judiciously chosen the other opinion, and represented the *Egyptian* doctrine as excluding God from the formation of the world; which is confirmed by *Cumberland*, *Mosheim*, *Brucker*, and *Banier*. According to the order here observed, the *Egyptian* philosophy seems to be preferred in point of antiquity to the *Chaldean*; upon which subject the learned are divided in opinion, since the controversy between *Conring* and *Borrichius*, most of them siding with the former, but our compilers, among others, with the latter. Of *Hermes* and *Thot* see *Ursinus*, *Fabricius*, and *Brucker*.

Pag. 29. *The* Babylonian *cosmogony*. Berosus.

The fragments of *Berosus*, which are preserved by the *Greek* writers, are collected and illustrated by *Fabricius* in his *Bibl. Gr.* *Beausobre* has attempted to compare this piece of the *Chaldean* cosmogony with the *Mosaic* account, and with the *Manichean* system, which last he endeavors to deduce from it. See some illustrations of it in *Banier*'s *Mythol.*

Pag. 32. Orpheus's *cosmogony*.

Banier, in his account of the *Orphic* cosmogony, has transcribed much from this introduction, without quoting it. The subject has been further discuss'd by *Eschenbach*, and *Mosheim* upon *Cudworth*, who, together with *Brucker*, is of the opinion here maintained, that the *Orphic* system excludes God from

from the actual creation of the world, and ſuppoſes a neceſſary exiſtence of matter in God, and a formation of it without any divine operation, tho' *Grotius*, *Huetius*, *Dickinſon*, *Cudworth*, and *Burnet* are miſled by their uſual prejudices, and the miſrepreſentations of the *Platonic* writers, to maintain the contrary.

As *Grotius*, *Dickenſon*, and others, have gone too far in attempting to reconcile the ancient *Theogony* of the *Greeks* to the *Moſaic* ſyſtem of the creation, ſo the opinion of *Cudworth*, on the other ſide, which is here approved, is too ſevere, or at leaſt it is expreſſed ambiguouſly. It is true this ſyſtem excludes, or wholly omits, God in the creation of the world; ſo far it may be called atheiſtical, as an atheiſt may receive it conſiſtently with his principles; but that it implies a denial of the exiſtence of a perfect ſupreme being, diſtinct from the world thus formed, and that all the profeſſors of this ſyſtem are therefore convicted of atheiſm, cannot be proved. See *Moſheim* upon *Cudworth*, and *Brucker*'s *Hiſt. philoſ.* *Pag.* 36. *Theogony of the* Greek *poets*.

In paſſing a judgment upon the doctrine of the origin of the world, delivered by *Thales*, whoſe anceſtors were *Phenicians*, and himſelf a *Mileſian*, we muſt obſerve the ſame medium, which was recommended above, with reſpect to the *Grecian Theogony*. So that this coſmogony is rightly placed among thoſe which exclude God from the creation of the world, without adding to the number of atheiſts the founder of the *Ionic* philoſophy. *Brucker*, in his *Hiſt. phil.* diſcuſſes the ſuſpicion of *Thales*'s atheiſm, and refers to his principal advocates. *Pag.* 37. Thales.

According to *Brucker*'s account, juſt mentioned, of the *Ionic* philoſophers, it is very difficult to decide upon the charge of atheiſm exhibited againſt them, as the true ſtate of their opinions, and the real meaning of their dark expreſſions cannot eaſily be *Pag.* 39. *and* 40. *The* Ionic *philoſophy*.

be aſcertained for want of immediate accounts concerning them. However, their moſt zealous advocates will admit, that their doctrine accounts for the origin of the world without the interpoſition of God, which, at the ſame time, does not imply a denial or doubt of the actual exiſtence of a ſupreme being diſtinct from the world. So that their philoſophy is not here miſplaced by the compilers, tho' their opinion of the atheiſm of its founders requires and will admit of great limitation, no leſs than the compariſon of *Anaxagoras*'s doctrine with that of *Spinoſa* and *Des Cartes*.

Pag. 40. *The* Atomic *ſyſtem.* The compilers, in favoring the antiquity of the atomic ſyſtem long before *Leucippus*, adhere too cloſely to *Cudworth*, without weighing and anſwering the objections of *Burnet* in his *Archæol. Brucker* likewiſe examines and refutes the harmony here alleged, of the *Italic*, *Megaric*, and *Eleatic* Schools, and all the ancient naturaliſts, with the *Atomic* ſyſtem. The bare agreement of a ſingle word, ſuch as *Indiviſibility*, hath heretofore occaſioned very different, ſometimes directly contrary, ſyſtems of philoſophy, to be miſtaken for each other, or at leaſt to be thought ſimilar, which hath rendered ſome opinions more conſiderable or more ſuſpicious than they might otherwiſe have been.

Pag. 43. *and* 44. Democritus. The account of *Democritus*'s doctrine, and the compariſon of it with *Malebranche*'s opinion are taken from *Bayle*, who was too precipitate in both. See *Brucker* and *Moſheim* upon *Cudworth*. Epicurus. *Brucker* examines the charge of atheiſm againſt *Epicurus*, which could not be done without previouſly removing the ambiguity uſual in theſe enquiries. It is indiſputable, that *Epicurus*, in his doctrine of the origin of the world, excludes the Deity from the creation of it, and that therefore a follower of his may be an atheiſt. It is likewiſe undoubted, that he maintained very groſs errors concerning God,

which

which interfere with the right notions of that most perfect and necessary being. But that he was, strictly speaking, an atheist, who denied the existence of God, is an assertion not only void of proof, but plainly disproved in many parts of his system. The question is not, Whether in those parts he delivered his full and real sentiments, since this is rather matter for conjecture than proof.

Pag. 45. Diogenes *of* Apollonia.

It is improbable that *Diogenes* of *Apollonia* maintained the opinion here imputed to him, since it must have led him to depart too far from the *Ionic* system. See *Brucker hist. Phil.*

Pag. 45. Heraclitus.

Olearius, who translated *Stanley*'s lives of the philosophers, has, in a dissertation, annex'd, *de principiis & genesi rerum ex mente Heracliti*, studied to defend *Heraclitus* from the imputation of atheism. But *Brucker* confirms the opinion of the compilers, and treats more at large of the doctrine of *Hippocrates*. However, the charge of atheism upon this last, is not so easily proved, at least has been more contested; for *Gundling*, who maintained it, has been answered by *Fabricius*, and several other writers in *Germany*, besides *Cudworth* and *Drellincourt*, in his Greek oration, since translated into *French*, upon the agreement of *Hippocrates* with the holy Scriptures.

Pag. 46, *and* 47. *The* Stoics.

The authors to be consulted upon the opinion of the *Stoics*, besides those referred to by the compilers, are, *Lipsius de physiologia stoica*, *Thomasius de exustione mundi stoica*, and his dissertations upon their history, *Buddeus de erroribus stoicorum* and *Brucker de fato stoico*, and in his *hist. phil.*

Pag. 48, *and* 49. *The* Chinese.

The different opinions of the *Chinese* may be seen in *du Halde*'s description of that empire, vol. 3d, where a conference is related with *Tchin*, a modern *Chinese* philosopher, concerning the origin of the world. See likewise, *Kempfer's histoire de l'empire du Japon*, for the *Chinese* doctrines have

 been

been propagated in that empire. It will appear, upon consulting these authors, that the doctrines of the followers of *Confucius*, are not sufficiently distinguished here from those of the *Tao-tsee*, or the followers of *Lao-kiun*, or *Roos*, and the modern Literati among the *Chinese*, and we shall find that these doctrines are surprisingly confused and uncertain, which partly proceeds from the obscurity and ambiguity of their most ancient religious books, partly from the difference between their public and private doctrines, partly from an endeavour to reconcile the most contradictory tenets, and in great measure, from the modern controversy between the Jesuits and the other *Chinese* missionaries, about the signification of the words *Tien* and *Chang-Ti*.

Pag. 50. *Sect of the* She Kia. According to the *Hist. du Japon*, before cited, the founder of the sect of *She Kia*, which hath spread itself over all the Eastern countries, came from Egypt. *Mat. la Croze* in his *hist. du Christianisme des Indes*, supposes him to be the famous *Buddas*, whom many confound with *Buddas* the *Manichean*.

Pag. 50. Japonese *doctrine adopted by the* Chinese. The opinion here attributed to the *Japonese*, is the doctrine of the modern Literati in *China*, who have studied to reconcile the secret tenets of *She Kia*, with those of their most ancient theology.

Pag. 52. Pherecydes. It being not only doubtful, but improbable, that *Pherecydes* maintained *time* to be a substantial self-existent principle, (as is falsely affirmed of other ancient theogonies,) he may more properly be ranked among those, who ascribe every thing to two principles perpetually changing, and supposed time to have effected the series or succession of those changes.

Pag. 54. Pythagoras. The opinion that *Pythagoras's Tetractys* was no other than the Hebrew *Tetragrammaton*, is founded on his pretended travels into the Eastern countries,

tries, and his conversation with the *Hebrews*. But the witnesses of these facts are not only too remote in point of time, but contradict the chronology of more ancient historians, and more authentic accounts, besides labouring under the suspicion of having reported them from mere conjecture, or perhaps from prejudice. It is moreover inconsistent with *Pythagoras*'s doctrine of numbers. We may therefore conclude, with more probability, that, as he considered the different proportions of numbers, and their relation not only to the proportions of greater numbers, but of all abstract ideas in general, to be a proper medium, in which to represent his philosophy and the doctrine of nature, he was induced to call the Deity *Tetractys*, by the proportion that number bears to others, which might be the case without any farther mystery, than his symbolical use of numbers. For the perfection of this number consists chiefly in this, that being added to the numbers preceding it, the amount is *ten*, that it stands in the middle of *seven*, that it is the first real square number, and the first geometrical progression of numbers, and that it is the first and least number capable of representing solid bodies, since a triangular pyramid requires only three planes. It is clear from hence, why *Pythagoras* chose this number as the symbol of perfection, and of the Deity, considered as the soul of the world, or as a symbol of God in his relation to the world, for out of that relation he stiled him the *Monad*.—The greatest objection to his doctrine is certainly this, that he asserted God to be the soul and nature of the world, and consequently the universe to be a necessary emanation of the Deity; which reduces it, in the main, to the *stoical* system.

The doctrine attributed to *Plato* by *Hierocles*, is a misrepresentation of his true meaning, forged by the *Pag. 57. Plato.*

the latter *Platonists*, particularly those of *Alexandria*, or of the *Eclectic* School. Many of the fathers, and some modern *Literati*, have been misled by this to imagine the *platonic* system more consonant to the christian doctrine than it really is, which cannot be supposed without prejudice to both systems. For some authors, *Bayle* in particular, have, upon the authority of this misrepresentation, charged *Plato* with downright atheism.

Pag. 59. Anaxagoras. The principle of *Anaxagoras*, *that a philosopher is not to have recourse to God*, may be taken in an innocent sense. It may mean no more, than that in accounting for natural events we are not to set aside second causes, and the laws of motion, by having immediate recourse to the Deity, nor to pretend miracles without proof or necessity. But it becomes a dangerous principle, if it be made the pretence for excluding God entirely from the connexion of causes and effects, and resting in contingencies for the account of natural events, or for confining the operation of the Deity to the production and establishment of the connexion of contingencies, or for denying the possibility of miracles. It is doubtful, however, whether this was the meaning of *Anaxagoras*, at least *Aristotle*, *Plato*, *Clemens* of *Alexandria*, and *Eusebius*, do not expressly charge him with impiety, for they only censure the exclusion of spirits from the events and changes of the material world. He seems to have differed very little both in his intention and doctrine from the first *Atomists*, and it is not determined, which of the two systems labors under most difficulties.

Pag. 60. Empedocles. The physiology of *Empedocles*, and his doctrine of the origin of all things, doth not agree so perfectly, as is here pretended, with the *Ionic* system of *Anaxagoras*, for he, like most of *Pythagoras*'s disciples, retained the substance of his physiology.

At

At least it is difficult to comprehend how his doctrine can be fundamentally the same with that of *Anaxagoras*, of *Democritus*, of *Epicurus*, and *Pythagoras*. Systems so very different should be compared with the utmost caution and restriction. There can be but little agreement between the *atomic* system and that of *Empedocles*, as the principal difference consists in the three opinions, in which the latter departs from the *atomists*, and as *Aristotle* expresly opposes him to them. The friendship and contention of *Empedocles* are applied only to matter as one of the principles he maintains, and are meant to shew how so great a diversity of creatures naturally arose from a matter originally uniform.

Plutarch, in different parts of his works, represents several philosophical systems, tho' not with equal accuracy and truth. But himself was a *Platonist* and of the *academic* sect, from which the account here given of the origin of the world is wholly borrowed. *Pag.* 61. Plutarch.

The whole account of *Hermogenes* is taken from *Cudworth*, who hath not stated *Hermogenes*'s doctrine exactly, and exaggerates in his account of modern errors. *Tertullian*, in relating his opinion, that God could not produce the world out of himself, says his reason was, because then all the creatures of God would be parts of himself, whereas he is indivisible, unchangeable, and for ever the same. The modern sects of christians here mentioned, must be chiefly *Socinians*, and perhaps some fanatics; but this is imputing to whole bodies of men the errors of some few writers, and without precisely determining the grounds and occasion of such errors. *Pag.* 61. Hermogenes.

It is not so unquestionable as is here pretended, that the creation of the world was admitted and asserted by the heathen nations alleged. After the *Pag.* 6 *Opinion of several heathen nations.*

 utmost

utmost endeavors to interpret favorably all the accounts we have of their doctrines, this interpretation of them will still remain suspicious and improbable. It is even more applicable to the two other opinions before exhibited, than to some of the systems under this third head.

Pag. 64. *Of the* Tuscans. It is not only possible but probable, that the system of the *Tuscans* was founded in the notion of the pre-existence of matter. For it could never have required so long a time to form the parts of the world, and the several kinds of creatures, without supposing a resistance and unfitness in matter; and the alternate dissolution and successive renovation of the world, as well as the whole opinion of the *great year*, imply such an eternity of the world, as was afterwards improved in the stoic system.

Pag. 65. *The* Oriental *writers.* The *oriental* writers here appealed to, are the *Arabian* historians, who not only lived at a great distance of time, but are justly suspected to have misrepresented the doctrine of the ancient *Magi* by additions of their own. The *Greek* remains of *Zoroastres* are, in point of authenticity, very suspicious and exceptionable.

Pag. 66. *The* Persian Magi. The *Persian* doctrine of the creation, especially as the opinion of the *Magi* stands amended by *Zerduscht*, approaches somewhat nearer to orthodoxy, by supposing the two principles subject to the supreme God and derived from him, whom they called *Zervan*, *Jezdan*, and *Mithram*. *Hyde*, *Prideaux*, *Beausobre*, and others, have confirmed this account of their doctrine. However, it is still embarrass'd with the eternity of the pre-existing matter and darkness, or rather with an eternal emanation of it from God himself,

Pag. 70. *The* Chinese. The account here given of the *Chinese* doctrine of the beginning of things, depends entirely upon the interpretation of the celebrated figures of *Fo Hi*, which the *Chinese* call *Yking*, and revere as their most

moſt ancient religious ſyſtem; but not the leaſt trace of the immediate operation of Deity occurs in this interpretation, tho' we frequently meet with the word *Shang ti*, i. e. heaven or nature. It is certain from *Du Halde*, that the modern diſciples of *Confucius* in their expoſition of the *Y king*, derive all things from *Tai ki*, the firſt original matter, and from *Li* the form of it. Whatever therefore might be the opinion of the ancient *Chineſe* and of *Confucius*, and ſome of his modern followers, it is undoubted that the people in general hold matter to be eternal, or perhaps the world to ariſe and periſh in an infinite ſucceſſion, conſequently that it was never ſtrictly ſpeaking created.

Pag. 71. *The* Japoneſe.

The religious doctrines of the *Japoneſe* are divided by *Kempfer* in his *Hiſt. du Japon*, into three kinds. Their moſt ancient idolatry *Sintos*, or *Sinſhu*, or *Kamimitſi*, i. e. the worſhip of *Kami*, contains the moſt abſurd fables of the origin of things, deriving every thing, ſpirits, gods and men from the chaos. The ſecond kind *Budſdo*, or the worſhip of foreign deities, or *Fotoke*, is the doctrine of *She kia*, which is much leſs conſiſtent with an actual creation. Now *Amida* being a deity of this ſect, preſiding over heaven and happineſs, eſpecially after death, the panegyrics here beſtowed upon *Amida* will hardly demonſtrate that this people believed the world to have been, ſtrictly ſpeaking, created. The third ſect, called *Siuto*, are their modern philoſophers, who embrace the doctrine of *Confucius*, according to the interpretation of his modern expoſitors, and admit no Deity but *nature* and *heaven*, by which ſome, indeed underſtand a ſpiritual governor, but not an author and creator of all things.

Pag. 75. *Objections to the* Carteſian *ſyſtem.*

In order to anſwer the good purpoſe here candidly attributed to *Des Cartes*, it is not ſufficient merely to intend it, but care muſt be taken that the

the means do not rather obscure and shake, than confirm and proclaim the wisdom and other attributes of God. This is manifestly the case with the *Cartesian* account of the origin of the world, as it not only affects the scriptural history of it, but imputes a needless and irregular conduct to the Deity; the production, for instance, of uniform matter, the division of it into such bodies as might be fit to compose the intended creation, and must pass thro' a tedious process before they become elements. Not to mention the intricacy and absurdity of this system, which hath induced *Huetius*, *Daniel*, and *Leibnitz*, justly to stile it an irregular romance. Besides the difficulties here stated, which are partly borrowed from hypotheses, it is evident that *Des Cartes* confounds motion itself, and the unchangeable laws of it, with the powers of motion; that his pretended division of matter into bodies closely joined together without a vacuum, leaves it inconceivable how either the division or the motion could take place; and that the bare difference of figure in the elements will not suffice to account for the composition of bodies and their various properties.

Pag. 78. *Objections to* Burnet's *system.* It is here said that oil, or any other liquor, could not possibly sustain such an immense heavy orb as Dr. *Burnet* supposes; but this must be understood only of the first gradual descent of the terrene particles, which would interfere with the laws of hydrostatics, or of the equilibrium and motion of fluid bodies; for the orb being once closed and fixed would need no support. But however specious this whole theory of the earth may seem, when considered by itself, it is involved in inextricable difficulties, when compared with the rest of the creation. For as the other great planets are supposed to have existed, and doubtless to have arisen according to the same laws of motion,

whence

whence did matter and chaos arise? What was the origin of the earth, or why did not the motion of it take place sooner? Or how is it that during so long a formation of the terrestrial globe no impression was made upon it by the neighbouring planets, or by the air which they agitated. For this hypothesis supposes the earth absolutely independent of the planets, with which it is undoubtedly connected, and the earth, as well as the vacuum taken for the formation of it, to be wholly separate from the regions contiguous to it, all which contradicts the most undeniable experience of philosophers.

Pag. 78. *The literal sense of scripture defended against Burnet.*

Dr. *Burnet*, in disputing the literal sense of the *Mosaic* history of the creation, confounds things very distinct, advances doubtful facts, and draws false conclusions. The *literal* and *verbal* sense are not the same, for the latter comprehends the figurative as well as the literal meaning. In like manner, figurative and sensible images, such as the rules of optics and human nature and passions will admit, are not to be treated as false, erroneous, and wrong. The advocates for the verbal sense of the *Mosaic* account of the creation do not deny that it contains words and phrases which depart from their natural signification; expressions and images, suited to our senses and perception; when it is said, for instance, that God spake and saw, when the moon is called a great light, when the sun is said to rule the day, and the moon the night; but the natural sense of the whole relation is not affected by this, for it was the only means of making it lively and comprehensible. Besides, we are to distinguish between a philosophical account of the possibility or nature of an object, or an event, and a true, sufficient, necessary, and intelligible account, and historical relation of it for general

general use. The former was not the intention of *Moses*, but this doth not derogate from his credit in the latter. And it is not very clear, that a writer whose veracity is disputed in his account of natural things, can retain his authority in moral truths; or that the stile of scripture is so very distant from common language. It is moreover somewhat inconsistent, sometimes to exaggerate in maintaining the condescension of scripture to the meanest capacity of the reader, and at other times to look for mystical, hieroglyphical, and mythological expression in a plain narration of matters of fact. It is certainly irregular to conclude from single cases of symbols and parables, that they were universally used, and in passages where the writer evidently meant to relate a fact as an historian.

Pag. 78---85. Whiston's Theory.

Mr. *Whiston*'s theory avoids indeed, most of the difficulties of *Burnet*'s, but it creates new and insuperable ones, requires more miracles and a more immediate interposition of the Deity, than the literal sense of the *Mosaic* account, and it presupposes many things, which are not clearly proved, nor so demonstrable as he pretends, particularly in the article of comets. One of the difficulties, besides those mentioned by the compilers, is, that the intense heat of the central solid could never admit a collection of watry particles so near it as is represented in the first day's work; another is, that the series of changes on the third and fourth day must be inverted, in one half of the globe, as it cannot be night and day at once on all sides of it; and a third is, that this planet, in its approach towards the sun, must, like all the other great heavenly bodies, necessarily have turned upon its own axis. That miracles are multiplied by Mr. *Whiston* is manifest, if we consider, that neither the first change of of the course of this body, nor the subsequent alteration in the manner of its motion, nor the preservation of the various seeds of plants and animals, which are supposed to be contained in the matter of the earth, was possible without the immediate interposition of omnipotence, under so frequent changes of place as this formation of the earth supposes, and much less possible in the former state of this original comet, especially in its transit through the region of the sun.

Pag. 85. *The* Mosaic *creation.*

Tho' *Moses* confined his history to our earth, and the planets related to it, and makes no other mention of these, than as they stand related to the earth, it doth not follow that the other planets out of the solar system existed before. For this would contradict not only the beginning of his account, and the history of the fourth day, but the divine perfections, and the origin of all things, especially our globe, and the relation they stand in to God. It would be affirming, either that God produced a chaos at different times and places, or suffered the chaos which was destined for some planets, to remain longer without form than that of others. This would manifestly contradict every cosmogony and philosophy founded in rational principles; for this new production of our solar system could not take place, without supposing a change in all the bodies then existing, unless we imagine an immense space to be left void for them between innumerable bodies on all sides, and so totally break the general connexion of things link'd together. The same analogy, by which the compilers conclude from the creation of one planet to that of the rest, at the same time, and in like manner, requires the contrary, and holds equally with respect to the sun. See *Carpzovius, Le Long Bibliotheca sacra, Petavius*'s *Dogm. theol. Picherelli Opuscul. theolog. Saurin Discours sur la Bible.*

In

Pag. 85, 86. *The first day.* In every miracle the course of nature is observed, as far as the end of the miracle will permit it; and as the work of the six days was undoubtedly a formation of the world from matter, or from simple elements, which had been immediately created before; as the work of each day proceeded gradually, not instantaneously, for God did not rest till the seventh day, and as the order of each day's work depended upon the natural relation, which the use and influence of the preceding works bore to those that were subsequent, it may very safely be admitted, that the work of the six days was, comparatively speaking, mediate; that the Creator made use of the powers of the elements, and of the bodies originally composed from them in the formation of the rest, and withal observed the laws of motion. But these natural powers of the bodies first created, and their laws of motion, are by no means sufficient to account for and explain the creation of the rest. The account of the first day's work, which is here rejected, is much better grounded than that received instead of it, which was merely owing to the mistaken prejudice, that the *mosaic* creation extended no farther than to our solar system, and that the other planets were then already in being. It does not, however, perfectly agree with this, for our sun must have pre-existed before the work of the six days, if the first day's work was to clear the atmosphere, that the luminous rays of the sun might pierce it. Besides, in that case, *Moses* would appear to have pass'd over the principal part of this day's work, and only to have mentioned a circumstance and effect of it, and in such manner as to render it necessary to depart from the literal sense. Whereas the other supposition should have been fairly stated thus; that the Creator collected together the fiery corpuscles, they being the lightest and best furnished with the powers of motion, or

disposed

disposed them in different parts of the immense space of original matter, where they began not only to burn and to cast forth rays of light, but to give motion to the matter around them; that this must have produced a great number of *vortices*, each of which was directed to the centre, and so a union and conjunction of fixed and caliginous bodies took place, and, by the circumvolution of our earth thus produced, night and day were distinguished. Upon this state of the hypothesis, the three difficulties mentioned by the compilers are obviated. For admitting the pretended proportion of the fiery corpuscles to the matter of the universe, it follows even from this objection, that they were at first collected and disposed in a natural way, and that without such collection and internal motion, they could no more burn and produce light, than other combustible bodies do, in which the fiery corpuscles are far superior in number to the rest. The universal gravitation of matter could not take place, till the *vortices*, and consequently the centres of such a property existed, which might arise in different places at the same time, without taking the terrene matter of the planets from the earth. Whereas, this gravitation renders the representation here given of the original rest of the terrene chaos impossible, since that had already a centre of gravity. As to the pretence of the earth's being in that case the centre of the world, it is so far from being a necessary consequence, that the contrary rather flows from it. For as all impulse and pressure occasions a resistance, all the caliginous bodies thus produced, must have obtained, by the means of this resistance, a common tendency to the side of the impulse and pressure; consequently the fiery body, being the cause of such motion, must have been the common centre of the contiguous dark bodies.

Accord-

Pag. 87. *The second day.* According to the laws of hydrostatics, the water and air must have separated themselves from the gross terrene particles, and the inferior grosser air become fit for the ascent of vapours, by the entire collection of the other matter of each *vortex* towards their centre. This must at once purify the expanse or the air in the intermediate space between the planets, and occasion and support their disposition both with respect to their mutual distance, and to the equilibrium requisite thereto, as well as the reciprocal effect of pressure and resistance, and the similar formation of what are here called the superior and inferior waters.

Pag. 87. *The third day.* The opinion here controverted is more agreeable to scripture, reason, and experience, than that of *Whiston*, which is preferr'd to it. The work of the third day is described and illustrated in the 104th psalm; in the 7th and 8th verse it is attributed to a violent thunder and earthquake, or to an inflammation of the fiery particles as well in the vapours which encompass the earth, or in the lower atmosphere, as in the earth itself; whereby the solid parts of it were dissolved, that in some places they might rise above the waters, and in others form proportionable cavities to contain them. This is very much confirmed by experience in the appearance of new mountains on the continent, and new islands in the sea, and in the swallowing up of whole countries by violent earthquakes. Whereas, the other opinion depends upon a principle not entirely demonstrable, it being particularly entangled with the difficulty of a preponderating gravity in the metals which are chiefly buried in and under mountains; and it consists of a conjecture, not very reconcileable to the laws of motion, and to the experience we have of the internal state of the earth. For the texture of long and high columns, particularly of so immense a bulk, interferes with the

the laws of ſtatics in the original connexion of ſolid bodies, and of the whole globe; and the different *ſtrata* we obſerve in the earth do not agree with the notion of columns precipitated and ſunk the deeper on account of their gravity.

The latter part of this day's work begun the production of organized bodies, which conſiſt of various parts differently formed, and deſtined for different uſes, and nouriſhed and ſupported by inward applications. The Creator here obſerved the order of their different degrees of perfection. The moſt imperfect were created before thoſe of a more perfect nature. Thus vegetables, whoſe life is mere exiſtence, were created firſt; animals of the irrational but ſenſitive kind came next, and laſt of all man, endued with liberty and reaſon. *Pag.* 87. *Order of the creation.*

As the ſun and moon became fit on the fourth day for the offices which *Moſes* aſſigns them, the Creator literally made them lights on that day to rule the day and the night, and to give light to the earth. For as the earth became fit, on the ſecond and third day, to receive and reflect the light, by the diſpoſition and purification of the ambient air, and by the production of the dry land and the ſeparation and collection of the waters; ſo this muſt have happened to the other dark planets at this time, when they, particularly the moon, firſt became lights. The ſame total purification of the air was neceſſary about the fiery planets; for, from the ſpots on the ſun it appears, that they are not only ſurrounded with thoſe globules of air, but likewiſe collect and admit vapours. As therefore all the planets in our ſolar ſyſtem thus receive their entire form and proper gravity, ſo by the ſame means their reciprocal action upon each other, and upon the ſun, takes place, conſequently their regular courſe at due diſtances from each other is eſtabliſhed. *Pag.* 88. *The fourth day.*

The

Pag. 89, 90. *The formation of plants and animals.*

The four questions started in this section, are not sufficiently answered, and in some measure such, that it is difficult to decide them, at least they are none of them indispensibly necessary towards a full understanding of the *mosaic* history of the creation. As to the first it is undoubted, that the bare laws of motion do not suffice to explane this formation of organized bodies, and that the subordinate operation of any agent impowered by God to form them, cannot be supposed. This last opinion was maintained by several ancient heretical parties, and has been defended by modern *Arians*, who revived it in order to invalidate the proofs of the Divinity of the Word or Son of God, drawn from the creation attributed to him. It is somewhat extraordinary, that no mention should be made here of the plastic nature or formative powers, especially as this opinion has had many zealous advocates in *England*, and among the rest *Cudworth* took particular pains to evince the probability of it. The great obstacle to it is the opinion of the impossibility of the operation of simple substances in compound ones, or bodies, which most modern philosophers reject as a prejudice. Else the doctrine of plastic powers would undoubtedly be more in vogue, and very well adapted to the latest systems of philosophy, and of use in explaning many things in nature. As to the *second* enquiry, it may be concluded from the perfection of man at his creation, that the same was the case with plants and animals, which also appears from *Moses*'s account, tho' it may be gathered from the same, that this perfect formation was not instantaneous, but a very quick growth. The opinion embraced upon the *third* question, is neither well grounded nor indisputable. The words of *Moses* retain their literal sense and force, tho' it should appear that only two of each species of animals, and

and one of each kind of plants were created. The neceſſity of planting vegetables all over the earth cannot be proved, unleſs it be ſhewn that the whole earth was inhabited from the beginning. The reaſons advanced in the *fourth* enquiry are not much more weighty, tho' the opinion maintained derives great probability from other grounds. The *firſt* reaſon proves too much; for the ſame argument deprives man of every clear idea, leſt the prerogative of God ſhould be invaded and leſſened, if that prerogative conſiſts merely in this, that the divine mind conceives every thing at once, whereas man arrives at knowlege only in part and by degrees. The *ſecond* argument contradicts experience, which inconteſtably proves, that brutes are capable of many things, which ocular demonſtration hinders us from denying to be works of art and reaſon; and many changes take place in man, without previous deliberation and enquiry into their poſſibility, and even without conſciouſneſs. The *third* argument proves no more than the general connexion of creatures, according to which each kind of animals contained the ſeeds of their young; but it doth not prove, that it was neceſſary the firſt of each kind ſhould contain all the ſeeds of the ſucceeding ones.

Pag. 92. The image of God in man.

If the image of God be underſtood in ſo large a ſenſe as to comprehend a likeneſs to God in general, which ſignification is, in ſome degree, authorized *Gen.* ix. 6. and *Jam.* iii. 10. Then the free and rational nature of the human ſoul, and its ſuperiority to brutes, was doubtleſs the principal part of that image. But if it be interpreted of the ſpiritual reſemblance to the divine attributes, or the original wiſdom, holineſs and juſtice of man, which he forfeited in his fall, then the rational nature of the ſoul is not properly a part, much leſs the principal part of the divine image. Conſequently the first signification, and the terms derived from it, must not be taken exclusively of the other, or as opposite to it.

Pag. 96---98. *The human soul.* Each of the three opinions concerning the origin of individual souls labours under difficulties. That of their being derived *ex traduce* from their parents, prevailed much in the Western church since the time of St. *Austin*, because it was thought more consistent with, and in some measure explanatory to, the natural propagation of original sin. The argument drawn from the similar propagation of their species in other animals proves nothing, since the propogation of their souls by generation is equally disputed by those who oppose this derivation of human souls, and no conclusion can be drawn from bodies to simple substances. The advocates for this opinion have indeed guarded it, by solemn assurances and cautious assertions of the truth, against the charge here brought of its inconsistency with the doctrine of the simple immateriality and immortality of the soul. But they have thereby manifestly rendered their opinion the more inconceivable. For the restrictions necessary to ward off all misinterpretation, have at last left nothing to give us any clearer idea of the nature of such a generation, than what arises from the usual illustration of it by the simile of lighting a candle or multiplying sound. The immediate creation of each soul by God is very difficult to be reconciled to the propagation of original sin, tho' it be not absolutely inconsistent with it. According to the doctrine of the mere accidental operation of second causes in natural changes, which supposes God the sole efficient cause of them, this would be easily accountable, and would soon solve the difficulty here raised from the indecency of supposing a divine creation to accompany a sinful act of generation; but that whole system is absurd, void of proof, and exposed

to

to inſuperable objections. We cannot, without erroneous and unworthy ideas of God's providence, preſervation, co-operation and government of all things, or of his operation by ſecond cauſes, ſuppoſe him an inactive ſpectator of his creation, and if we could, the ſuppoſition would lead us too far.

The third opinion of the creation of all human ſouls at once, at the immediate and inſtantaneous production of all ſimple ſubſtances by God, and that they exiſted before the particular generation of each individual, is generally rejected by the Weſtern church, notwithſtanding the authority of many teſtimonies of antiquity, and foreign parties to the contrary. The attempts to revive this doctrine have met with little ſucceſs, becauſe it was connected with many erroneous tenets of the *platonic* or cabbaliſtic ſyſtem, and even made uſe of to protect the errors of *Arianiſm*, at leaſt to repreſent ſuch ſouls in a full ſtate of conſciouſneſs and in the perfect uſe of intellectual powers. The ſtate of this doctrine in the philoſophic ſyſtem of *Leibnitz*, removes all theſe difficulties, and at the ſame time obviates the objection here made concerning the loſs of memory and conſciouſneſs of ſuch pre-exiſtence. Upon the whole, this opinion is ſo connected with that before maintained concerning the firſt creation of all organized bodies, that both hypotheſes muſt ſtand or fall together.

Pag. 100. *The time of the creation.*

The opinion of ſeveral of the fathers, that the world was created at once, and that *Moſes*'s account means only a review and ſurvey of the creation, was owing to a falſe tranſlation and miſinterpretation of that paſſage in *Eccleſiaſticus* xviii. 1. where no more is ſaid than that God created all things in general.

Pag. 100. *The season of the creation.* Besides the two equinoxes, from one of which most chronologers date the beginning of the world, some have thought the longest day, or summer solstice the most probable date, among whom are *Mercator*, *Kepler*, and *Alph. des Vignoles*, in his *Chronologie de l'histoire sainte*, where the opinion of *Moses*'s having introduced the distinction between the civil and ecclesiastical year is examined.

Pag. 101. *Doctrine of the* Sadducees *concerning* angels. The doubt whether the *Sadducees* among the *Jews* denied the existence of angels, arises from the difficulty of reconciling such an error to their belief of the scriptures, at least of the books of *Moses*, and from the silence of *Josephus*, and every other part of the New Testament. Some carry their doubt on this subject so far as to suspect *Acts* xxiii. 8. of an interpolation of the words, *neither angels*, especially as the next words are, *but the pharisees confess both*; and in the 9th verse the possibility of a spirit or an angel speaking, is mentioned to the whole assembly as a matter out of dispute; and moreover the modern *Jews* acquit the sadducees from the imputation of such an error. But the error was very consistent with the belief of the books of *Moses*, and of all the inspired writers of the Old Testament, which were common to them with other *Jews*, if we suppose, agreeably to the opinion of some, that by the angels there mentioned they understood the attributes, powers and operations of other beings, even of God himself, and only rejected their personality; or, which is yet more probable, and consonant to their doctrine of the human soul, that they considered them as creatures of God, of short duration, destined to particular extraordinary purposes, and consequently denied their eternity. The silence of *Josephus* arises from hence, that this error was only a consequence of that capital error which denied a future state and the immortality of the soul, and they

they fell into the other to rid themselves of an unanswerable objection drawn from the nature of angels; at least the silence of *Josephus* cannot be opposed to so plain express a testimony, much less the silence of other passages concerning the Sadducees, which did not require a full account of all their errors and the consequences of them. The word *both*, in the verse above cited, is justifiable by the rules of language, because the denial of angels and spirits, as similar beings, is compounded and referr'd to as one. As to the words of the scribes in the next verse, they were not only pronounced by scribes of the Pharisees part, and so may have been meant as their own doctrine, which the sequel seems to shew, but besides they do not really contradict the doctrine of the Sadducees, for they admitted such appearances of angels. The design with which modern *Jews* may endeavor to render St. *Luke*'s narrative suspicious, is sufficient to render their opinion on this subject suspected, especially as it is unsupported by any ancient testimony. See *Ode*'s *comment. de angelis.*

How many of the fathers maintained the opinion after *Origen*, that angels existed before the *mosaic* creation, may be seen in the large collection of their declarations on that head compiled by *Ode* in his *comm. de angelis*, and by *Dion. Petav.* in his *dogm. theol.* who likewise cite the sentiments of other fathers that maintained the contrary. *Petavius* takes great pains to shew the indifference of both opinions, that either of them may be received by the faithful without incurring error, and that the decree of the Lateran synod under *Innocent* III. has left the matter undecided. The *Socinians* and *Arians* have patronized this opinion in modern times, in order to weaken the proofs of *Christ*'s divinity, drawn from the expression, *before the foundation of the world.* Among the remonstrants

Pag. 102. *Angels when created.*

it has been favoured by *Episcopius* and *Limborch*, and so easily made its way into *England*. The passages quoted in the *Univ. Hist.* to prove it, are not demonstrations; for that of *Job* xxxviii. 7. is perfectly consistent with the contrary opinion, even tho' it be understood, as it is probably meant, of angels, who immediately after their creation were capable of admiring and praising the works of their Creator. The fall of man, the time of which cannot be precisely ascertained, proves indeed that the fall of angels must have preceded it, and not that it consisted in this, as some have pretended, but it gives us no room to conclude, that their fall was longer before that of man, than from the beginning of the *mosaic* creation till *Adam* was tempted; especially as it is not impossible that the tempter engaged in this undertaking soon after his own fall, and as the fall of the angels was probably soon after their creation. Both appear probable from the words of *Christ*, *Joh.* viii. 44. and the latter may, in some measure, be concluded from the unavoidable perseverance in virtue, which results from a long practice of it. Other arguments drawn from the silence of *Moses*, and from the improbability of a total absence of creatures, and of a total inactivity in God before the *mosaic* creation, prove too much, and the superior nature and excellency of angels rather shew the contrary, if we suppose the creation to have risen gradually.

Pag. 102. *Bodies of* angels. The fathers, who attributed subtil and delicate bodies to angels, are cited by *Petavius* in his *dogm. theol.* by *Norris* in his *Vindic. Augustin.* and *Dallæus de usu patrum.* Among the moderns *Cudworth* has maitained the opinion from the testimonies of christian and heathen antiquity, and of scripture itself, as well as from other grounds. But *Mosheim*, in several of his notes, objects to the notion. See

Loersius

Loerſius de angelorum corporibus, and *Ode comm. de angelis*, who likewiſe treats at large of the abilities, powers and employments of angels. *Leibnitz* embraced it from other philoſophical principles, and ſince then it has been very favorably and generally received.

The diviſion of the angels into nine orders and three hierarchies was firſt made in the writings of the ſpurious *Dionyſius Areopagita de cœleſt. hierarchia*, and was afterward received and propagated by the ſchool-divines both in the Eaſtern and Weſtern church. *Pag. 105. Orders of angels.*

It is conjectured by ſome, from *Gen.* i. 31. that the fall of angels did not take place till after the creation was compleated; but that paſſage may refer only to the creatures whoſe formation was before related. The *Jews* place it on the ſecond day, becauſe *Moſes*, in his account, omits the divine approbation of that day's work, whereas he mentions it twice on the third day, before which the collection of the waters was not finiſhed. That they fell before the *moſaic* creation, is founded in a prejudice which hath been already examined. It is hard to determine the nature and circumſtances of their offence. The fathers have indeed been led, by miſtaking in the tranſlation and ſenſe of *Gen.* vi. 2—4, to aſſert the carnal mixture of angels with men; but they did not make their firſt fall to conſiſt in this, which indeed would have been very abſurd, ſince the fall of man by the ſeduction of Satan had happened long before. Several fathers have placed their fall wholly in the ſeduction of man, but againſt all probability, tho' it fulfilled and confirmed their rebellion againſt God. If it be imputed to inordinate ſelf-love and pride, it remains to demonſtrate what was the object of that pride, what occaſioned ſuch an attempt and arrogance of unbecoming ſuperiority. It could not be the Deity itſelf, or the ſupreme Lord, whom *Pag. 105. Their fall.*

whom ſome ſuppoſe to have been the object of it from *Gen.* iii. 5. for this would preſuppoſe a confuſion and error inconſiſtent with their primitive ſtate. Others imagine, that they envied and were diſguſted at the preference and dominion of the Son of God, particularly in his human nature; but theſe either preſuppoſe an erroneous diſtinction of the Son of God, and his power from the ſupreme Being, and his eſſential power, which hath very much recommended this opinion to perſons inclined to *Arianiſm*; or it remains a myſtery how the angels could know of his human nature and the prerogatives of it, unleſs we admit the doctrine of his celeſtial humanity, or ſuppoſe an immediate revelation of the divine decree concerning the great ſcheme of man's redemption, which would hardly conſiſt with the perfection of God. The moſt natural conjecture is, that they ſtrove for the dominion of our globe and its inhabitants. This inordinate ambition might ariſe from the employment of angels in the care and adminiſtration of ſome parts of the creation, and it partly accounts for their ſollicitude to ſeduce mankind, and for their perſeverance in this, and the divine permiſſion of it; it is likewiſe moſt agreeable to the ſcriptural term, *the God of this world*, *Heb*. vi. 12. *Rev*. xii. 9, 12. 1 *Job*. v. 19. See *Ode comm. de angelis.*

Pag. 107. *Opinion of the heathens.*

The ſame M. *Ode* proves in his 4th ſect. ch. 1. *de exiſtentia malorum angelorum*, § 4. that the heathens were not entirely unacquainted with the diſtinction of good and evil angels.

REMARKS

REMARKS

ON THE

UNIVERSAL HISTORY.

REMARKS

ON THE

UNIVERSAL HISTORY.

BOOK I.

The Asiatic *History to the time of* Alexander the Great.

CHAP. I.

The General History of the World till the Flood.

THE first opinion, which places Paradise near *Damascus* in *Syria*, hath, besides the writers here quoted, been supported by *Berruyer* in his *Histoire du peuple de Dieu*. But it is rather grounded in the partiality of the *Jews* to *Palestine*, which frequently misled them to make it the scene of every important transaction before the deluge, than in the *mosaic* account, to which it can never be reconciled, even tho' we avail ourselves of the *Chrysorrhoas*, and carry the alteration of the course of the rivers ever so far. *Pag.* 114. *Situation of Paradise.*

The *Roman* historians give *Trajan* the honour of having cut this *Nahar Malcha* in his expedition into *Parthia* in the year of *Christ* 115, and pretend that *Julian* repaired it. But the much earlier antiquity *Pag.* 117. Nahar Malcha.

quity of this canal appears probable, not only from the more ancient *Greek* historians, and several old geographers, but from the necessity of digging such a canal to prevent inundations from the *Euphrates*. See *Prid. Connex. of the Old and New Test.* vol. 1. p. 131. However, it is certain that this was not dug early enough to be meant by *Moses*. As to this third scheme, it is greatly confirmed by *Moses*'s description of the situation of the garden of *Eden* toward the *east*, since neither *Armenia* nor *Syria* lay eastward to the residence of *Moses* at that time.

Pag. 118. *The* mosaic *description of* Eden.

What is here asserted is undoubtedly true, that more hath been written, and with more zeal, on the subject of the situation of Paradise, than was necessary. Abbé *Calmet* reckons nine treatises at large upon this head, to which another author adds nineteen more, tho' some of those quoted in the *Univ. Hist.* are not in either of the lists. It is likewise certain, that *Moses* neither intended to give a full geographical description of the country where Paradise was situate, nor of its rivers, nor could he represent the countries otherwise than as they were then, nor describe them but in reference to the time and place when and where he wrote. But it is a bold and groundless assertion, to say, that his description neither answers to the present, nor former situation of the country at any time, and is founded in false accounts. For it is far from being absurd, and rather confirmed by similar undoubted cases in other parts, to suppose such changes in the situation and course of some rivers, as to render it impossible to reconcile their present appearance with the accounts of the most credible historians of former times. Besides, the modern writers of travels are not all equally credible, and frequently contradict each other in fixing the situation of places. It would be therefore injurious

to

to question the credibility of an old historian, upon their hasty and perhaps defective reports of the nature and situation of places.

Pag. 121. Adam *giving names.*

As the act of giving names denoted among the ancients, particularly the oriental nations, dominion, property, and taking possession (2 *Kings* xxiii. 34. xxiv. 17.) So God gave to *Adam* dominion over all beasts, and permitted him, by this act, to take possession of them. The beasts might possibly then receive such an impression concerning man, as might serve to support their relation to each other. But this was, at the same time, such an exercise of the understanding in distinguishing the variety and the similarity of objects before him, in separating general ideas into different sorts and kinds, and connecting these with symbols or marks of distinction, that the use and facility of clear expressive powers and of a rational language, was speedily promoted, or rather produced by it. But that *Adam*, or his creator, intended it as the means of matching and propagating each species, or of a gratification to their natural passion for each other, or to shew the impossibility of this without a new interposition of the Deity, doth not appear from the relation of *Moses*, but is a pretence to which the ancient and modern inventors of it were led by erroneous prejudices, that the appetites of *Adam* were inordinate before his fall, that the institution of matrimony, contrary to the original design of God in the formation of man, was for the prevention of a greater evil, and that the literal sense of this whole account of the primitive state of man and his subsequent fall was impossible.

Pag. 121, 122. *The day of the fall.*

The opinion here mentioned, that a day and a year were the same before the fall, labours under the same difficulty, which was just before mentioned, the divine approbation of every thing created

created on that day. For it is equally absurd to suppose the fall on the sixth day, whether that day consisted of a year, or only of twenty-four hours.

Pag. 123, 124. *The allegorical sense of the fall.* As the assertors of the allegorical explanation of the *mosaic* account of the fall differ very much in determining the sense of the emblems and the things signified by them, so they had different views in opposing the literal sense of this history. It is certain, however, and much to be lamented, that the objections and pretended difficulties extend farther, and prove more than the objectors apprehend or avow, and hence the adversaries of the scriptures have availed themselves of them. Besides *Philo* and *Origen*, the allegorical sense has been maintained by *Tho. de Vio*, *Cajetan*, *T. Burnet*, *Corn. Agrippa*, *Van Helmont*, *Beverland*, and the author of *Democritus redivivus* concerning the fall of *Adam*. The emperor *Julian*'s ludicrous treatment of this history was answered by *Cyrill* of *Alexandria* in his 3d book. The *mosaic* account, as it is here stated, and the difficulties of its literal sense, seem to be extracted from Dr. *Middleton*'s letter to Dr. *Waterland*, which hath been answered by several hands. Besides the arguments here urged for the literal sense, from the connexion of this account with the rest of *Moses*'s history, those who believe the scriptures may prove the same from the quotations of that account and references to it in other passages, all which are literal, and therefore confirm the literal sense, 1 *Tim.* ii. 14. 2 *Cor.* xi. 3. *Rev.* xii. 9.

Pag. 125. *The serpent.* The opinion that no natural serpent was concerned in the seduction of the first man, but that Satan was the only seducer, either invisibly, or in the disguise of a serpent, or in that of an angel of light, was advanced so early as by *Steuchus Eugubinus*, and has been embraced and very well defended by many modern writers. But as it departs

too

too much from the literal sense of the *mosaic* account, the other opinion here adduced is preferable, and has been vindicated at large by many eminent writers.

This whole conjecture, that the tempter pretended to be a celestial spirit, or at least was considered as such by *Eve*, is not so consistent with the use of a natural serpent, as with the notion of a mere assumed appearance of a body. It is besides entangled with great difficulties. For the serpent's pretended ignorance of the nature of the divine prohibition, and the least appearance of a contradiction to it, must have disgusted *Eve* much more than she could be captivated by discovering a new faculty in a creature well known to her before, of which she imagined, and was persuaded by him, that she saw the cause. Indeed the more artful we suppose this disguise of *Satan*'s to have been, the more difficult it is to account for the divine permission of it, and for the subsequent punishment of the fall, and consequently for the whole history. For instead of accounting for the seduction, and shewing it possible, it shews it to have been necessary and unavoidable, especially if we suppose, with *Epiphanius* and others, that he represented to *Eve* the appearance of the Shechinah, or of the Son of God. *Pag.* 127. *Whether he appeared a celestial spirit?*

The serpent's address to *Eve* will be better understood, if we consider, that he designedly avoided accosting both our first parents, and chose to address *Eve* rather than *Adam*, not only because she was created last, and so was not arrived to the same degree of perfection with him in the use of his faculties, for he had exercised his considerably before she was created (See *Gen*. ii. 19—24.) but because she had not received the prohibition of the fruit of this tree immediately from God, but from the report of *Adam*. In the first part of the conversation, *Pag.* 128. *The serpent's address to* Eve.

ſation, *Gen.* iii. 1. the tempter pretends ignorance, and deſires to be informed of a matter quite new to him, in order to introduce himſelf to her, and to engage her confidence and ſecurity, under the opinion that ſhe was converſing with a creature inferior to her in knowlege and deſirous of information. After this preamble he begins his attack, *v.* 4, 5. which conſiſts of two parts. In the firſt part, *v.* 4. in order to remove one great obſtacle to the deſign he was meditating, he denies the puniſhment ſhe apprehended, but without any mention of God, or any impeachment of his veracity. He rather leaves it undetermined, whether this prejudice of *Eve*'s had been inſtilled into her by *Adam*, or aroſe from a miſtake of the words of God, which herſelf had not heard, or whether it was derived from God. In the ſecond part, v. 5. he allures her by a tempting repreſentation of the great benefits ſhe might infallibly expect from eating this fruit. For the truth of this he appeals to God himſelf, and quotes his knowlege as an inſtance to exemplify his aſſeveration. All this had a tendency to perſuade her, that as the fruit had no pernicious effect upon the ſerpent, but had raiſed his mental powers to an equality with man, with reſpect to the principal diſtinguiſhing characteriſtics, reaſon and ſpeech, ſo ſhe might look for a proportionable improvement of her condition by yielding to his perſuaſions. Thus her mind was gradually alienated from attention to the divine command, and brought to diſbelieve it by indulging doubts concerning the truth, the equity, and the obligation of it.

Pag. 129. *The tree of life.* The account here given of the tree of life is adapted to the *Arminian* doctrine concerning a ſtate of innocence. Immortality is ſuppoſed, by that ſyſtem, to have been a ſupernatural grace of God, and a reward for well-doing, man being naturally mortal

mortal then, as he is at present. But as it plainly appears from *Gen.* ii. 17. iii. 3, 19. *Rom.* v. 12. vi. 23. viii. 10. 1 *Cor.* xv. 21, 22. that death was a mere consequence and punishment of sin, and therefore that the original state of man was not necessarily mortal; that, on the contrary, part of the image of God in man was his immortality, or the possibility of it, or even the impossibility of natural death; it follows that the virtues of this tree did not consist in securing the continuance of human life. It seems more probable, that the intended effect of it was such a change of the human body as was necessary towards its translation from earth to a more perfect state in heaven, after he had passed thro' his time of probation, and sufficiently persevered in the practice of virtue. This gives some probability, at least, to the opinion of St. *Austin*, which hath been farther discussed by later enquiries into the covenants between God and man, and their different conditions and establishment. His opinion was, that as in the subsequent institution of his covenant of grace, God appointed certain meats as the means of grace, and gave them a supernatural power, so this tree of life, and the participation of it, was such a means of grace in the primitive covenant, and was not only ordained as a seal and assurance of an immediate enjoyment of God, but provided with a supernatural power to produce salutary effects in man, *Rev.* ii. 7. xxii. 2. See *Chemnitius de arbore vitæ*.

Pag. 130. *The tree of knowlege.*

The tree of knowlege is, by some authors, supposed to be the same with the tree of life, and that this name, common to both trees, was not given to the tree of knowlege till after the fall, it being called only the tree in the midst of the garden before the fall; and tho' *Gen.* ii. 9. and 17. contradict this, yet the appellation is only accidental, not emphatical there; and in the former of those passages the particle *and* signifies much the same as *namely*. But this opinion is very exceptionable, If the tree of life be considered as a means of divine grace in the primitive state of man, why should not this tree be considered in like manner? for God might in due season, after a sufficient trial of man, and after he had used all the preparatory means of attaining to higher perfection, have permitted him to eat of it, and it might, by its supernatural virtues, have produced the same salutary effects upon the mind of man, which the tree of life was to have upon his body and vital powers. At least, this removes the objection, how God could create a tree, either prejudicial or useless, and merely dangerous, and in some cases noxious to man, and it extends the use of this tree somewhat farther than mere speculation.

Pag. 130. *The words of God,* Gen. iii. 22. *not ironical.*

The words, *Behold, the man is become as one of us, to know good and evil,* cannot, without great difficulty, be interpreted ironically; especially as they follow immediately after the promise of the redemption of man. They are rather a bitter compassionate complaint, of the loss of man's former perfection, which obliged his Creator to withdraw from him the innocent and beneficial, but now dangerous use of other things. It interferes with the connexion, and does some violence to the words, to apply them to the happy change of the state of man by the promise of his redemption.

Pag. 132. *The equity of the punishment.*

When the divine law is divided into arbitrary and natural, this is meant in a comparative or relative sense, with respect to the knowlege of his creatures, for all the laws of God are founded in reason and equity, consequently no law can be supposed without any other grounds than the mere will of God. Man, indeed, is bound to make the revealed will of God the rule of his conduct, whether he sees the good and evil consequences

naturally

naturally resulting from what is commanded and forbidden, or not. So that the will of God is our best characteristic to distinguish good from evil, tho' the grounds of it are not to be supposed in the divine will itself, but in his wisdom and knowlege of what is best.

Pag. 133. *God made them coats of skins.*

It is not necessary to ascribe to angels those acts which are expresly attributed to God, or to make them consist in a mere command and direction. We may easily reconcile them, if we avoid such ideas of the immediate operation and transactions of God, as are unworthy of the supreme being. For all his immediate operations are performed by his will, and by the means of his stated exercise of his power. Hence this divine condescension to cloath man, is not only a proof of the continuance of his paternal care for him, after the promise of the redeemer, but might probably tend to the institution of sacrifices, if we consider that some animals were to be slain upon the occasion, which was, at the same time, the first example of corporal death exhibited to man.

Pag. 134. *Man's despair.*

Despair would have been the natural unavoidable effect of the fall, and the punishment ensuing upon it. But God himself guarded against this. He excited faith and hope in man by promising a redeemer, at the same time when he denounced the guilt and punishment incurred. And the punishment of the unhappy pair and their posterity, was attended with such circumstances of providential care for them, that they had sufficient assurance, that it was the gracious intent of God to preserve, restore, and save them.

Pag. 135. *Imputation of* Adam's *guilt.*

The compilers have here committed two errors in history. First, in calling those who maintain the imputation of *Adam*'s guilt, *supralapsarians*, an appellation peculiar to those, who, in the order of divine decrees, place that unconditional one of the salvation of some men, and the damnation of others, before the fall, and so make this an effect and necessary consequence of that divine decree, which is so far from being the doctrine of those who assert the imputation of *Adam*'s guilt, that it is not even maintained by all the defenders of such an unconditional decree. In the next place it is pretended, that those who impute the guilt of *Adam* derive the unhappy state of his posterity merely from that imputation, which is a groundless assertion. For the natural depravity and sinfulness of *Adam*'s posterity contributes, at least, as much to expose them to divine wrath and damnation, as the imputation of his guilt, and indeed the former is implied in the latter. And all who deny this imputation, do not, at the same time, deny, that the posterity of *Adam* became children of wrath by the fall, and the propagation of the natural depravity arising from it.

Pag. 136. *Apathy before the fall.* In asserting the opinion, that human passions took their rise from the fall, some caution is necessary to avoid the *stoic* and *platonic* doctrine of the sinfulness and turpitude of all sensual affections and appetites, which was patronized by many of the fathers, and hath been productive of many bad consequences. No finite spirit, much less man in his terrestrial state, can be free from sensuality and passions, and their subordination to his superior powers in great measure constitutes his perfection.

Pag. 136. *Temper of the body before the fall.* The tenderness here attributed to the human body before the fall, could have contributed but little towards its perfection; for a very delicate sensation of external things is a painful infirmity, and the result of a diseased body. It seems more fitting to make the advantages of this primitive state, with respect to the body, consist in a more extensive sensibility of all the internal motions of its parts, and a power connected with this to deter-

mine

mine their changes. This would suppose a power over the functions and operations of natural life, of which man is at present incapable.

Pag. 138 ---142. *Mr.* Whiston's *theory of the change of the earth after the fall.*

Mr. *Whiston*'s theory is rather subject for an ingenious poem, than built on the principles and experience of philosophy. For the revolution of the earth about the sun is still elliptical, and the primary planets in their rotation about the sun cannot describe this figure but in revolving about their own axis, or even by the means of such revolution. Nay if, in defence of this hypothesis, the motion of the moon about the earth without such revolution should be alleged; (tho' no argument can be drawn from the motion of secondary to that of primary planets) yet it could not take place. For the motion of the moon about its centre, having one and the same side constantly turned towards the earth, requires quite another disposition of this imaginary course of the earth without revolving upon its own axis. Besides, the rules of probability are strangely violated, both in supposing two collisions of a comet against the earth, in a space which does not amount to a third part of the age of the world, and nothing like it to have happened or to have appeared since; and in admitting effects, so very different, from these two impulses of comets, and that of a third still impending. Not to mention that so unequal a division of day and night, which were to each other as 1 to 51, or at the most as 4 to 48, or 1 to 12, could be neither agreeable nor suited to the necessary changes in the vegetable and animal creation.

Pag. 142. *The* Hebrew, Samaritan *and* Greek *copies of the* Pentateuch.

The opinion, that the *Hebrew* and *Samaritan* copies, and the *Greek* version by the septuagint, are to be considered as the three principal copies of these ancient records, and of equal value, and consequently, as their computations differ, that we we are at full liberty to prefer any one of them upon other principles, is perhaps the chief source and occasion, or at least the most frequent and most specious pretence for controverting the *Hebrew* or *masoretic* chronology. This is done upon one of these two principles, either that the *Greek* translators adhered most accurately to the original, without the least alteration, or that the *Samaritan* copy of the books of *Moses* is older and more accurate than the *Hebrew*, which frequently varies from it. But neither of these principles is evident, and both may be disproved and confuted from other grounds and passages, which have no relation to chronology. Without mentioning other particulars, both the *Samaritan* and the *Greek* version abound in various readings, with respect to their different chronologies, and frequently contradict themselves. Whereas the *Hebrew* is uniform and consistent in all its copies, and in all the versions from it. It is besides much easier to convict the two other chronologies, than the *Hebrew*, of a wilful corruption. There is not the least probability in the charge commonly brought against the *Jews*, that they falsify their copies in order to invalidate the proofs of the advent of the Messiah drawn from the prophecies; for they had the same, if not stronger, reasons for falsifying the *Greek* version, as the Christians attacked them from this, and not from the *Hebrew* copy; and as these arguments might be as conclusively drawn from the *Greek* as from any other copy or version. On the other side, it cannot be denied, that the *Greek Jews*, and the seventy translators were strongly disposed to remove whatever was a stumbling block to the heathen world; and hence it is not improbable, that they so settled the chronology of their sacred books, as to accommodate it, as much as possible, to the great pretences to antiquity in heathen historians.

rians. The same appears plainly from *Josephus*'s books against *Appion*. And this is farther confirmed by another conjecture, made so early as by St. *Austin* in his book *de civit. Dei*, that the septuagint, in order to reconcile the great age of the patriarchs to the procreation of their children, supposed the years to be months, and allowed to each of them before the deluge only an hundred additional years, as that number of months would be too small for the purpose, which hundred years they constantly deducted from that part of their age which was subsequent to the birth of their sons. The same endeavor to render the history of the patriarchs more probable, and to clear it from objections, seems to have induced the *Samaritans* to abbreviate their great age before the deluge, and to prolong the years of those after it, in order to remove the great disparity of those numbers. This pretence is frequently made use of by *Is. Vossius*, *Pezron*, and *Rob. Cary* in his chronological account of ancient time, where he opposes *Petavius* and *Usher*, the great advocates for the *Hebrew* chronology. The *Samaritan* system is maintained by *Whiston*, whom the authors of the *Univ. Hist.* follow in this respect.

Pag. 142. *Variations of* Josephus.

As the assertors of the *Greek* chronology have taken great pains to shew its agreement with *Josephus*, even by manifestly falsifying many passages, in which all copies and editions of his works agree, so *Whiston* has done the same in the service of the *Samaritan* chronology. This variation of *Josephus*, both from the *Greek* and *Samaritan*, is fully set forth in *Pet. Brinch*'s *examen chronologiæ & historiæ Josephi*, which is incorporated with the second volume of *Havercamp*'s *Josephus*; and in *Spanheim*'s *chronol. sacra.* M. *Des Vignoles*, in his *chronologie de l'histoire sainte*, shews, with great probability, from the amount of the aggregate sum of years before the deluge, that *Josephus*, in the antediluvian part of his history, strictly observed the *Hebrew* chronology, tho' frequent corruptions in various passages afterwards took place; insomuch that even at this time the separate numbers of the age of each patriarch do not agree with the aggregate sum.

Pag. 144. Shem *born in* 1556. The birth of *Shem* belongs more properly to the year of the world 1556, than that of *Japhet*. For tho' the latter might be the eldest son of *Noah*, yet the chronological series is continued thro' the line of *Shem*, and his birth should therefore be connected with the 500th year of *Noah*, which is authorized by the order in which the sons of *Noah*, mentioned *Gen.* v. 32. are placed. This does not indeed affect the sum total of the years in this table, but it does affect those of the postdiluvian patriarchs.

Pag. 145. *Sum total in the* Septuagint. The aggregate sum of years before the flood, according to the *Greek* version, is taken from the reading of the *Alexandrian* manuscript, where the age of *Methusalah*, at the time of his son's birth, is said to be 187, instead of 167 years. But this seems to be a later correction of an error observed in the *Greek* version, and was probably made by *Julius Africanus*, and afterward adopted by *Epiphanius* and the *chronicon Alexandrinum*; whereas *Eusebius*, *Jerom*, *Austin*, and *Syncellus* read 167 in all copies, and *Petavius*, in his *doctr. temporum*, judges this to be the true genuine reading of the *Greek* version, whence the aggregate sum is commonly reckoned 2242. As the compilers have thought fit to receive the emendation, they should have taken care to make the age of *Methuselah* in page 143, amount to 989.

Pag. 147. *The* Samaritan *corrected from the* Greek. There is great probability in the conjecture of *Spanheim*, in his *Chron. sacr.* that the *Samaritan* computation was corrected and settled according to the *Greek*. This appears yet more manifest after the deluge, for before that period 100 years are

are constantly cut off from the *Greek* computation in the age of each patriarch. And we have here a farther confirmation that the years of *Methuselah* were at the birth of *Lamech* 167, consequently the aggregate sum before the deluge is 2242 years.

As the nature of the offerings made by the two brothers is circumstantially specified by *Moses*, *Gen*. iv. 3, 4. in a narrative very concise in other respects, the different reception they met with, seems to have arisen from the difference of their sacrifices, tho' these again were founded in their different temper and characters. For as the bloody expiatory sacrifices were probably instituted and ordained by God himself, and even founded in the promise made *Gen*. iii. 15. of the painful redemption of mankind by the seed of the woman, so the bloody offering of beasts slain was more agreeable to the divine institution and design, than the mere oblation of an unbloody sacrifice, without any connexion with those that were properly expiatory. And herein consisted the faith of *Abel*, so celebrated *Heb*. xi. 4. that by this act he manifested his acceptance and appropriation of that divine promise concerning the redemption of man, and consequently grounded his confidence and expectation of God's favor in that future propitiation, of which this divine institution was the type and assurance.

Pag. 151. *Offerings of* Cain *and* Abel.

The words of God to *Cain*, *Gen*. iv. 7. are variously interpreted. Some suppose them intended as an intimation of the true reason for giving so different a reception to the two sacrifices, and as a general exhortation. Others think they were meant to convince him strongly of the iniquity of his anger and displeasure, or to warn him of the propensity to murder which was then growing in his breast. Some again vary their interpretation on account of the different sense that is put upon the

Exposition of Gen. iv. 7.

the last expression in this verse, which is thought to be a mark of divine approbation, or of remission of sins, or of an intended reward, and the preservation of the rights of primogeniture, or in opposition to the *falling* of his countenance, it is rendered *lifting up* his eyes and countenance. Others are perplexed by the meaning of the word *sin*, which is explained to signify the inward propensity to sin, or the punishment of sin, or an expiatory sacrifice for it; and others again are at a loss how to interpret the reference, thou shalt rule over *him*, which is applied either to *sin*, or to *Abel*.

Gen. iv. 8. It is frequent in scripture to use the expression, *Gen.* iv. 8. for a dialogue or discourse with another in general, without repeating the words that pass'd. *Ex.* xix. 25. 2 *Chron.* xxxii. 24. *Ps.* iv. 5. cxxxix. 20. So that there is no room for supposing a chasm in this passage. See *Pfeifferi dub. vex* in the appendix *de colloq. Caini & Abelis. Fabricii Codex Pseudepigr. Glassii Philolog. sacr. Carpzov. crit. sacra.*

Gen. iv. 13. The words of *Cain*, *Gen.* iv. 13. are consider'd by some interpreters as a penitent supplication, that he thought his sin so great as to be ashamed of it, and not to venture to lift up his eyes. *Seb. Schmid* and Dr. *Schuckford* favor the opinion, that they are to be understood interrogatively, *Is* my sin too great to be forgiven? The latter, however, supposes them an expression of penitence. It is a needless and improbable conjecture, that *Cain* was afraid of being killed by wild beasts.

Pag. 157. *Origin of society.* It was owing to many prejudices, derived chiefly from *platonic* societies, that the fathers and several commentators ascribed the institution of civil societies, and even of property amongst men, to wicked founders, and esteemed it a great evil.

The

The *Jewish* opinion here mentioned, which derives idolatry from *Gen.* iv. 26. *Then began man to call upon the name of the Lord*, is supported by *Selden de Diis Syris proleg.* and *Van Dale de orig. Idol.* *Pag.* 162. *Origin of idolatry.*

Tho' the intermarriages of the descendants of *Seth* with the race of *Cain* are mentioned *Gen.* vi. 1, 2. as having occasioned the general propagation of sin amongst men, yet this corruption of the posterity of *Adam*, or even of *Cain*, is not wholly to be confined to the sin of incontinence, the account of which is too much exaggerated, and not to be reconciled to the genealogy of the family of *Cain* in the fourth chapter. The compilers have likewise too abruptly decided the question, Whether idolatry prevailed among the antediluvians, by absolutely denying it, and limiting the decay of religion merely to a denial of God. *Pag.* 170, 171. *Corruption of the posterity of* Adam.

Of the passage, *Gen.* vi. 2. consult *Ode*'s *comm. de angelis*, where the foundation of this absurd pretence of angels defiling themselves with women is fully examined, and authorities are cited against it from the fathers. The same author, *sect.* 4. *c.* 6. § 8. adduces several proofs, some of which are indeed of no great weight, that the spurious prophecy of *Enoch* was not, as is commonly supposed, prior to the times of the apostles, but was invented after. *Pag.* 171---175. *Angels mixing with women.*

The existence of giants is examined in two dissertations, of which extracts may be seen in the *Histoire de l'academie des inscriptions & belles lettres.* In the first *tom.* 1. *p.* 158—163. *Abbé Tilladet* maintains it; in the second, *tom.* 2. *p.* 262—269. it is controverted by *M. Mahudel. Calmet* in his second preliminary dissertation to the book of *Genesis* confirms the first opinion more at large. See the several writers *de gigantibus*, *Ryckius*, who confutes *Becanus*, *Cassianus*, *Magius in Crenii fascic.* 8. *Sennert*, *Mollert*, *Carpzov*, *Hiller*, &c. *Pag.* 176. *The giants.*

To

Longevity of the antediluvians. To the history of the antediluvian patriarchs appertain two other enquiries, concerning their longevity, and concerning the eating of flesh, which was even in those early times lawful and usual. See *Heidegger*'s *Histor. patr. Tarnovii Methusela, Major de optima temperie, vivacitatis patriarcharum ante diluvium causa.* Of the pretended writings of those patriarchs, see *Collier*'s *histoire des auteurs sacrés.*

Pag. 181. Sanchoniatho's *design in writing his history.* This whole fragment of *Sanchoniatho* is illustrated by *Banier* in his *Mythol. expliq.* from Bishop *Cumberland*'s edition. But the exposition of him here given, is founded in the principle that his history is genuine, which is a matter very disputable, and in the three following conjectures; 1. That it was *Sanchoniatho*'s design to apologize for idolatry by arguments drawn from history; 2. That he was possessed of the writings of *Moses*, and made use of them in compiling his own history; 3. That he chose to make the offspring of *Cain*, they being the real ancestors of *Noah*, the founders of his religion. All these conjectures, particularly the first and the third, are highly improbable. For the design here imputed to him might have been as easily, if not better and more speciously obtained, either by acknowleging the deluge, and deriving it from some other cause, or by corrupting the accounts of the posterity of *Seth*, or at least by concurring more strictly with the *mosaic* history. It is therefore reasonable to suspect, that as other commentators upon heathen mythology discover more philosophy and history in it, than the authors themselves ever thought of, so these represent *Sanchoniatho* or *Philo*, more artful, ingenious and learned, than they really were. Other interpretations of this genealogy may be seen in *Scaliger*'s Appendix to his *emend. temp.* who shews that several of the names were manifest conjectures and errors of the *Greek* translators.

translators. See likewise *Bochart*'s *geogr. sacra*; and a further account of *Sanchoniatho* may be found in *Brucker*'s *histor. philos.*

The antiquity of the kingdom of *Egypt*, and of the whole *Egyptian* chronology, has been the subject of much controversy in modern times, and both parties have undoubtedly run into extremes. The enemies of revealed religion have made use of the great antiquity pretended to by the *Egyptians* to controvert the *mosaic* history, and the advocates for revelation have denied all those pretences in general, and reduced the age of this kingdom to a very late date. This was particularly done by Sir *Isaac Newton*, whom Dr. *Warburton* answers in his second volume of his *divine legation of Moses*, and endeavors to confirm the *mosaic* history by vindicating the higher antiquity of the *Egyptians*. *Pag.* 196. 197. *Antiquity of* Egypt.

An account of *Manetho* may be seen in *Ger. Joh. Vossius de historic. Græc.* and *Fabricius*'s *Bibl. Græc.* Concerning his credibility see *Conringius in adversar. chronologicis*. His remains were extracted from *Julius Africanus* and *Eusebius* by *Syncellus*, and explaned by *Jos. Scaliger* in the appendix to his *emend. temporum*. *Pag.* 197. Manetho.

The months, in this computation, must be supposed to consist alternately of 30 and 29 days, in which case the 9000 years will amount to 265,500 days, which being divided by 365, the exact sum is 727 years 145 days, which, according to the best reading, is the number of years in *Syncellus*, and not 724. If we suppose the months to consist all of thirty days, then the amount of days will be 270,000, which make 739 years 265 days, and so the pretended mistake of *Syncellus* vanishes. Of his various readings see *Goar in emend. ad Syncell.* *His computations.*

The comparison of *Osiris* and *Typhon* with *Noah* and the deluge, is not much more probable than the opinion of *Huetius*, who interprets every thing in *Pag.* 200. Osiris *and* Typhon.

in antiquity of *Moses*; or of Sir *Isaac Newton*, who imagines *Osiris* to be *Sesostrem*, *Backum* or *Sesac*, tho' this conjecture is more agreeable to chronology. See *Banier*'s *dissert. sur Typhon*, in the fourth vol. of the *Memoires de litterat. de l'Acad. des inscript.* and his *mythol. expliq.*

Pag. 201. Egyptian *chronicle.* M. *des Vignoles* has, in his *Chronol.* fully treated of this ancient *Egyptian* chronicle, and the comparison of it with *Manetho*.

As to what is said in the conclusion of this section of the *least pretence* to antiquity, it must be understood of a well-grounded, at least an ancient claim, and must be limited to that, else the inventions of *Annius*, and the like, would be equally entertaining and curious.

Pag. 208 ---212. *Conjectures concerning the deluge.* In *Saurin*'s *Discours historiques sur les evenemens du vieux & du nouveau testament*, and in *Delany*'s *Revelation examin'd*, &c. may be found more conjectures and essays towards explaning the internal evidence of the deluge, by shewing the possibility of it. The latter of those authors considers the deluge as the means of taking off the curse of God from the earth; the former as an effect and final execution of the curse pronounced against the *earth* after the fall. One of the most specious conjectures, besides those here mentioned in the *Univ. Hist.* is that of *Scheuchzer*, that the rotation of the earth being suddenly stopt, the waters which moved with it, upon it, and in it, not only of necessity continued their motion for some time, but overflowed and left the cavities which contained them. But this, like all the other conjectures, is exceptionable, for two reasons; 1. It is an attempt to explane a miracle to the sagacious enquirers into philosophy and the laws of motion, by another miracle, as incomprehensible at least, if not more so, by subverting the laws of motion. 2. After all this, it is no satisfactory account of the fact as related by *Moses*.

Besides the objections here stated to *Burnet*'s account of the deluge, and the general improbability of his whole system of the origin and nature of the earth, upon which that account is built, the following may deserve notice; 1. The incredible heat here supposed must have exhausted all the moisture of the earth, and have rendered it wholly unfruitful, long before it could be dry enough to crack and burst. 2. Both men and beasts, besides laboring under the want of meat and drink, must, in that case, have perished by mere heat. 3. If the heat of the sun had penetrated thro' the earth into the inner waters of the abyss, it could not have occasioned such a change as must arise from the disruption of it, since heat operates more powerfully in a fluid body, than upon a solid vessel containing it. 4. If the rarefaction of the subterraneous waters, and the vapours it occasioned could have the effect of bursting the earth, it would follow, that the earth is void of all pores and apertures whatever; for the least pore would convert the whole earth into a ball of air; and yet according to *Burnet*'s account, it must have been porous, as this inward heat of the abyss, and the subterraneous vapours could not be otherwise than gradually produced. So that this whole theory is, in general, very rightly considered as a philosophical dream.

Pag. 212 ---214. *Objections to Dr.* Burnet'*s theory.*

Mr. *Whiston*'s account of the deluge is founded in the doctrine of comets, which is hitherto pretty uncertain; and it is rather invalidated and become improbable, than confirmed by the calculation of the time of the trajection of the comet in the year 1688. It interferes, moreover, with the laws of motion which regulate the circumvolution of the superior planets, for the approach of a comet to the earth

Pag. 214 ---217. *Mr.* Whiston'*s theory.*

earth in the manner pretended in this theory, must have produced greater and very different changes from those which took place at the deluge; the gravity of the earth would have been surprizingly increased by this accession of weight, and the attractive power of the planets, which is admitted throughout *Whiston*'s system, must have totally altered the course either of such comet, or inevitably of our earth. *Don Joseph Anton. Gonzalez de Sales*, in his *dissert. paradoxica de duplici viventium terra*, annexed to the *Frankfurt* edition of *Burnet*'s theory, advances an hypothesis concerning the deluge more improbable than that of either *Burnet* or *Whiston*; that the whole earth was dissolved or annihilated by the deluge, and a new one created afterwards.

Pag. 218. *Preservation of the world a miracle.* It is here rightly intimated, that miracles require no greater power in God, and no higher exercise of it, than natural events and changes. For as the continuance of the powers of his creatures demands a perpetual influence and immediate co-operation from God, so all the laws of motion, the observation of which constitutes the course of nature, depend upon the divine will. If this were always duly considered, men would be cautious both of groundlessly multiplying miracles, and of indiscretely denying and disputing them.

Pag. 223. *The time of building the ark.* It is certain that from the words of *Moses* no time can be fixed in which the ark was built. So that the objection vanishes which greatly distressed some of the fathers, how the timber could be preserved, which must rot in a hundred and twenty years, tho', by the way, this last is not better supported by proofs than the other.

Pag. 226. *Its form adapted to the sea.* That *Noah*'s ark was incapable of swimming and of resisting storms and waves, hath not been so fully proved, but the contrary is maintained, and with some probability, that it was fit for both purposes, considering its proportions in length, breadth, and height,

height, which are as 10, 5, and 3, especially if only a sixth part of the height was under water, as is more fully set forth by *Pelletier* in his *Dissert. sur l'arche.*

It is not easy to determine with certainty, either the season of the year when the deluge took place, or the real length of the year at that time. That it began in harvest is exposed to this difficulty, that men and beasts could find no sustenance upon the dry earth in winter, especially if we suppose them to have left the ark at the end of *November* or beginning of *December*; and *Scheuchzer* produces other arguments in favour of the spring, drawn from many petrified remains of the deluge, which indicate the cessation of it at that season. But the express mention of the second month interferes with this opinion; for the historian having himself related the alteration of the ecclesiastical year, and of the computation of months, which first took place in his time, could not, with propriety, mean that second month but according to the old stile, which even in his time was not totally abolished. M. *des Vignoles* in his *Chronol. de l'hist. sainte*, treats at large of the year of 360 days before the flood, and Dr. *Shuckford* is of opinion, that this ancient civil year of 360 days agreed, till that period, with the natural year, which then first began to consist of 365 days. The contrary opinion, that the natural solar year was complete before the deluge, is most fully set forth in *Alph. a Carranza tract. de partu naturali & legit*, and which is annexed to it, in his *Diatrib. super primar. temp. doctrina Petavii*, likewise in *Bengel*'s *Ord. temp.*

Pag. 227, 228. The time of the deluge.

As it is probable from *Gen.* ii. 2, 3. and *Exod.* xvi. 23, 25. xx. 8, *&c.* that the religious observation of one day in the week, and particularly of the seventh day, was earlier than the deluge, which is confirmed by the intervals of weeks

Pag. 229, 230. Religion of the antediluvians.

obſerved by *Noah*, *Gen.* viii. 10, 12. So from the undeniable diviſion of years into months, *Gen.* viii. 4, 5, 13. compared with *Gen.* i. 14. and from *Gen.* iv. 3. it may, with great probability be concluded, that monthly and annual feſtivals were then kept, or that the new moon and the commencement of the year were ſolemnized.

Pag. 230. *Arts and ſciences of the antediluvians.* As on the one ſide the arts and ſciences of the firſt men are groſsly, without foundation, and even incredibly magnified, ſo on the other their ignorance is equally exaggerated. When the age of man was of ſo great a length, the invention of arts, and the extenſion of their knowlege was not only eaſy, but almoſt unavoidable, and we have evidence of it in the early building of cities, *Gen.* iv. 17. The *Mexicans* are a proof that many arts may be carried to a conſiderable height without the uſe of iron.

Pag. 230, 231. *Their policy.* The inſtitution of civil ſociety among the antediluvians ſufficiently appears from the early date of violences amongſt men, and the earlier foundation of cities. And tho' the ſeveral civil communities were more cloſely connected under the ſupreme ſociety of mankind, by the remembrance of their common origin, which was preſerved by the longevity of men, by the propagation of the ſame cuſtoms tranſmitted thro' the means of tradition, and by the uſe of one common language, yet it was impoſſible that the whole human race ſhould form but one commonwealth, eſpecially when they were ſo much more numerous than ſince the deluge; for great empires can neither ariſe without violence, nor long ſubſiſt without the wiſeſt regulations of policy.

Pag. 232. *Numbers of the antediluvians.* Mr. *Whiſton*'s table is not quite agreeable to the principles here laid down, and determines the years of doubling too arbitrarily, and, in general, too improbably, eſpecially in the firſt numbers. The

following

following computation is better founded in these principles, and in itself more probable, as the numbers at first are rather too few than too many.

Number of mankind.	*Years of the world.*	*Number of doubling.*
4	41	1
8	82	2
16	123	3
32	164	4
64	205	5
128	246	6
256	287	7
512	328	8
1024	369	9
2048	410	10
4096	451	11
8192	492	12
16384	533	13
32768	574	14
65536	615	15
131072	656	16
262144	697	17
524288	738	18
1048576	779	19
2097152	820	20
4194304	861	21
8388608	902	22
16777216	943	23
33554432	984	24
67108864	1025	25
134217728	1066	26
268435456	1107	27
536870912	1148	28
1073741824	1189	29
2147483648	1230	30
4294967296	1271	31
8589934592	1312	32
17179869184	1353	33
34359738368	1394	34
68719476736	1435	35
137438953472	1476	36
274877906944	1517	37
549755818388	1558	38
1099511627776	1599	39
1299023255552	1640	40

 Josephus's

Pag. 234. *Longevity of the antediluvians.* *Joſephus*'s quotation from *Heſiod* may be admitted as genuine, without having recourſe to *Voſſius*'s conjecture *de hiſt. Gr.* which is founded in the falſe reading of ſome copies of the *Latin* tranſlation of *Joſephus*, or ſuppoſing this ſome loſt piece or paſſage of *Heſiod.* For it is not abſolutely neceſſary, amidſt ſo many quotations and appeals to teſtimonies, that a quotation ſhould be literally the ſame in every writer cited. It is ſufficient, that the point in queſtion is deducible from the writings and teſtimonies referred to. Now, as *Heſiod* fixes the infancy and adoleſcence of men in the ſecond generation at 100 years, we muſt ſuppoſe their age, tho' comparatively ſhort, to have amounted to ſeveral hundred years, and the age of the firſt generation, which laſted much longer, to have been very little ſhort of a thouſand years. The longevity of the firſt men was owing to a complication of various ſecond cauſes, tho' in conſidering it we ſhould keep divine providence as the ſupreme cauſe in view, ſince God could ſo eſtabliſh the courſe of nature, without an actual miracle, as to have ſet ſhorter bounds to the life of man.

Pag. 234 ---238. *Exceptions to* Burnet *and* Whiſton *on the changes made by the deluge.* The opinions both of *Burnet* and *Whiſton* are exceptionable; for, 1. This imaginary ſtate of the earth, tho' it were poſſible, could not anſwer the end of its fertility ſo well, as a ſtate like the preſent. Mr. *Whiſton*'s miſts could never produce the benefit of a moderate rain, eſpecially as thoſe miſts were beſides to ſupply the ſprings of rivers; and *Burnet*'s ſcheme of watering the earth with rivers, could not poſſibly, without an inundation, ſupply the want of rain, as is evident from the caſe of *Egypt*. 2. The theories of thoſe gentlemen, if narrowly examined, will appear to have more difficulty than at firſt ſight they ſeem to be embarraſs'd with, and to contain many things which can never be explaned, nor accounted for upon the right principles

ciples of philoſophy, but directly contradict them, however *Whiſton* may be underſtood with reſpect to the origin of rivers. Thus it is impoſſible to ſuppoſe an air ſo pure and thin, tho' clogg'd with ſo many vapours for ſo long a ſpace; or in *Burnet's* theory, to admit ſo perfect an equilibrium in the air in all places, without a thought of the revolution of day and night; or to admit it in *Whiſton's* ſyſtem, where the ſun muſt be ſuppoſed more powerful, and the exhalation of vapours ſtronger in ſome places than in others, conſequently that equilibrium to ceaſe, which indeed was inconſiſtent with the diurnal rotation of the earth, always attended with winds and collections of vapours. 3. Theſe accounts are not conſiſtent with other parts of thoſe theories. This is particularly the caſe with *Burnet's*, where the perpetual flowing of ſuch quantities of water upon the earth, render it impoſſible that ſuch a drought of the earth ſhould enſue, ſince the general law of gravity and the nature of vapours ſuffer us not to ſuppoſe any of the matter of the terreſtrial globe to periſh. And *Whiſton*, in his account, ſeems to forget the continuance of rivers and ſeas during their perpetual exhalations. 4. Both theſe writers contradict *Gen.* i. 6, 7. and *Gen.* vii. 4, 11, 12. for if it had never rained, before God warned *Noah* of the deluge, and if rain were contrary to the courſe of nature at that time, then *Noah* could not have underſtood the divine denunciation, and a miracle would have been requiſite in order to produce the effect. They likewiſe depart from *Gen.* viii. 22, compared with chap. i. 14.

If the opinion of a total want of rain in the primeval world fall to the ground, then the conſequence here drawn from the firſt appearance of the rainbow after the deluge muſt likewiſe vaniſh. It is an aſſertion unſupported by proofs, that all *Pag.* 238. *The rainbow.*

signs and seals of a covenant divinely instituted, or assurances of a promise made by God require something new and strange, The contrary appears from several institutions of religious acts with that intent, which acts or exercises were before well known. *Delany*, in his *Revelation examined*, draws a proof from *Heb.* xi. 7. which is no better grounded than the above assertion, since the threatened deluge, and the promised deliverance in the ark were things which *Noah* had not yet seen, but could only believe, even tho' he had frequently before seen heavy rains.

Pag. 239. *Whether flesh might be eaten before the flood.*

The *first* objection here alleged against the permission of eating flesh before the deluge, from *Gen.* ix. 3. is removed by considering the whole connexion. For as it doth not follow from the 2d verse, that God then first gave to man dominion over the brute creation; nor from *v.* 1. that the increase and propagation of the species was before unlawful, so the revival of the permission to eat flesh cannot prove it to have been before prohibited; and *Lev.* xi. 3. doth not prove that the beasts there permitted to be eaten, such as parted the hoof, and were cloven footed, and chewed the cud, were before interdicted. The *second* objection from *Gen.* i. 29, 30. is fully answered here, for the dominion granted to man over beasts, and the property therein, must have consisted in a permission of every possible use of them, among which we may reckon the eating of flesh, unless we take things for granted, which ought to be previously examined: besides the 30th verse by no means shews, that the eating of flesh and of reptiles, by beasts, was not originally permitted, or that it was contrary to the ordinance of God. The distinction between beasts that were fit or unfit for sacrifices, certainly arises from their fitness or unfitness for the use of man, and is a remote argument of the custom

of

of eating flesh before the deluge, even tho' *Gen.* vii. 2. be understood merely of the distinction for the purpose of sacrifices, which by the law of *Moses* afterwards was confined within yet narrower limits.

CHAP. II.

The general history from the deluge to the birth of Abraham.

AS in the former comparison of the *Hebrew*, *Samaritan*, and *Greek* computations, so in this table of the *Hebrew* computation, the numbers stated are neither indisputably certain, nor founded in the most apparent probability. The numbers here computed are taken from *Usher*'s chronology, who connects the call of *Abraham* from *Haran* with the death of *Terah*, and places it in the year of the world 2083, consequently 427 years after the deluge; so that he computes 352 years from the deluge to the birth of *Abraham*. M. *Godfr. Kohlreif* augments this sum, and places the call of *Abraham* in the year of the world 2086, or even in 2091. *Bengelius* fixes that call in the year of the world 2021, consequently 365 years after the deluge, and supposes his birth to have been in the year of the world 1946, and 290 years after the deluge. Their difference arises from the two former having connected the birth of *Abraham* with the 130th year of *Terah*, whereas the last fixed it in the 70th; from the two former having included the two years after the deluge before the birth of *Arphaxad*, which the last omits, and calculates his series only thro' the years of the age of the patriarchs at the birth of their sons; and from the

Pag. 254. Hebrew *chronology.*

second having inserted many years to supply the defective years or months which had not been taken into the computation. And the greatest chronological difficulty in this period, particularly with respect to the age of *Terah* at the birth of *Abraham*, arises from this variation in ascertaining the *Hebrew* chronology; for as to the confusion in the *Greek* and *Samaritan* computation, it might be much sooner regulated, or rather intirely set aside.

Pag. 256, 257. *The birth of* Abraham

Abraham's going forth from *Ur* is not to be confounded with his subsequent call from *Haran*. It will appear hereafter, that the scripture not only admits, but requires this distinction. But as to the controversy about the birth of *Abraham* in the 130th or 70th year of his father, the grounds of the former opinion, as they are here stated by the compilers, are neither solid nor conclusive, and far outweighed by the opposite arguments for the other opinion. The first of those grounds is taken from *Gen.* xi. 26. but is rather a confutation of the strongest proof on the other side, than a real argument. This confutation is built on two uncertain deductions. The *first*, that *Abraham* must have been the eldest son, is not demonstrable; for as it does not follow from *Gen.* v. 32. that *Shem* was the eldest son of *Noah*, so neither can this order of the sons of *Terah* infer the primogeniture of *Abraham*, which the reasons here alleged, and *v.* 28, 29. do not sufficiently prove. Compare *Gen.* x. 1. and xxv. 9. with 1 *Chron.* i. 28. and *Josh.* xxiv. 4. The contrary opinion contains nothing inconsistent with the account of *Moses*. For as these three sons of *Terah* were not born at once, *Nahor* and *Haran* must have been born before or after *Abraham*, consequently before or after the seventieth year of their father; the former of which is perfectly consistent both with the account of *Moses* and with the years of the procreation of children

children among the antecedent patriarchs, conſequently it is probable, for three of them begat children in their 30th year, *Nabor* in his twenty-ninth. The *ſecond* deduction, that if *Terah* was two hundred and five years old at his death, *Abraham* being then but ſeventy-five, he muſt have been one hundred and thirty when *Abraham* was born, is founded on the prejudice, that *Abraham* left *Ur* as well as *Haran* in the year of his father's death, and the latter after his death. But the contrary of this appears, *Gen.* xi. 31. xii. 1, 5. *Acts* vii. 2, 4. *Judith* v. 6, 7. where it is expreſly ſaid, that *Terah* dwelt with *Abraham* and the reſt of his family in *Haran*, and that they got ſouls in *Haran*; that *Abraham* in leaving *Haran* quitted his friendſhip and his father's houſe, ſo that he was then alive. And from *Gen.* xii. 1, 5. compared with xi. 32. or from *Acts* vii. 4. it cannot be concluded, that his call from *Haran* was after the death of his father; for the firſt of theſe objections preſuppoſes, that the account *Gen.* xii. 1, &c. muſt have been ſubſequent to the death of *Terah*, mentioned ch. xi. whereas it is frequent in chronology to avoid interrupting the ſeries by reporting ſome things out of the exact order of time. See *Gen.* v. 32. vi. 1, &c. As to the *ſecond* objection from *Acts* vii. it is certain that *Moſes*'s account is more authentic than *Stephen*'s, ſuppoſing the ſeeming contradiction could not be reconciled; for the latter was no hiſtorian, but only mentions theſe facts incidentally, and perhaps followed the order of *Moſes*'s narration, without a particular regard to chronology. It is beſides very clear, that *Stephen*'s deſign was not ſo much to relate *Abraham*'s call from *Haran*, as the whole conduct of providence in placing him in *Canaan*, which was effected gradually, and in particular by his purchaſe of a property in *Canaan*, *Gen.* xxiii. 25, 9. which he did after

after *Terah*'s death. See *Wolfii curæ philologicæ in Nov. Test. ad Act.* vii. 4. The preponderating arguments for the other opinion, concerning *Abraham*'s birth in the 70th year of his father, are drawn partly from the express mention of that year, *Gen.* xi. 26. where no sufficient reason can be assigned for departing from the literal sense of the words; and partly from a twofold probability of the thing itself, which may be shewn from the connexion of the circumstances, and strongly confirms this opinion. For all those of the posterity of *Shem*, who were ancestors to *Abraham*, begat children much earlier, the first at thirty-five, the second at thirty, the third at thirty-four, the fourth at thirty, the fifth at thirty-two, the sixth at thirty, and the seventh at twenty-nine. Hence it is much more probable, that *Abraham*, the son of the eighth, was born in the seventieth year, and was not the eldest, than that he was born so late as the 130th year. Besides, how could it appear so strange and unusual to *Abraham*, as we find it did, *Gen.* xvii. 17, that a child should be born to him in the 100th year of his age, if himself was born in the 130th year of his father's age. The testimonies of *Philo* and *Josephus* might moreover be alleged, tho' they contribute but little towards deciding the question. *Scaliger*, *Calvisius*, *Petavius*, *Heidegger*, and *Spanheim*, have all declared for this opinion.

Pag. 258. Cainan *interpolated in the Septuagint.*

The various readings of the *Greek* chronology are set forth in *Spanheim*'s *Chron. sacr.* That *Cainan* is interpolated in the *Greek* version. *Gen.* x. 24. xi. 13. is undoubted, tho' he is omitted in 1 *Chron.* i. 24. of the same version. But it is not so certain, whether this was done designedly, in the translation itself, in order to support the pretence of the great age of the old world, or whether it was done after, which however must have been early, and before

before the time of *Christ*; and, in this case, it is doubtful what could occasion the interpolation. There is therefore more probability in the conjecture, that the grandson of *Seth* was, by a mistake of some copyist or other writer, confounded with the grandson of *Shem*, and here inserted in the genealogy as his real grandson, than that *Salah* had the surname of *Cainan*, and so a distinct patriarch was formed. At least a subsequent alteration of that kind might more easily gain ground and become general, as it agreed with the great augmentation in the number of years in those early times made by this version. As to St. *Luke*, it is neither necessary nor probable to suppose *Cainan*'s name a false reading, or a late interpolation in his gospel; for without any prejudice to the credibility of this historian, or to his divine inspiration, he might follow the *Greek* version, as the sacred writers frequently did, where it departs from the *Hebrew*; and the general agreement of the copies and translations shew the improbability of a modern interpolation. See *Bengel*'s *Gnomon Nov. Test.* and his *ordo temporum*, and *Wolfii curæ phil. & crit.*

Pag. 258. *The* Hebrew *and* Samaritan *computations in this period.*

The great question in comparing the *Hebrew* and *Samaritan* reckonings is, whether the *Hebrew* pentateuch is genuine and uncorrupted? for in examining any facts the trial of the witnesses must supersede all other grounds of credibility. As to the inconcistencies charged upon the *Hebrew* computation, they are easily removed, if we consider, 1. That the kingdoms of *Canaan* and the state of the adjacent countries at that time, suppose *Abraham* to have lived much earlier, and nearer to the deluge, than the *Samaritan* computation will admit, whereas the *Hebrew* determines it. For *Abraham* and his 318 servants smote four considerable kings, *Gen.* xiv. 9, 14. and he was respected by the monarchs of those countries as a powerful prince,

prince, and their equal, and the same is mentioned of *Isaac*, ch. xxvi. 26--29. 2. That the quick increase of the *Israelites* in the time of *Moses*, in the fourth generation from *Jacob*, and the sixth from *Abraham*, as well as the populous condition of other nations descended from *Abraham* and *Lot*, in the time of *Moses*, such as the *Ishmaelites*, *Midianites*, *Edomites*, *Moabites* and *Ammonites*, account for the great increase of mankind in the time of *Abraham*, in the tenth generation from *Noah*, especially as the longevity of the patriarchs of that time must have greatly contributed to that increase. 3. That the dispersion of mankind did not require so great a number of men as the peopling of the earth, so that it might very well take place in the time of *Peleg*; tho' there are some who interpret the division of the earth, mentioned *Gen.* x. 25. not of this dispersion of mankind, but rather of a natural separation of some great parts of the globe.

The other principal objections to the *Hebrew* chronology in this period, are removed by the following observations; 1. The late procreation of children begins with *Abraham*, supposing him to have been born in the seventieth year of *Terah*, and not to have been the first-born; for had it been regular and usual at that time for men far advanced in years to propagate their species, then *Abraham*'s faith would not have been tried, nor *Isaac* have been the fruit of a divine promise. The case of *Isaac* and *Jacob* arose from the delay of their marriages, for their brothers *Ishmael* and *Esau* had children long before; and that delay was an effect of the religious separation of the families of those who were immediate parties in the covenant with God; and it ended with the sons of *Jacob*, many of whom, as well as their immediate posterity, had children very early, tho' some instances of later

later marriages perpetually occur, which might arise from the custom of not marrying out of their own kindred. 2. The longevity of some patriarchs, who survived many of their posterity, is by no means improbable, since the days of man after the deluge were shortened by degrees, and to secure the oral tradition of some truths, it might seem expedient to divine providence to preserve the lives of some patriarchs longer than those of the rest of mankind. *Abraham* and *Isaac* indeed are said to be old, tho' neither of them reached the age of their ancestors, but this was in comparison with other men, particularly most of their cotemporaries, as appears from the words of *Jacob*, *Gen.* xlvii. 9. where it is both intimated, that an hundred and thirty years was at that time a very extraordinary age, and that the lives of his fathers lasted much longer.

Pag. 265. *The birth of* Japhet.

According to the *Hebrew* marks of distinction, it may be proved from *Gen.* x. 21. compared with ch. ix. 24. that *Japhet* was the eldest son of *Noah*. But the other reason here alleged is not well grounded, for according to the order and connexion of the words, *Gen.* v. 32. the birth of *Shem* must be placed in the 500th year of *Noah*, and the design of *Moses* undoubtedly was to fix a chronology of the patriarchs by the years he mentions. Hence it has been pretty justly concluded by some, that *Gen.* xi. 10. is to be understood of the second year after the beginning of the deluge, or the year of *Noah*'s leaving the ark, consequently that these two years are not to be included in the aggregate sum of the whole chronology.

Pag. 268. *Comparison of the age of the patriarchs with the present.*

The comparison of the present age of man with that of the patriarchal times, is carried too far, particularly with respect to the proportion of intellectual faculties to the age of men, or the number of their years. For if that proportion were to be strictly

strictly observed, we could hardly suppose the patriarchs to arrive at maturity of reason and understanding till they had lived a century.

Pag. 268, 269. *The curse of* Canaan. The design of *Moses* here alleged, to animate the *Israelites* to attack the *Canaanites*, may perhaps have been the reason for recording this prophecy, but affords little or no help towards explaning the motive which induced *Noah* to curse *Canaan* and his posterity. However, it is certain, *first*, that these words of *Noah* are, like other predictions of the patriarchs concerning the fate of their posterity, to be placed among the prophecies which they were divinely inspired to deliver, and which were confirmed by the subsequent exact completion of them. *Secondly*, That the curses contained in those prophecies are not properly imprecations, or the fruit of warm vindictive passions, but predictions of impending calamities and afflictions in after-times; consequently, in the *third* place, they neither affect the eternal happiness or misery of men, nor can be considered merely as the actual punishment of certain crimes committed by their immediate sons, the remote ancestors of such posterity, *Rom.* ix. 11, 12, 13. *Mal.* i. 2, 3, 4. Hence, *fourthly*, it becomes needless exactly to measure and calculate the proportion between a calamity so denounced, and crimes previously committed, even tho' the evil was denounced on occasion of the misconduct of the progenitors of those unhappy people; it is needless, at least, to compare them by way of proof, that the proceedings of divine administration in such instances are not arbitrary, but grounded in the circumstances and condition of men, and that the virtues and vices of forefathers have an undoubted influence upon the external condition of their posterity, even by the appointment of divine providence. Therefore, *fifthly*, these words of *Noah* must neither be explaned

nor

nor vindicated with reſpect merely to the offence of *Ham*, nor is that to be wholly tried by the overt act, but by the diſpoſition of mind which it diſcovered in him, and from the entire connexion of all the circumſtances, many of which are unknown to us. It follows, in the *ſixth* place, that the offence of *Ham* was not ſo ſlight as it may appear to ſome, even without aggravating it by falſe additions. For the mockery of ſo venerable a father on ſuch a trifling occaſion, with ſo thorough a contempt of all ſhame and decency, muſt have been the reſult of a profligacy very deeply rooted, and betrayed a vicious mind, as well as an extreme contempt of his parent, whom many circumſtances, beſides his paternal conduct, rendered an object of the higheſt eſteem and reverence. For he was the ſurviving father of the whole human race, the inſtrument of their preſervation, particularly a benefactor to thoſe whom he had preſerved from the deluge, a preacher of righteouſneſs ſo highly endowed from above, the witneſs of divine truths, and indiſputably under God the ſupreme head and ruler of the world then exiſting. So that he could not be contemptuouſly or ignominiouſly treated, without a violation of many duties, religious, civil and natural. As to the conceit of thoſe, who imagine the blackneſs of *Ham*'s poſterity to be a conſequence of this curſe, the conciſe anſwer to it is, that neither all the poſterity of *Ham*, nor they alone, are diſtinguiſhed by this colour, and that the turpitude of it is only a prejudice of cuſtom and an arbitrary opinion.

The beginning of *Nimrod*'s reign, as it is here ſtated by the compilers, is in all probability wrong, and dated much too late: For as *Nimrod* was the great grandſon of *Noah*, conſequently at the ſame diſtance from *Noah* as *Salah* the grandſon of *Shem*, who was born in the thirty-ſeventh, or even in the thirty-fifth year after the deluge, there appears no reaſon

Pag. 281. *Time of* Nimrod's *reign.*

reason for placing the beginning of *Nimrod*'s reign in the fifth century after the deluge, especially as *Cush* his father was the eldest son of *Ham*, and marriages and births were not less early or frequent in this line, than in that of *Shem*.

Pag. 296. Peleg. The frequent and very improbable conjectures concerning *Melchisedeck*, and the insertion of him in the line of *Shem*, hath been occasioned by the *Jewish* prejudice, adopted by some of the fathers, that the true religion and divine grace were confined to that line. The great difficulties in the *Hebrew* chronology, so often mentioned with respect to *Peleg*, may be removed by the three following observations. 1. That *Gen*. x. 25. is not to be understood of a civil division of the world and its inhabitants into several nations and commonwealths, but of a natural separation of considerable parts of the globe from each other; for it is past dispute that such changes in the surface of the earth, and disruption of many parts of the continent, have happened at different times, and were more violent, more frequent, and more general, in the first ages after the deluge than since. 2. That there were more dispersions of nations than one, which are to be carefully distinguished. For as the compilers, in the sequel, admit of several dispersions subsequent to that at *Babel*, so it is possible, that before this great and total dispersion some nations began to be separated, and created an apprehension of being all scattered abroad upon the face of the earth, which they endevored to prevent, *ch*. xi. 4. So that the birth of *Peleg* might happen at the time of such previous separation, and there is no necessity of connecting it with the building of the tower at *Babel*. 3. The division of the earth, which took place in the time of *Peleg* is mentioned by *Moses* as the reason of his name. Now this name might be given him by *Eber* prophetically, with a view to that division; or it might, without any

any particular prophecy be a mere disposition of providence, that the signification of his name, which was given him for other reasons, should be fulfilled by this event happening in his life, in order the better to perpetuate the memory of it by that seemingly accidental circumstance. And both these completions of the names of particular persons are confirmed by other instances in scripture. The compilers seem to have forgot the ancient tradition, mentioned by Bishop *Patrick* and others, that *Peleg* built the city of *Phalga*, called by *Ptolemy Pharga*, on the *Euphrates*, at the confluence of the *Chaboras*.

From the continuation here given of the history of *Sanchoniatho*, it appears yet clearer than from the beginning of it, in chap. 1. sect. 5. of the *Univ. Hist.* that there are grounds for the suspicion, that *Philo* either greatly corrupted, or wholly invented this history himself. This suspicion is confirmed by the conclusion of the whole fragment in *Eusebius*, where *Philo* seems himself to betray his design to render the theological mythology of the *Greeks* more specious and credible, by separating from it, and apologizing for, the absurd additions, and to endeavor to support it in general by testimonies drawn from the earliest antiquity. This induced the authors of the *Universal History* to judge of it, in this section, more doubtfully and cautiously than before. And Bishop *Cumberland* has, in his illustration of this history, rather distinguished his great reading and fertile genius, than done any service to ancient history, or to the authority of the books of *Moses*; especially as the contradictions in his remarks proceed not only from prejudice, but from the precipitancy of crude reflexions. The best use that can be made of this spurious or at least very corrupted fragment is, to learn from it to observe and rightly estimate the value of the books of *Moses*.

Pag. 320, 321. *Observations upon* Sanchoniatho.

For we see, in this instance, how miserable a figure ancient history would make, and what kind of authorities we should have to rely on, if we wanted these records. And it is observable, how few true and genuine records and traditions of the earliest antiquity were extant in other nations, since they were necessitated to borrow some events from the *Jewish* accounts, in order to give some air of probability to the absurdities they had to relate. Our sentiments concerning *Sanchoniatho* have been delivered before. The observation made in the *Univ. Hist. p.* 318. in the note *B*, that at the time when these accounts were first drawn up by the *Cabiri*, a considerable part of mankind might bear testimony to the deluge, even tho' the memory of it should have been lost, or purposely suppress'd among some, is certainly just; for *Shem*, and perhaps his brothers, were then living, and their posterity might very authentically testify a fact, which had been reported to them by immediate eye-witnesses. So that the conclusion here drawn, that these accounts could not proceed from the *Cabiri*, nor from *Thot*, is much more probable than the conjecture, that *Sanchoniatho* wrote an account of the deluge, which was left out in his remains, for the whole series of events related by *Sanchoniatho* doth not admit of any deluge.

Pag. 322. *The migration to* Shinaar.

It is owing to the prepossession in favor of the *Samaritan* chronology, that the migration to *Shinaar* and the dwelling there, is here dated after the death of *Noah*. The first of the four opinions upon the expression *from the East*, *Gen.* ix. 2. is a great violence done to the words, not to be justified from *Gen.* xiii. 11. nor from 1 *Sam.* xiv. 5. both which passages are alleged in vindication of it by *Drusius* and others. The second opinion is a bold accusation of *Moses*, unsupported by proofs. Instead of it, and for want of other solutions of this difficulty,

ulty, it would be much more decent and specious o suppose, with *Bochart*, that *Moses*, and several oriental writers after him, considered all the countries beyond the *Tigris* as lying eastward, and those on this side of that river as lying westward. The hird and fourth opinions, which are the right explanations, may be joined together, and very consistently be both admitted. So that there is no necessity for the invention of an unknown country by the name of *Kedem*. The Septuagint render the name *Shinaar* by *Babylon* in *Zach*. v. 11. and *Is*. xi. 11.

Perizonius's interpretation depends rather upon the apparent sense and connexion, particularly of the subsequent words, than on any proof of the meaning of the expression itself, which occurs frequently in other passages of scripture, 2 *Sam*. viii. 13. 1 *Chron*. xvii. 8. *Isa*. lxiii. 12, 14. *Dan*. ix. 15. But the design, which is gathered from the subsequent words, is not so very clear, if narrowly examined. For the people concerned in the building must have known from experience, that neither a single city, nor such an extent of country as this tower, and the signals upon it, even by fire, could command, would suffice for the sustenance of their posterity, continually increasing and multiplying, especially if we suppose, with the compilers, that the whole human race conspired and were employed in this enterprize. On the other hand, if we consider, that the dispersion of mankind was already begun, and had in some degree taken place, and that a more general dispersion into remote countries, must unavoidably be foreseen without the aid of divine revelation, an ambition to perpetuate their name, which gave rise to the prodigious structures of the most ancient times, accounts very naturally for this attempt to secure their origin and establishment in these countries from oblivion, and

Pag. 235. *Design of the tower of* Babel.

this plain of *Shinaar* might be fixed upon for the conveniency it afforded of materials for building. See *Deylingii obs. sacr.* lib. 3. obs. 4.

Pag. 326. *The time of the building.* The time of the building of the tower cannot be assigned with any certainty. The opinion adopted by the compilers is partly founded in the prejudice, that this dispersion took place in the year of *Peleg's* birth, and partly in their partiality to the *Samaritan* computation. But, besides other arguments against the latter, it is difficult to conceive (especially when that is connected with the opinion here insisted upon, that all mankind assisted at this undertaking) how the human race could continue together till the fifth century, considering their speedy increase in the primitive times, and how particular nations could be propagated in the remotest parts of the earth, by the sons and grandsons of *Noah*, which yet appears undeniable from their names and traditions compared with *Gen.* x.

Pag. 329, &c. *The tower of* Babel. Besides the authors here cited, the following treat fully of the tower of *Babel*; *Calmet*, *Delany*, *Saurin*, *Strauchius* in his *dub. hist. & chronol.* *Shuckford*, *Bochart*'s *Phaleg*. *Prideaux* in his *connexion*, and *Rollin hist. ancien.* The ill-grounded conjectures concerning the design of this structure have been, in great measure, occasioned by a misinterpretation of *Gen.* xi. 4. *whose top may reach unto heaven*, which words are only meant to express an extraordinary height. That the whole human race were concerned in the building, doth not appear so clearly from the arguments here alleged, as the compilers seem to imagine. The tenth and eleventh chapters are not so immediately connected, as is pretended; it is rather evident, that to avoid interrupting the genealogical series, many things are joined together in the tenth chapter, which are explaned more at large in the next. So that it doth not follow from the meaning of the word *earth*,

earth, *ch.* x. 32. that *the whole earth*, *ch.* xi. 1. is to be understood of all the habitable globe, which is the sense upon which all the arguments here alleged are chiefly founded. Now, tho' nothing can be gathered either for or against this opinion from *ch.* xi. 5. yet it is much more probable from *ch.* x. 10. that this building was undertaken by *Nimrod*, or the posterity of *Ham*; without giving into the opinion of M. *Von der Hardt*, that the race of *Ham* designed it as a fortification against the race of *Shem*, or as the means of subduing them. This conjecture, however, is more tolerable than another extravagant conceit of the same gentleman, that *Joshua*, who was high-priest at the time of the destruction of *Babylon* by *Cyrus*, was the author of this account of that event.

The ruin here described would exceed any monument extant in point of antiquity, if the genuineness of it, which is here justly disputed, could be better evidenced than that of *Noah's* ark. For the bare concurrence of the circumstances of situation and materials, will not suffice, in a country abounding by nature in one sort of materials, and wholly destitute of every other convenience; and considering how long and continually this country hath been inhabited, and how it hath been desolated and new-peopled by many wars, the preservation of this monument will appear highly improbable. The reports and accounts of travellers must, in cases of this kind, be tried by the rules of credibility, which will very much detract from the credit of many pieces of antiquity described by them; for their accounts become extremely suspicious, if we recollect on the one side the ignorance, self-love, ostentation, and mercenary disposition of the inhabitants, particularly of the Eastern countries, and on the other, the want of judgment, the credulity, strong imagination, and propensity to any thing

Pag. 337 --340. *Ruins of* Babel.

curious and marvellous on the part of travellers, encouraged by the hope of security from all contradiction.

Pag. 342, 343. *Extent of the primitive language.* The reasons here given by our authors for the poverty and narrow limits of the primitive language consist in prejudices, and the conclusion built upon them is vastly exaggerated. *Adam*'s knowledge of the creation must have extended much farther than is here pretended, for the exhibition of the fish to him required no greater miracle than that of other animals, particularly birds, and his observation of the world before him was not in the least interrupted or impeded. But besides these images impressed upon his mind by sensation, the extent of his ideas and reflexions, and the operations of his understanding must have been considerable, as appears from *Gen.* ii. 24. and this must naturally have improved his language and the use of symbolical characters. The declaration of *Gregory* of *Nyssa* here cited, upon which *R. Simon* builds an important argument in his critical history of the Old Testament, is very extravagant, and to be understood with great restriction, or it may be applied to censure, as unworthy of God, his whole work of creation, particularly of our world. The opposite opinion, however, may be carried too far, as has been the case, especially in denying the arbitrary appointment of the primitive words, and pretending to discover an internal signification of each letter, and from thence forming the signification of the words compounded of such letters. See *Carpzovii crit. sacr.*

Pag. 346. *Claims of several languages.* *Carpzovius* in his *critica sacra*, treats at large of the claims of several languages to the honor of being primitive, and cites the writers on that subject. The *Greek* has been zealously defended by M. *Von der Hardt*, but Dr. *C. B. Michaelis*, has thoroughly examined his opinion in a particular dissertation

dissertation *contra hypothesin Hardtianam de Hebræâ & aliis adfinibus orientis linguis a Græcâ derivandis.*

Pag. 348. Of the Hebrew.

As the kindred oriental languages, particularly the *Hebrew*, *Chaldæan*, *Syriac*, *Arabic* and *Ethiopic*, have so many words, phrases, and even grammar rules, in common, that it can hardly be denied that they were originally the same language, or proceeded from the same root, and are therefore justly considered as various dialects of one and the same original tongue, most of the arguments urged in favor of the *Syriac*, will, in some measure, serve to prove the antiquity of the *Hebrew*. See *Rhenferd's rudim. gram. harm. ling. orient.* in his *opera philolog.* and in the same work his *specimen litteraturæ Phœniciæ eruendæ*. *Reinesii* ἱστορούμενα *linguæ Punicæ* in *Grevius's syntagma dissertat. rarior.* and *Schultens's origines Hebrææ*, likewise his *instit. ad fundam. ling. Hebrææ*, where he answers the arguments here alleged against the antiquity of the *Hebrew* tongue. See also *Wolfii Biblioth. Hebr.*

It is true, that many have miscarried in their attempts to derive other languages from the *Hebrew*, and to shew the similarity of some words in foreign languages with *Hebrew* words. *Lud. Thomasinus*, who published a *Glossarium universale Hebraicum* at *Paris* in 1697, is one of those who made this attempt without success; for tho' his preface discovers much reading, and abounds with useful observations, yet he was neither sufficiently acquainted with the Oriental, nor the principal *European* languages. But the miscarriage of these individuals is no argument against the derivation of other languages from the Eastern, and particularly from the *Hebrew*; for neither were the warmest opposers of the antiquity of the *Hebrew* perfectly qualified for this enquiry by their fundamental knowlege of languages, especially of the Eastern, as may be proved to have been the case with *Morinus*, *Simon*, *Huetius*, *Grotius*, and *Job. Clericus*; for they undoubtedly confined the *Hebrew* language within too narrow limits, and formed their judgment of the primitive extent of it, from the few surviving books that were originally written in it, and their works sufficiently discover, that they were ignorant of some of the principles of the *Hebrew* tongue, and of the signification of some of the words.

Pag. 352 ---357. *The confusion of tongues.*

The opinion controverted by our authors, that no new languages were formed immediately by God at the building of the tower of *Babel*, is not so absurd and improbable as they pretend. The words of *Gen*, xi. 7. may very well be interpreted of a misunderstanding among the builders; this might consist in a miraculous confusion of their language or memory, or more probably in their refusing to give attention and mutual compliance to one another. *Moses*, in *Gen*. x. 5, 20, 31. expressly derives the origin of languages from the dispersion and separation of the several families and people, and it is not yet proved, that *ch*. xi. 1, *&c.* intimates that the whole human race assisted at the work. The immediate formation of new languages would be the greatest miracle that ever was performed. The number of men was infinite, whose ideas and characteristical marks of expression were to be so totally changed; and there is not an instance in the whole history of the world of a divine operation like that upon the faculties of the human mind, so as totally to remove and efface an infinite number of images from the memory, and instantaneously to replace them by others, especially as the connexion between words and the thoughts and ideas of men is so close, that every man must have entirely ceased to recollect any of his former thoughts; all which bears no similitude to the miraculous gift of speech at the effusion of the

the Holy Ghost. It is somewhat extraordinary, that the compilers, who were so averse to a miracle in the first origin of language in the case of *Adam*, should here be so ready to admit an accumulation of much greater miracles. Besides, many languages, even of the earliest times, are so rough and uncultivated, that the immediate formation of them cannot, with decency and respect, be attributed to God. It is no argument against the descent of all the present race of men from *Noah*, that not one of them can possibly trace his genealogy back to that patriarch; in like manner, the impossibility of proving the extraction and affinity of all languages is not so clear an argument as some imagine, against their common derivation from one primitive language. Nor can we conclude, from the slow and inconsiderable change of languages among nations of a later date, whose histories are still extant, that in the primitive times the change was as gentle and gradual; for when the earth was first peopled, and frequent migrations took place, new languages might much more easily arise than in succeeding times, when nations became more numerous, more cultivated in comparison, and better connected. The multitude of languages in *America*, and their great disparity, sometimes in a small district, and in islands at a very small distance from each other, sufficiently shews, that new languages arise more easily, the more a people is uncultivated, wild, ignorant, and unsociable. This doth not, however, in the least, affect the particular interposition of divine Providence, whose measures are represented after the manner of men. See on the subject, *Vitringæ observ. sacr. Perizonius*'s *orig. Babyl. Heidegger*'s *Hist. Patriarch.* and others. But if the other opinion maintained by our authors be admitted, it doth not follow from it, either that the primitive language was

was totally lost, since the preservation of it was very consistent with such a miracle; or that it became impossible to learn it. The confusion of tongues at *Babel* is more fully discuss'd in *Crinesii disput. de confus. ling.* which is preserved in *Crenii analect.*—*Buxtorf*'s *diss. de confus. ling. ebr. & plur. linguar. orig.* and his *diss. phil. theol. Ziegra de confus. ling. Babylonica, Gesner's disp. in cap.* xi. *Gen. Meisner de confus. ling. Babyl.*

Pag. 357. *Effects of the division of mankind.* The great division of nations and their sudden dispersion after building the tower of *Babel*, undoubtedly occasioned the uncivilized state of a great part of mankind, and precipitated the ignorance and neglect of true religion which soon after prevailed. Here was sufficient employment for a divine over-ruling providence, both to punish the neglect of known and confessed truths, and to provide for the good of mankind in the midst, and even by the means, of their punishment.

Pag. 361, 362. *Calculations of the increase of mankind.* The exact calculations of the increase of mankind in the early ages, are not only needless, but the three calculations here exhibited are each of them extravagant. For 1. The tower of *Babel* might be built by a much less number of men than is generally imagined. Some augment the number because they misinterpret the words *Gen.* xi. 4. others form an arbitrary supposition, that the amazing structures at *Babel*, mentioned in the historians of subsequent times, were most of them raised so early as at the first building of the city. 2. The dispersion and separation of mankind might be gradual, and in all probability was so, consequently as the original institution of common wealths was upon the plan of natural and domestic societies, the new colonies might consist of much fewer in number, than these calculations presuppose. 3. The fabulous accounts of immense armies brought into the field in these early times, are both improbable

improbable in themselves, and may be confuted by irrefragable authorities. 4. There is no apparent necessity to place this event at *Babel* in the year of the birth of *Peleg*, which creates an improbability in the age of *Nimrod*. These four observations being admitted, the necessity ceases of crouding so great a number of men into the second century after the deluge, tho' it be certain, that the increase and propagation of mankind was much quicker then, than in succeeding times. Of the three calculations here exhibited, the incredibility of the two first is very obvious. Mr. *Whiston*'s is likewise very hypothetical, but somewhat more tolerable than the other two. He is most arbitrary and improbable in the manner of determining the years of doubling in the first fifty years after the deluge, and indeed in the eight first centuries in general. The following things are observable with respect to Mr. *Whiston*'s exceptions to the *Samaritan* chronology, which he made before he gave it the preference to every other. 1. That it is a matter of great uncertainty to fix the age of some men after the deluge, till the times of *David*, and most of these are extraordinary cases, from which no conclusion can be drawn in favor of the usual longevity of men in those times, since human life was shortened much earlier, as appears from the frequent deaths of the descendants of the patriarchs before their ancestors. So that Mr. *Whiston*'s calculation is extremely erroneous. 2. Mr. *Whiston* does in fact calculate the doubling of mankind in a much shorter space, than is here presupposed, he doth not fix the period of the doubling at sixty years till the fifth century, and shortens it considerably before that time. 3. That the compilers have proceeded in the sequel upon Mr. *Whiston*'s calculation, tho' his table being formed on the principles of the *Hebrew* chronology, cannot be made use of in the *Samaritan*, as the generation

generation of men was much later upon this system; and consequently the doubling of mankind must be proportionably slower.

It appears from the lowest of these calculations, how impossible it was, that so great a number of men should continue so long together, especially under no other than the paternal form of government and fifty years after the death of *Noah* without some previous separation or division; and how improbable it is, that seventy languages should arise at the confusion of *Babel*, since it is so difficult a matter to count fifty three nations, and their number is not certain, because the fathers are separated from their immediate sons.

Pag. 366. *Uncertainty of ancient names.* The general principles here laid down by our authors are indisputably true, that a narrow inquiry into the names of ancient people, and their original habitations, is of a nature quite indifferent, neither important nor trifling, and that it is impossible to arrive at any degree of certainty in it. But their other assertions require some limitation. It is owing to the want of ancient writings and records, and the frequent changes of names occasioned by the frequent migrations of those early times, that many names of people, countries and cities mentioned in scripture occur no where else, at least under the same denomination. So that this renders the sacred history neither suspicious nor uncertain, nor does it prove, that *Moses* and other historians did not retain the original names of nations foreign to them or before their time, but translated them as they thought fit. The complaint here made of the want of authentic antiquities among the *Jews* must be confined to those *Jewish* historians, who wrote after the inspired writers. Among these *Josephus* is the eldest, if not the only one, that falls under this observation. For if it be meant to extend farther, it is not only void of proof,

proof, but demonstrably false. For it is manifest in the latest historians among the *Israelites*, and particularly in the writings of *Moses*, that many records and monuments of antiquity were extant in their time, so that we need not ascribe the whole of their ancient history to a divine revelation.

Pag. 367---381. *Migrations in the first dispersion of mankind.*

Beside *Bochart* and *Shuckford*, who are referr'd to in this full enquiry into the settlement of the first nations after the deluge, it will be of use to consult the following authors; *Eusebius Cæsar in lib. de locis Hebraic. Jo. Martianæus, Jo. Clericus,* and *Jac. Rhenford* in his *exerc. philol.* upon the *onomasticum* of *Eusebius* in his *opera philolog. Havercamp* upon *Josephus*; *Schulten*'s *index geogr. in vitâ Saladini*, *Calmet*'s *comment. litter.* upon *Gen.* X. and his *dict. hist. de la bible.* See likewise *Shaw*'s and *Chardin*'s Travels.

Pag. 381---384. *Second migration.*

Of the *Arabian* nations and their origin, see *Sale*'s preliminary discourse to his *Koran*, *Ockley*'s history of the *Saracens*, *Pocock*'s *specim. hist. Arab.* and more particularly *Assemanni dissert.* 4. *de arabum origine ac religione* in *Pet. Rahebi's chron. orient.* in the *Venice* edition of the *scriptor. Byzant.* p. 220—270.

Pag. 385---387. *Origin of civil societies.*

The representation here given of the origin of civil societies has very much the air of a *Platonic* commonwealth. We read in the scriptural history of early misunderstandings between persons nearly allied in blood, even between brothers in the houses of their fathers, and we there find the contrary of what is here pretended concerning the jurisdiction of the patriarchs over their descendants, especially with respect to the external coercion of punishments. So that the necessity of instituting commonwealths seems to have arisen from the violences unavoidable by any other means. Besides the property of vassalage obtained by conquest in war, the history of *Joseph* in *Egypt* points out another very natural method

method of acquiring that right, by the relief and ease of persons in extreme distress, upon the condition of total slavery, or by a contract under which they sold themselves and theirs.

Pag. 388. Original arts and sciences. The great simplicity of the earliest times, when men were strangers to many things, which are now esteemed indispensibly necessary, and the longevity of men, which lasted for a considerable time after the deluge, render it probable, that men had at that time leisure enough to apply themselves to some arts and sciences. The choice of these was doubtless determined by their utility in social life. In this respect astronomy must be placed among the earliest occupations of men; for every division of time, which is of so great importance to human society, must, from the beginning, have been regulated by the course of the heavenly bodies, and the observation of these, and of the changes of weather at different seasons, must have been of evident use and indispensibly necessary to agriculture and pasture, as well as to determine the situation of countries, and to direct the traveller. This will further appear, if we consider, that the first civilized people begun very early to devote particular persons, and even whole families, to the study of the sciences, particularly of astronomy; and the most ancient writings extant, of all nations, shew the great antiquity of this study amongst men, which in all probability gave rise to the first idolatry.

Pag. 389. Of navigation. It is a matter not easily decided, whether the invention of shipping was prior to the deluge. *Sanchoniatho's* accounts prove only this, that navigation was one of the earliest attempts made by man, which is in itself not improbable. The particular and extraordinary preparation of *Noah's* ark, and the nature of the deluge, sufficiently shew, that a common vessel built in the usual way, which in in those times could have been of no very large size, would have been too weak to have withstood the tempests and the waters of the deluge. As to the passage which some refer to, *Heb.* xi. 7. it will not amount to an argument in this case, since *Noah*'s faith was sufficiently exercised, tho' navigation might not, at that time, be wholly undiscovered. But the pretence of others is highly improbable, that the posterity of *Noah* should neglect this art after the deluge, and that it was discovered anew a long while after. See *Wisd.* xiv. 17.

CHAP. III.

The History of Egypt *to the time of* Alexander the Great.

THIS elaborate account of *Egypt* is carefully extracted both from the proper sources in ancient history, and from the best reports of modern travellers. The three following learned enquiries into the ancient and present state of that country have been published since the first edition of the *Univ. Hist.* and deserve to be consulted; *Description de l'Egypt sur les Memoires de Monsieur de Maillet, par M. l'Abbé le Mascrier*; Dr. *Shaw*'s *Travels*, and Dr. *Pocock*'s *Description of the East.*

Cairo, or *al Kahira*, the capital of *Egypt*, being also called *Masr*, or *al Masser*, the whole country may have born the same name, which is still in use, and derived by Dr. *Shaw*, according to an oriental tradition, from *Mizraim*. *Pag.* 390. *Name of* Egypt.

Egypt has always been reckoned among the Eastern, and the rest of *Africa* among the Western nations, in the division of the *Roman* provinces, and afterwards of the Christian bishoprics. The question, *Pag.* 391, 392. *Situation and extent of* Egypt.

question, whether *Egypt* appertains to *Asia* or *Africa*, is of so early a date, that *Herodotus* treats of it in his second book. *Pliny*, in his *Natural History*, likewise places it in *Asia*. Dr. *Pocock* measures the length of *Egypt* at no more than five hundred and sixty miles, or eight degrees of seventy miles each, and observes that *Herodotus*, in measuring the length according to the course of the *Nile*, must have included all the windings of that river, else it would be impossible to make the extent of it from the sea to *Elephantis*, amount to eight hundred ninety-five miles.

Pag. 402. *The nomes of* Egypt. The division of the country into nomes or prefectures, has been frequently changed by the sovereigns, which accounts for the different numbers of them in ancient authors, and hence that diversity of numbers is very consistent without contracting or extending the limits of the whole country. This division of the kingdom into three parts, and of each of these into subordinate prefectures, hath, in general, been continued thro' all the subsequent revolutions in the government, insomuch that even at present, under the *Turks*, the number of those prefectures is much the same with the original institution. The passage in *Isa.* xix. 2. is rightly translated by the Septuagint, but we must take care not to confound the words νομὸς and νόμος, for the false reading νόμος ἐπὶ νόμον, instead of νομὸς ἐπὶ νομὸν, occasioned the old *Latin* translation, *lex super legem*, which hath since been corrected by the Vulgate, *regnum contra regnum*.

Pag. 406. *Accession of land to* Egypt. The opinion here disputed, that either all *Egypt*, except only *Thebais*, or at least that which is strictly called the lower *Egypt*, and particularly the *Delta*, is a country formed from the soil brought down from the *Nile*, is generally asserted by the ancients, and mentioned as a tradition of former times, as may be seen in *Herodotus*, *Diodorus*, *Aristotle*'s *meteorol.*

teorol. and *Pliny*'s natural history. Many of the moderns too have assented to it, as an opinion very well grounded, and particularly in two evident matters of fact. One of these is the continual accession of land to *Egypt*, when the *Nile* discharges itself into the sea, which is past all doubt, both from history and experience. Not to mention the great distance, in former times, of the isle of *Pharos* from the continent, taken notice of by *Plato*, *Pliny* and *Seneca*, upon the authority of *Homer*'s *Odyssey*; it is undoubted, that *Damietta* was a maritime place, and a harbour in the middle of the thirteenth century, at the time of S. *Lewis*'s expedition, and is now ten miles distant from the sea-coasts. The city *Fouah*, which is now seven miles from the sea, was a sea-port three or four hundred years ago. And *Maillet* assures us, that *Rosetta*, which an hundred years ago was washed by the sea, acquired half a mile's length of land in so small a space of time as between the years 1692 and 1718, of which he was convinced by his own observation. The other undeniable fact is that of the land being raised in *Egypt*. For as the cities, particularly those of lower *Egypt*, were all built upon natural or artificial eminences, in order to guard against inundations, yet the circumjacent plain has been gradually observed so to raise itself, that it became necessary either to raise the cities higher, or to encompass them at a vast expence with *Dams*. Hence the temple in the midst of *Bubastus* was lower than the rest of the city, because at the raising of the city it was thought too costly an edifice to be pull'd down and rebuilt. And hence the places where *Heliopolis* and *Babylon* were situate, are level with the rest of the country, and annually overflowed; tho' they were formerly considerable eminences. To the same cause may be imputed the loss of so many ruins and remains of antiquity, which are wholly or in great part buried under ground. The great quantity of sand, which the wind conveys into upper *Egypt* might contribute to this, and must at the same time increase the quantities of soil brought down from the *Nile*. There is no great weight in the argument drawn by *Maillet* from the shells and scales of sea-animals found in the midst of the country, that being a very common case in othes countries; and the proof, which some gather from *Herodotus*'s account of the different height of the *Nile*, requisite to overflow the country in his time, and in the reign of king *Moeris*, nine hundred years before, is, upon very probable grounds, disputed by the learned Dr. *Pocock*; for the height not only differs, from the different measure, by taking in or omitting the depth of the *Nile* in its real bed, but the infinite number of trenches and capacious reservoirs, particularly that of the lake *Moeris*, must occasion a prodigious difference in the height of the river, when overflowing its banks. The same author adds several curious observations against the regular accession of land to *Egypt*, with respect to the proportion in which it is raised, and in some measure shakes Dr. *Shaw*'s conjecture, that the land is raised a foot in an hundred years. However, the latter draws one good conclusion from it against the monstrous chronology and incredible antiquity of the *Egyptians*; for those fables are confuted by the natural condition of the country, which could not even be habitable so many thousand years, as they pretend to look back. But another conclusion drawn from the same premisses, that in proportion as the land increases in height, the inundations must gradually decrease, and totally cease at last, is ill-grounded, for the bed of the *Nile* must necessarily be raised in the same proportion, especially in lower *Egypt*. The name of *Baheira*, given by *Sicard* to the

Western

Western part of the *Delta*, is confirmed by Dr. *Pocock*.

Those passages in the ancients, which mention the want of rain in *Egypt*, must be understood of *upper Egypt*, or *Thebais*, and are generally meant in a comparative sense, which is undoubtedly the sense of *Deut*. xi. 10. *Maillet* says, that it seldom rains at *Cairo*, and higher up in the country, and only for about a quarter or half an hour in the evening; that in the years 1692, 1693, and 1694, it rained five or six times from *November* to *April*; that it is frequently the case in *upper Egypt*, to pass three or four years without any rain, and that it is such a rarity as to occasion public rejoicings. Dr. *Pocock* confirms this, and mentions, that the rains are frequent and heavy on the sea-coasts, and in *lower Egypt*, particularly from *November* to *March*, but that at *Cairo* they are moderate, and only in the Months *December*, *January*, and *February*, and that in *upper Egypt* they had rain but twice, half an hour each time, in the space of eight years. The case is the same with earthquakes, of which *Pliny* in his *Natural History* says, *ideo Galliæ & Ægyptus minime quatiuntur*. But *Maillet* mentions two earthquakes, one in 1694, the other in 1698, and *Pocock* mentions a more violent one in 1740, which demolished some houses. The common husbandmen wear nothing but linnen, as the cold is not very sensibly felt but in the morning and evening. Pag. 411. *Rains in* Egypt.

The supplying of *Rome* from *Egypt* lasted no longer than till the building of *Constantinople*, for from that time this city became the granary of *Rome*; and the heaviest charge alleged against *Athanasius* before *Constantine* was, that he obstructed this exportation. *Maillet*, upon the authority of a *Coptic* writer, attributes the draining of *Egypt* to *Joseph*. At least it is undoubted, that the project Pag. 412. *Fertility*.

of cutting canals thro' the country, must have rendered many wet marshy lands habitable.

The Nile. Tho' there was a little river on the eastern coasts of *Egypt*, distinguished by the name of *Sihor*, yet it is generally thought, and upon probable grounds, that the *Nile* was meant by that name in *Jer.* ii. 18. The name of *Nile*, which is now the only one in use, is more properly derived from the *Hebrew* word *Nabal*, which signifies a river in general, and so might easily, by way of eminence, become the appellation of this principal river of the whole country, than from the *Greek* μελας *black*, by changing μ into ν. The seven principal mouths of the *Nile* are mentioned so early as by the prophet *Isaiah*, ch. xi. 15. The difficulties arising from their various numbers and appellations, are fully considered in *Cellarius*'s *notit. orb. antiqui*, and by Dr. *Shaw* and Dr. *Pocock*.

Pag. 414. *Miraculous rise of the* Nile. *Maillet* reports this event from *Arabian* writers, but differs in the circumstances, for he represents it to have happened under the caliph *Omar*, in the 21st or 23d year of the *Hegira*. Dr. *Shaw*, in a large extract from *Kalkasendu*, concerning the *Nile* and the *Nilometers*, gives a circumstantial account of this event, that it happened in the time of the vice-gerency of *Amru Ebn Al Als*, in the reign of *Abdallah Omar Ebn Al Khattab*, for the truth of which he appeals to the writing *Abdal Rahhman Ebn Abdallah Ebn Abhsakam*, and to other testimonies; so that by a mistake of modern travellers, an event, which happened at the beginning of the reigns of the *Moslemim* or *Mohammedans*, is dated much later under the government of the *Turks* in *Egypt*. This removes one of the difficulties here complained of. As to the solution of the other, it is not improbable, that the *Egyptians* annually cast a graceful image or statue of a virgin into the river, which was a practice intolerable to *Mohammedans*,

medans, who were warm zealots against images. For image-worship and superstition were at that time arrived to a very great heighth, and over-ran the Eastern countries, and the practice of throwing a cross with great solemnity into the *Nile*, at the fall of that river, renders it probable that the same superstitious usage prevailed at the rise of it; which is confirmed by the caliph *Omar*'s order, in case the *Nile* did not swell to a sufficient heighth, to throw into it the following letter or warning of his: "*Abdallah Omar*, ruler of the faithful, to the *Nile* in *Egypt*. If thou wilt not spread thyself freely, and of thine own accord, know, that there is a superior power able to compel thee to flow. In the mean time we shall earnestly pray to him to compel thee to flow."

Kalkasenda gives an account, at large, of all the several kinds of *Nilometers*, used in former times, till the ninth century of the *Hegira*, and mentions that the inspection of them was at first left to Christians, till the reign of *Al Motawakkel*, who gave an hereditary grant of this office to *Abul Radad Abdallah Ebn Abdul Salam al Mudab*, in whose family it continued. The greatest difficulty consists in the calculation and comparison of this measure. *Maillet* reckons a pike at twenty-four inches; *Bernard de mensuris* at twenty-eight inches nine lines. Dr. *Shaw*, upon the authority of *Gabrieli*, fixes it at twenty-eight inches; to which *Kalkasenda* agrees, tho' with respect only to the twelve lowest pikes of the *Mikyas*, the rest differ as follows; to 16 of 28 inches, from 17 to 20 of 26 inches, and the uppermost from 21 to 23 of 24 inches, as *Pocock* hath accurately shewn. This solves many contradictions, otherwise irreconcileable, between ancient and modern writers, and amongst the latter when they vary from each other. It likewise accounts for the different height requisite to water the coun-

Pag. 414, 415. *The* Nilometers.

 try

try at different times, tho', besides the different measure, this might be partly occasioned by the foulness and cleansing of the canals, and the formation of new ones, particularly the improvement of them undertaken by *Petronius* in the reign of *Augustus*.

Pag. 415. Sphinxes. The *Egyptian* Sphinxes had a twofold design and meaning. When they stood alone, which was particularly the case of that prodigious one on the *Nile*, they denoted, in the manner here mentioned by the compilers, at what time the waters of the *Nile* would swell, as is explained in *Horapollini's Hieroglyp.* But they are, in general, according to the explanation of *Clement* of *Alexandria*, *Strom.* 5. symbolical representations of prudence and strength united; and, according to the same author, *Strom.* 7. and to *Plutarch de Isid. & Osir.* when they were placed before temples, they signified that their theology, and all their religion, consisted of *symbols* and *enigmas*. The largest and most celebrated Sphinx, which is placed eastward of *Cairo*, near the pyramids, and less distant from the *Nile*, and much lower in point of situation, is hewen out of a rock, and so much of it as appears above the earth is very little hurt, except only that his nose is maimed, probably by the *Mohammedans*, from their bitterness against images. At the top of its head is a hole, which has occasioned some to conjecture, that this image was made use of as an oracle, because the hole is five or six foot deep, and large enough to contain a lusty man. At the back of it is an aperture, four feet in length and two in breadth, whence it is conjectured, that the Sphinx was quite hollow, and perhaps had a subterraneous communication with the pyramids. Besides the two here mentioned by the compilers, there are a great number of them near *Thebes*. In *Baddam's Abridgment of the Philosophical Transactions*, is is an extract from N°. 71. of the *Transactions*, where avenues or alleys are described consisting of sixty Sphinxes on each side, which account is indeed but short and defective, but doth in general coincide with Dr. *Pocock*'s account of *Thebes*.

Many disputes, and sometimes bloodshed, have arisen between the several districts of *Egypt* about the opening of the trenches, to convey and equally divide the water, which hath occasioned the strictest provision of law duly to observe the times. In *lower Egypt* they are commonly opened nine days later than in *upper Egypt*, and always in the presence of a magistrate. In the high lands immense pains are taken to draw the water from the lower trenches to the upper, which is often done to a prodigious height, sometimes by five pumps above one another, from a lower reservoir into a higher, in which they employ many more kinds of wells and engines than are here mentioned. *Maillet* reckons that fifty thousand oxen are daily employed in drawing water, but we may safely double the number. *Pag.* 416. *Manner of conveying the water.*

The fecundity of *Egypt* hath declined of late years, but not so much through any defect in nature, as thro' the negligence of the inhabitants, and the want of due culture of their lands. This is particularly the case in the countries remote from the *Nile*, many of which were heretofore populous and fruitful, and are now a desart, which is principally occasioned by the obstruction of the corn-trade, and the reduction of the number of inhabitants. But wherever the land is at all cultivated, the fertility is still amazing; for in some places there are pieces of land which yield four crops a-year, and in the greatest plenty. This is partly owing to the powerful influence of the sun upon so moist and manured a soil; but as the rains in the southern parts, near the source of the *Nile*, *Pag.* 417. *Fecundity occasioned by the* Nile.

contain an incredible quantity of sulphureous and oily vapors, and as whole villages are annually burnt to stop the flame of an immense quantity of reeds, canes, and rushes, the ashes of which are afterwards carried off by the *Nile*, it is an easy matter to account for the extraordinary fertility of the land.

Pag. 417, 418. *Fecundity of men and animals.* It is certain that the waters of the *Nile* are very salubrious, except only during a few weeks of the year, when the river first begins to swell; but the fruitfulness of men and animals may be ascribed to other causes. The period which the compilers fix for child-bearing is not general, and may arise from their long confinement at the time of the inundations, which is spent in idleness and pleasures, rather than merely from drinking the waters of the *Nile*.

Pag. 418. *Change of seasons in* Egypt. The commodious changes of the nature and appearance of the country at the two seasons here mentioned, must render the weather of this climate both tolerable and pleasant; for else the summer months would be intolerably hot, if the air was not seasonably cooled by the inundation. Hence, in former times, during the florishing state of *Egypt*, this season was almost constantly spent in ships upon the water, and the Great made a magnificent appearance in enjoying the refreshment.

Pag. 419. *Causes of the inundations.* Beyond the cataracts, the *Nile* receives vast accession, not only from the white river or sea, and many other considerable rivers which discharge themselves into it, but as it runs the length of several days journey between great mountains, it receives many large and small rivulets, which are produced by the rainy months. Dr. *Shaw*, beside the passages of *Diodorus* and *Plutarch*, quotes *Ebn Sinai* in *Abulfeda*, and *Al Rhodoi* in *Kalkasenda*, in confirmation, that this cause of the winter rains, was not unknown to the ancients. *Maillet* gives a yet

yet more circumstantial account of this reason of the swelling of the *Nile*, and mentions, that not only many wooden boats, but ships laden with earthen ware manufactured in *Ethiopia*, pass thro' the falls of the *Nile*, without being at all intimidated by the apparent danger of being shattered to pieces. Of the source and swelling of the *Nile*, see *Lobo*'s *Voyage historique d'Abissinie*, p. 105, &c.

Pag. 420. Deut. xi. 10, 11, 12.

The words of *Moses* here cited plainly intimate, that tho' the watering of *Egypt* by the *Nile* be so very beneficial, yet the labor and care of the inhabitants is much greater than in other fruitful countries, as *Canaan* doubtless was; which deserves to be considered as a singular instance of the wisdom of divine providence, since, in the present state of things, some degree of labor and useful employment is, in all places, indispensibly necessary to man.

Pag. 420. The Crocodile.

The *Crocodiles* are at present called *Timsah*, which agrees pretty well with the appellation *Champsa*, given them by *Herodotus*. Some travellers assure us, that they are now very scarce, and indeed they were always scarce in *lower Egypt*, the utmost extent of those gentlemen's travels; for they are apt to avoid a strong current of water, and therefore seldom come farther below *Cairo*, than to *Ahmim*, which accounts for their scarcity here much better than the pretence of the *Coptic* priests in the convent of St. *Anthony*, that they were banished from these parts. So that Dr. *Shaw*'s account, that the *Egyptians* are as curious to see a crocodile as the *Europeans*, must be limited to *lower Egypt*, tho' he makes them a rarity as far as the cataracts. *Maillet* likewise observes, that there are none below *Cairo*, but mentions their great number in the upper parts, particularly about *Girgey*, or the ancient district of *Sais*, where they do considerable mischief. Dr. *Pocock* saw many of them, and mentions,

tions, that they seldom venture far from the water, not even above thirty or forty paces in the night. Their chief strength is in their tail, with which they beat down every thing, and tear with their claws what they cannot swallow at once. Among other methods of catching them, one is that of digging holes not far from the banks, and having covered them with straw, to allure the crocodile that way by the cry of some animal.

Pag. 421. *The* Hippopotamus. *Ludolf*, in his *Hist. Æthiop.* treats at large of the Hippopotamus, which is more common in *Ethiopia* than in *Egypt*. He asserts at large, in concurrence with *Bochart*, that this animal is the *Behemoth* in the book of *Job*, and maintains this opinion against *Pfeiffer* in his *dub. vex.* It is generally allowed, that this animal is now almost unknown in *Egypt*, except that some years ago one was found near *Damietta*. The appellation of a river-horse is not derived from its shape, which rather resembles that of an ox, tho' twice as big, and is only like a horse in its ears. But it very much resembles a horse in neighing and sneezing, which is done with such violence, the head being projected above the water, that it is heard at a vast distance. This animal having but one small vulnerable place in his head, is very dangerous and mischievous, as he not only feeds upon corn, but fruits. The only security against him is his dread of fire, which will effectually drive him away.

Pag. 421. *The* Cynocephalus, *&c.* The Cynocephalus was held in great veneration among the ancient *Egyptians*, because that animal was most accurate in observing the changes of the moon, which were to be distinguished remarkably in both sexes. See *Horapollini's Hieroglyph*. The Cameleon, and the great number of lizards, are highly beneficial to the country in destroying flies and moths, which without them would become intolerable.

It

It is said, that the Land-Crocodile never drinks. His flesh is very hot, and made use of in the eastern countries as a provocative to venery. He is likewise pretty common in *Arabia*. *The Land-Crocodile.*

The Ichneumon is now likewise called *Pharaoh's Rat*. Besides the great use of it in destroying the eggs of crocodiles, of which there are sometimes no less than four hundred together in the sands; this animal also serves for the destruction of other noxious creatures, particularly field-mice and rats. It is now as much despised as it was formerly honored, and is therefore become very scarce, which might partly arise from the great regard with which cats are treated by the *Mohammedans*, especially in *Egypt*, to whom even particular hospitals are appropriated. *The Ichneumon.*

The black Ibis is at present very rare, but the white and grey one, whose female is marked with red, is very common. Their likeness to storks still preserves them the veneration which the *Mohammedans* pay to the latter bird, upon the supposition that its cry, attended with emotions of the body, is a species of worship. *Pag. 422. The Ibis.*

The Cashouc seems to be the Gurgur mentioned by Dr. *Pocock*, of which fish it is said, that when swallowed by the crocodile, it works itself out; so that it is not an improbable conjecture, that *Pliny's* account of the dolphin, and of his wounding the crocodile, may be applied to the Cashouc. *Pag. 423. The Cashouc.*

Fruits, in general, thrive very indifferently in *Egypt*. Dr. *Pocock* deserves to be consulted on the subject of the difference of sexes in palm-trees, which, in many places, where none of the one sex grow, occasions the other to bear no fruit. He likewise treats of the Doms, or Theban and wild Date trees. In Dr. *Shaw's Travels* may be seen a catalogue of several scarce plants of *Barbary*, *Egypt*, and *Arabia*, where he reckons six hundred and thirty- *Fruit-Trees.*

thirty-two different kinds, and marks those that are most uncommon.

Pag. 423. *The* Papyrus. The little value that is put upon the reed Papyrus in modern times, seems almost to have occasioned the loss of it; at least, it is now so little known that we can only conjecture which of the vegetables of *Egypt* comes nearest to the descriptions of it in the ancients. Dr. *Pocock* makes no mention of it at all; Dr. *Shaw* only treats of it among the hieroglyphical images of the ancient *Egyptians*. *Maillet*, indeed, mentions it, but with such uncertainty, that, at length, with the utmost improbability, he makes it the fig-tree of *Adam*, which the *Arabs* call *Mons*. Of the ancient Papyrus, a fuller account is given by the following authors: *Montfaucon*, in his *Palæogr. Græca*, and in the *Dissertation sur la plante appellée Papyrus, sur le papier d'Egypte, sur le papier de coton, & sur celui dont on se sert aujourdhui*, which is preserved in the *Memoires de l'academie des inscriptions*, &c. *Scip. Maffei* in his *Istoria diplomaticâ*, *Mabillon de re diplomaticâ*, *Nigrisolus de chartâ ejusque usu apud antiquos*, which is extant in the *Galleria di Minerva*, tom. 3. *Melch. Guilandinus de papyro*, or a Comment upon *Pliny* the elder on that subject, *Jos. Scaliger*'s animadversions upon *Guilandinus*, *Salmasius* in his remarks upon *Vopiscus* and *Solinus*, *Holmius de scripturâ*, *Crenii anal. philol. crit. hist. Prideaux*'s *Connexion*, and *Calmet dissertation sur la matiere & sur la forme des livres anciens.*

Pag. 424. *Flax.* Tho' the soil of *Egypt* was very favorable to the growth of flax, and hemp still continues to grow there in great plenty, yet the manufacture of linnen is very much decayed, and negligently carried on in later times, which partly arises from the general use of fine cotton in the Eastern countries.

The Lotus. Dr. *Shaw*, in his *Phytographia*, mentions several kinds of the Lotus, and there is, in the second

part

part of the *Memoires de l'academie des inscriptions*, a piece of *M. Mabudel*, intitled, *Examen des divers monumens, sur lesquels il y a des plantes, que les antiquaires confondent presque toujours avec le Lotus d'Egypte*, in which he gives several representations of this plant. That M. *Maillet* had no account or idea of the *Lotus* of the ancients, appears evidently from his uncertainty and conjectures about it. As this plant, in some measure, resembles the figure of the sun, and its changes seem to be exactly regulated by the motion of the sun, and as it is only seen on the surface of the water, when the sun shines, it has been treated as a representative of the sun and of Osiris.

The Henna. The Henna is the seventeenth article in Dr. *Shaw*'s *Phytographia*, where this plant is called *Alhenna* and *Alcanna*, and is accurately described. The excellency and plenty of plants and vegetables in *Egypt*, together with the temperate climate, accounts for the subsistence of that incredible number of hermits and monks who have swarmed in this country ever since the fourth century, and have frequently lived without the aid of bread or corn.

Pag. 425. *The* Pyramids. Except the three most celebrated pyramids of *Gize*, near the ancient *Memphis*, most of them are near *Saccara* and *Dashour*, of which *Pocock* gives a description at large, and some are not far from *Faiume* near the lake *Moeris* and the labyrinth, in which situation, so distant from the *Nile*, it must have been much more expensive to raise so amazing a structure, on account of the difficulty of conveying the stones and other materials requisite, than to build one of those on the *Nile*.

Pag. 428. *Imperfection and uncertainty of the ancient accounts of* Egypt. The sepulchre of *Osymanduas* is described by *Diodorus* as a superb temple at *Thebes*, which was not at all inferior to the pyramids in magnitude, as well as elegant and sumptuous ornaments, and

some

some considerable remains of it are still extant, in confirmation of *Diodorus*'s account. So that he does not differ in this from *Herodotus*, for they treat of different buildings. From the uncertainty and contradictory accounts in the most ancient writers, of the builders of these pyramids, and from the impossibility which *Herodotus*, *Diodorus*, *Strabo*, and *Pliny* have confessed, of determining any thing concerning them which may be depended upon, notwithstanding the helps they had of many writings since lost, we have sufficient grounds to conclude the imperfection of the most ancient histories of *Egypt*, and the weakness of their pretended, extravagant and celebrated claims to antiquity, and the accounts they give of it. We may likewise conclude, how much more authentic written accounts are in preserving the memory of former times and events, than other monuments and memorials, which pretend to perpetuate them, and can only answer this purpose, by being connected with oral traditions, which end is defeated by the changes and unavoidable uncertainties to which the latter in time are subject.

Pag. 429. *The end for which* Pyramids *were erected.* The end here assigned for the erection of *Pyramids*, that they were destined for sepulchres, which is supported by the highest probability, and by many testimonies of antiquity, is particularly controverted by Dr. *Shaw*. But his arguments are of no great weight, and some of them do not prove the point, for which they are alleged. The apartments, the wells, and the whole disposition of the interior parts of the greatest pyramids are easily accounted for by admitting the conjecture, that living persons were immured along with the dead, which will appear probable from the sequel, and is not disproved, but rather confirmed by the contrary opinion. For we are not only unacquainted with most of the religious rites of the

Egyptians,

Egyptians, but cannot any other way account for the shutting up, and the pains that were taken to prevent the opening of the interior part of a Temple separated for religious worship. It cannot be proved, that the two other pyramids had no inner apartments and passages; on the contrary it is probable they had, for they have never yet been opened. The difference of the tomb, which is extant in this pyramid, from other Repositories of preserved bodies, and the different position of it, is a mere prejudice founded in the groundless supposition, that all corpses were placed erect, and that all the tombs were formed exactly alike, both which are manifestly contradicted by numerous instances. Some conjecture, that it was either the repository of religious mysteries, or a vessel for the consecrated water, both which were in use among the *Egyptians*. But before this conjecture assumes an air of probability, it should first be proved, that any religious service was, or could be performed in the pyramid. It is however by no means repugnant to the general opinion, but rather confirms it, to suppose the form and inward disposition of all the pyramids to have had a religious meaning and tendency. For the *Egyptians* not only fixed upon their sepulchres many emblems of their deities and mysteries, but had sepulchres too within temples, as appears from *Diodorus*'s account of the sepulchre of *Osymanduas*, and *Herodotus*'s of those of *Appianus* and *Amasis*, and this was objected as a reproach to the heathens by *Clemens Alexandrinus* in his admonition to them. But that the pyramids as well as obelisks were representations of the deity, particularly of the sun, is undeniable, both from the accounts of the most ancient idolatry, especially of the oriental nations, who have been the last that retained the custom of representing their gods by columns and heaps of stones,

stones, without any other images, as may be seen in the history of *Heliogabalus*; and from the plainest testimonies of antiquity, *viz. Porphyry* in *Eusebius*, *Plutarch de Isid. et Osir. Tertullian de spectac. Pliny, Pausanias, Clemens Alexandrinus strom.* 1. and *Suida* in the word ἀγυιεύς. The same custom of erecting eminences and piles of stones for that purpose obtained among the old northern and *German* nations.

Pag. 431. *Dimensions of the* Pyramids. The different accounts of the dimensions of the pyramids, arises partly from the different sizes of the instruments they were measured with, and from the variable condition of the ground in which they stand, which is not quite level, and is covered by the wind with heaps of sand, but it is chiefly owing to the different abilities, care and instruments of the measurers. In these respects *Greaves* has undoubtedly excelled all the rest. He affirms the perpendicular height of this great pyramid to be four hundred ninety-nine feet.

Pag. 432. *Outside of the* Pyramids. Some pretend to have found traces of a statue and a fortification on the uppermost flat, which *Greaves* measures at upwards of thirteen feet; but others have exploded this conjecture. The variation in the numbers of the degrees may, besides the reasons already assigned, arise from some of them being broken and unequal. *Wansleb* says, the great pyramid has no more than 206 degrees, whereas *Thevenot* makes it consist of 208, which mistake is occasioned by his not observing, that two degrees are broken into two parts each, and so he was misled to reckon them four degrees. It is generally thought that this pyramid had always the same external appearance, which it has at present, and was never covered, as the other two are in some measure, whence it has been concluded, that they were never completely finished. But *Maillet* and *Pocock* have shewn the contrary, and proved that it was covered with white marble, which

which in succeeding times were stript off, and made use of in other buildings. The principal arguments, by which they evince the probability of this, are, that there is still chalk and mortar to be found upon some of the degrees, which must have been the cement of that marble; that amongst this chalk, or lime, there are still some pieces of white marble, of which the pyramid is not composed, and which *Egypt* doth not produce, but import from *Arabia*; that *Pliny*, in his natural history, mentions it as an extraordinary piece of agility in the inhabitants of *Busiris* near *Memphis*, that they could ascend to the top of these pyramids, which would be no extraordinary performance with respect to the greatest, if they were always provided with steps, by which any one may, without difficulty, ascend them at present; and that the inequality of the steps, and their different breadth, by the projection of many stones, argues the covering to have been laid on immediately after raising the structure; tho' *Herodotus* mentions another method of building, by finishing the whole with steps, and then drawing up stones by machines, which cannot well be understood of any other stones, than those made use of to cover the whole building, and fill up these steps.

Maillet is the first, who has examined and luckily hit upon the nature, the probable design and curious contrivance of this pyramid, in the seventh letter of the first part of his description of *Egypt*, from whence *Pocock* has given us an extract of his descriptions and conjectures. It must have been a work of immense labor and expence to open this pyramid, for the builders had employed all their art in making the inner parts of it impenetrable. According to an oriental tradition, the merit of opening it is attributed to the Caliph *Aron al rachid*, but the more general opinion gives it to the Caliph

Pag. 434. Inside of them.

Mahmud, who died in the 205th year of the *Hegira.* It appears from the accounts of ancient writers, that they knew something of the inner construction of the pyramid from tradition, tho' it is manifest from the same accounts, that it was not open in their time. *Strabo* expresly mentions, that the avenue to the inner apartments was shut up by a stone in the middle. But notwithstanding the light given by these directions and accounts, it is certain that this avenue was not opened without frequent attempts and inexpressible labor, for the two long galleries were filled with stones, and in order to penetrate the aperture of the second rising gallery, it was necessary to demolish part of the main building, on the right side, in order to get at this gallery sideways.

Pag. 435, 436. *The well.* The well in this pyramid does not sink directly perpendicular, but in a slope, towards the west, and this is broken in the middle by a passage fifteen feet long, at the west end of which the declivity of the well is continued. *Maillet*'s conjecture concerning this well is, that it served for a private outlet to the number of workmen, who were employed in walling up and securing the inside of the galleries, and that after they were gone it was an easy matter to close this up again. The survey of this well plainly shews, that the inner part of the pyramid was not the work of masons, for the lower passages are partly cut thro' a firm gravel, partly thro' a natural rock. On the east side of this lower gallery, there is in the side-wall a cavity eight feet high, and three feet in breadth and depth, of which the design probably was to place erect in it a corpse swaddled in the *Egyptian* manner. There was, besides, a breach made in the wall of this apartment, twenty five paces wide, by which means it is so filled with rubbish; which fruitless labor was doubt-

less

leſs occaſioned by the hopes of finding ſome hidden treaſures.

Maillet conjectures, that both the heighth and the different breadth and cavities in the ſide walls of this large and ſpacious gallery, were neceſſary for depoſiting the ſtones and materials, and for erecting a ſcaffold, which was covered with ſtones at top, and ſerved to keep a paſſage clear underneath, into the laſt-built upper apartments; ſo that when a corpſe was depoſited, and the avenues were cloſed by thoſe ſtones, the two lower paſſages might be filled up and walled, which was neceſſary to be done from within. *Pag.* 437. *Contrivance of the gallery.*

The only reaſon why the tomb of *Cheops* was left where we find it, was perhaps the impoſſibility of conveying it farther through the many windings and narrow paſſages. The upper border of it ſhews, that it was incloſed by a covering, which ſeems to have been broke in the opening. The two inlets here mentioned in the ſide-walls, are conſidered by *Maillet* as an argument, that beſides the royal corpſe, ſome living perſons were immured in this apartment. That on the north-ſide, which is the larger, is a foot wide and eight inches high, and tho' it be now ſtopp'd up five or ſix feet deep, and filled with ſtones, ſeems to have been formerly continued in a direct line thro' the whole pyramid, and to have anſwered the purpoſe of conveying to them freſh air and proviſions. The other round cavity, which is only a foot deep in the wall, opens at the bottom into the loweſt foundation of the pyramid, and might ſerve them for neceſſary evacuations. This is much more probable, than to ſuppoſe theſe inlets to have been made uſe of for receiving lamps, which would have required a different and a higher contrivance, The blackneſs might ariſe from the ſmoak of that infinite number of lamps and torches, with which *Pag.* 438. *The tomb of* Cheops.

these apartments were necessarily lightened, and which might blacken and disfigure all the walls. That the corpse, for which this pyramid was erected, was not brought thither, is hard to be proved; the contrary rather appears from the care that was actually taken in keeping it closely shut.

Pag. 439. *The* Echo. The hard and smooth surface of the walls and vaults in this building account perfectly well for the repetition of the Echo. Some have thought it observable, that the sound of the tomb, when it is struck, is the same with that of the whole apartment and its walls; but this might be caused by the equal hardness of the marble, of which the whole consists, without supposing an equal proportion in the dimension, which is not to be found here.

Pag. 439. *The second* Pyramid. On the north-side of the second pyramid, there is the appearance of great pains taken to find an aperture for the entrance, which is the reason of its being so broken and damaged half way up on that side. Dr. *Pocock* judges, by the eye, that it is as high as the first.

Pag. 441. *The third* Pyramid. The third pyramid is, in great measure stripp'd, but there are still, in many parts of it, intire pieces of granite marble, with which it was covered. Dr. *Pocock* found the top to measure fourteen foot on the north-side, and twelve feet on the east-side, and counted 78 steps, of a foot and nine inches each, which agrees with *Herodotus*'s measure. Near it are several lesser pyramids, but most of them demolished, and there are the ruins of a magnificent temple.

Pag. 442. *A fourth* Pyramid. The fourth pyramid near *Saccara*, is placed among a great number of others, which have remained very intire, and are not much less. It is commonly called *Il-Herem Elkebere-El-Barieh*, or the great pyramid toward the north, by way of distinction from another not far from it, which is called

called the great pyramid toward the south. Dr. *Pocock* has given an accurate description of it, and his admeasurement agrees pretty well with *Thevenot*'s. There is likewise a complete description of it in a piece of *Mascrier*, intended as a continuation of *Maillet*, intitled, *Idée du gouvernement ancien & moderne de l'Egypte*, &c.

Herodotus seems to mean only, in his account, the manner of covering the pyramids with the external stones, by which the sides became a smooth even slope; this must have been a laborious work, if the whole building was first raised with steps, and afterward covered; which was undoubtedly the case with some of them, whereas others were built with their coverings at once from the foundation. Mr. *Greaves*'s conjecture is hardly reconcileable to the ingenious contrivance of the interior parts of the pyramids. It is difficult, however, and indeed hardly possible, to comprehend how stones of an amazing size could be raised so high, and especially at such a distance, as from the ground at the foot of the pyramids, to the part they were destined for. Even the raising of the scaffolding, and other apparatus, is hard to be imagined, and must have been an immense expence. So that many very rightly place this kind of architecture among those arts of antiquity that are lost.

Pag. 442. *Manner of building the* Pyramids.

Wansleben mistook and exaggerated a conjecture, which, by being duly limited, hath been rendered probable by others, and consists in this, that eminences, rocks, and mounts were chosen for building the pyramids, in order to prepare the sepulchres upon or within them, and that then they raised the walls on all sides. This appears undeniably from some lesser pyramids, almost totally in ruins, of which the inner and lower parts are earth or rock, which was walled round.

Pag. 443. *The materials.*

Remarkable circumstances of the Pyramids. There are still some considerable remains of the magnificent ascent to the rock, upon which are the large pyramids near *Giza* or *Memphis*. As a great part of this rock is cut away as far as the sphinx before the second pyramid, and the stone was made use of in building the pyramids, so the exact proportion observed in these different structures, and the multiplicity of ornaments, particularly that sumptuous ascent, shew them to have been erected soon after each other, and upon one and the same plan; an amazing evidence both of the power and perfection of arts in those early times.

Pag. 445. *Two in* al Feyyûm. The two large pyramids in *al Feyyûm* stand in the neighbourhood of *Dashour*, and are described by that situation. The country of *Saccara* abounds most in these structures.

Pag. 445---449. *The* Labyrinth. Dr. *Pocock* gives a very accurate and circumstantial account of that magnificent piece of antiquity, the labyrinth, and exhibits in his 22d and 23d plate, an exact draught of the whole structure, and a plan of the sumptuous temple. The same author treats at large of the ancient architecture of the *Egyptians*, and particularly examines, with great accuracy, the form of their columns and pillars, from the representations of which, in his plates, it appears what variety of columns were in use among the *Egyptians*, and how different from the orders which were afterwards established, and that they are not at all inferior to the *Grecian* and more modern inventions, and tho' formed in a different taste, are by no means irregular.

Pag. 450 451. *The lake* Moeris. *Herodotus*'s account of the lake *Moeris*, is justly treated by *Pocock* as incredible, and after accurately describing the two openings and sluices, as well of *Joseph*'s canal, as of that which lies eastward near *Taminea*, he raises a probable conjecture, how this lake might arise without digging the earth for it,

and

and mentions particularly, that the water of it is very salt.

The isle is not situate, at present, in the middle of the lake, and there are very few remains worth notice, of any former public buildings in the island. *Pag. 451. The isle.*

The compilers of the *Universal History* seem, in their account of a palace near the cataracts, to confound two distinct buildings. There is at *Elephantis*, not far from *Asswan*, near the cataracts, a considerable ruin of a temple, and in the island *Philæ*, we meet with another magnificent edifice, which appears by many intire pieces to have been a large temple, and of which Dr. *Pocock* gives a circumstantial account. But the particulars they mention denote the great temple at *Thebes*, the remains of which are of such extent, so curious and sumptuous, that they far excel every other building of antiquity. See *Pocock*. *A palace near the cataracts.*

There are at *Dandera* large and magnificent remains of four temples pretty near each other, but they are by no means comparable in point of magnitude and expence to that at *Thebes*. Dr. *Pocock* very sufficiently explodes the pretence of a town built on the ruins of one of those structures, for he shews the dimensions of that temple upon which the *Arabs* built some small houses with unburnt bricks, to have been no more than 200 feet in length, and 145 in breadth. It is to be wished that the compilers, instead of *Lucas*'s accounts, which appeared at that time the best, had been possess'd of the more circumstantial and accurate descriptions of the learned doctor just mentioned, which far exceed all former accounts of these antiquities, and must give the reader very high ideas of ancient *Egypt*, which it is impossible to survey without pleasure and admiration. *Pag. 454. Temples at Dandera.*

Pag. 455. *Antiquity of the Egyptians.* That the *Egyptian* accounts of their ancient chronology are false and fabulous, is too evident to need any proof. It is therefore impossible to ascertain any part of the scripture chronology by arguments drawn from thence, since that must first be corrected upon other principles, before it can be admitted to any degree of probability. This will appear to those, who consult *Conringii adversar. chronolog. de Asiæ et Ægypti antiquiss. dynastiis*, which may be seen in *Grævii syntagmata dissertationum rariorum*; and *Perizonii Egypt*. The account given by the compilers of the customs and antiquities of the *Egyptians* far exceeds that of M. *Rollin*, and besides the general use arising from a knowlege of such antiquities, they may enable us rightly to examine and decide a twofold controversy. For without this knowlege it is impossible to judge about the question concerning the *Egyptian* origin of the law of *Moses*, and the religious rites there established, in which both sides have gone too far, and of that other pretence of some modern deists, chiefly embellished by *Morgan*, of the fraudulent introduction of religion among the *Egyptians* by the patriarch *Joseph*. However it is necessary previously to observe, how defective and uncertain are all the accounts now extant. This hath partly arisen from the frequent revolutions of government in these countries, which could not take place without a change of customs by the introduction of foreign ones, particularly of those nations, to whom they were subdued, nor without a loss of ancient monuments, records and accounts. Another cause to which those defects may be computed, is the great rarity, and almost total want of ancient historical books of this country; for all the traditions we have, passed thro' the hands of *Grecians*, who either dwelt in *Egypt* in the later times of the *Grecian* dominion there, or picked up some

ſome wild accounts in their travels there. A third reaſon is the myſterious method of teaching, and cloathing, not only the ſciences, but even hiſtory in ſymbolical repreſentation, and the pains they took to confine all learning to the prieſthood, whoſe intereſt it was to conceal to the utmoſt of their power, all accounts both of ſpeculative truths, and of matters of fact.

Pag. 456, 457. Reſtraints laid on the kings of Egypt.

The ſtrict reſtraints, that are ſaid to have been laid upon the kings of *Egypt*, did not always take place, as appears from the hiſtories of their kings, and from the many revolutions, which happened in the government. For whilſt the power of doing hurt was reſtrained, great and fortunate exploits were at the ſame time ſuppreſſed. It is certain, however, that a free and voluntary obſervation of eſtabliſhed cuſtoms and ſolemn ceremonies, a regular conduct and ſtrict adherence to laws, are very conſiſtent with abſolute power, of which we have a remarkable inſtance in the conſtitution of the *Chineſe* empire.

Pag. 459. Judgment upon them after death.

From the judgment paſſed upon the *Egyptian* kings after death, ſome have attempted to deduce the defective ſtate of the ſeries of their Dynaſties, pretending that the names of vicious and worthleſs kings were omitted or expunged from the public fables and monuments, tho' the reigns of thoſe nameleſs kings were, for the ſake of chronology, taken into their computations. But theſe chaſms may be otherwiſe accounted for, eſpecially as we find many kings of very infamous character, in the liſts that are preſerved. However, the opinion of a life after death was univerſal among the *Egyptians*, and of ſo much the greater force and efficacy, as the future ſtate of the departed ſoul was according to their doctrine ſo cloſely connected with the fate of the body, in its burial and preſervation, that the happineſs and miſery of it depended wholly upon

upon the sentence pronounced by those who were the appointed judges on this occasion. Hence it has been conjectured with some probability, that the whole *Grecian* mythology concerning the infernal deities, and the rewards as well as punishments of deceased men, was derived from *Egypt*, and that even the Eleusinian mysteries were a symbolical representation thereof. See Dr. *Warburton's divine Legation of Moses*, B. ii. Sect. 4.

Pag. 459, 460. *The* Egyptian *priests.* Among other articles in the dress of the *Egyptian* priests, it is observable, that their shoes were made of the reed *Papyrus*, because they were not allowed to wear any thing appertaining to beasts, and consequently wore neither leather nor wool. Some modern libertines have taken occasion from these accounts of the *Egyptian* priests, and the extraordinary immunities they enjoyed, to deduce from them the real origin of all external worship and superstition, and to consider them as irrefragable proofs, of the actual designs of the priesthood, and of the danger and mischief arising to a community from that order of men. Lord *Shaftsbury* first paved the way for this sort of reasoning, but some of his successors have departed much farther from the accounts of antiquity, and from probability, and have transgressed all bounds of modesty in their inventions. These writers seem either to forget, or not to know, that if the ancient *Egyptian* division of men into different ranks and orders still prevailed, they themselves would be members of this order, and probably not be so free in calumniating and depreciating it. For the order of priesthood in *Egypt* comprehended all the learned, consequently all magistrates, lawyers, philosophers and physicians, of whom only some few were selected for sacrifice, and other religious rites. It is possible that these last offices might not be displeasing even to those writers; for, according

to

to them, the whole regulation of divine worship, and all morality, ought to be in the hands of magistrates and philosophers; so that this constitution of *Egypt* might, in that case, come to be considered as a very proper model, and as it is customary with those gentlemen to change both their attacks and armour, the bitterness with which they have hitherto treated the *Egyptian* priests, might possibly be converted into the highest and most extravagant esteem. For there is as much, if not more, room to extol, as a policy worthy of universal imitation, this institution of the *Egyptians*, whereby all doctrines and religious rites are submitted to the opinion and direction of great philosophers and intelligent magistrates. In short, they are ready to acquiesce in any thing, to rid themselves of the stated interpreters of a divine revelation, but, unfortunately for them, that was likewise part of the province of the *Egyptian* priests.

Pag. 463. Hereditary arts and trades.

The custom of transmitting employments from father to son, seems to be attended with various advantages. It is undoubtedly a good foundation for knowlege and skill in any art to be early trained up to it, and any one will be much sooner qualified for those occupations, to which, from his cradle, he hath been formed and accustomed, than to others. There is besides, under such an establishment, less opportunity and temptation to disturb the peace of civil society, or to murmur at the obligations and prerogatives of the state, and of domestic, particularly paternal authority; and the improvement of trades, arts and sciences, is very much facilitated and encouraged by the hereditary tradition of new inventions from father to son. But this institution is, on the other side, attended with many mischiefs and inconveniencies. For, as the natural abilities of men, and the propensities arising from them, are various, this constraint would

would not only render them useless, but could not, in many cases, take effect without great violence and difficulty. In the next place, the number of persons devoted to this or that trade or occupation, might easily become too great or too small, and a due proportion of them to the exigencies of human societies, might be neglected, which there is less room to apprehend where the probability of better success in an employment determines the choice of it, than when it is wholly left to the involuntary determination of birth and parentage. Not to mention, that the impossibility of being excelled by others of a different extraction, and of improving one's fortune by attempting another employment, if the paternal one should be overstock'd with hands, are great motives to idleness and negligence. So that to render such an institution perfectly innocent, there must be some exceptions of extraordinary cases, of which indeed there were not wanting instances among the *Egyptians*, amongst whom the old institution was in great measure introduced and preserved by several opinions concerning the transmigration of souls.

Pag. 463, 464. *The courts of justice.* The three courts of justice at *Heliopolis*, *Memphis*, and *Thebes*, seem to have been united after the union of the lesser kingdoms under one head, and to have formed one general supreme tribunal, in order to prevent a fresh separation. It is probable, however, that besides the general sessions of this supreme court at stated times, for the decision of important causes, there were afterward particular sessions of the ten judges of each of the principal divisions of the kingdom, in the three cities abovementioned, for the dispatch of inferior litigations; for it would have been highly burthensome to the people to be obliged to carry their misunderstandings, sometimes from very remote places, to the supreme tribunal. *Diodorus* mentions, that this whole

whole assembly of the thirty judges is represented in a stone-carving in the temple of *Osymanduas*'s sepulchre at *Thebes*. There are still to be seen over a gate, eleven carved images of men, sitting in a semicircle, one of which in the midst, having his five assessors at some distance from him on each side, is distinguished by a particular ensign. It is more natural to interpret this of the ten judges at *Thebes* with their supreme judge, than to make it a representation of *Osiris* and other deities, for these were not usually represented in human shape, nor does the number agree with that of their supreme deities. Dr. *Pocock* exhibits this monument in his forty-third plate, but without any notice of the *Egyptian* judges, makes it an assembly of Gods. However, if the conjecture here offered be admitted, then the ensign which the supreme judge holds in his right-hand before his breast, and which might thus be very easily directed to either party in deciding the cause, is at first sight a fresh argument, that the breast-plate of the high-priests of *Israel*, and the divine arbitration of matters by that, cannot be deduced from this *Egyptian* ensign of truth.

As the *Egyptian* laws are too much magnified by some, in order to make them, with greater propriety, the foundation of the *Jewish* law; so others have unjustly depreciated them, and charged them with injustice in some cases and absurdity in others, in both which they may be excused and vindicated by a right interpretation. Even *Herm. Witsius* in his *Ægyptiaca*, is apt to run into the latter extreme. The last of the laws here cited, has labored under such a misinterpretation, many having considered it as a solemn permission of theft, as a regular occupation. *Gellius* laid this to the charge of the *Egyptians*, upon the testimony of

Pag. 464 ---467. Egyptian *laws.*

of *Aristo*, and many modern writers have been led into the same mistake. Whereas it is certain, that the *Egyptians* not only judged all theft, and even a private breach of trust to be sinful, as appears from the prayer and the justification of them after death, cited by *Porphyry*; but they inflicted corporal punishments upon persons convicted of fraud and male-practices, as appears from the eleventh of the laws here cited. It is besides not very clear, that *Diodorus* did not mistake a mere singular custom for a law, or gave it that appellation in a vague undetermined sense. In some *European* countries bands of robbers have sometimes been under the same or simular regulations, and in that case, the search after them has not been so strict, tho' their proceedings were not deemed lawful, and all that were apprehended and convicted of theft underwent the legal punishment of it. Many considerable cities and commonwealths would think themselves greatly injured, if such laws should be laid to their charge, tho' it were upon the printed reports of travellers. A farther account of the laws and customs of the *Egyptians* may be seen in *Nicolai de Ægyptiorum synedrio & legibus insignioribus*, and *Casalius de ritibus Ægyptiorum.*

Pag. 467, 468. Egyptian *Gods.* Of the *Egyptian* gods see *Casalius*, *Marsham*, *Witsius*, *Kircher*, *Vossius* in his *theol. gentil.* and *Banier's* mythology. The secret account of them is partly drawn from historical facts, such as the adventures and exploits of illustrious heroes and great patriots, and this is the most antient account of them; partly from philosophy, and particularly astronomy, which was improved by considerable additions and alterations taken from the modern systems of *Grecian* philosophy in *Egypt*. Hence arose the many repeated and very different accounts of one and the same deity. The obscurity and uncertainty of these accounts is considerably increased by the intermixture

ture of foreign religions with the *Egyptian*, which was greatly facilitated in *Egypt* by the many instances of a like extraction and of similitude in other respects, which they observed in comparing the hymns addressed to foreign deities with their own, and by its being usual among the *Grecians* to compare foreign religions and gods with theirs, and to take occasion from thence to give them *Greek* appellations. So that in order to avoid this confusion, it is very necessary to examine with caution the reports not only of *Plutarch*, *Porphyry*, *Jamblichus* and other modern *Grecians*, but even those of *Diodorus* and *Herodotus*. However the real religion of *Egypt* hath not only maintained its ground under the government of *Persians*, *Grecians* and *Romans*, but besides being the original fountain of the religion of *Greece*, it hath spread very far in succeeding times, thro' the western and northern countries, particularly *Gaul* and *Germany*, and over the *East*, where the modern idolatry called *She-kia* is wholly attributed to the same source. A farther account of the *Egyptian* theology may be seen in *Brucker*'s *Hist. crit. philos.*

The opinion that *Serapis* was a foreign deity, introduced into *Egypt* in the reign of the *Ptolemys*, is founded in *Tacitus*'s story, that *Serapis* appeared to *Ptolemy* the first, the son of *Lagus*, and commanded him to order his image to be fetched from *Sinope* in the *Pontus*, which was accordingly done, and occasioned the worship of him in *Egypt*. It is supported too by the testimonies of *Origen*, *Clemens* of *Alexandria*, *Plutarch de Iside et Osiride* and *Macrobius*, by the silence of *Herodotus* on the subject, and by the omission of the image of that deity on the famous table of *Isis*. But as this last argument supposes all the *Egyptian* gods to be recorded on that table, and *Herodotus* to have omitted the mention of none of them, both which are absolutely false,

Pag. 468. Serapis.

false, the testimonies here alleged are so far from proving the pretence, that they rather confirm the contrary. For the accounts themselves contradict each other, and acts that are ascribed by some to *Ptolemæus Lagi*, were according to others done by *Ptolemæus Soter*, and some put *Seleucia* for *Sinope*. It is likewise observable, that *Origen* and *Clemens*, in order to shew the modern origin of heathen deities, quote such opinions and Traditions as best serve their purpose. But besides all this, *Tacitus* and *Plutarch* expresly cite the contrary more prevailing opinion, which is very consistent with the date of the fact in the reign of *Ptolemy*, that he revived the worship of an ancient *Egyptian* deity, which was particularly idolized at *Memphis*, and that he both improved and propagated it even as far as *Athens*. For the deity of *Sinope* was *Pluto*, whose image the *Egyptians* immediately acknowleged to be their *Serapis*. Since that time the worship of this God, who was neither *Osiris* nor *Bacchus*, but *Pluto*, hath outdone the honors paid to almost all the other deities, as appears from the history of *Vespasian* in *Tacitus*, from *Hadrian*'s letters in *Vopiscus*, and from *Pausanias*, with which the reader may compare *Spencer*'s *annot. ad Originem contra Celsum*, *Cuper de Harpocrate* and *Banier*. The last of these seems indeed not to have had recourse to the fountain-head for information, when he takes notice that *Tacitus* doth not mention under which *Ptolemy* this happened, and that it was the son of *Lagus*, but that *Macrobius* is the first who records this, which is so manifestly false, as to afford one instance among others, that his work is only extracted from modern writers. *Bochart* and *Witsius* are of the first opinion, and *Vossius* maintains the second.

Pag. 469. *One God.* The notion of the worship of one supreme God among the *Egyptians*, is in all probability as ill-

grounded

grounded, as the pretence of ſome modern writers, of the trinity being known and adored by the *Egyptians*. *Kircher* and *Franc. Fluſſus Candalla* and *Hannibal Roſſel* have endeavoured to gloſs over this invention. (See *Witſius* and *Brucker*). *Cneph* ſeems rather to have been a ſenſible repreſentation, than an actual deity among the *Egyptians*, at leaſt the worſhip of him was never univerſal, and either rare, or of very ſhort duration in upper *Egypt*; for the many monuments and remains that are extant of the religion of antiquity in theſe countries, ſhew that the worſhip of other deities prevailed in preference to this.

The various images, names and ways of worſhipping the ſame Gods, and the ſolemn celebration of particular favors received from them in different cities, occaſioned in time the Gods themſelves to be multiplyed. Many however have ſtrangely increaſed their number by confounding with the deities themſelves thoſe things which were dedicated to ſome of them, and conſecrated either for their ſervice, or for ſenſible repreſentations of them. *Pag.* 469. *Multiplicity of Gods.*

Oſiris is frequently repreſented as a ſwaddled corpſe, or a mummy; and among the ſymbols of *Iſis*, that of a ſhip is the moſt celebrated, and was very uſual out of *Egypt*. *Pag.* 470. Oſiris *and* Iſis.

It appears from *Euſebius* in his life of *Conſtantine*, from *Socrates* and *Sozomen*, that *Conſtantine* had removed the *Nilometer* from the temple of *Serapis* into a chriſtian church, but that *Julian* replaced it in that temple, where it remained till the year of Chriſt 389, when *Theodoſius* demoliſhed the *Serapium*, and all the temples and idols in *Egypt*; ſo that the annual feſtival of the inundation of the *Nile* was in honor of *Serapis*, which purpoſe it would anſwer, if he had been the *Diſpater* or *Pluto*, to whom, even according to the foreign theology, the fruitfulness of the earth was, next to *Ceres*, to be attributed. And this gives a light into the source of the emperor *Hadrian*'s error; nay, it may serve to justify the main substance of his letter to *Severian* which we find in *Vopiscus*; for the general observation of that festival not only by heathens, but by the *Jews*, *Samaritans* and *Christians*, who were in *Egypt*, might lead him to conjecture, that since the heathen *Egyptians* devoted this feast to *Serapis*, that deity was the common object of worship to the professors of all other religious systems however different. *Jupiter Ammon* is supposed by some to be *Ham* the son of *Noah*, and *Osiris* to be *Mizraim*, or by others, *Menes*.

Pag. 472. *Two bulls.* The keeping of two bulls in *Egypt* at the same time, one at *Heliopolis*, the other at *Memphis*, hath led some into the improbable conjecture, that the one represented *Osiris*, the other *Isis*; whereas, others have judged, with more probability, that such custom arose from the time of the division of *Egypt* into distinct sovereignties, and particularly into two principal kingdoms, in each of which such a living representation of *Osiris* was worshipped, which in process of time, after the union of those kingdoms, were both retained, tho' the *Apis* was considered as much more respectable than the *Mnevis*.

Pag. 473. *Isis.* The worship of *Isis* constituted greatest part of the religion of the ancient *Egyptians*. Besides the celebrated table of *Isis*, which is still preserved at *Turin*, and the interpretation of which may be found in *Brucker*'s *hist. crit. philos.* there is a pregnant monument of the religion of the ancient *Egyptians* in *Martin*'s *Explications de divers monumens singuliers, qui ont rapport á la religion des plus anciens peuples.* It consists of a vessel or repository of *Isis*, full of many symbolical figures and representations of the rites performed in that worship; in the exposition of which, in the *dissert. sur la religion des Egyptiens*, many

many other festivals and religious rites of the *Egyptians* are illustrated. See likewise the dissertation *des differentes années des Egyptiens*; *Isis singuliere*; *Banier's mythol.* where he gives an explanation *de la table Isiaque*, but by mistake intimates, that it is totally lost.

There was in the most ancient times an annual festival of twelve days solemnized at *Thebes*, during which the image of *Jupiter*, and those of other Gods, were carried about the country with religious ceremonies. This custom is attributed to the *Ethiopians* by *Homer* in the first book of his Iliad, for the inhabitants of upper *Egypt* were called *Ethiopians*. See *Martin*. *Pag. 474. Jupiter.*

The Phallus was more frequently used among the *Egyptians*, than any other nation, in their religious ceremonies at the worship of *Osiris* and other deities. The later *Egyptians*, in the fourth century after Christ, were very much ashamed of these images, and extremely provoked, when *Theophilus*, bishop of *Alexandria*, caused many of them which he had found in the ruins of a temple, to be carried about and exposed publickly; for after the appearance of Christianity the idolaters endeavor'd, as much as possible, to avoid indecency in their worship. *Martin*, who wrote the rest of his work in *French*, explanes, in a *Latin* dissertation, the mystical meaning of those images. *Pag. 475. The Phallus.*

The feast at *Papremis* was celebrated in honor of *Anubis*, the son of *Nephthe*, who represented not only the *Grecian Mars*, but more frequently *Mercury*. The club, which is commonly seen in the hand of *Anubis*, and some figures of dogs heads and staves before the temples, are applied by *Martin* to this festival, and the history of it. See *Pocock*, *Shaw*, and *Maillet*. *Pag. 476. The feast at Papremis.*

M. *Blanchard* has written a dissertation at large *sur les animaux respectes en Egypte*, but his enquiries are *Pag. 477 ---479. Worship of animals.*

are of no great moment. That the *Apis* was sometimes drowned by the priests, appears from the testimony both of *Marcellinus* and *Pliny*, and is very consistent with the natural death of some of these animals by age; for many of them might not arrive at this honor very young, and the time, when it was expedient they should die, might not be regulated and determined merely by the duration of their lives, or by the adoration they had received, but by other rules and limits. That this worship of animals was very ancient, appears not only from the worship of a calf among the *Israelites* in the wilderness, *Exod.* xxxii. but from the answer which *Moses* returned to *Pharoah*, *ch.* viii. 26. when he offered him permission to sacrifice in the land of *Egypt*. *It is not meet so to do; for we shall sacrifice the abomination of the* Egyptians *to the Lord our God; lo, shall we sacrifice the abomination of the* Egyptians *before their eyes, and will they not stone us?*

Pag. 479 ---482. *Apology for it.* *Banier* hath given us two large dissertations by way of apology for this religious worship of animals among the *Egyptians*, one of which is in the *Memoires de l'Academie des inscriptions*, the other in his *mytholog. expliquée*. In both of them it is observable and surprizing, that the author, in excuse and justification of this idolatry, should make use of the distinction invented by the modern advocates for image-worship, between *Latreia* and *Douleia*, or *divine* and *religious*, *mediate* and *immediate*, *direct* and *relative* worship. He did not probably recollect, that this honest confession of these absurdities was a strong argument against the modern tenets of his church, since it is certain, that the grossest idolatry may be deduced from them. At least this great depravity among the *Egyptians*, in the midst of all their wisdom, illustrates the truth of St. *Paul*'s observation concerning the heathens, *Rom.* i. 21—23, &c. *When they knew God, they glorified*

glorified him not as God, neither were thankful, but became vain in their imaginations, and their fooliſh heart was darkened. Profeſſing themſelves to be wiſe, they became fools; and changed the glory of the uncorruptible God, into an image made like to corruptible man, and to birds, and four-footed beaſts, *and creeping things*, &c. It likewiſe ſhews, how dangerous it is to introduce and retain in public worſhip, cuſtoms of mere human invention, the uſe of which muſt depend upon the recollection of far-fetched conceits and reflexions;' for as theſe myſtical interpretations are above the conception of the multitude, they, not being equal to theſe abſtruſe reaſonings, neceſſarily fall into ſuperſtition or idolatry. Among other heathen writers, who expoſe the abſurdity and indecency of this worſhip of animals, *Lucian* ridicules it with great bitterneſs.

The beſt among the ancient writers make ſo frequent uſe of the fabulous accounts of the Phœnix, or ſun-bird, that we have no right to be ſevere in our cenſure of ſome of the fathers, who being unacquainted with natural hiſtory, came into this prejudice of their times. It may, however, be very ſafely concluded from thence, that ſuch writings, as *Clement*'s epiſtle from *Rome* to the *Corinthians*, were not divinely inſpired. *Pag.* 482. *The* Phœnix.

The manner of conſulting oracles, mentioned by *Pauſanias*, was this; after performing the ſacrifice, and offering a preſent, the perſon conſulting held his ears before the image of the deity, then kept both ears ſhut with his hands, till he was out of the temple, when the firſt words he heard were ſuppoſed to be the anſwer of the oracle. Our compilers, in the ſtory of *Germanicus*, mean the oracle of *Serapis* at *Alexandria*, whoſe name we find in the *Latin* verſion, but the *Greek* words are expreſs of the *Apis*. As the *Egyptian* deities were cloſely connected with the planets and ſtars, which *Pag.* 483. *Oracles*.

were supposed to be their habitation, and to the motion and influence of which upon our earth, most of the sacred hymns refer and are applied, and from which the signs in the zodiac took their name, it should seem, that the *Egyptians* were the first who made astrological predictions, or at least were very early and deep in that science, and it may be concluded, that they had originally a kind of divine oracle.

Pag. 485. Human sacrifices. If we may credit the testimony of *Ruffinus*, human sacrifices were offered in *Egypt* till the fourth century after Christ; but from his account of them it appears, that they were performed very privately in later times, and probably were an offering to *Serapis*, for the annual overflowing of the *Nile*.

Pag. 484. Leeks, onions, &c. The authority of *Juvenal* is of no weight at all in the subject of *Egyptian* idolatries; for he has not only committed manifest mistakes in the immediate connexion of his account, but the whole contents of the fifteenth satire are a fabulous event. However, the introduction is very true. *Prudentius*'s testimony is of no very great moment. But *Pliny*'s account, in his natural history, *allium cæpasque inter deos in jurejurando habet Ægyptus*, would be more credible, had he not, by the express limitation of that worship to oaths, shewn both the grounds of his whole narrative, and at the same time what kind of worship this was. For the *Egyptians* might swear by their riches, and by their most common food, and might consider certain vegetables as symbols of the Deity, without ranking them among the gods, which would not have been very consistent with their constant consumption of them in the way of food. *Pythagoras*'s abstinence from beans seems to have been derived from *Egypt*, and has been the occasion of many conjectures about the secret causes of that custom. See *Brucker*'s *Hist. crit. Philos.* and *Heuman*'s *act philos.*

Ruffinus

Ruffinus gives a circumftantial defcription of the magnificent temple of *Serapis*, from which *Alexandria* hath, according to the cuftom of *Egypt*, been fometimes called the city of *Serapis*. And tho' this amazing ftructure was not erected, till the *Grecians* were Lords of the country, yet it is probable, that the moft effential and confiderable parts of the model of the moft ancient and celebrated temples were retained. One circumftance, in particular, is obfervable, that fuch an aperture was made in the eaft wall of the temple, as might daily admit the fun for a fhort time to fhine upon and falute the face, and efpecially the mouth of the idol. As to what is mentioned, that there were no images in the moft ancient *Egyptian* temples, the fame may be affirmed and fhewn of the moft ancient temples of all nations. Before real ftatues were contrived, large ftones and unformed pillars were ufed as reprefentations of the deities. The cuftom of making animals reprefentatives of the gods arofe, probably, from the ancient manner of dreffing in whole unprepared fkins of beafts. This drefs was afterwards retained in the images of deified heroes, and at length, when the myftical meaning of religious fymbols was introduced, it was exchanged for the figure of beafts themfelves. Human figures have not been unufual among the *Egyptians* in later times, but they were imported from foreign countries, which was particularly the cafe with the image of *Serapis* at *Alexandria*. *Pag.* 484, 485. *Temples.*

In the hotteft parts of *Africa* it is extremely difficult to make and preferve wine, for the grapes are very foon dry, and the wine in a fhort time turns to vinegar. The Chriftians of that country, particularly in *Abyffinia*, have found this very inconvenient at the celebration of the facrament, and been obliged generally to make ufe of the juice of raifins foftened in water; fee *Renaudot's* additions *Pag.* 486. Egyptian *wine.*

 to

to *Lobo's Voyage d'Abyssinie*. So that wine was never much in use in these countries, especially in *upper Egypt*.

Pag. 487. *Feasts.* The custom of carrying about the image of a dead person, or a real corpse at a feast, seems to have been introduced with a very good design, to admonish every one present in the strongest manner, to remember death in the midst of their festivities, by which means all vicious excesses of intemperance might most effectually be guarded against. *Ecclus.* vii. 40. *Ps.* xc. 12. xxxix. 5. *Eccles.* xi. 9. But this wise provision had unfortunately a contrary effect, for the remembrance of death and of the transitory condition of human life was misapplied by them as a motive to the most dissolute voluptuousness, by way of enjoying a short life during its continuance. And other nations, who imitated the custom, have made use of the same kind of emblems and warnings of mortality, as encouragements to be the more active in their feasts and diversions, and neglect none of the short time and opportunity, which they conceived to be allotted for the purpose. The second chapter of the book of *Wisdom*, alludes plainly to this, and the book was probably written in *Egypt*. *Our life is short and tedious, and in the death of a man there is no remedy. —Come on therefore, let us enjoy the good things that are present, and let us speedily use the creatures like as in youth,—Let none of us go without his part of our voluptuousness; let us leave tokens of our joyfulness in every place, for this is our portion and our lot is this.* A passage in *Petronius*, where he describes the gluttony and debauchery of *Trimalchio*, shews how much the *Romans* imitated this abuse of a good institution. The custom mentioned immediately after this of their neatness and separation of strangers at *Egyptian* feasts is confirmed by the narrative of

Joseph's

Joseph's entertainment of his brethren, *Gen.* xliii. 24, 32.

The account of the manner of embalming bodies in *Egypt*, may serve to illustrate *Moses*'s account of *Jacob*'s funeral, in explaning which, *Calmet* discourses at large upon the *Egyptian* manner of embalming bodies, and the accounts of it we meet with in the ancients. *Fabricius* in his *Bibliographia antiquaria* gives a long list of writers upon the subject. Dr. *Pocock* besides representing the figure of a mummy, and that of an embalmed sacred bird, in copper plates, treats separately and at large of the *Egyptian* manner of embalming human bodies and birds, illustrates *Herodotus* and *Diodorus* on the subject, and gives a full description of a mummy swaddled up, which he had narrowly examined. The present scarcity of mummies is occasioned by an old prejudice, that they were of use in medicine, and by the frequent destruction of them, when new inhabitants of the country expected to find mony and treasures in and near them. *Maillet* informs us, that it is a difficult matter to find a fresh mummy, which has not been inspected and examined, at any expence, for the people of the country have learned the trade, and keep a stock of mummies which they pretend to be fresh. The same author takes notice, that the air and the soil of *Egypt* contribute greatly towards drying the corpses and preserving them from putrefaction; insomuch that the corpses of *Europeans*, which were deposited in tombs have after some time been found quite dry and sound. *Pag.* 489---492. *Embalming bodies.*

We find in *Martin*'s *explication de plusieurs textes difficiles de l'ecriture*, &c. a plate of a mummy, with two written leaves in his hands, from whence that author hath been led to conjecture, that the substance of any complaints alleged against the deceased, as well as of their absolution and the praises consequent *Pag.* 492. *Judgment upon the dead.*

consequent upon it, was sometimes given them in writing. In the passage of *Diodorus* here referred to, the word which is rendered *beyond*, may be very well understood of *this side*, or *close by* the lake, which signification of περαν is not very unusual in *Greek* authors, so that the difficulty or contradiction vanishes, which the compilers seem to observe in the historian here.

Pag. 494. *Mummy pits.* Dr. *Pocock* and *Maillet* give us plates of the *Mummy-pits* near *Saccara*. The opening of the well is commonly four feet wide, but the holes in the walls are so broken and damaged, that it is hardly possible to descend by them. The best bodies, such as were in coffins, and in hollow trunks formed to the human shape and joined together in the middle, have been long since removed from these catacombs, so that we now find none but ordinary corpses indifferently embalmed, sometimes mere bones wrapped up in cloth, or covered with rosin, others deposited in reeds and many remains of dismembred bodies.

Pag. 494. *Arts and sciences in Egypt.* There have been great controversies among the moderns on the subject of the antiquity and state of the sciences in *Egypt*, since *Herman Conringius* in his piece *de hermetica Egyptiorum veterum* attacked the common opinion of the extraction of all sciences from *Egypt*, and was answered by *Olaus Borrichius de ortu et progressu Chemiæ*, &c. The learning of the ancient *Egyptians* hath since that time been very much controverted. One side undoubtedly has gone much too far. In point of antiquity, they have treated the learning of *Egypt* as a tradition of *antediluvian* sciences, which had been preserved in writing in subterraneous vaults, pretending that it was prior to the *Chaldæan*, and even that the latter was derived from it. In point of greatness and extent of those sciences, they have been preferred far before all modern knowlege and inventions.

inventions. But on the other side, many things have been taken for granted without proof, and greatly exaggerated. Such is the opinion which many maintain, that the *Egyptians* owed all their sciences to the *Hebrews*, that not only all their Gods are derived from the race of *Abraham*, which *Fourmont* hath taken most pains to prove, but that they obtained all their learning from *Abraham*, *Joseph* and *Moses*. The medium between these extremes will shew, that the *Egyptians* are justly reckoned among the most ancient civilized people, who were not only distinguished very early by their learning, but carried it farther than other oriental nations, whom in every respect they excelled, whether prior to them in knowlege or not; that their arts and sciences are of an earlier date, than any true authentic history now extant, and that from them was derived all the wisdom and learning of the *Grecians*, whose lawgivers, philosophers and poets, all spent some part of their time in *Egypt*. Such were *Orpheus*, *Musæus*, *Melampus*, *Dædalus*, *Solon*, *Lycurgus*, *Pythagoras*, *Thales*, *Democritus*, *Plato* and even *Homer* himself;—that the progress of these sciences in *Egypt* was not proportioned to the antiquity of their origin, for some of them did not improve upon the first invention, others declined and were lost, which seems to have been chiefly occasioned by the hereditary restriction of them to certain families, by the mystical and intricate method of teaching, as well as the hieroglyphical characters, and by the early rise and quick growth of superstition, which must naturally introduce an infinite number of superfluities to the great detriment of useful learning. In the sciences themselves great mischief was done by the separation of particular branches, to which some of the learned were confined in exclusion of the rest, tho' they were indispensibly necessary to a thorough fundamental knowlege of the whole,

whole. See *Brucker*'s *hist. crit. philos. Reimman*'s *idea systematis antiquitatis literariæ. Warburton*'s *divine legation of Moses.*

Pag. 496. *Astronomy.* If we consider the exactness with which the great pyramid was built, so as to mark the true meridian of the place where it stands, and the early introduction of the solar year among the *Egyptians*, their skill in astronomy must have gone somewhat farther, than seems here to be asserted, tho' it is not to be denied, that the imperfect state of geometry and arithmetic, and their constant study of astrology must have retarded and obstructed the progress of astronomical enquiries. *Weidler*'s *historia astronomiæ* contains a particular dissertation *de astronomia veterum Ægyptiorum*, in which tho' he acknowleges several astronomical discoveries and opinions to have been ascribed to them by the ancients, yet he shews how imperfect they were in that science, and examines their claim to the invention of it. Of the *Egyptian* year, and the use of astronomy in chronology see M. *des Vignoles*'s *chronologie de l'histoire sainte.*

Pag. 498. *Physic.* The restriction of the knowlege and labors of physicians to certain diseases and parts of the human body, is not so very beneficial, as seems to be here supposed. For considering the nice dependence of the several parts of the human body upon each other, the common sources and frequent connexions as well as changes of several distinct diseases, it is impossible to be secure or well grounded in the care of any particular disease in all individual cases. without an insight into other diseases and a knowlege of the whole science. And hence it is much to be wished, that skill in chirurgery might be joined as far as possible to knowlege in medicine in general. The *Egyptians* are supposed to have learned the use of clysters from the Ibis, who is said to perform that operation upon himself with his bill; and

and, according to *Pliny*, they were inſtructed in bleeding by the Hippopotamus. Beſides the controverſy before mentioned between *Conring* and *Borrichius*, which was chiefly on the ſubject of the ſcience of phyſic in *Egypt*, it is treated of very fully by *Dan. le Clerc*, in his *Hiſtoire de la medicine*, *Schultzen*'s *hiſtoria medicinæ*, *Goelicken*'s *hiſtor. medic.* and *Barchuſen de medicinæ origine & progreſſu.* Dr. *Shuckford*'s opinion is anſwered at large by Dr. *Warburton*, who, at the ſame time, enquires into the antiquity and ſtate of phyſic in *Egypt*.

The moſt ſpecious argument, that can be alleged for the antiquity and great improvement of chymiſtry among the *Egyptians*, is doubtleſs that of *Moſes*'s reducing the golden calf into powder, which could not poſſibly be done without great ſkill in the tranſmutation of metals, and ſeems to be part of the wiſdom he had learned in *Egypt*. However, the pretence of alchemiſts, and of ſeveral commentators upon the heathen, particularly the *Egyptian*, fables of the Gods, and of the hieroglyphics, as to the myſteries of the ſeparation and tranſmutation of metals, is certainly unſupported by proofs. For *Meyer*'s *arcana arcaniſſima*, and *Tollius*'s *fortuita*, are rather works of learning and genius, than ſtrict pieces of reaſoning. But it is nevertheleſs a falſe concluſion to infer from the firſt mention of the tranſmutation of metals, ſo late as after the reign of *Conſtantine*, that it was wholly unknown in more ancient times, and among the *Egyptians*. For we can only judge from the few books of antiquity that are now extant, that many arts were formerly known long before they were committed to writing. *Pag.* 499. *Chymiſtry.*

It ſufficiently appears, from the manner of embalming deſcribed before, that but little advantage could ariſe from it to the knowlege of the internal part of the human body; or to anatomy in general. *Pag.* 499. *Anatomy.*

The

The edict of the *Egyptian* kings, reported by *Pliny*, to dissect bodies in order to investigate the causes of diseases, seems to have been dated in the later times of the *Grecian* monarchy. And there cannot be a weaker argument of the existence of this science, than the *Egyptian* custom of exhibiting a skeleton at entertainments, for it was either a swaddled corpse, or a carved wooden image of a dead man.

Pag. 500. *Natural philosophy.* It is necessary, in this branch of learning, to distinguish collections and observations in natural history, from the knowlege requisite to explane them, and to assign their causes. The *Egyptians* made very great progress in the former of these studies, but were defective in the latter, on account of the imperfect state of mathematical learning, and of the narrow limits to which the laws of the country confined each man's attention and study.

Pag. 501. *Magic.* If we compare the words of *Joseph*'s servant, who was sent after his brethren, *Gen.* xliv. 5. with the words of *Joseph* himself, recorded in the 15th verse, and if the circumstance of divining by the cup, be considered as a mere addition of the servant to aggravate the offence of taking it away, *Joseph* will stand clear of the charge of superstition, or of a guilty dissimulation, and this incident will serve, at the same time, to shew the different ways of divining and of magic practised in *Egypt*.

Pag. 501 ---503. *Whether possible?* It would be quite inexcuseable in historians and philosophers to be tempted by the imposture that has been practised in some instances of magic, to believe the same of all the rest. For historians must see the falsity of such a conclusion by experience, and philosophers must know it by argument. As one single undeniable case fully evinces the possibility of a fact, tho' its nature be neither demonstrable nor comprehensible; so, on the other side, the want of ocular proof and personal observation, or or the intrinsic difficulty of conceiving it, together with the infinite number of manifest falshoods arising from deceit or imagination, do not suffice to prove the contrary; they only serve to shew the necessity of a nice and regular examination of the truth of those accounts, which are generally received as true. The modern objections against all possibility of magic, drawn from the inconceivableness of the operations of spirits, and from the impossibility of actual contracts between men and invisible beings, are grounded in prejudices, and doubtless prove too much. The second of the grounds of *Egyptian* magic here recited should certainly be dated much later, for it is a system of the *eclectic*, or modern *platonic* philosophers in *Egypt* after the birth of *Christ*. It might, at first, have a specious and a religious appearance, after the introduction of polytheism, and particularly of the *Egyptian* theology, to pretend that every thing unusual and extraordinary was the operation of the gods; and they never ascribed their magic to the interposition of evil spirits, which were unknown to most heathen nations, but to their gods. So that all that was esteemed *magic* among the ancients, cannot, with propriety, be comprehended under the idea which we usually afix to the word. See *Brucker's*. *Hist. philos.* and *Reimman's ant. litt. Ægypt.*

Pag. 304. *Navigation on the* Nile.

Most of the navigation for commerce, even with *Ethiopia*, is now carried on upon the *Nile* by the means of floats; of which see *Maillet*, who treats of them at large, as well as of the ancient navigation and solemn voyages of the *Egyptians* on the *Nile*. This author gives us great reason to lament the total want of authorities for such accounts, especially as he relates many things, which appear very improbable and greatly exaggerated.

As

Pag. 505. *Literary monuments.* As the *Egyptians* accounted *Hermes* to be the original inventor of writing and science, they have pretended almost all the inscriptions of antiquity in their country to be columns and monuments of his, which may be so far true, that they are composed in the characters according to the art invented by him; and this reconciles to us the number and the date of many columns attributed to him. The account before given of the grottoes and amazing subterraneous cavities near *Thebes*, confirm the almost incredible reports of ancient writers, and render it highly probable, that these very caves and the hieroglyphical images they contain, are the famous pillars of *Hermes*, to which ancient historians so often appeal, as is evident from comparing *Manetho* with *Ammianus Marcellinus*. The most ancient method of writing upon stones hath lasted longest in the northern countries, where the subsequent more commodious inventions have not been so early received.

Pag. 506. Egyptian *learning.* The circumstantial accounts of *Pythagoras*'s travels in *Egypt* and other *Eastern* countries are chiefly taken from the later and very suspicious accounts of the *Platonics*, particularly *Porphyry* and *Iamblichus*, which have much the air of romances. It is certain however, that the ancients had two sorts of learning, which may probably have been derived from *Egypt*; and tho' it seem'd in those times to be greatly beneficial, both to prepare noviciates and disciples for higher attainments in the sciences, and to avoid the misleading of the latter by ignorant hands; yet it was undeniably of the utmost prejudice to the increase and establishment of the sciences, as it must occasion a needless perplexity and loss of time, a studied obscurity, unavoidable misinterpretation, false imagination and pretence of great mystery, as well as a narrow restriction of the discoveries that are made.

The

The *Egyptian* writing is properly divided into two ſorts. The firſt was an immediate repreſentation and expreſſion of *things*, the other of *words*. The firſt was practiſed two ways, either by painting, which kind of language came by degrees into great vogue on account of its conciſeneſs and general utility, and was ſoon divided into various kinds, by repreſenting general ideas of properties, actions and relations, under corporeal figures, or under more eaſy ſigns, which were introduced inſtead of the laborious method of images, and reſembled the *Chineſe* characters, by means of which ſeveral nations of different languages may uſe the ſame ſigns of expreſſion, tho' they annex ſuch ſigns to very diſſimilar words. The other method of writing by letters was likewiſe twofold amongſt the *Egyptians*, for beſides the common letters, they had private and more myſtical marks, to render their writing illegible to the vulgar. The firſt, or the hieroglyphical kind, was in all probability the moſt ancient, and was an immediate imitation of nature, which hath ſince been retained by many *American* nations. So that *Shuckford*'s opinion is totally groundleſs and improbable, and *Warburton*'s extremely well-grounded. *Pag.* 507, 508. *Characters.*

Both the opinions here oppoſed to each other, may very well be connected. It is undoubted from many teſtimonies of antiquity, particularly from *Diodorus* and *Tacitus*, that events and common tranſactions of human life are expreſs'd in hieroglyphics; but that the gods were ſo repreſented, and abſtract ideas and maxims, nay even many myſteries, is demonſtrable from many more ancient teſtimonies. For one ſort of figures had a direct hiſtorical, another ſort an indirect ſymbolical ſignification. So that not only the different times, when monuments filled with hieroglyphical in- *Pag.* 508. *Hieroglyphics.*

ſcriptions were erected, but the particular view and intent of them, muſt have given a key to their ſignification, which was loſt in ſucceeding times. Hence we cannot in the preſent times hit upon any, even uncertain conjectures, in the explanation of thoſe writings. And this uncertainty hath been conſiderably increaſed both by the writings of the modern *Greeks* in *Egypt*, and by the extravagant dreams of modern interpreters. The former expected to find in thoſe inſcriptions their *Platonic* or *Eaſtern* philoſophy, or at leaſt applied them to it in their explanation; and the latter, particularly *Kircher*, have with incredible fertility of imagination ſought or rather diſcovered great myſteries in trifles. See *Joh. Pierii Valeriani Hieroglyphica*, and *Shaw's Travels*.

Pag. 509. *Sacred characters.* It appears from the remains of *Manetho*, in *Euſebius*, that the *Egyptian* prieſts, beſides the ſacred characters, had alſo a ſacred language to conceal their myſteries.

Pag. 509---511. *Affinity of the* Coptic *and* Greek *letters.* The great affinity between the *Coptic* and *Greek* letters, may be deduced from a much more ancient cauſe than the dominion of the *Greeks* in *Egypt* from the times of *Alexander*. For, according to the account of *Herodotus*, *Pſammetichus* having ſubdued all *Egypt* with the aſſiſtance of the *Carians* and *Ionians*, planted many colonies there, and placed *Egyptian* children amongſt them to learn their language; at this time it is very poſſible their characters might be introduced, and their language might begin to be mixed, and the new writing might become uſeful and be received in common life, whilſt the more ancient characters were gradually loſt. After this *Cadmus*, who firſt introduced the *Greek* letters among the people of *Greece*, might derive them from *Thebes* as well as from *Phenicia*.

Maillet

Maillet aſſures us, that during his ſtay in *Egypt* the laſt *Coptic* prieſt died, who underſtood the language. Hence the performance of divine worſhip in that language was not very rational, but became tolerable by the principal parts of it being repeated in the *Arabic*, or the language of the country. *Pag.* 512. Coptic *language.*

REMARKS
ON THE
UNIVERSAL HISTORY,
VOL. II. BOOK I.

CHAP. III.

The Egyptian *Chronology to the time of* Alexander the Great.

Pag. 4--18. Egyptian *chronology.*

THE *Egyptian* chronology, even after it was published by *Syncellus*, hath pass'd thro' so many hands, some of which were wanting both in abilities and discretion, that this hath not a little contributed to increase the confusion of old traditions, and of the sources of this whole enquiry. Besides *Scaliger*, *Petavius*, *Usher*, and *Pezron*, the subject hath been examined by *Marsham*, *Conring*, *Perizonius*, *Cary*, *Tournemine*, *Newton*, *Bedford*, *Vignoles*, *Bengel*, *Whiston*, *Vitringa*, *Witsius*, *Shuckford*, and *Leidecker*, together with most of the considerable writers of the ecclesiastical history of the Old Testament. As to the old chronicle, it has been already treated of before. The learned *Des Vignoles* hath fully confirmed the first conjecture, that the vast sum of 36525 years is an astronomical period; for by multiplying the great

great cynic cycle of the *Egyptians* of 1461 years, by the cycle of the moon of 25 years, the produce will be this very sum of 36525. The second conjecture has been so stated by others, that the fifteen first Dynasties form the list of the gods and demi-gods, who are indeed said to have been sixteen in number, but either *Vulcan* must be excluded, as being without time, or *Jupiter*, that is, *Ammon* or *Ham*, the last of the demi-gods, must belong to the beginning of the sixteenth Dynasty, and have been the founder of it. It is supposed, that these fifteen fabulous Dynasties might have been occasioned by the fourteen generations from *Adam* to *Mizraim*, *Gen.* v. and x. to which the inventors of them might have an eye, after taking away the deity and the world, that is, *Vulcan* and the sun, and that they comprehended *Menes* as the fifteenth. *Bengelius* imagines the sixteen names of the gods and demi-gods to have been derived from the ten patriarchs from *Adam* to *Noah*, the three sons of the latter, and the three brothers of *Mizraim*. If we suppose the years in the extravagant numbers of this calculation to have been days, which attempt has been made by M. *Gibert* in settling the chronology of the most ancient people, the pretence even of such an ambiguous appellation would be demonstrable enough, not only with respect to days, but in some measure to months, and would, in some degree, save the principal large sums, which would thereby become tolerable and specious; but the difficulty would increase with respect to the lesser numbers, which would then be altogether condemned as fictitious, and in that case we should have but little left to depend upon, among all the accounts and remains of antiquity, which authorize both sorts of the determined numbers.

Manetho has been treated of already. Since *Goar*'s edition of *Syncellus*, which is not equally successful *Pag.* 18. Manetho.

cessful throughout in the emendations, particularly those of the calculations, some pains has been taken more fully to examine and to make use of or to controvert *Manetho*'s remains and his Dynasties, which last has been done with the most spirit by *Conring* and *Perizonius.* Before this, the learned were forced to content themselves with that imperfect piece of *Syncellus*, published by *Scaliger*. It seems indeed the shortest and readiest solution of many difficulties, totally to reject all those difficulties; but this would be a dangerous step, and would not only tend greatly to depreciate the accounts of antiquity, with which we do not abound, but would tend to weaken the credibility of all other records of the like kind, none of which are free from difficulties, which may be solved or removed by other methods. If *Marsham*'s *Abris* be corrected according to the intimations of *Vignoles* and *Bengel*, we shall then bring this chronology into some connexion, and need not wholly reject, but, in the main, save the credit of *Manetho*.

Pag. 19. *Note* (O). *concerning hieroglyphical characters.*

The conjecture of the compilers in the note (O) is perfectly well grounded, and extremely probable. For it appears not only from the express mention of letters, but of a language or dialect, that those signs could not be hieroglyphical, since no language can exist without words, and the hieroglyphical characters are not words. Hence Dr. *Warburton* has received this emendation of *Eusebius*, or rather of *Syncellus*; but he disputes the first conjecture of the preceding note (N), because *Greek* words might be written with the sacred letters, and the *Greek* language seems to have been known much earlier in *Egypt*, especially among the priests, than is generally supposed. The other conjectures give a clearer insight into this whole difficulty. The *Hieroglyphical* characters being an invention of the first *Hermes*, and letters being attributed to the second,

second, it is very possible, that all accounts of great antiquity drawn up in these different kinds of writing, were ascribed to those two. At least *Manetho* might appeal to these records merely on account of their great antiquity. Another writer, M. *Koch*, has disputed all the Dynasties and accounts of *Manetho* upon other grounds; for he charges him with having changed old inscriptions, which contained accounts of important events, into proper names, and palmed them upon the world for lists of *Egyptian* kings. Of this he gives several instances, such as the words *Toegar*, *Amachus*, *Momcheri*, *Venephes*, *Usophaedus*, *Miebidus* 26, *Semempsis*, *Bienaches*, *Bochos*, *Keuchos*, *Binothris*, *Tlas*, *Sethenes*, which he renders *Toegar (heros strenuus) imbellis seu impotens factus labe membrorum obscænorum et respirationis (faucium), sed lugens, pœnitens, a familiari seu sectatore ab Abrahamo Semi (Patriarchæ postero) restitutus est per preces. Interim fletus, animorum compunctio, anxietas, ad numen placandum in coetu supplicationum publico, ubi agnum victimam statuerat misere ægrotus.* From hence he concludes, that the *Pharaoh*, who took *Sara* from *Abraham*, *Gen.* xii. was the *Toegar Amachus Momcheri* of *Eratosthenes*, as he belongs to this period, according to the years mentioned in the lists of *Eratosthenes* and *Manetho*. There are more such applications to *Pharaoh* in the same author, and these, together with his account of the *Israelites* going out of *Egypt* under the shepherd king *Assis*, are made the foundation for his whole examination of the *Egyptian* history, which by such means must of necessity become very arbitrary. Were we not well assured, that the ancient *Egyptian* and the *Hebrew* tongue are too widely different to suffer words of the former to be thus explaned by the latter, the contrary would be sufficiently proved by the explanation *Eratosthenes* gives of every name in his

his lift. Even if the *Coptic* language retained no traces of the old *Egyptian*, the contrary of which is undeniable, and confirms the interpretations *Eratofthenes* gives, yet in the time of *Manetho* and *Eratofthenes* it is a thing quite incredible, that the *Egyptian* tongue fhould be fo utterly unknown, as that they themfelves either thro' ignorance miftook thefe words for names; or could venture upon fo daring an enterprize, as defignedly to forge the whole, and that it fhould neither be obferved in their own time, nor after by *Jofephus* and others, who had the writings of *Manetho*, and were not unacquainted with the *Hebrew* tongue. Not to mention, that in the courfe of fuch an interpretation many names are derived and explaned from the *Greek*, tho' no *Greek* words could have been admitted into fo ancient a *Hebrew* monument, and even many *Hebrew* words and rules of conftruction are received, which are quite unfupported by Proofs.

Pag. 21. *Difficulties in* Manetho. The fhortnefs of the ancient *Egyptian* year, which confifted only of 360 days, is not taken notice of here, tho' the difference of five days and a quarter becomes very confiderable in fo large a number of years. But even with this help, *Manetho*'s computation is not reconcileable either to the *Samaritan* or *Greek* chronology, if the Dynafties he reckons are to be confidered as fucceffive in the order in which he places them.

Pag. 22. Marfham. Sir *John Marfham* fecured himfelf by the clue of the *Hebrew* chronology from wandering in this *Egyptian* labyrinth, or running into the extravagancies of others, who were mifled by the *Greek* and *Samaritan* chronology, which was particularly the cafe of *Is. Voffius* and *Pezron*. He has certainly the credit of having paved the way for others, tho' he did not remove all difficulties, and committed fome errors. After *Perizonius*, M. *Fourmont* attacked

tacked his chronology, and *des Vignoles* confirmed and amended it. Sir *Iſaac Newton* indeed came into the ſingular opinion of *Marſham*, that *Seſoſtris* was *Seſac*, but by advancing the other notion, that he was likewiſe *Oſiris*, he hath thrown all this chronology into the utmoſt confuſion, as will appear more plainly in the ſequel.

F. Pezron, beſides building his chronology upon weak and arbitrary grounds, hath increaſed the difficulties of it by a vaſt number of miſtakes, many of which are judiciouſly pointed out by *Fourmont*. *Pag.* 22. F. Pezron.

The medium is the ſecureſt way of judging of the credibility of *Manetho*. The accounts he gives of the *Iſraelites* do not a little affect his credit, tho' *Joſephus*, thro' mere partiality, received and confirmed them; and undoubtedly another queſtion ariſes, whether his miſtakes are to be imputed to him, or to the authorities he followed? The amazing corruptions of the tranſcribers, in the catalogues of the Dynaſties, cannot be denied, tho' it is not a ſufficient plea for totally rejecting him. As theſe catalogues contain no expreſs intimation that the ſeries of the ſeveral Dynaſties is collateral, ſo neither can it be gathered from them, that it is ſucceſſive. Now, as it appears unqueſtionably, from other ancient authorities, that there were, at one time, ſeveral kingdoms and ſovereignties in *Egypt*, as this is the only method of ſaving the whole of *Manetho*'s account, and rendering it intelligible, this ſeems to be a tolerable foundation for that opinion. *Fourmont* conjectures, with ſome degree of probability, that the *Auritæ*, *Meſtræans*, and *Egyptians*, who are commonly ſuppoſed to have been the gods, demi-gods, and men, were the inhabitants of different parts of *Egypt*, the firſt having lived near *Abaris* and *Tanis* in *lower Egypt*, the ſecond, or the *Mizraim*, in *midland Egypt* near *Memphis*, *Pag.* 24. *Judgment upon* Manetho.

phis, the third in *upper Egypt*, and that they successively possess'd themselves of the supreme power; which is confirmed in *Jer.* xliv. 1. *Isa.* xi. 11. xix. 2. *Ps.* lxxviii. 12, 43.

Pag. 24. Eratosthenes. The public is highly obliged to Dr. *Paul Ernest Jablonsky*, for the pains he has taken with *Eratosthenes*, both in illustrating his explanation of the *Egyptian* names from the *Coptic*, and in proposing many lucky conjectures about various corrections. The work is incorporated in the second part of *Vignoles*'s *Chronology*, and is intitled, *Annotationes in Eratosthenis catalogum regum Thebæorum Ægypti*, &c.

Pag. 25. *His chronology connected with the* Grecian. As by the passage of *Dicæarchus* here cited, *Eratostenes*'s chronology is connected with the foreign *Grecian* system, so by the introduction of the five intercalary days, and the alteration of the old *Egyptian* year, it is connected with *Manetho*'s chronology, which would be yet more useless without such a *Theban* succession of kings.

Pag. 26. *Series of* Syncellus. The series of *Syncellus* contains, to all appearance, the kings of *Heliopolis*, or *lower Egypt*, by connecting which with the *Theban*, or those in *upper Egypt*, the chronology of the whole nation is brought to some degree of perfection, and even *Manetho*'s Dynasties will have their use. There is great improbability in the charge here brought against *Syncellus*, that he pick'd out his names at random, and it is refuted by one evident proof, that he mentions the years of the reigns of unknown kings, which he would doubtless have distinguished by some name, had he compiled his fable in so hasty and arbitrary a manner, and not followed an old record, which he had in his hands, to some author perhaps unknown to himself.

Pag. 27, 28. Osiris The most received opinions concerning *Osiris* are of two kinds. Some who apply all the fables of the heathen gods to the scriptures, and derive all

all those inventions from thence, have ventured at several conjectures. *Huetius*, in his *Demonstratio evangelica*, applies the whole of this history to *Moses*, but at the same time supposes, with the highest improbability, that *Theuth* or *Mercury*, *Serapis*, *Orus*, *Anubis*, *Vulcan*, and *Typhon*, were likewise *Moses*; and, in his opinion, there is hardly a heathen deity, whose character does not correspond to that of the *Jewish* lawgiver. *Fourmont*, on the other hand, in his *reflex. crit. sur les histoires des anciens peuples*, takes great pains to shew, that *Osiris* was *Esau*, and that *Typhon* was *Jacob*. Others, again, place him among the *Egyptian* kings, and Mr. *Koch*, a *German* author before-mentioned, supposes this *Osiris* to have been *Salatis* or *Pharaoh*, who exalted *Joseph*. Sir *Isaac Newton* endeavors at large to prove, that *Osiris* was the same king with *Sesostris* or *Sesac* in scripture, but *Warburton* fully confutes this opinion. The fable of the delivery of *Rhea* in the five new days, which *Mercury* won from the moon, undoubtedly alludes to the addition of five intercalary days to the old *Egyptian* year, five being the 72d part of 360. However, it does not follow from thence, that *Osiris* lived about the time of such alteration of the year, it rather proves him to have a claim to much higher antiquity; for the *Egyptians* frequently gave to the planets the names of their deified heroes and kings.

Pag. 29. Egyptian gods.

The *Greek* writers have intermixed the whole history of the heathen gods with many fables from their own theology, and thereby rendered it very dark and intricate. See *Banier*'s *Mythology*.

Pag. 29, 30. Hermes.

Brucker in his *Hist. crit. philos.* treats at large of *Hermes*, and both refers to the other authors concerning him, and examines the several opinions which derive his character from the scriptures, particularly from *Moses*.

According

Pag. 31, &c. *Death of* Osiris.

According to the account of *Julius Firmicus Maternus*, *Isis* had an intrigue with *Typhon* during the absence of *Osiris*, and thereby promoted the conspiracy against her husband. The whole narrative savours very much of a mixture of different transactions of different persons, which arose from the confusion of the *Grecian* with the eastern theology, which was considerably increased by the *Grecians* in applying the history of foreign gods to their own heroes.

Pag. 36. *Temples of* Isis.

The accounts of the temple of *Isis* at *Busiris* are confirmed by Dr. *Pocock* in his *Description of the East*. There is another very sumptuous one at *Tentyra*, described by the same author, who adds his own conjectures, where the *Typhonia*, mentioned by *Strabo*, was situate. He likewise gives a full account of two statues of *Osiris* and *Isis* sitting in a very unusual posture.

Pag. 37---39. Menes.

Diodorus ascribes the building of the city *Arsinoe*, and of a labyrinth, to *Menes* or *Mendes*, but he must have lived much later, and several subsequent kings bore this name, tho' commonly with some other name, as *Ramesse Menes*. It is highly probable, that this first *Menes* is to be placed in the remotest antiquity, and the objections of modern writers have not yet been able to discredit this assertion. As to the objections of *Perizonius* in his *Orig. Ægypt.* it is to be observed, *first*, that but little can be gathered from the account of the *Mestræans*, it being not yet decided, whether they were demigods, or inhabitants of different countries; and *Menes* may notwithstanding continue to be reckoned a son and successor of the demi-gods, especially as being one of the *Mizraim*, by only placing the gods and demi-gods before the deluge, which must be done independently of this. *Secondly*, The pretence of the invention and introduction of many things is not sufficient to determine with certainty

a

a point of chronology. For it has been the custom of all nations to magnify the excellence of their arts and the foundation of their most celebrated cities, by attributing them to the greatest names in the remotest antiquity. Besides, the luxury introduced by *Menes* may have been only more commodious contrivances for the ease of human life, which must have been greatly wanting before the erection of civil societies. *Thirdly*, The *Egyptian Hammon* may have obtained the surname of *Jupiter* very late from the *Grecians*, tho' he might not only be *Ham* the son of *Noah*, but likewise the last of those men, whom the *Egyptians* deified. Indeed the order of these gods may be occasioned not so much by the time and the genealogical series, as the different merit of their actions and extent of their power, which becomes probable from the characters of *Osiris* and *Isis*. *Pezron* and his predecessor *Is. Vossius* have fallen into monstrous chronological errors from their prejudice in favor of the *Greek* version preferably to the *Hebrew* numbers. Sir *Isaac Newton* has displayed his great powers of invention by raising a structure of *Egyptian* chronology and history, which is neither consistent with the accounts of Holy Writ, nor with those of any other ancient historians. There was a kingdom regularly established in *Egypt* so early as the times of *Abraham*, which in *Joseph*'s days, and before, not only comprehended several cities and countries, but had most of those civil institutions, of which we read in the ancients, and which cannot possibly be reconciled to the modern erection of a kingdom or state. The antiquity of the city of *Hebron* is expressed, *Num.* xiii. 22. by this circumstance, that it was built seven years before *Zoan* in *Egypt*. But it is a difficult and doubtful matter to decide, whether this *Menes* was *Ham* himself, or *Mizraim*, or another

another unknown son of *Ham*'s, brother to *Mizraim*; for *Menes* being the first king of *Thebes*, or rather of upper *Egypt*, seems to have been the son of *Ammon* or *Jupiter*, and is distinguished from *Mizraim*, the first king of lower *Egypt*, unless we suppose *Ham* to have been called *Menes*, after the cultivation of *Egypt*, which is called the land of *Ham*, *Ps.* lxxviii. 51. cv. 23, 27. and that after some time he left lower *Egypt* to *Mizraim*, and reserved upper *Egypt* to himself, because *Eratosthenes*'s table gives sixty-two years to *Menes*, and *Syncellus*'s only thirty-five to *Mizraim*.

Pag. 39---41. *The shepherds.* The shepherd-kings of *Egypt* are very rightly placed in the earliest and darkest times of antiquity. The observations to be made upon them, particularly with respect to the abuse and misapplication of this event to the prejudice of the *Mosaic* history, will be answered in the Appendix, in a separate examination of the several opinions concerning the dominion of *Abraham*'s posterity in *Egypt*.

Pag. 46---51. Sesostris. Sir *Isaac Newton*'s opinion concerning *Sesostris*, how specious soever it may be, will, if narrowly examined, appear highly improbable. It is founded partly in fabulous accounts of the heathen gods, such as antiquity, particularly that of *Greece*, produced, partly in some similitude and harmony of circumstances and events in the accounts of *Osiris*, *Sesostris* and *Sesac*. But both these grounds are very exceptionable. The histories of the gods are so filled with inventions, and contain so much confusion of distinct persons and contradictory narrations, that they must needs prove a very precarious and arbitrary foundation for chronology. As to the accidental similitude of circumstances and events, that is often observable to a great degree, in persons notoriously different, but in these very ancient times it might arise or be increased from the general custom, which prevailed greatly in *Egypt*, of attributing to their kings the names of old

old heroes and gods, for in aftertimes this consonance of the names hath occasioned several, if not all, the exploits of a later king of the same name, to be ascribed to the first hero, who bore it, in order to excite the greater admiration at his extraordinary merit; which in all probability was very much the case of *Osiris*. But the greatest difficulty attending that great man's opinion is, that it manifestly contradicts all other accounts both of sacred and prophane historians. For it is inconsistent not only with *Manetho*, but with *Herodotus* and *Diodorus*, to suppose this *Sesostris* to have been the inventor of agriculture, of social life, of civil constitutions, and of religious establishments, and that he even was the first, who, with the assistance of *Mercury*, introduced all sciences, and the use of arms and horses in war, and regulated the spreading and the beneficial overflowing of the *Nile*. But to attribute all this to *Sesac* is manifestly contradicting the express words of holy writ; for, according to scriptural accounts, all these inventions existed not only before the times of *Moses*, but before those of *Joseph*, and there is particular mention in the histories of *Moses* and *Solomon*, of the famous cavalry of the *Egyptians*, and of their sciences and idolatry. See *Warburton*'s *Divine Legation*, &c. Besides the other opinions here cited by the compilers, M. *des Vignoles* has, in his *Chronologie de l'histoire sainte*, confirmed the conjecture of *Scaliger* and *Usher*, that *Sesostris* was the *Sesonchis* of the twenty-second Dynasty, and asserts, upon good grounds, that several *Egyptian* kings must have born this name, whose transactions were afterward confounded.

Tournemine, in the *Memoires de Trevoux* of *September* 1702, has endeavored to shew, that *Sesostris* must be supposed to have reigned before the departure of the *Israelites* out of *Egypt*, and to be that *Pharaoh* in scripture who oppressed the *Israelites*, and

Pag. 66. *His insolence.*

and in whoſe reign *Moſes* was born; conſequently, that he reigned 1400 years after *Menes*. *Perizonius*, in his *Orig. Ægyptiac.* takes great pains to confute this opinion, but *Tournemine* attempts to ſupport and eſtabliſh it in his *diſſert. de primo ſacræ & profanæ chronologiæ vinculo, epocha Seſoſtris*, which is the twelfth piece in the *Supplement ad Menochium*.

Obeliſk of Rameſſes *at* Rome. The obeliſk at *Rome*, by which king *Rameſſes* ſtudied to perpetuate his memory, is one of the moſt magnificent monuments of antiquity, tho' *Kircher* was induced, by his hieroglyphical prejudices, to ſtudy to diſcredit and explode the hiſtorical explanation of the inſcription. *Auguſtus* intended to have ordered it to *Rome*, but either a ſuperſtitious caution prevented him, or rather the apparent impractibility of the undertaking deterred him. *Conſtantine* ordered it to be brought to *Alexandria*, with a view of adorning *Conſtantinople* with it. But it was *Conſtantius* who executed this deſign, and who for religious reaſons, becauſe it was dedicated to the ſun, and idolatry was totally extirpated at *Conſtantinople*, erected it at *Rome*, where it ſuffered from the deſtructions of the ſucceeding centuries, and was not replaced till the year 1588, in the reign of *Sixtus* V. See *Ammianus Marcellinus*, *Marſham*, and *Vignoles*, the laſt of whom ſuppoſes it to be a work of the *Iſraelites*, whoſe bondage in *Egypt* he places under this *Rameſſes*.

Pag. 79. Sethon. *Rollin*, in his *Ancient Hiſtory*, makes it very probable that this *Sethon Sevechus* was the ſon and ſucceſſor of *Sabaco*, whoſe overthrow by *Sennacherib* fulfilled ſeveral prophecies of ſcripture againſt *Egypt*, tho' the *Egyptians* falſely apply to themſelves the miraculous event which happened before *Jeruſalem*, in order to conceal and aboliſh the diſgraceful memory of their defeat. See 2 *Kings* xviii. *Iſ.* xviii--xx--xxx--xxxi. *Nah.* iii. 8. *&c.* The

ſame

same author briefly shews, that the *No Ammon* mentioned in scripture was not *Alexandria*, as the Seventy interpret it, but *Thebes*. The same is done more largely by *Pet. Zora*, in a piece intitled *de Historiâ & antiquitatibus urbis No Ammon*, which is in the second volume of his *opuscula sacra*, and contains many illustrations of *Egyptian* antiquities, and of the history of these times. See also *Vignoles's Chronol.* where these *Ethiopian* or *Egyptian* kings are explaned according to the different opinions of chronologers.

A collection of the several accounts of *Apries* or *Pharaoh Hophra*, and a comparison of them with the many passages of scripture where he is mentioned, may be seen in *Prideaux*, *Rollin*, *Marsham*, *Perizonius*, and *Vignoles*. *Mascrier*'s account is rather confused and unsupported by proofs. *Pag.* 86--90. Apries

The four and forty years assigned to the reign of *Amasis* are not sufficient for his many acts, particularly those by which his kingdom was restored to a florishing condition. *Diodorus* therefore seems to be better grounded in allowing him ten years more. For else it will be hard to find the forty years, of which *Ezekiel* had foretold, *ch.* xxix. that during that space *Egypt* should lie desolate. These years must commence at the period when *Nebuchadnezzar* plundered and ruined this kingdom, which was a work of time, especially as *Amasis*, according to the confession of *Herodotus* himself, was not then king of *Egypt*. And tho' *Diodorus*'s account should be true, that he was the immediate successor upon the death of *Apries*, yet he could not, in less than fifteen years, perform all the things that are related of him. But if, as some pretend, *Nebuchadnezzar* only appointed him his viceroy in *Egypt*, and he did not ascend the throne till after that monarch's death, in that case his time was yet more contracted, and considering how horrid a devasta- *Pag.* 90--96. Amasis.

tion the *Babylonians* inflicted on the country, it is ſcarce credible that this kingdom ſhould, in ſo ſhort a ſpace, be reſtored to a floriſhing ſtate. Or perhaps *Herodotus* was, in this inſtance, likewiſe impoſed upon by the *Egyptian* prieſts, and ſo aſcribed to *Amaſis* what was really done by other *Egyptian* kings. It is therefore probable, that the forty years in which *Egypt* was deſolate, expired in the reign of *Cyrus*, and that it was indeed, in ſome meaſure, reſtored under *Amaſis*, but continued in a ruinous condition, in compariſon with other kingdoms, as *Ezekiel* himſelf intimates.

Beſides the two inſtances here mentioned, in which *Diodorus* and *Herodotus* differ, the former attributes to *Amaſis*, and the latter to *Pſammis*, the wiſe anſwer that was returned to the *Grecian* ambaſſy to *Egypt*, from the people of *Elis*, on account of the *Olympic* games. *Herodotus* in reporting the ſeveral opinions of the cauſe of this war, only mentions it as a *Perſian* cuſtom, not to ſuffer an illegitimate ſon to rule, during the life of the legitimate heir. *Prideaux*'s conjecture may be connected with *Herodotus*'s accounts of the *Egyptian* marriages of the *Perſian* kings; that *Nebuchadnezzar* having ſubdued *Egypt*, *Cyrus*, who afterwards conquered all his countries, aſſerted his claim to the ſovereignty over this kingdom, and *Cambyſes*, ſucceſſor to the latter, would not depart from that claim. This renders it highly probable, and agreeable to the oriental cuſtoms, that both *Cyrus* and *Cambyſes* increaſed the number of their wives from *Egypt*, and did not even ſpare the royal family of this now tributary kingdom. Of this *Amaſis* ſee *Prideaux*, *Rollin* and *Marſham*.

Pag. 98--107. Egyptian *kings after* Pſammenitus.

Rollin concludes his ancient *Egyptian* hiſtory with *Pſammenitus* and the conqueſt by *Cambyſes*, tho' the reigns of the ſucceeding kings of *Egypt* were of a conſiderable length, and are no ſmall part of the hiſtory

history of this nation, and have their separate place in *Manetho*'s Dynasties, where they seem to be a strong evidence, that the series and number of the Dynasties doth not import a regular succession of sovereignties after each other, but that several of them were collateral, or subsisted at the same time. *Mascrier* gives a concise account of these reigns in his usual manner, in the first part of his *idée du gouvernement de l'Egypte*. *Perizonius*'s account in his *Orig. Ægypt.* is likewise very short, as his design was chiefly to confute the chronology of *Marsham*, who does not descend so low. *Prideaux* is more circumstantial in this part of the *Egyptian* history, in the first volume of his connexion. To the reasons here alleged why the *Persian* yoke proved intolerable to the *Egyptians*, may be added the oppressive measures of the *Persian* satrapæ, or governors of provinces, especially in these remote provinces, and the custom of the *Persians*, who never suffered a conquered people to retain their own laws. All this is confirmed by the fidelity of the *Egyptians* in after-times to their *Grecian* kings, and this allegiance was very much promoted and supported by the union and mixture of the religions of *Greece* and *Egypt*.

Pag. 107 ---119. *Series of the kings of* Egypt *according to the oriental historians.*

Athan. Kircher gives an account, in his *Oedipus*, of the oriental traditions concerning the *Egyptian* kings. The same is done by *Fourmont* in his *reflexions critiques sur les histoires des anciens peuples*, where he cites the *Jewish* traditions concerning them from *Juchasim*, which differ very much from the *Arabic*. However it is evident, that these *Arabic* historians drew from *Jewish* sources, and intermixed the scriptural history in their narrations. It is undeniable, that the kings of antiquity had different names, some of them many, and those frequently changed; this, together with the different manner of pronouncing some names among different nations, according to their several languages, in which respect the *Greeks* took great liberties with oriental names, hath occasioned much confusion in the most ancient history, and in some cases hath rendered it extremely difficult, if not wholly impossible, to compare and make use of the traditions of several nations. *Reimman* in his *idea system antiq. litt. Ægyptiacæ*, gives a large catalogue of *Arabic* historians of *Egypt*, but which is not to be entirely depended upon. We may judge in how great reputation the *Egyptian* history or *Tarikh Mesr* of the celebrated *Jousaf ben Tagri Bardi*, which was translated into *Turkish* in the reign of the emperor *Selim*, still continues among the *Turks*, from this circumstance, that the translation of the abridgment of it, with the continuation of *Schamseddin Ahmed Ben Soliman Ben Kamal*, was one of the first books published from the *Turkish* printing-office erected at *Constantinople*. The great partiality of the compilers to the eastern historians and traditions, seems to have been only in opposition to the blind and extravagant contempt they are treated with; for else that partiality must be limited. Facts not heard of before may become more probable, merely from their being uncommon, than they are in themselves, and than they can remain after a narrow examination. The world would certainly lose more than it could gain, by exchanging the *Greek* and *Roman* for the oriental taste. As to these eastern accounts of *Egypt*, it is not only certain that all the *Arabic* historians were at a very unequal distance from those ancient times, but it is hard to conceive, how they should have better sources, records and original accounts of *Egypt*, than the *Grecians*, whose constant commerce with this nation and long possession of the country, must give them much greater advantages in this respect, than the *Arabs* could possibly have.

A P-

APPENDIX:

BEING

An EXAMINATION of the several opinions of those who pretend, that *Abraham's* posterity reigned in *Egypt*.

THE

CONTENTS.

THE opinions here to be examined, are divided into two Classes, § 1. *The* first *contains the opinion of those who hold, that the* Israelites *did rule over* Egypt; *on which occasion* Morgan's *opinion is considered,* § 2; *and after having shewn who the* Hycsos *were,* § 3, Morgan's *opinion is stated at large,* § 4, *and refuted,* § 5 *to* 7. Boivin's *opinion, and the grounds of it are stated,* § 8, *and refuted, both with respect to chronology,* § 9 *to* 11, *and to the passages of scripture quoted by him,* § 12 *to* 15. Lastly, *Mr.* Koch's *opinion is stated,* § 16, *and refuted,* § 17 *to* 20.—*The* second Class *comprehends the opinion of those who make others of* Abraham's *posterity, besides the* Israelites, *kings of* Egypt; *some giving that honour to* Esau's *descendants,* § 21, 22, *others to the* Ishmaelites, § 23 *to* 25.

A P-

APPENDIX:

BEING

An EXAMINATION of the several opinions of those who pretend, that *Abraham's* posterity reigned in *Egypt*.

SECT. I.

IT is very well known, of how great importance it is in explaning the books of holy writ, and vindicating their truth and divine authority, that the sacred writings, and the history of God's select people, be duly compared with the ancient accounts of the neighbouring nations; and with how much caution a narrative of facts, authorized by God himself, and needing no other testimony, ought to be secured against the danger of suffering by this comparison, and of being rather shaken than confirmed by the allegation of foreign evidence.

I flatter myself, therefore, that I shall have the ready approbation of the public for entering into an examination of this matter, and considering the different opinions of modern writers concerning the *reign ascribed to* Abraham's *posterity in* Egypt. These opinions may be divided into *two classes*. To the *first*, we refer such as hold, that the *Israelites* ruled some time in *Egypt*; and to the *second*, those who pretend, that another branch of *Abraham's ham's* posterity, descended either from *Esau* or *Ishmael*, were formerly the lords of that country. I shall therefore have two objects in view, and endevor to shew, *first*, that *Egypt* never was subject to the *Israelites*, and that none of that nation ever ruled there, which will be the point chiefly in question; and *secondly*, I shall consider somewhat more briefly, the pretended government of the *Idumeans* and *Ishmaelites* in *Egypt*.

SECT. II.

The first class comprehends particularly three opinions, which I have undertaken to examine. The *first* is advanced by *Morgan*, who, with a view to undermine the authenticity of *Moses's* writings, has (in his very long introduction, consisting of 121 pages, to the third volume of the *Moral philosopher, or superstition and tyranny inconsistent with theocracy; occasioned by the Rev. Dr.* Leland's *second volume of the divine authority of the Old and New Testament asserted, and the Rev. Mr.* Lowman's *dissertation on the civil government of the* Hebrews *by* Philalethes) attempted to prove, from *Manetho*, that the *Israelites* were those celebrated shepherds of antiquity, who, by various artifices, made themselves masters of the kingdom of *Egypt*, and, after a long and injurious possession of the country, and an oppressive course of government, were by force and with ignominy driven out, and thence removed to *Palestine*. This dangerous opinion, which *Morgan* published in 1740, was answered in the year following, by a piece intitled, *The ancient history of the* Hebrews *vindicated; or remarks on part of the third volume of the Moral Philosopher, wherein a particular account is given of the shepherds in* Egypt, *and of the origin of circumcision in that country; by* Theophanes Cantabrigiensis.

SECT.

SECT. III.

Before we proceed in our examination, we shall briefly state the antient history of the *Hycsos* or shepherd-kings, as they are called, which has given rise to this opinion, and mention the thoughts entertained on this subject by the most eminent modern writers, who have particularly applied themselves to the study of the antiquities of the *Hebrews* and the *Egyptians*. We are obliged to *Manetho* for the whole of this history. The memory of it is preserved in the two fragments we have of his writings. A shorter narrative of the steps these kings took in order to become masters of *Egypt* is contained in his account of the *Egyptian Dynasties* which is twice communicated to us by *George Syncellus* in the *Chronographia*, published by *Jacob Goar* and may be met with there, page 60 of the *Paris* edition; the one being taken from *Julius Africanus*, and the other out of *Eusebius*'s *Chronicon*. Both differ much from one another, the former placing the government of the shepherd-kings in the *fifteenth*, and the latter in the *seventeenth Dynasty*; and their departure from *Josephus*'s account, is taken notice of by *Syncellus*. *Flavius Josephus* has preserved to us a more *circumstantial* account of this matter, lib. 1. *contra Appionem* § 14—16. which he has borrowed from the second book of his *Egyptian* history, page 144; likewise § 26—33. according to *Haverkamp*'s edition, from which *Eusebius* also extracted a part, in the *Præpar. evangel.* l. 10. c. 13. p. 500. Some of the moderns apply this whole narration, entirely to the *Israelites*, and pretend, that the *Egyptian* kings, whose reigns coincide with the dwelling of the *Israelites* in *Egypt*, were distinguished by this name on account of their tyrannical government over these strangers; and that the foreign shepherds, who invaded *Egypt*, were no other than the *Israelites*,

elites, whose departure from that kingdom by the immediate interposition of God, brought such heavy judgments upon that realm, and so not only perpetuated the melancholy remembrance of this people, but excited an implacable hatred against them. So that it is not matter of wonder, if the *Egyptians* in succeeding times invented this account of a forcible irruption and expulsion of the *Israelites*, in order to blot out the dishonour of their ancestors, and lay the blame of all violence and crimes, of fruitless attempts and foolish hopes, on the *Israelites*. *Flavius Josephus* is the first patron of this opinion; whom a great number of moderns have followed. The principal of them are *Nich. Abram in Pharo*. l. 8. c. 3. *Herm. Witsius in Ægyptiacis* l. 3. c. 2. *Jacob Perizonius in originibus Ægypt.* c. 19. & 20. *Campeg. Vitringa comment. in Jesaiam in protheoria ad* c. 19. § 32. *John Franc. Buddeus in histor. ecclesiast. vet. test. period.* 1. *sect.* 3. § 20. and *John Alb. Bengel in ordine temp.* c. 3. § 5. p. 409. *Others*, on the contrary, are of opinion, that either the abode of the *Israelites* in *Egypt* must be placed in another period, or that they were very ill treated by these shepherd-kings, after they had the government, and were a very distinct people from them. This opinion is subscribed to by Sir *John Marsham in canon. chron.* § 8. p. 100. *Paul Pezron* in his *antiquité des tems retablie* p. 76. *Jos. Ren. Tournemine in supplem. ad Menoch.* p. 842. *Sam. Shuckford* in his *connection between the sacred and profane history of the world*, l. 7. vol. 2. p. 140. *Steph. Fourmont* in his *Reflexions critiques sur les histoires des anciens peuples* l. 3. c. 9. vol. 2. p. 131. and *Alph. des Vignoles* in his *Chronologie de l'histoire sainte*, vol. 1. l. 3. c. 1. p. 599; not to mention *Joseph Scaliger*, *Sam. Bochart*, *Usher*, *Herman Conring*, Sir *If. Newton*. *Rollin*, *Guyon* and the authors of *the Universal History*. This last opinion not only appears

appears to us more probable than the first, as it serves better to establish the credit of the rest of *Manetho*'s accounts, (except those incidental fictions wherewith the *Jews* are unjustly charged) and to justify the whole system of the Dynasties stated by him; but it may likewise discover to us the true reason of the hatred, the *Egyptians* bore against the shepherds, whereof mention is made *Gen.* 46. v. 33; though we cannot deny, that the difference in religion and the prevailing superstition of the *Egyptians*, must have given some, if not the greatest occasion, to this contempt and hatred. The limits of this piece, will not allow us to examine, whether or no these shepherds were *Arabs*, as *Manetho*, who doth not in this respect agree with himself, maintains; or *Phœnicians*, as *Africanus* and *Eusebius* pretend, on the authority of this very *Manetho*; or *Egyptians*, that dwelled in the marshy grounds of *lower Egypt*, as *Scaliger* conjectures; or whether they were those *Canaanites* that had been expelled by *Joshua*, as Sir *Isaac Newton* holds; or whether they were those *Horites* driven out by *Esau*'s posterity, as *Shuckford* pretends.

SECT. IV.

But to return to *Morgan*. He has treated his subject very artfully, considering how little he was acquainted with it, or with learning in general. But he might have embellished it to much greater advantage, and have prevented the imposition from being so easily discover'd, if he had ever read *Manetho*'s account in *Josephus* himself, or the depositions of those other writers that are mention'd there, *Tacitus*, *Justin*, *Martial*, and the inventions of others concerning the *Jews*; whereof *Christ. Worms in corruptis antiquitatum Hebræorum vestigiis apud Tacitum* &c. gives a large account. This disingenuous

ous writer proposes three things; first an history of *Egypt*, how it was enslaved by the patriarch *Joseph*, and usurped by his family; which narration he most impudently pretends to have taken out of *Moses*. Next he relates, corrupts and amplifies *Manetho*'s calumnies concerning the expulsion of the *Jews* by the native *Egyptians*, in such a manner, that it is visible, that he either has never read *Manetho*, but taken perhaps a casual and cursory view of what is quoted from him in *Shuckford*, *Marsham* and others, or that he treats profane authors as licentiously as he has done the sacred ones, in setting aside entirely that part of the holy scripture, which he calls supernatural, and in very plain terms charges with being mere invention. After having thus misrepresented the *Mosaic* history, and treated *Manetho*'s testimony in a manner suitable to his own purpose, he endeavours to persuade his readers that the *Israelites* certainly ruled over *Egypt*, which they had fraudulently conquer'd; that they were banished on account of their leprosy and infamous crimes, but that their departure was very different from that supernatural description of it given by *Moses*; that, after having left *Egypt*, of which he says, the conquest had even been meditated by *Abraham*, they colour'd their invasion of *Palestine*, with a divine promise, and introduced the superstition of their ancestors there by the assistance of *Moses*; whom, upon the credit of *Manetho*, he calls an *Egyptian*. These monstrous opinions are so very remote from all probability, contradict the very proofs he alledges for them, and betray so much ignorance, rashness and petulancy, scarce distinguishable from madness, that it requires no great pains to confute them. However, we shall briefly run through all the arguments alleged, in order to shew the reader, what honesty, and what weapons

pons are now-a-days made use of for attacking our most holy religion, and to what a miserable condition, learning and the history of times past, and even reason itself, must be brought, should the mockery of such men, who treat so ludicrously of sacred matters, be ever capable of raising attention.

SECT. V.

He sets out with undertaking to exhibit a short view of *Moses*'s account of the sojourning of the *Israelites* in *Egypt*, and insists previously, page 5, upon this principle, that no book or writing can prove itself, and ought not to be admitted upon its own authority, against the plainest marks and appearances of fraud, artifice and deception, unless we are willing to receive the *Koran* of the *Mohammedans* and the *Zerdust* of the *Persians*, as equally divine with *Moses*'s writings, and to submit to *Moses*, *Zoroaster* and *Mohammed*, as true prophets, all sent from God. This preamble, in which he gives a particular proof of his learning by confounding the *Persian Zendavest* with *Zerdust*, which is the name of *Zoroaster*, was doubtless intended to premonish his reader, what were his sentiments of the *Mosaic* history, lest he should ignorantly mistake what follows hereupon, as a confirmation and illustration of that history. The substance of what follows afterward is this: "*Joseph* a young "man of great art and incredible good fortune, had "the charge of his fellow prisoners in the king's "goal in the house of *Potiphar*, an eunuch, with "whose lady, it seems, he was reconciled. Here "he acted the part of an interpreter of dreams, "and laid the king's chief butler, whose restora-"tion to his former dignity he knew, under an "oath, to remember him to *Pharaoh*. But he, "jealous

" jealous of his disposition of mind, did not re-
" member him till two years after, when he intro-
" duced him to *Pharaoh*, just at a time when the
" latter was anxious about a dream which he want-
" ed to have interpreted. The butler introduced
" him, with a view to ingratiate himself both with
" the king and with *Joseph*, though to the mani-
" fest ruin of his country and the loss of its liberty.
" For, this politic slave perswaded *Pharaoh*, to
" appoint a general surveyor of provision over
" *Egypt*, who was to gather in and keep the fifth
" part of all the grain in the seven plentiful years,
" to guard against a famine, which was to follow
" thereupon during the seven succeeding years.
" Thus it became very easy for him, to obtain this
" place to himself and a great power annexed to it,
" so that *Pharaoh* reserved nothing to himself but
" the royal title, and resigned the whole govern-
" ment to this sooth-sayer. Upon this, *Joseph*
" caused an astonishing quantity of grain to be
" carried into the cities and castles, which of ne-
" cessity must have been fortified, in order to se-
" cure them against those, whom hunger might
" have prompted to commit robbery and violence.
" This buying up of corn in *Egypt* as well as in the
" neighbouring countries, which continued for
" seven successive years, caused vast dearth, and
" when it prevailed universally, the *Egyptians*
" were reduced to the loss of their substance,
" estates and liberty; for nothing was tender'd
" them for their subsistence and the sowing of their
" lands, till all *Egypt* was reduced to slavery, and
" the inhabitants made the King's bondmen, the
" priests only excepted; with whom *Joseph* had
" allied himself by marriage, and consequently
" taken care to enrich them. And by the whole
" of this conduct he at the same time first taught
" the

" the world, how a yoke is to be laid on freemen, " how a monarchical government may be intro- " duced, and how the people may be kept in awe " by arms and fortresses. However, he did not " forget the nation from whom he was descended, " on the contrary, he prepared matters for putting " them in possession of that kingdom which they " had long wish'd for. For, when the famine " became general, and very severe, he invited " his father and brethren, and the whole " patriarchal family to *Egypt*, where they pass'd " for shepherds, presented them with the most " fertile provinces, raised them to the highest " places of trust, subjected the provinces under " their command, and contrived things so, that, " in a short time, they might not fail to become " lords over *Egypt*. The King soon perceived the " irreparable mischief done to himself and the " whole country, which groaned heavily under " the insupportable slavery of the foreign " shepherds, as well as the priests, who were " now exalted to the highest dignities; he " therefore endeavor'd, tho' too late, to suc- " cour his distressed subjects, and to lessen the " power of *Joseph*. And it is on this account, " that no public funeral, like that which *Jacob* " was honoured with, was ordered for *Joseph*. " And, at the approach of his death, this wise " politician warned his people of the impending " change of the fortune they had till then enjoyed; " and, after giving them counsel how to maintain " themselves in possession, advised them to prepare " for an irruption into *Palestine*, whenever they " should be turned out, or find no hope of sup- " porting their power any longer against so nu- " merous a people. And these shepherds were " not wanting in any activity on their parts, but maintained "maitained themselves in the unwarrantable possession of the kingdom by arms, for the space of one hundred years, computed from the time when the successor of the King had attempted to shake off the *Hebrew* yoke, and during this time they cruelly oppressed the people, whom they had infected with the itch, leprosy, and nauseous eruptions, till they were at length, after long wars, overcome, and so much humbled, that, in all appearance, they must have been totally extirpated, had not *Moses*, who perfectly understood the *Egyptian* magic and incantations, by means of his magical wand, and astonishing plagues, which he brought all over *Egypt*, delivered them, and at last obtained their liberty; whereupon he, with the whole race of shepherds, endeavor'd to save themselves by flight."

To such a degree of impudence did this perfidious apostate from the doctrine he once preached himself arrive, that he quotes none but *Moses* as the author, and appeals to him as a witness of all that he relates and adds of his own invention. He reports, upon his credit, things which no one before himself ever discovered, and which none after him, with the utmost sagacity, ever will discover, unless he be very far advanced in this new art of converting a narrative, drawn up with a most noble simplicity, into a theatrical fiction; of extracting from it events which were never heard of, and of believing a delusion with their eyes open. We are therefore of opinion, that the reading of *Moses*'s narration will be quite sufficient for exploding these inventions; nor let any one apprehend, that he advances these facts upon the credit of *Manetho*, or perhaps some other foreign historian, and thus, at least, had some authority.

If

If we only give proper attention, we ſhall obſerve, with how much virulency this writer proceeds in that ſecond part of his attempt.

SECT. VI.

For, he endeavours there to ſhew, that the ſhepherds, mentioned by *Manetho*, are no other than the *Iſraelites*, and that the narration of that author is more conſiſtent than the *Moſaic* ſtory, which, according to him, not only gives a greater confirmation to *Manetho*, but is itſelf reſtored by him to its firſt accuracy and order. To this purpoſe he 1. denies, "That there ever was a people diſtinguiſhed by "the name of *Shepherds*, except the *Iſraelites*, who, "according to the teſtimony of *Moſes* himſelf, "publickly bore that name; 2. He appeals to a "conformity in both relations with reſpect to the "chief circumſtances, *viz.* that the ſhepherds, "through incredible artifice, without violence "and bloodſhed, made themſelves maſters of the "*Egyptian* realm, gariſon'd all the ſtrong places, "and cruelly waſted the country, till the natives, "whoſe patience was at length exhauſted, at-"tacked them in an hoſtile manner, and obliged "them to take to flight; 3. He ſays that *Manetho*, "in his narration, doth not vary from *Joſephus*, "tho' the latter expreſsly denies, that his anceſtors "had been afflicted with the leproſy; in which, "however, *Moſes* himſelf contradicts him, among "whoſe laws there are many to be met with, "wherein a method of curing the leproſy is pre-"ſcribed, beſides other regulations for preventing "this diſeaſe by frequent purifications; and in-"deed, it is by all antiquity agreed, that the *Iſ-*"*raelites* were plagued with this contagious and "hereditary diſeaſe." But how much this malicious reviler imposes on the reader, will appear upon our considering, 1. That both his pretences in the first article are invented and manifestly false. For, this illiterate man might have been convinced of his imposition or ignorance out of *Manetho* himself, who not only says of these shepherds in *Josephus*, that they were held by some to be *Arabs*, but likewise in *Africanus* and *Eusebius* cited in *Syncellus's Chronographia*, calls them *Phœnicians*; in case even he had not known those other vouchers in which mention is made of several people, who, on account of their living the life of shepherds, and their unsettled abode, are called *Nomades*, or *Scenites*, and may still be met with. But this denomination can no where be found to have been given to the *Israelites*, nor is it deducible from *Gen. ch.* xxxvii. 13, or *ch.* xlvi. 32, 33. For *Joseph*, who very exactly conformed himself to the constitution of the *Egyptian* government, subjected his brethren to a very ancient law, quoted by *Herodotus* and *Diodorus*, according to which none had liberty to settle in *Egypt*, without previously acquainting the magistrate with his profession, or ranking himself among one of the five orders, *viz.* that of the priests, soldiers, husbandmen, shepherds, or mechanics. See the *Universal History*, Vol. I. 2. As for the second article, this absurd writer would have been able to give his narrations a more regular appearance, had he read *Manetho* himself. For, he would not have limited the abode of the *Israelites* to two hundred and ten years, and repeated the same at different times, had he known that *Manetho* assigns almost six hundred years to the government of the shepherds in *Egypt*. He would likewise have had the most distinguished modern chronologers, who ascribe a longer abode to the *Israelites* in *Egypt* on his side. Besides, *Moses* no where

expresly

expresly fixes a term of two hundred and ten years, and the incredible propagation of the race of shepherds, descending from one parent, may certainly be far more easily comprehended by allowing a longer time; especially if we consider, that, after the death of *Joseph*, they were continually intangled in wars. It is plain, therefore, that *Morgan*'s ignorance was the occasion of these defects and improbabilities. In the remaining part of his story, we find a great number of palpable falshoods proposed in a most impudent manner. The *Israelites* came into *Egypt* after a previous invitation; whereas *Manetho*'s shepherds invaded that kingdom by surprize; the former, he tells us, consisted of a small number, and made themselves masters of *Egypt* by tricks and artifices; whereas the latter by open force, and with hostile troops, brought the people under their yoke, who being seized with a sudden panic, were thus prevented from making resistance, and conquered without effusion of blood. The first are reported to have been given to superstition, and that they had first made use of priests to carry on their designs; whereas we read of the latter that they demolished the temples, threw down the idols and subverted the whole religious worship. The first occupied but one single province in *Egypt*; whereas the latter inhabited and destroyed all *lower Egypt*. Not to mention the disparity that occurs in the numbers, reported by *Moses* and *Manetho*, and with respect to the kings and their successors, in which they very widely differ from one another 3. The *third* article is the most amazing piece of effrontery in the whole. *Manetho* is so far from making these foreign shepherds suspected of leprosy, that he rather ascribes this nauseous distemper to the *Egyptians*, and says, that a great many of their *Lepers* went over to the ſhepherds, and departed with them. *Joſephus* likewiſe clears them from this calumny, and in the ſequel entirely frees them from any ſuſpicion of Leproſy. That the Leproſy was a common diſtemper in *Egypt*, or that the *Elephantiaſis* ſo called, was natural to this kingdom more than to any other country, ſhould not have been unknown to this writer, who ſo oſtentatiouſly pretends to the knowledge of antiquity. For, *Lucretius*, l. 6, *Pliny*, l. 6. § 5, *Marcellus Empiricus*, l. 19. deſcribe this *Elephantiaſis* as a diſtemper quite peculiar to the *Egyptians*.

Eſt Elephas morbus qui propter flumina Nili
Gignitur Ægypto in media, neque præterea uſquam.

And the moſt modern travels of *Maillet*, *Pocock* and others, mention this cutaneous malady, as a diſtemper owing to the climate or ſome quality of that country. What *Flavius Joſephus* mentions on this ſubject, is of no weight, as he appears not to have been willing in general to contradict all that is reported by *Manetho*, but rather to embrace whatever might contribute towards proving the great antiquity of his nation: However, he differs in all thoſe points in which this vain ſuperficial writer endeavoured to correct *Moſes* out of *Manetho*.

SECT. VII.

The concluſions, which *Morgan* draws from the above, fall to the ground, together with thoſe arguments on which he founded them, and are of the ſame ſtamp with what has been hitherto quoted. His opinion is, that *Abraham*, *Iſaac* and *Jacob* had never ſo much as thought of taking poſſeſſion of the *Land of Promiſe*, of which God had given them hopes, becauſe they did not like this barren and uncultivated country, and on the contrary, were

were much more intent in their views upon *Egypt*. This he endeavours to prove; in the first place by *Abraham*'s journey into *Egypt*, of which mention is made, *Gen.* 12: here this calumniating spirit ascribes to him such an anxious desire after this country, as even to prostitute the honour of his wife to gratify his ambition. *Secondly*, because they never shewed any earnest desire to possess themselves even of the least part of *Palestine*. *Thirdly*, that *Joseph* neglected to make use of the *Egyptian* armies under his command, for conquering this country in favour of his kindred, which he very easily might have done, had he had an inclination for it, and not been rather willing to procure something better for them—All these illusions will vanish, upon consulting *Moses*'s account, from which nevertheless he pretends to have taken every thing. For *Moses* alledges quite another reason of *Abraham*'s journey into *Egypt*; he gives us likewise a far more advantageous description of *Palestine*, and contradicts the neglect imputed to the patriarchs in not taking possession of the *Land of Promise*, *Gen.* chap. xxiii. 9. and the following; likewise chap. xxxiii. 10. chap. 49, 30. and the following; and chap. l. 13. He, on the contrary, mentions of the patriarchs, that they never had given up their intention and hope of once possessing this *Land*, *Gen.* chap. xlviii. 21. chap. xlix. 13. chap. l. 24, 25; though they waited with patience to obtain from the hands of the same God, who had made them this promise and raised this hope in them, as well as acquainted them with the delay of its completion, an appointment of the right time when they should become possess'd of it. On this testimony we have certainly more cause to rely, than on the ribaldry of this impious man, who stands so convicted of imposture and ignorance, that scarce any further proofs can be judged necessary.

SECT. VIII.

I proceed now to the second opinion, which is founded indeed on no better grounds; but shews more respect to the testimony of holy writ, and savours much less of a dissolute libertine disposition of mind. I shall therefore examine it with all possible candor. We find it in the *Histoire de l'academie royale des inscriptions & des belles lettres* tom. II. p. 31 to 52, and the author of it was *Lewis Boivin*, who distinguished himself by rashly inventing opinions, by obstinacy and moroseness in defending them, and by a general biass to singularity of sentiments, all which qualities were taken notice of in the panegyric bestowed on this extraordinary genius by his fellow members and collegues; see of this *l'histoire suivie de l'acadamie royale des inscript.* tom. II. p. 90 to 109. He holds, in substance, "that "the *Israelites* continued in *Egypt* 430 years, as "appears from *Exod.* xii. 40, *Gen.* xv. 13, "*Acts* vii. 6. That this time of their abode was "divided by three great periods, in which their "condition had varied. The *first* comprehends "71 years, or the time when they attended the "calm and peaceable employment of shepherds "under *Jacob* and *Joseph*; the *second*, 259 years, "when they ruled the conquer'd kingdom of "*Egypt* under *Ephraim*, *Beriah*, *Kephah*, *Resepb*, "*Thelah* and *Thahan*, 1 *Chron.* vii. 23—25, or "under *Salati*, *Beon*, *Apachna*, *Apophi*, *Jania*, "and *Asse*, which are *Egyptian* names given to the "same persons by *Josephus*, who has taken them "from *Manetho*; the *third* period contains 99 "years and two months, during which their fortune being miserably changed they lived in bondage

"dage, oppreſſion and captivity, under *Landan*, "*Ammihud*, *Eliſama*, *Nun*, and *Joſhua* 1 *Chron.* "vii. 26, 27. ſo that theſe thirteen generations "amount to 430 years, allowing, according to "the uſual computation of chronologers, 30 years "to each generation". Our laborious inventor, in order to give an air of probability to this threefold change of their condition, from ſhepherds, to kings, and then to captives, appeals firſt to *Manetho*, and the concurrent teſtimony of *Joſephus*. But leſt the ſilence obſerved in this reſpect in holy writ, ſhould prove prejudicial to his ſyſtem, he, in the ſecond place, quotes ſome books mentioned there, *viz.* the *Book of the wars of the Lord*, *Numb.* xxi. 14, the *Book of Jaſher*, *Joſhua* x. 13, and 2 *Samuel* i. 18, which containing a full account of this government and theſe wars of the *Iſraelites*, *Moſes*, for that reaſon, had paſs'd them over in ſilence. In the *third* place, he pleads, that there are not wanting ſcriptural paſſages, which in his opinion plainly allude to theſe circumſtances. He quotes for this purpoſe, *Jeremiah* xxxi. 9. where *Ephraim* is called God's firſt-born; likewiſe *Gen.* xlix. 22—28, where *Joſeph*, on account of the enſuing ſhepherd-government which was to ariſe from his family, receives the name of *Shepherd and the ſtone of Iſrael*; further 1 *Chron.* vii. 20—24, where the overthrow of the children of *Ephraim*, and the building of three cities by his daughter which was conſequent upon it, cannot be underſtood, as he pretends, without theſe wars, which the *Ephraimites* carried on with their neighbours the men of *Gath*; wherefore that very country hath alſo been called *Goſhen* or *Goethſen*; and, *laſtly*, the victory of *Vaheb* and the conquering of the whole country, mention'd *Numb.* xxi. 14. He likewiſe quotes *Pſalm* lxxviii, 9—12, where mention is made of ſeveral battles and marvellous things that happen'd before the going-out of *Egypt*, and punishments inflicted on the *Israelites* on account of their falling to idolatry, which they are upbraided with, *Joshua* xxiv. 23. He alledges the 105th *Psalm*, where it is said in the 23d verse, that the *Israelites* multiplied more than their enemies that stood up against them; and 1 *Chron.* iv. 18, where it is said, that *Mered* married the daughter of *Pharaoh*, which, he says, is quite incredible, unless we take her to have been a daughter of the dethron'd king.

SECT. IX.

Boivin's opinion has been refuted by two of his collegues; first by *Ant. Banier*, whose observations upon him and his antagonists may be met with in the above-cited *Histoire de l'Academie*, &c. and afterwards, by *Steph. Fourmont* in his *Reflexions critiques sur les anciens peuples*, livr. 3. chap. ix. vol. 2. p. 132. Yet notwithstanding these refutations, several points remain still to be inquired into. To proceed in order, we shall begin with inquiring into the time, which the *Israelites* spent in *Egypt*. For if it can be proved, even that this was but a small space in comparison, and not half so long as is pretended, the arguments built upon it will fall to the ground. Many have very much inlarged the time of the abode of the *Israelites* in *Egypt*, for no other reason than to make out the 430 years which are here taken for granted; the chief of these are, besides *Genebrardus*, *John Gerhard Vossius in Isagoge chronol. sacræ diss.* 8, and *Nic. Abram in Pharo veteris testam.* ch. 7; the opinion of the latter we find reported in the *Supplementa ad Menochium* p. 428 with *Jos. Ren. Tournemine*'s confirmations. We have however a much greater number of learned men, who have with more accuracy examined this matter;

matter; among these are, besides *Lyranus*, *Caietanus*, *Ar. Montanus*, *Lud. Capellus*, and *John Meyer*, *Dionysius Petavius de doctr. temporum*, l. 9. cap. 25. *Usher in chronol. sacra & profana*, l. 9. cap. 25. *Shuckford in his connection of the sacred and prophane writers*, vol. 2. l. 9. p. 313. *Usher in chronolog. sacr. & prof.* and *Joh. Alb. Bengel in ord. temp.* c. ii. §. 6. p. 61; to whose opinion we subscribe for the following reasons. St. *Paul* mentions in express terms *Gal.* iii. 17, that the law was given four hundred and thirty years after the promise made to *Abraham* and his seed; whence it follows, that this number of years do not commence from *Jacob's* journey into *Egypt*, but from *Abraham's* going out of *Chaldæa*. Moreover *Kohath*, who was born before the *Israelites* went into *Egypt*, as well as his younger brother *Merari*, *Gen.* xlvi. 11. compared with verse 8, lived *one hundred and thirty three* years; his son *Amram* came to the age of *one hundred and thirty seven*; and his grandson *Moses* was *eighty* years old about the time of the *Israelites* departure from *Egypt*, *Exod.* vii. 7. These years aggregated amount to *three hundred and fifty*; from which sum no inconsiderable part falls away, or is to be deducted for the years *Kohath* spent in *Palestine*, as well as for the years of *Amram*, computing those before the death of his father (for some of his brethren were born after him) as well as those after the birth of his son *Moses*, who, at least, was not a posthumous child, but perhaps even born in the life time of his grandfather *Kohath*, as may be gathered from *Hebr.* xi. 23; whose sister *Jochabed*, a daughter of *Levi*, born in *Egypt*, *Numb.* xxvi. 59, was his mother. (Compare *Numb.* chap. xxvi. 59, with *Gen.* chap. xlvi. 11.) This genealogical account of *Moses*, reduces the time of the abode of the *Israelites* in *Egypt* to very narrow limits, at least it can never exceed three hundred years; and it it certainly agrees, as to the number of descendants, with most of the other families, which may be seen by consulting *Numb.* xxvii. *Joshua* vii. 18. 1. *Chron.* ii. 18, *Matth.* i. 2, 3. And this computation of ours particularly receives an additional confirmation by considering the posterity of *Hezron*: For *Hezron* was born in *Palestine*, *Gen.* xlvi. 12; in the 60th year of his age he married the daughter of *Machir*, 1 *Chron.* ii. 21, by whom he had *Segub*; whose son *Jair* conquer'd in the 40th year after the going-out of *Egypt*, the cities of *Bashan*, *Numb.* xxxii. 41, *Deuteron.* iii. 14. The *Acts of the Apostles* too confirm this computation, for it is said there, ch. xiii. 20. that from the time of the call of the patriarchs, about four hundred and fifty years had passed till the partition of *Palestine*; which number of years may be made out by adding the four hundred years which passed from the birth of *Isaac* to the going out of the *Israelites*, to those forty years, which they spent upon their journey through the wilderness; and five years more that passed before the partition was taken in hand, which must have been some years negociating, according to *Joshua*, ch. xi. 23. ch. xiii. 15. ch. xviii 1. ch. xix. 51. ch. xxi. 33. 35. The arguments made use of for doubling the said two hundred and fifteen, or rather the two hundred and ten years of their abode in *Egypt*, and extending them to four hundred and thirty years, are of no weight, at least those on the other side greatly preponderate. If we especially compare, together, as we ought to do, those three passages of *Exod.* xii. 40. *Gen.* xv. 13. *Acts of Apostles* vii. 6; we shall find that they comprehend the whole time of their bondage and journey. If *Achior*'s evidence be alleged from *Judith* v. 8, it proceeds from misunderstanding, *Exod.* xii. 40, and would prove nothing, even though the same should be found in

the

the *Greek* text, where neverthelefs nothing of that kind occurs. The incredible multiplication of the people, which happen'd in fo fhort a time, may be very well accounted for, where fuch account is properly requifite; on the other hand, this circumftance is of no ufe to *Boivin*, who is obliged to admit a far more incredible multiplication to have happen'd only during a fpace of feventy-one years, in cafe he will bring together a fufficient army for conquering all *Egypt*, which, according to *Manetho*'s report, muft have confifted of two hundred and forty thoufand fighting men. An opinion like this, can never be made to agree with the chronology of holy writ, nor are his other arguments, which we fhall now but briefly handle, of weight fufficient to convince us.

SECT. X.

Boivin agrees indeed fomewhat better with *Manetho* than *Morgan*, but not entirely. The difference with refpect to time, is very great in both authors, and they differ likewife confiderably with refpect to the manner in which the conqueft was brought about. *Manetho* fays, that it happen'd fuddenly, unawares, and without any effufion of blood; whereas *Boivin* pretends, that they fpent well nigh feventy years in it, and that the overthrow of the *Ephraimites*, had produced a bloody victory attended with miracles. The difpofition of the conquerors is likewife very differently defcribed by thefe writers; the *firft* reprefents them as a cruel people and enemies to the *Egyptian* worfhip; and the latter, as very humane and inclining to the *Egyptian* idolatry, in which they were at length involved. *Laftly*, this people's going out of *Egypt* is not lefs differently exprefs'd by both. *Jofephus*'s teftimony, to which *Boivin* appeals,

peals, favours him very little. For, besides what has been already said (§ 6.) concerning this writer, nothing is mention'd in his *Jewish Antiquities* of those things which our author alledges, though it is scarce to be believed, he would have pass'd them over in silence had he ever given the least credit to these things, as *Manetho*'s account was not unknown to him and others.

SECT. XI.

As to the argument drawn from the silence observed in holy writ, which *Boivin* denies, knowing how much it affects his new opinion, the denial of it would not much avail him, even tho' all the supports which he has gathered with so much labour to gloss over his cause, should appear quite unexceptionable, and though the passages he quotes from scripture were to be understood in the manner he explains them. We shall make no objection against the *Book of the Wars of the Lord*, nor the *Book of Jasher*, nor some *Hymns* mention'd here and there in holy writ, which are quoted as pieces really extant. We are willing to grant it, and may do it without impeaching the uncorrupted perfection of holy writ; and indeed the passages expresly quoted oblige us to admit that these writings were distinct from those which now compose the body of the holy scripture; nor shall we contradict their contents, which, in all probability, were historical. *John Christopher Wolf* may be consulted on this head, in his *Biblioth. hebr.* vol. 2. l. 1. § 1. p. 9. and § 4. particularly § 1, 5, 6. p. 211, and the following, where the different opinions and their assertors are cited in great numbers. Yet, whatever stress *Boivin* may have laid on this support, it will be found, notwithstanding all that has been granted, that it will

will be rather against, than for him. For, supposing that it was true that the throne of *Egypt* had been filled successively by six *Israelites*; supposing further, that *Vabeb* had obtained the great victory related by *Boivin*, and that it had been attended with all the miracles and marvellous consequences he pretends; supposing likewise, that all this had been reported in those lost writings, which, it is true, may be conjectur'd, but never can be proved; and supposing *lastly*, that all those passages quoted by *Boivin* and interpreted by him to the advantage of his cause, did really relate thereto, which is undoubtedly far from being the case, as shall be made appear hereafter: There remain still two chief difficulties to solve with respect to this silence, which make his whole allegation extremely improbable. *In the first place*, it cannot be imagined, that *Moses* should have pass'd over entirely in silence, such a considerable and important part of the history of the *Israelites*, comprehending events that had happen'd during the space of some hundred years. Whereas we may clearly gather from the writings of his which are extant, that his principal view in books, which he was divinely authorized and directed to compile, was, to record in writing not only the most ancient accounts of the origin of the human race, but chiefly that of the *Israelites* and the fate and revolutions that happen'd to the latter, down to his own time. Now it is not likely that he should have lost sight of this intent by omitting so remarkable an event, nor could it ever be excused in him, chiefly if an account of it was contained in writings that were still extant in his time. He would have acted directly against this intent, had he passed over such a considerable space of time without mentioning a single word or alledging a reason for

for it; nay much more in relating the occasion of the oppression of the *Israelites* in *Egypt* quite differently; which could not but make the credibility of his reports, with respect to other events, very suspicious and precarious. *In the second place*, it is still less to be imagined, that *Joshua* and the other men of God, that lived in the following times, nay God himself, should not have mention'd these memorable revolutions attended with many miracles, in the several speeches which were made to the *Israelites* either for rebuking, instructing, or comforting them, and which are handed down to us. And can we believe, that on these occasions, they should not have been more frequently and explicitly mention'd, than in the passages quoted by *Boivin*, which shall be examined hereafter? whereas we find innumerable instances of mention being made in those speeches, of the journey of the patriarchs into *Egypt*, the *Egyptian* bondage, the triumphant going out of *Egypt* and the wonderful taking possession of the *Land of Promise*.

SECT. XII.

We shall now consider the passages quoted (§ 8.) from holy writ. It is neither necessary nor warrantable to take occasion from the words of *Numb*. xxi. 14, 15. concerning the *Book of the wars of the Lord* mention'd there, to speak of an *Egyptian* king, named *Vabeb*, as the same place manifestly shews, that the words of that passage relate to an event that happen'd without the borders of *Egypt*, that is to say, in the land of *Moab* or the river *Arnon*, and so it is more probable that *Vabeb* was the name of a conquer'd city there, than that of a king. As for the other passage from *Joshua* x. 12, 13. it is so far from proving that the miracle of of the sun's standing still and the prolongation of the day, for the destruction of *Vaheb and his Army* by the *Israelites*, should have been written in the *Book of Jasher*, that the immediate following 14th verse rather expresly testifies, that there had never been an instance of such a miracle, either before or after the time of *Joshua*, and that there never had been a day like that. The *third* passage from 2 *Samuel*. i. 18. contains nothing from which it might be proved, that the *Book of Jasher* contained an account of the government of the *Israelites* and their victories over the *Egyptians*. The *fourth* passage from *Jeremiah* xxxi. 9. only confirms the promise given to the *Israelites* of their restoration from their misery, and mentions the particular blessings bestowed on the *Ephraimites*; whereof so indisputable an account is to be met with in holy writ, that there is no necessity, for the sake of shewing the right meaning of the words of God, to invent and ascribe to this people a particular kingdom in *Egypt*. The *fifth* passage taken from *Gen.* xlix. 24. has but very little chance of adding the least degree of probability to the opinion in question, whether we understand the words referred to, of *Joseph* himself, who by the direction and power of the almighty God of *Jacob*, was become a shepherd and stone of *Israel*, to whom his brethren and their families owed their preservation, security, life and fortune, according to chap. xlvii. 12, 25. chap. l. 21. or whether we interpret them of *Joseph*'s posterity, which was to produce some valiant heroes, who were to charge themselves with the care of all the happiness and prosperity of *Israel*, such as were *Joshua*, *Gideon*, *Jair*, *Jephtha*, *Abdan*, not to mention the kings of *Israel* from and after *Jeroboam*. Or the words may likewise be understood of the *Messiah*, to whom the name of the *Shepherd* and

Stone

Stone of Israel belongs by way of eminence, and of whom *Jacob*, in his prophecies of the future fate and fortune of his other sons, makes mention, though he was not to descend from them, chap. xlix. 18. Besides, *Boivin*'s interpretation cannot be made to agree with the other part of this prophecy, which relates to the sway of the tribe of *Judah*; nor with *Jacob*'s omitting to mention any thing of this nature, in his declaring the prerogatives of the tribe of *Ephraim*; which, without so much as hinting a particular government or kingdom, he solely places in a speedy and numerous increase of his family.

SECT. XIII.

The next following passages quoted by *Boivin*, appear to be more in his favour; but, however, are far from being able to bewilder us. The *sixth*, taken from 1 *Chron*. vii. 20, especially, comprehends three points, which we shall examine; as this author flatters himself they tend greatly to the support of his opinion. The first is the overthrow of the *Ephraimites*, mentioned in the 20th and 21st verses; which, it must be allowed, has perplexed many interpreters, and is certainly attended with some difficulty. For, not to mention the intricacy of the genealogical register, which *John Peter Grünenberg*, in *tabulis sacr. genealog*. tab. 14. has taken much pains to adjust and amend, but which has been really amended by *John Henr. Michaelis in annot. uberior. in hagiographa*, Vol. 3. p. 369. the historical account itself of this action and overthrow of the *Ephraimites*, has been differently expounded by the interpreters. There are many *Jews*, who place the time of its having happened either shortly before the departure of the *Israelites* out of *Egypt*, or immediately after it;

it; the former are supported by the authority of the *Targum* (a) on the *Song of Solomon*, chap. ii. ver. 7. in which *Moses* is represented exhorting the *Israelites* to make no irruption before the expiration of the forty years, which were prescribed for the punishment of their sedition and murmuring; upon which occasion, he is said to have inforced his exhortation by alleging the unfortunate attempt of the *Ephraimites*, who thirty years before had made an irruption out of *Egypt* into the country of the *Gathites*, and suffered a great overthrow. Others are of opinion, that the very rash expedition of the *Ephraimites*, undertaken without *Moses*'s consent, was meant in the above passage quoted from the first of *Chronicles*; and *David Kimchi*, one of the advocates for this opinion, seems so confident that his interpretation is right, that, from the comparison he makes between *Numb*. i. 33. and ch. xxvi. 37. he judges, eight thousand *Ephraimites* to have been slain at that time. But, unfortunately for this last opinion, upon comparing *Numb*. xiv. 44, 45. with *Deut*. i. 44, we may gather, that the business in question concerns quite another country, and that those who caused this overthrow, were different enemies from those above: And both opinions are quite overset by the express mention of *Ephraim*'s mourning, and the birth of *Bariah* in 1 *Chron*. vii. 22, 23; both which events, it is impossible, can fall in with the time of the departure out of *Egypt*. For this reason, some interpreters, upon better grounds, place this overthrow in the first years of the abode of the *Israelites* in *Egypt*; tho' they cannot agree who occasion'd it. Some charge the *Ephraimites* with it, among whom are, besides the *Jewish* authors, *Lavater*, *Grotius*, *Calvius*, *Calmet*, *Berruyer*, and several others; whilst

(a) The *Targum* is a name which the *Jews* give to their *Chaldee* glosses and paraphrases on the Scripture.

others, upon more probable grounds, take the *Gathites* for the authors; among whom the principal are *Lightfoot*, *Clericus*, *Gussetius*, and *Michaelis*, who prove their opinion not only from the words in which this event is recorded, but from the well known condition of this people. Of these proofs, taken from the text itself, the following are worth our notice. In the *first* place, immediately after the account of this irruption, mention is made of the *Gathites* without any intermediate mention of the *Ephraimites*. *Secondly*, The journey from *Palestine* to *Egypt* may be called a *Going down*, rather than the journey from *Egypt* to *Palestine* a *Going up*. As for the proofs taken from the condition or state of the *Gathites*, they have shewn that the *Jews*, at that time, were still a weak people, and under dependance, and only had a great superfluity of cattle, which the *Gathites* were in want of, tho' they took by fraud or violence whatever they could meet with upon the borders. Now all this can be of no advantage to *Boivin*, unless we have a mind to make of the *Gathites* another people, *viz*. *Philistines*; which shall be considered in the sequel. He will gain as little support from the second part of this controverted passage, where it is said, that *Sherah*, *Ephraim*'s daughter, had built three cities, *Beth-horon the nether*, and *the upper*, and *Uzzen-sherah*. For the two first-named cities, without the least doubt, belonged to *Palestine*, and were part of *Ephraim*'s portion, according to 1 *Chron*. vi. 8, *Joshua* x. 10, xvi. 3—5, xviii. 13, 14. which may be conjectured likewise of the last city, as no author has ever mentioned one of that name in *Egypt*. *Sherah* also, may very well have been one of *Ephraim*'s posterity, and perhaps a daughter of *Bariah*, to whom the beginning of the 24th verse of the above 1 *Chron*. vii. seems to relate, and she might, nevertheless, be called a daughter of

Ephraim.

Ephraim. The *third* point of *Boivin*'s argument, taken from this passage, is of less difficulty than the others, and entirely founded on ill-grounded conceits and inventions. The country of *Goshen* never was a part either of *upper Egypt*, or the *Arabian Egypt*, nor did it receive its name from a city called *Goeth*. It always was placed in *lower Egypt*; which, as well as the derivation and signification of the name *Goshen*, hath been very learnedly discussed by Mr. *Paul Ernst Jablonsky*, in his academical dissertations *de terra Gosen*, chiefly in the 6th and 7th dissertation. Nor is there any room for inventing any other city of the name of *Gath*, besides that famous and powerful one of the *Philistines*, so called, whereof so frequent mention is made in holy writ, and whose inhabitants fell upon the *Ephraimites*. We cannot however deny, that there appears some difficulty with respect to the 21st verse, where they are said to have been natives of *Egypt*. For the words, *that were born in that land*, can neither be understood of the *Ephraimites* born in *Egypt*, nor of the *Gathites* born in *Canaan*, nor of the *Ephraimites* born in *Palestine*. The last would certainly be false, and the two first might have been understood of either, without such a particular description. 'Tis therefore to be supposed, that some of the *Gathites* had settled in *Egypt*, which country was always open to strangers, tho' for some time shut to the *Grecians* in the earliest times. 'Tis likely that the septennial famine was the occasion of their resorting to *Egypt*, and that their children, in their return from that country, were those that overthrew the *Ephraimites*. But be this as it will, at least every other circumstance of this passage is so clear and evident, that no one, who is not particularly inclined to make a parade of new opinions, need either object any thing further

 against

against what has been said, or seek for grounds upon which to invent a particular kingdom or sovereignty of the *Israelites*, or force a long story from a word manifestly falsely derived.

SECT. XIV.

The *seventh* passage quoted from *Psalm* lxxviii. is likewise a very weak support to *Boivin*'s opinion. Though the *Chaldean* interpreter holds, that the 8th verse alludes to the rash irruption of the *Ephraimites* into *Palestine*, which is said to have happened shortly before the going out of *Egypt*, and is invented from 1 *Chron*. vii. 21; and though this interpreter has, besides the *Jews*, several other learned men on his side, yet there is no doubt that the author of this psalm had an eye to the times subsequent to the going out of *Egypt*, in which this tribe was, on many occasions, distinguished by its pride and temerity. So that we may either, with *Kimchi*, apply this passage to that rebellious attempt mentioned, *Numb*. xiv. in which, for ought we know, this tribe may have led the van; or we may, with *Seb. Schmid*, suppose it to relate to their impetuous disposition of mind described in *Judg*. viii. 1. and xii. 1—6. What follows in the 11th and 12th verses, is of no weight against this application, because their defection from God is there only described as the more inexcusable, because, in former times, they had had so many opportunities of experiencing God's providence and power, and been eye-witnesses of so many miracles. We need therefore no other miracles, for explaning this passage, than those which were performed by the hands of *Moses* at the departure of the *Israelites* out of *Egypt*. As for the perfidy and crimes wherewith the *Israelites* are upbraided in the fol-

lowing

lowing verses, they, without doubt, relate to their ungrateful conduct after they left *Egypt*; which *Moses* has very fully described, without even omitting the violent inclination of this people to the *Egyptian* worship, and other idolatries, and which the other sacred writers frequently expose, in representing to us their conduct in the wilderness during the forty years. Thus there is no apparent necessity why, for the sake of explaning this psalm, we should have recourse to a fictitious kingdom of the *Israelites* in *Egypt*, which is pretended to have been afterwards destroyed on account of their introducing a foreign idolatrous worship.

SECT. XV.

The eighth argument, taken from *Psalm* cv. 23, is such, as may easily be answered by comparing it with *Exod*. i. 9—20. Besides, the multiplication of the *Israelites* becomes subject to still greater difficulties, if we allow that so early as in the 71st year after their entering *Egypt*, they were more numerous and stronger than their enemies. The last passage quoted by *Boivin* from 1. *Chron*. iv. 18. can never make for his opinion, unless we will admit in support of it a mere fiction; 'tis even doubtful, whether or no *Boivin*'s opinion deserves much preference before that insipid fable of the *Jews*, by which they make *Caleb* out of *Mared*, *Jochabed* out of *Judijah*, and the daughter of *Pharaoh*, who received *Moses* and his brethren and sisters, out of *Bithia*. At least both are founded on equal grounds, and do not in any manner, excepting only the bare name of *Pharaoh*, affect the present case. Let us only suppose, that a certain *Jew* bore this *Egyptian* name, which it is possible, may have happen'd more than once; and neither of these fables will appear of any weight against us.

SECT. XVI.

I come now to the *third* opinion, which I shall examine with greater exactness, as it has the reverend Mr. *Jacob Koch* for its author, whose respect for the divine truth, and unwearied application in removing difficulties started against it, deserve the utmost esteem, though we cannot subscribe to his opinion in the present case, and could have wished, he had had more recourse to learned authors, and been more cautious and diffident of himself, and less fertile in inventions and conjectures. We shall first of all give his opinion, and afterwards set forth the reasons we have for not assenting to it. The opinion is to be met with in his *Pharos, or an unexpected dawn of Light among the thickest darkness of the earliest* Egyptian *accounts*, published in 1741, in which he has endeavour'd to clear up these ancient accounts. The substance of his doctrine is, that *Manetho*'s shepherds were *Israelites*, but their kings, *Egyptians*; among these he numbers, 1. *Salatis*, who he pretends was the *Osiris* killed by his brother *Typhon*, the *Concharis Silites*, likewise the same *Pharaoh*, who exalted the patriarch *Joseph*, and intrusted him with the administration of all his affairs, whom he likewise calls *Saophis*, *Seesaophis*, *Soris Syphis*, *Use Ramasses*, and *Thusimares*. 2. *Banan* or *Orus*, *Mustis*, *Othonon*, under whom *Manasses* was in high esteem, who is likewise called *Ramasse Menes*, *Ramasse Vaphres*. 3. *Pammus Archontes*, or *Phius*, *Apachna*, under whom *Ramasse Seos* raised himself. 4. *Apappus* the great, *Phiops* or *Apaphes*, under whom lived *Janias* or *Jannes* the High Priest, and *Sethos*, a royal prince, or or *Ramasses Tubartes*. 5. *Chescus Ocarus* or *Assis*, *Montesuphis* or *Aseth*, who was drowned in the *Red Sea*. He adds, that these kings had been succeeded by *Nitrocris*, a woman of *Jewish* extraction, married to *Ramasses Tubartes*, whom she survived. After God had destroyed the *Egyptian* army, by the means not only of those unclean *Israelites*, who, not having been permitted to eat of the Paschal-lamb, had remained in *Egypt*, but likewise by the mixed multitude descended from intermarriages of both nations, whereof a part had followed *Moses*, *Exod*. xii. 38, and returned to *Egypt* after many seditious practices, *Levit*. xxiv. 10. *Numb*. xi. 4. this woman had possessed herself of the throne, governed the *Egyptians* with cruelty, and threatening them with the return of the *Israelites*, kept them in awe, even disposing them to circumcision. This had given occasion to the song of the Leprosy of the *Israelites*, though those that left *Egypt*, had been entirely free from this distemper, and such as were subject to it, never left that country notwithstanding the fabulous account of *Manetho* on this head. This celebrated author attempting from § 40 to 48, to prove his opinion, adds, for that purpose, an interpretation of an inscription out of *Manetho*, whose accounts of the most ancient *Egyptian* kings, as well as those given by *Eratosthenes* and *Syncellus*, he represents to consist of various collections of inscriptions, wherein every thing is falsely turned into proper names. This inscription is conceived in the following words: *Achenchres Rathotis Acheres Armais Ramesses*, *Armesses*, *Miamum*, *Amenophis*; which is thus interpreted: *The Brethren of a foreign Woman have excited the last Terror. To wit Aramæa*, i. e. the *Israelitish Woman*, *the Wife of Ramesses*, *has subdued the country of* Egypt, *after Amenophis was drowned in the Sea.*

 He

He conjectures besides this, that *Sherah*, of whom mention is made 1 *Chron.* vii. 24, was married to a *Palestine* prince, and that therefore this marriage of an *Egyptian* prince with an *Israelitish* woman, had nothing in it that could seem improbable.

SECT. XVII.

As we are about to shew the reasons which hinder us from subscribing to this opinion; we think proper, previously to declare, that, in doing this, we accept in no manner that of the celebrated *Alph. des Vignoles*, who holds, that *Pharaoh*, upon pursuing with his army, the *Israelites* that went out of *Egypt*, was not at all drowned in the *Red Sea*, but did return from his unhappy expedition, and for the space of fourteen years after it, rule over *Egypt*; and that the name of this king was none else but that of *Ramesse Barta*. For, notwithstanding those things advanced by this learned author in *Chronologie de l'histoire sainte*, l. 7. c. iii. § 11, n. 7. tom. 2. p. 530. we think his arguments not sufficient for overthrowing the common opinion that *Pharaoh* was drowned in the *Red Sea*, it being founded on so very clear and evident proofs, as *Exod.* ch. ix. 15, 16. ch. xiv. 4, 6, 8, 10, 13, 17, 18, 28. xv. 19. *Psalm.* cvi. 10, 11. *Psalm.* cxxxvi. 15, which proofs Mr. *Bengel* quotes *in Ordine temp.* c. iii. § 3. p. 142. and, besides adding other instances for further corroborating these proofs, likewise enlarges on the silence observed in holy writ concerning the above allegations, concluding with the following words; *Ignosce, magne vir: pereat potius totus regum catalogus, quam aperta scripturæ verba violentur.* We shall therefore not dwell upon these arguments, but

but produce other reasons, which dissuade us from adopting Mr. *Koch*'s ingenious invention.

SECT. XVIII.

The first we take from the accounts of *Herodotus*, *Manetho* and *Eratosthenes*, those being the only historians we can consult concerning what relates to this queen. Now *Herodotus* expresly tells us, that *Nitocris* was an *Ethiopian*, and succeeded her brother, who being murdered by the *Egyptians*, she avenged his death on the principal *Egyptians* at an entertainment, though she had been raised by them to that crown. *Manetho*, according to what is mentioned by *Jul. Africanus* in *Syncellus*, under the sixth *Dynasty* of the *Memphites*, represents *Nitocris* as a beautiful woman, and the builder of the third *Memphitian* pyramid. And *Eratosthenes* says in the 22d table, that *Nitocris* had ruled six years instead of her husband, adding, that her name signifies *Minerva victrix*, *sospitatrix*; as it is explaned by Mr. *Paul Ernst. Jablonsky*, tom. 2. p. 755. of Mr. *Des Vignoles*'s *Chronology*. With these must be compared *Flavius Josephus*, who, in his *Antiquat. Jud.* l. 8. c. vi. § 2 and 5, mentions this queen of the *Egyptians* and *Ethiopians* upon the authority of *Herodotus*; yet calls her *Nicaulis*, and places her in the time of *Solomon*, nay, even supposes her to be the queen from the *South*, that visited *Solomon*. Hence *Marsham* in *Canon. chron.* § 7. p. 91. concludes, that in those times both kingdoms of *upper* and *lower Egypt* were united, and the first distinguished by the name of *Ethiopia*; which certainly cannot be questioned. Of all these things we find not the least mention in Mr. *Koch*'s writings, unless we mingle them so together, that nothing

nothing more remains distinguishable than the bare name of *Nitocris*.

SECT. XIX.

My second argument is founded on the improbability itself of this opinion, as well as the silence observed, in so important an article, in holy writ, and in the works of *Josephus* and *Manetho*, which contain copious accounts of the *Egyptian* affairs, and in them there is not the least trace of a sovereignty of the *Israelites*. It is in the first place excessively improbable, that during the oppression of the *Israelites*, a prince of the royal blood, who ruled over the land of *Goshen*, should have married an *Israelitish* woman, and at the same time continued and increased the oppression. Or, that the overthrow of the *Egyptian* army, should have had the effect of so dispeopling the country, as to reduce it to the necessity of submitting to an *Israelitish* woman, and to the government of a despised and obnoxious people that were left. It is likewise improbable, that the number of lepers and others troubled with cutaneous diseases among the *Jews*, should, at that time, have been so great, as to enable them to seize the *Egyptian* government; or that the lepers, supposing there were some among the *Jewish* people, should have remained in *Egypt*, as the laws were not yet extant, which prescribed the manner of proceeding with this distemper; and even circumcision itself, was likewise put off on account of the circumstances of those times. It is improbable again, that a mixed multitude descended from intermarriages of *Egyptians* and *Israelites*, who followed *Moses*, should have returned, and kept more rigorously to circumcision and other religious ceremonies, than the *Israelites*, who suspended that rite,

rite, during the forty years they were upon their journey thro' the wilderness. Nor is it likely that divine providence at the time of the *Israelites* going out of *Egypt*, should have settled the government of that country upon the afore mention'd people, who had a distaste to the long journey and the wars to be carried on against the *Canaanites*; and this is still less likely, if we consider that all the *Israelites* were often disposed to murmur by remembring the fertility of *Egypt*, and certainly would have been encouraged in their mutiny, had they known, that those who disobeyed *Moses*, fared better than those who followed him. Nor can we suppose, that *Moses* could have been ignorant of the above transactions, or able to conceal them from the people if we compare the following passages, *Exod*. xxxii. 12, *Numb*. xiv. 3, 4, 13. *Deuteron*. chap. xxiii. 7. chap, xvii. 16. It is besides not to be imagined, that such a part of the genealogical register of *Jacob*'s descendants could have been lost, as the number of them was far from being inconsiderable, and must have been missed at the frequent mustering and numbering of the people. We may farther add, that the difficulty of the incredible multiplying of the *Jewish* people which happen'd during the space of two hundred years, is not a little increased, if, besides those that really left *Egypt*, so considerable a number as this should be taken into the account. All these and many more arguments may be urged against this opinion, from the omission of divine care in calling those people to repentance and amendment of their lives, from the silence of the inspired writers with respect to the matter in question amidst the fullest narrations of the many vicissitudes and adventures of this people, and amongst all the reproaches for their sins, and all the warnings of impending dangers; so that we we cannot, unless conclusive reasons are shewn and unquestionable evidence produced, both which are wanting in the proposition of this learned man, acknowledge this pretended *Israelitish* empire over *Egypt*.

SECT. XX.

We shall now shew the weak foundation of Mr. *Koch*'s arguments, which is the *third* reason that prevents us from subscribing to his opinion. They consist of the three following particulars, *first*, an interpretation of *Manetho*'s and *Eratosthenes*'s accounts, as they are found in *Syncellus*, from which our ingenious author has only learned so much, that *Nitocris* is the *Armais* or *Aramea*, consequently an *Israelite* by birth; *secondly*, in computing the time in such a manner, as to make it tally with his opinion; and *lastly*, in calling *Manetho*'s *Fiction* to his assistance, concerning the lepers said by him to have seized *Egypt* and to have been driven out of it afterwards, which *Justin* and others have likewise repeated after him. As for the *first* and *second* arguments, they have already been refuted in one of my remarks upon what is said of the Dynasties of *Manetho* in the *Universal History*, and by Mr. *Bengel* in *ordin temp.* c. ii. § 6. p. 69. to which may still be added, that our author regulates and computes the years in an arbitrary manner, changes them at pleasure, omits many that are set down in *Manetho*'s and *Eratosthenes*'s accounts, and were added to the common names, which he in the inscription, by mistake, transmutes into proper names. His *third* argument will little or nothing avail him. For, the mention of the lepers is all he retains of the whole narration of *Manetho*, upon which it is much more reasonable to form the conjecture, that in this case the same thing happen'd

to

to *Manetho*, which did in his narration of the ſhepherd-kings, that in order to caſt a reproach and diſgrace upon the *Jews*, he ſet down ſuch things as he found relating to that event in the *Egyptian* Annals, whereof the inſurrection in the kingdom occaſioned by a great number of lepers is one; under which, it is very poſſible that true events might be concealed and might anſwer his purpoſe, of vilifying that people, though to apply ſuch events literally to the *Iſraelites* is againſt all manner of probability.

SECT. XXI.

We have now done with thoſe opinions that relate to the firſt part of our examination. We ſhall at preſent, in a few words, conſider thoſe who do not aſcribe ſuch a kingdom in *Egypt* to the *Iſraelites*, but to other deſcendants of *Abraham*. Some of them attribute this honour to *Eſau*'s offspring, others to that of *Iſmael*. *Steph. Fourmont* has adopted the firſt, in his *reflexions critiques ſur les hiſtoires des anciens peuples*, and ſo much enlarged on it and embelliſhed it, that one diſſertation would not be ſufficient only to give an abſtract of what he alleges. For the firſt and ſecond book of the ſaid learned *reflexions* entirely treat of this opinion, and there is ſtill a good deal relating thereto mention'd in the third. The ſubſtance of it is in few words; that *Eſau* is the *Oſiris*, or *Bacchus* and *Sirius*, likewiſe the *Buſiris* of the *Egyptians*, or the *Alluph*, that is the *Ox* or *Bull*; who, in moſt ſucceſsful expeditions, had conquered and made *India*, *Egypt*, and *Ethiopia* tributary, and thereby acquired ſuch great repute that he had been deified, and the higheſt honours and worſhip paid him. The grounds on which he builds this opinion, are twofold. The

firſt

first consists in a similitude he discovers in some *Oriental* words, which he knows how to connect and compare with a surprising address. He compares the sacred writings not only with the *Phœnician* mythology from *Sanchoniatho*'s fragments, but with the *Grecian*, nay even with the *Indian* mythology of the present *Bramins*. The following genealogical register relating to our purpose, and which he either has proved or invented, may serve as a specimen. *Thara*, he says, is the *Uranus*, originally derived from *Ur*: *Abraham* is the *Cronus*, or *Ilus*; among his wives *Sarah* is the *Isis* or *Rhea*; *Hagar* the *Ocha*, *Pallas*, *Minerva*, *Neith*; *Kethura* is the *Bersabean Persephone* or *Ceres*; *Lot* is *Atlas*, who was attacked by the *Titans*, *Gen.* xiii. but succour'd and delivered from them by *Uranus* with the help of *Eshcol* or *Hercules*; *Eliezer* is *Mercury* or *Hermes*; and *Ismael* he pretends to be *Pluto*; *Isaac* is the *Sadid* or *Jupiter*, who by *Rebecca* or *Juno*, had *Osiris*, a brother of *Typhon*; his wives were, first *Rachel* or *Astarte*, who brought forth *Pothos* and *Eros*, that is to say, *Joseph* and *Benjamin*; afterwards *Leah* or the *Didane*, *Silpah* or *Rhea* II. *Bilhah* or *Eunarmene*; and his daughter *Dina* is the *Ora*. *Osiris* had married *Bashemath*, *Gen.* xxxvi. 3. who, according to his opinion, is not a distinct person from *Aholibamah*; his son *Korah* is *Orus* or *Apollo*, and had in his army the *Satyrs* or *Sheirim*, nay even *Eshcol* or *Hercules*; and many other things of that nature.——The *second* argument on which he builds, is taken from holy writ itself; partly from *Gen.* xxvii. 39, 40, and partly from the history of the *Amalekites*, whom he derives from *Amalek*, *Esau*'s son, *Gen.* xxxvi. 12, and who intended to take vengeance of the *Egyptians*, and make themselves masters of their country.

SECT.

SECT. XXII.

As this opinion so visibly contradicts holy writ, and has not the least probability in it, we shall need but few words in confuting it. The following, we think, will be sufficient to that purpose. In the *first* place, *Esau* did not keep at a great distance from his father, when *Jacob* went to *Haran*, *Gen.* xxviii. 6, he met him when returning from *Seir*, chap. xxxii. 1. xxxiii. 16; he also assisted at his father's burial, being then one hundred and twenty years old, *Gen.* xxxv. 28, compared with xxv. 26; and hereupon returned to *Idumea*, chap. xxxvi. 6. From this time to *Jacob*'s journey into *Egypt* are ten years, *Gen.* xlvii. 9. before which *Joseph*'s rise in that country was at the distance of eight years. Hence it follows, that it is impossible to point out so much time as would be required for an expedition of that extent which *Fourmont* ascribes to *Esau*, and which he supposes to have been made before *Joseph*'s being intrusted with the administration of the *Egyptian* government. In the *second* place, though we should allow that there had been a king of *Egypt*, different from *Esau*, but tributary to him, which nevertheless can neither be reconciled with the *Egyptian* history of *Osiris*, nor with the account which the scripture gives of that *Pharaoh* under whom *Joseph* flourished: yet it is in no manner conceivable how it came to pass, that neither *Joseph* nor *Jacob* made the least mention to *Pharaoh* of *Esau* or *Osiris*, the sovereign of both; and much less, how it was possible, without a violation of the divine prophesy, *Gen.* xxvii. 29, for *Jacob* and his family to have been in *Esau*'s dominions and served him. *Thirdly*, *Moses* shews plainly, that the civil as well as religious

gious constitution of the *Egyptians*, was very well established in *Joseph*'s time; so that we cannot look for the beginning of arts and sciences in those days, which all the ancient accounts unanimously place in the time of *Osiris*. According to *Gen.* xli. 20—25, priests had been long ago appointed; and even the hatred of the *Egyptians* against the shepherds, chap. xlvi. 34. xliii. 32, seems to imply their idolatrous worship, chiefly dedicated to *Osiris*, and perhaps may have taken its rise from it, as appears by *Exod.* viii. 26. *Lastly*, if we compare this opinion with what is said of *Esau*'s posterity in *Numb.* xx. 14—21, *Deut.* ii. 4—12. and xxiii. 7, it cannot have the least appearance of foundation. All that Mr. *Fourmont* adds, for giving it a specious colour, is of no moment. To explain mythology in an historical manner, is an undertaking of vast latitude; it may, according to every one's fancy, be explaned sometimes in this, sometimes in another manner, especially when the fables of several nations are interwoven, and the alterations of them are even acknowleged to have been merely arbitrary, and so nothing certain and authentic can be deduced from thence. Let us add, that the whole invention is defeated by *Isaac*'s prophesy, rather than confirmed, as appears by what has been said before. And as for the *Amalekites*, they are falsely made to descend from *Esau*; for, in *Abraham*'s time mention is made of the *Amalekites*, *Gen.* xiv. 7, so that they must be numbered among the most ancient nations.

SECT. XXIII.

I have but one opinion more to enquire into, of which *Theophanes Cantabrigiensis*, the concealed writer of the treatise against *Morgan*, mentioned

§ 2.

§ 2. is the author: He, with great confidence, and many ſpecious arguments, endeavors, in the 25th note from page 53—64, to maintain, that the *Iſhmaelites* were thoſe that ruled in *Egypt*. *Manetho*'s ſhepherds, he pretends, were *Iſhmaelites*, in whoſe bondage the *Iſraelites* had been; and for proving this, he makes uſe of three kinds of arguments. The *firſt* conſiſts in a compariſon of *Manetho*'s narration with the condition of the *Iſhmaelites*, to which he ſays that his deſcription well agrees; to wit, that they, for the greateſt part, were ſhepherds, lived in liberty, and each man was his own king, till in *Egypt* they choſe one from among themſelves; that they were formerly deſpiſed by the *Egyptians*, partly on account of their manner of living, partly becauſe they were deſcended from *Hagar*, a bond-maid; that they invaded *Egypt* from the ſide of the eaſt, and were called *Arabs* by ſome; that they fortified the eaſtern part of *Egypt* againſt the *Aſſyrians*, whoſe neighbours the *Iſhmaelites* had formerly been, and ſpoke the *Phœnician* tongue, ſo that they might eaſily be taken for *Phœnicians*; and that they had the *Egyptian* deities in abomination, having been inſtructed in the pure religion of *Abraham*. The *ſecond* branch of his arguments he borrows from holy writ, and is of opinion, that not only what is mentioned *Gen*. xvi. 10—12, was thus accompliſhed moſt glorioully, but that the words of *Exod*. i. 8, would be better underſtood, if, inſtead of domeſtic ſhepherds, we ſuppoſe foreign ones to be meant, and if the 10th verſe is explaned of domeſtic enemies who were ſo long oppreſſed till the *Iſraelites* joined with the *Iſhmaelites*. His *third* argument, upon which he lays the greateſt ſtreſs, is taken from circumciſion, which, he ſays, was very differently inſtituted among the *Iſhmaelites* by the

the founder of their family, for that their males were not circumcised till the 13th year of their age, *Gen.* xvii. 25; and *Moses*, when he was found, might, by this mark, very easily be discovered to be an *Israelite* or *Hebrew* child, *Exod.* ii. 6. This kind of circumcision, he adds, was introduced by the *Ishmaelites* into *Egypt*; wherefore those colonies which at that time went over to *Greece*, had detested this rite, but the later ones, *viz.* that at *Colchis*, made use of it.

SECT. XXIV.

There are many objections against this opinion. It is erroneous in the *first place*, in point of time. For, *Ishmael* was, by one generation, older than *Jacob*, and died in the 137th year of his age, when *Isaac* was 123, and *Jacob* 64 years old. This happen'd at least, 45 years before *Joseph* was sold; but, according to this opinion, this last event must be placed in later than the irruption of the shepherds into *Egypt*. Now things being thus circumstanced, there is no possibility to account, how *Ishmael*'s posterity could have increased to a multitude sufficient to oppress *Egypt* in the life time of *Isaac*, who died long after *Joseph*'s being sold, and at the same time to maintain *Arabia*, which was before possess'd by them, and which according to history they never abandon'd. *Secondly*, if it is true, that the *Ishmaelites* ruled over *Egypt* in *Joseph*'s time; 'tis inconceivable, why the *Egyptians* should hold the *Hebrews* in such abomination, and abhor the shepherds so far, as that *Joseph*'s brethren were merely by this employment excluded from court and public places of honour. *Thirdly*, *Egypt* was at that time in tranquillity, had plenty of all things, and the people were much more free than afterwards, when the

the long famine occasion'd an alteration in their condition: All this cannot be conciliated with the unsupportable tyranny and desolation said to have been brought upon *Egypt*, by the shepherds. *Fourthly*, the rulers as well as the people of *Egypt* were in *Moses*'s time given to idolatry and false worship, having their own priests appointed for it, who were already introduced among them before *Joseph*'s time. Our author endeavours in vain to evade this, by quoting *Exod*. ix. 20; for the fear that is spoken of there, was on account of the plagues denounced against them by *Moses*, which they were sure would happen, having to their cost been before convinced of the certainty of these predictions; and, it is very absurd to pretend that this fear was a religious awe of the almighty, if we compare with that text chap. x. 7, 16, 17. chap. xi. 3. His attempt to distinguish the *Egyptians* from the *Ishmaelites Exod*. viii. 26. is likewise of no advantage to him; for the *Israelites*, who in religious matters agreed with the *Ishmaelites*, had nothing to fear from a people long ago oppress'd and reduced to extremity. *Lastly*, and which is most decisive in this matter, we find the *Israelites* about this time, expresly distinguished from the *Egyptians*. Witness *Gen*. xxxvii. 25, 27, 28. xxxix. 1. Above all, it is not agreeable to the manner of *Moses*, that he should so often have given to those people which oppress'd the *Israelites* the name of *Egyptians*, unless they were such; we rather find him carefully distinguishing the people and the countries wherein they dwelt from each other; and it is not to be supposed, that he would have departed from his usual accuracy in this case, or at least not have mentioned, that the native *Egyptians* were to be distinguished from their foreign rulers. The expression in *Exod*. i. 8. that a *new king*

king arose over Egypt *which knew not* Joseph, is wrongly and very forcibly explained by our author, by his taking it for a disregard of the services done by *Joseph* to the country; it may, with better ground, be accounted for from the frequent changes in the *Dynasties* and *Lines* of the royal house.

SECT. XXV.

The arguments on the other hand, which our author makes use of for supporting his opinion, are not so conclusive, as to prevail with us to alter our sentiments. The resemblance or conformity, which he finds between the *Ishmaelites* and *Manetho*'s shepherds, is partly in some instances uncertain, in others far fetch'd, in others again manifestly false, and in others the circumstances in which they differ from each other, are far superior in number to those in which there appears a resemblance or conformity. The passage of *Exod.* i. 8, 10, may very well be interpreted of the whole *Egyptian* people and its foreign enemies, chiefly if the kings, whom the *Israelites* served, reigned only over *lower Egypt*, which seems very probable. As for his argument taken from circumcision, it is not likely that the *Egyptians* would of their own free choice have retained that custom even after the expulsion of the shepherds, had it taken its rise from a nation who were their enemies. Besides, that custom was never so universally introduced in *Egypt*, that all the males were circumcised; which nevertheless was done by the *Ishmaelites*. And the antiquity ascribed, to the custom of circumcising among the *Egyptians*, is inconsistent with what is said, *Joshua*. v. 5, 9; even if the objection drawn from *Exod.* ii. 6. that *Moses* by his being circumcised was known to be of *Israelitish* offspring, were removed

removed by what is alledged in the anſwer. *Laſtly*, it is not practicable to fix ſo exactly the epochas of thoſe different colonies that went out of *Egypt*, that any thing certain could be gathered from thence. Thus much may be affirmed upon the whole, that the boaſted great antiquity of circumciſion in *Egypt* can but very little be depended on, if we conſider, that this cuſtom was for a long time unknown in *Greece*, though all arts, ſciences and religions, were carried thither by the *Egyptians* and *Phœnicians*.

INDEX.

Note, *The words marked* pref. *are to be looked for in the* Supplement to the Preface of the Univerſal Hiſtory, *and thoſe marked* †, *in the Notes.*

N. B. *The ſheet* Z *being, by miſtake, paged like* Y, *the articles occurring in* Z *are diſtinguiſhed by this mark* *.

A.

INDEX.

B.

C.

Curiosity,

D.

E.

F.

Fresnoy,

G.

H.

I.

K.

L.

Letters,

M.

N.

O. *Observations*

INDEX.

O.

P.

R.

S. *Samaritan*,

INDEX.

S.

T.

Tongues,

V.

U.

W.

X.

Y. *Year*,

INDEX.

Y.

Z.

FINIS.